BLACKSTONE'S GUIDE TO

The Serious Organised Crime and Police Act 2005

BLACKSTONE'S GUIDE TO

The Serious Organised Crime and Police Act 2005

Tim Owen QC, Alex Bailin, Julian B. Knowles, Alison MacDonald, Matthew Ryder, Debbie Sayers, Hugh Tomlinson QC

OXFORD

UNIVERSITY PRESS

OXFORD

UNIVERSITY PRESS

Great Clarendon Street, Oxford OX2 6DP

Oxford University Press is a department of the University of Oxford.
It furthers the University's objective of excellence in research, scholarship,
and education by publishing worldwide in

Oxford New York

Auckland Cape Town Dar es Salaam Hong Kong Karachi
Kuala Lumpur Madrid Melbourne Mexico City Nairobi
New Delhi Shanghai Taipei Toronto

With offices in

Argentina Austria Brazil Chile Czech Republic France Greece
Guatemala Hungary Italy Japan Poland Portugal Singapore
South Korea Switzerland Thailand Turkey Ukraine Vietnam

Oxford is a registered trade mark of Oxford University Press
in the UK and in certain other countries

Published in the United States
by Oxford University Press Inc., New York

© Tim Owen, 2005

British Library Cataloguing in Publication Data

Data available

Library of Congress Cataloging in Publication Data

Data available

Typeset by RefineCatch Limited, Bungay, Suffolk
Printed in Great Britain
on acid-free paper by
Biddles Ltd., King's Lynn

ISBN 0-19-928906-9

1 3 5 7 9 10 8 6 4 2

Contents—Summary

TABLE OF CASES   xi

TABLE OF STATUTORY INSTRUMENTS   xiv

TABLE OF STATUTES   xv

TABLE OF ABBREVIATIONS   xxv

1. INTRODUCTION   1

2. SERIOUS ORGANISED CRIME AGENCY: ESTABLISHMENT AND POWERS   7

3. ORGANISED CRIME: NEW INVESTIGATORY POWERS   19

4. OFFENDERS ASSISTING INVESTIGATIONS AND PROSECUTIONS, AND THE PROTECTION OF WITNESSES   45

5. FINANCIAL REPORTING ORDERS, INTERNATIONAL OBLIGATIONS, AND THE PROCEEDS OF CRIME   59

6. POLICE POWERS   71

7. PUBLIC ORDER AND CONDUCT IN PUBLIC PLACES   91

8. MISCELLANEOUS   103

APPENDIX   Serious Organised Crime and Police Act 2005   119

INDEX   349

Contents

TABLE OF CASES   xi

TABLE OF STATUTORY INSTRUMENTS   xiv

TABLE OF STATUTES   xv

TABLE OF ABBREVIATIONS   xxv

1. INTRODUCTION

    A. Overview   1.01

    B. New Powers of Investigation   1.06

    C. Cooperating Criminals   1.07

    D. The Need for Change?   1.09

    E. Conclusions   1.12

2. SERIOUS ORGANISED CRIME AGENCY:
   ESTABLISHMENT AND POWERS

    A. Introduction and Overview   2.01

    B. SOCA's Functions   2.05
        1. Serious Organised Crime   2.05
        2. Information Relating to Crime   2.08
        3. General Considerations   2.10

    C. Powers of SOCA   2.11

    D. Structure and Supervision of SOCA   2.13
        1. Structure of SOCA   2.13
        2. Powers of SOCA Staff   2.14
        3. Supervision of SOCA   2.17

    E. Use and Disclosure of Information   2.19
        1. Disclosure by SOCA   2.20
        2. Disclosure to SOCA   2.23
        3. Restrictions on the Use of Information Disclosed by or to
           SOCA   2.24
        4. Compatibility of these Provisions with the ECHR   2.26

    F. SOCA's Relationship with the Police   2.30

    G. Prosecutions Arising out of SOCA Investigations   2.34

3. ORGANISED CRIME: NEW INVESTIGATORY POWERS

A. Investigatory Powers Created by SOCPA 3.01
B. Overview 3.04
C. Who can Exercise the New Investigatory Powers? 3.05
D. Offences to which the New Investigatory Powers Apply 3.07
E. Disclosure Notices 3.12
F. Production of Documents 3.21
G. Restrictions on Requiring Information 3.23
  1. Privilege 3.24
  2. Excluded Material 3.34
  3. Banking Confidentiality 3.35
H. Restrictions on Use of Statements 3.37
  1. Protection against Self-incrimination 3.37
  2. Limits of the Protection against Self-incrimination 3.43
  3. Derivative Use 3.51
I. Enforcement 3.55
  1. Power to Enter and Seize Documents 3.55
  2. Offences in Connection with Disclosure Notices or Search Warrants 3.59
J. Procedural Issues 3.66
K. The Approach in Other Jurisdictions 3.68

4. OFFENDERS ASSISTING INVESTIGATIONS AND
PROSECUTIONS, AND THE PROTECTION OF WITNESSES

A. Overview 4.01
B. Offenders Assisting Investigations and Prosecutions 4.03
  1. Immunity from Prosecution 4.04
  2. Undertakings as to Use of Evidence 4.09
  3. Reduction in Sentence 4.11
  4. Review of Sentence 4.16
  5. Proceedings under Section 74: Exclusion of Public 4.20
C. Protection of Witnesses and Other Persons 4.21
  1. Protection Arrangements 4.23
  2. Duty to Assist Protection Providers 4.28
  3. Offences of Disclosing Information Relating to Protection
    Arrangements and new Identities 4.29
  4. Protection from Liability 4.34
  5. Transitional Provisions 4.35
  6. Duty to Provide Information and the Interpretation of Chapter 4 4.38

5. FINANCIAL REPORTING ORDERS, INTERNATIONAL
OBLIGATIONS, AND THE PROCEEDS OF CRIME

A. Financial Reporting Orders 5.01

Contents

1. Introduction 5.01
2. Making a Financial Reporting Order 5.05
3. The Effect of a Financial Reporting Order 5.11
4. Failure to Comply with a Financial Reporting Order 5.15
5. Verifying the Information in a Financial Reporting Order Report 5.16
6. Variation and Revocation 5.21

B. International Obligations 5.23
1. Enforcement of Overseas Forfeiture Orders 5.23
2. Mutual Assistance in Freezing Property or Evidence 5.28

C. Proceeds of Crime 5.36
1. Confiscation Orders in Magistrates' Courts 5.37
2. Civil Recovery: Freezing Orders 5.39
3. Appeal in Proceedings for Forfeiture of Cash 5.42
4. Money Laundering: Defence where Overseas Conduct is Legal under
   Local Law 5.46
5. Money Laundering: Threshold Amounts 5.49
6. Money Laundering: Disclosures to Identify Persons and Property 5.51
7. Money Laundering: Form and Manner of Disclosures 5.66

6. POLICE POWERS

A. Overview of Part 3 of SOCPA 6.01
B. Powers of Arrest without Warrant by Constables 6.04
C. Powers of Arrest without Warrant by Other Persons 6.22
D. Exclusion Zones 6.28
E. Search Warrants 6.31
F. Stop and Search for Prohibited Fireworks 6.36
G. Photographing of Suspects 6.37
H. Fingerprints 6.44
I. Footwear Impressions 6.48
J. Intimate Samples 6.50
K. Staff Custody Officers 6.52
L. Additional Matters in Part 3 of SOCPA 6.56

7. PUBLIC ORDER AND CONDUCT IN PUBLIC PLACES

A. Overview 7.01
1. Introduction 7.01
2. Freedom of Expression and of Assembly 7.03

B. Harassment 7.06
1. Introduction 7.06
2. Amendments to Protection from Harassment Act 1997 7.07
3. Harassment of a Person at Home 7.12

C. Trespass on Designated Sites   7.18

D. Demonstrations in the Vicinity of Parliament   7.25

E. Anti-social Behaviour   7.31
    1. Anti-social Behaviour Orders: General   7.31
    2. Reporting Restrictions   7.34
    3. Contracting Out   7.36
    4. Protection of Witnesses   7.37
    5. Parental Compensation   7.38

8. MISCELLANEOUS

A. Overview   8.01

B. Protection of Activities of Certain Organisations   8.02

C. Vehicle Registration, Insurance, and Road Traffic Offences   8.10
    1. Provisions Relating to Vehicle Registration   8.11
    2. Provisions Relating to Unlicensed and Uninsured Drivers   8.17
    3. Provisions Relating to Drink-driving Offences   8.22
    4. Payments by Secretary of State to Police Authorities   8.28

D. The Publication of Local Policing Information   8.29

E. Other Miscellaneous Police Matters   8.32
    1. Responsibilities in Relation to the Health and Safety etc of Police   8.33
    2. Investigations: Accelerated Procedure in Special Cases   8.35
    3. Investigations: Deaths and Serious Injuries During or After Contact
    with the Police   8.37

F. Abolition of the Royal Parks Constabulary   8.38

G. Criminal Record Checks   8.41

H. Witness Summonses   8.47

I. Private Security Industry Act 2001: Scotland   8.51

APPENDIX   Serious Organised Crime and Police Act 2005   119

INDEX   349

Table of Cases

References are to Paragraph Numbers

A v Boulton [2004] FCA 56; [2004] FCAFC 101 .... 3.75
Air Canada v the United Kingdom (1995) 20 EHRR 15 .... 8.21
Al-Fayed and others v Commissioner of Police for the Metropolis and others
  (CA 25 November 2004) 6.13
Allen v UK [2003] Crim LR 280 .... 3.54
An Enquiry Into Mirror Group Newspapers plc, Re [2000] Ch 194 .... 3.67
Arrows Ltd, Re [1992] Ch 545 .... 3.62
Aston Cantlow Parochial Church Council v Wallbank [2003] UKHL 37 .... 3.42
AT & T Istel Ltd v Tully [1993] AC 45 .... 3.38, 3.42
Attorney-General's Reference (No 3 of 2003) [2004] Cr App R 23 .... 3.64
Attorney-General's Reference (No 7 of 2000) [2001] 2 Cr App R 19 .... 3.51, 3.54
Australian Competition and Consumer Commission v Amcor Printing Papers
  Group Ltd (1999) 163 ALR 465 .... 3.73

Barclays Bank v Taylor [1989] 1 WLR 1066 .... 3.32
Bennett v Richardson [1980] RTT 385 .... 8.11
Bowman v Fels [2005] EWCA Civ 226 .... 3.31, 3.32
Brown v Stott [2003] 1 AC 681 .... 3.54

Cobb v Williams [1073] RTR 113 .... 8.11

Doe v United States (1988) 487 US 201 .... 3.51, 3.77

Fayed v UK (1994) 18 EHRR 393 .... 3.38
Ferreira v Levin (1996) 1 BCLR 1 .... 3.68
Friedl v Austria (1995) 21 EHRR 83 .... 6.41
Funke v France 16 EHRR 297 .... 3.37, 3.38, 3.54

Hammond v DPP (2004) 168 JP 601 .... 7.11
Heaney and McGuiness v Ireland (2001) 33 EHRR 12 .... 3.54
HKSAR v Lee Ming Tee [2001] 1 HKLRD 599 .... 3.68

IJL, GMR and AKP v UK (2001) 33 EHRR 11 .... 3.37

James and others v the United Kingdom 21 February 1986 .... 8.21
JB v Switzerland [2001] Crim LR 748 .... 3.54
Jones v DPP 8.11

Kastigar v United States 406 US 441; 460 (1972) 3.78

Marlwood Commercial Inc v Kozeny [2004] 3 All ER 648 .... 3.62

Mohammed-Holgate v Duke [1984] AC 437 .... 6.13

Norwood v DPP [2003] Crim LR 888 .... 7.11

Osman v UK [1999] 29 EHRR 245 .... 4.23

Pyneboard Pty Ltd v Trade Practices Commission (1983) 152 CLR 328 .... 3.73

R v A and B (1999) 1 Cr App R (S) 52 .... 4.01
R v Allen [2002] 1 AC 509 .... 3.54
R v Blastland [1985] AC 41 .... 3.49
R v Brady [2004] 3 All ER 520 .... 3.40
R v Central Criminal Court ex p Francis and Francis (a Firm) [1989] AC 346 .... 3.31
R v Chesterfield JJ ex p Bramley [2000] QB 576 .... 3.58
R v Chief Constable of South Yorkshire Police ex p Marper [2004] 1 WLR 2196 ..... 6.41
R v Cox and Railton (1884) 14 QBD 153 .... 3.31
R v Debbag and Izzet (1991) 12 Cr App R (S) 733 .... 4.01
R v Derby Magistrates' Court ex p B [1996] 1 AC 487 .... 3.26, 3.32
R v Director of the Serious Fraud Office ex p Evans [2003] 1 WLR 299 .... 3.06
R v Director of SFO ex p Smith [1993] AC 1 .... 3.20
R v Gill [2004] 1 Cr App R 20 .... 3.54
R v Goodyear [2005] EWCA Crim 888 .... 4.12, 4.13
R v Hasan [2005] UKHL 22 .... 3.48
R v Hayter [2005] UKHL 6 .... 3.48
R v Hertfordshire CC ex p Green Environmental Industries Ltd [2000]
    2 AC 412 .... 3.38, 3.42, 3.54, 3.61
R v Home Secretary ex p Finivest SpA [1997] 1 All ER 942 .... 3.15
R v Hundal and Dhaliwal; The Times 13 February 2004 .... 3.54
R v Kearns [2003] 1 Cr App R 111 .... 3.54
R v King (1985) 7 Cr App R (S) 227 .... 4.01
R v Lam Chi-Wing [1991] 2 AC 212 (PC) 3.53
R v McDonald 77 Cr App R 196 .... 4.05
R v Metropolitan Stipendiary Magistrate ex p SFO, The Independent,
    24 June 1994 .... 3.20
R v Myers [1998] AC 124 .... 3.49
R v Rosenthal (unreported) Southwark Crown Court 3.49
R v Self [1992] 1 WLR 657 .... 6.24
R v SFO ex p Maxwell (Kevin) The Times; 9 October 1992 .... 3.19
R v Sivan (1988) 10 Cr App R (S) 282 .... 4.01
R v Sweetbaum (unreported) Southwark Crown Court 3.49
R v Turner [1970] 2 QB 321 .... 4.12
R v Wood (1997) Cr App R (S) 238 .... 4.01
R (D) v Central Criminal Court [2004] 1 Cr App R 41 .... 3.46
R (Daly) v Secretary of State for the Home Department [2001] 2 AC 532 .... 7.04
R (Kent Pharmaceuticals Ltd) v Director of Serious Fraud Office
    (Secretary of State for the Home Department) [2004] EWCA Civ 1494;
    [2005] 1 All ER 449 .... 3.43
R (McCann) v Crown Court at Manchester [2001] 1 WLR 358 .... 7.31

R (Morgan Grenfell & Co Ltd) v Special Commissioner for Income Tax
  [2002] UKHL 21; [2003] 1 AC 563 .... 3.26
R (Stanley) v Commissioner of Police [2005] EMLR 5 .... 7.34
Rio Tinto Zinc Corp v Westinghouse Electric Corp [1978] AC 547 .... 3.42
RJS v The Queen (1995) 121 DLR 589 .... 3.68

S v Customs & Excise Commissioners [2004] EWCA Crim 2374 .... 5.40
Saunders v UK (1996) 23 EHRR 313 .... 3.01, 3.13, 3.17, 3.37, 3.38,
                          3.39, 3.40, 3.41, 3.48, 3.49, 3.51, 3.52, 3.54, 3.61
Schmerber v California 384 US 757 (1966) 3.77
Serves v France 28 EHRR 265 .... 3.37
Sorby v The Commonwealth (1983) 152 CLR 281 .... 3.73
Sunday Times v United Kingdom (No 1) (1979) 2 EHRR 245 .... 7.04

Three Rivers DC v Bank of England (No 6) [2004] UKHL 48;
  [2004] 3 WLR 1274 .... 3.26, 3.30
Trade Practices Commission v Abbco Ice Works Pty Ltd (1994) 52 FCR 96 .... 3.73
Triplex Safety Glass Co v Lancegaye Safety Glass (1934) Ltd [1939] 2 KB 395 .... 3.42

United States v Hubbell 530 US 27; 34–35 (2000) 3.77

Westminster City Council v Haw [2002] EWHC 2073 .... 7.25
Willmott v Atack [1977] QB 498 .... 3.64

Table of Statutory Instruments

References are to Paragraph Numbers

Criminal Justice (International Co-Operation) Act 1990
  (Enforcement of Overseas Forfeiture Orders) Order 1991 (SI 1991/1463) 5.26, 5.27
Criminal Justice (Northern Ireland) Order 1996 (SI 1996/3160) 4.15
  Art 2 .... 4.15

Insolvency Rules 1986 (SI 1986/1925)
  r 9.5(4) 3.62

Rehabilitation of Offenders Act 1974 (Exceptions) Order 1974 (SI 1975/1023) 8.41
Rehabilitation of Offenders Act 1974 (Exclusions and Exceptions) (Scotland)
  Order 2003 (SI 2003/231) 8.41

Serious Organised Crime and Police Act 2005 (Commencement No 1,
  Transitional and Transitory Provisions) Order
  Art 4(2) 7.26A

Table of Statutes

References are to Paragraph Numbers

Animal Enterprise Protection Act
  1992 .... 8.03
Animal (Scientific Procedures) Act
  1986 .... 8.04
Anti-Social Behaviour Act 2003
  s 59 .... 8.03
Australian Crime Commission Act
  2002 .... 3.70, 3.75
Australian Evidence Act 1995
  s 128 .... 3.74

Children and Young Persons Act
  1933 .... 7.34
  s 39 .... 7.34
  s 49 .... 7.34
Companies Act 1985
  s 447(5) 3.22
Countryside and Rights of Way
  Act 2000
  s 2(1) 7.21
Crime and Disorder Act 1998 .... 7.31,
                     7.33, 7.34, 7.36
  s 1(10C) 7.32
  s 1(10D) 7.34
  s 1(10E) 7.34
  s 1C(4A)–(4C) 7.32
  s 1CA 7.33
  s 1D 7.32
  s 1F(7)(a) 7.36
  s 1F(9) 7.36
  ss 13A–13E 7.38
  s 13A(1) 7.39
  s 13A(2) 7.39
  s 13A(5) 7.40
  s 13A(6) 7.40
  s 36ZD 7.40
  Sch 3 .... 8.50
Criminal Damage Act 1971 .... 8.03
Criminal Justice Act 1987 .... 3.04
  s 2 ...... 3.15, 3.18, 3.20, 3.36, 3.49, 3.62
  s 2(1) 3.11

s 2(1)(a) 3.11
s 2(3) 3.13, 3.22
s 2(8) 3.13, 3.39, 3.49
s 2(8AA) 3.39
s 2(9) 3.24
s 2(10) 3.36
s 2(11) 3.05
Criminal Justice Act 1988
  Part VI 5.24, 5.26
Criminal Justice Act 2003 .... 1.04
  Chap 2 .... 3.45, 3.46
  Part 4 .... 3.46
  s 118 .... 3.48
  s 119 .... 3.45
  s 120 .... 3.45
  s 126 .... 3.46
  s 128 .... 3.49
  s 174(1)(a) 4.15, 4.19
  s 270 .... 4.15, 4.19
  Sch 3 .... 4.13
Criminal Justice and Police Act
  2001 .... 6.38, 7.06
  Chap 1 .... 6.38
  Part 1 .... 6.38
  Part 2 .... 3.33
  s 42 .... 7.12
  s 42(1) 7.12
  s 42(4)(a) 7.17
  s 42(4)(b) 7.17
  s 42(7) 7.12
  s 42A 7.13, 7.15, 7.16
  s 42A(4) 7.14
  s 42A(5) 7.16
  s 42A(7) 7.13
Criminal Justice and Public Order
  Act 1994
  s 34 .... 3.41
  s 68 .... 7.19, 8.03
Criminal Justice (International
  Co-Operation) Act 1990
  s 9 .... 5.24, 5.26

Criminal Justice (International
   Co-Operation) Act 1990—*contd*
  s 9(1) 5.23, 5.26
  s 9(6) 5.23, 5.24
Criminal Procedure and Investigations
  Act 1996 .... 8.47
Criminal Procedure
  (Attendance of Witnesses)
  Act 1965
  s 2 .... 8.47

Data Protection Act 1998 .... 2.21, 2.23,
                      2.28, 5.20

Education Act 1996 .... 6.38
  s 444A 6.38
Enterprise Act 2002
  s 188 .... 4.05
  s 190(4) 4.08
  s 242 .... 3.40

Football Spectators Act 1989
  Part 2 .... 2.20

Health and Safety at Work Act
  1974
  s 51A 8.33
  s 51A(2B) 8.34
  s 51A(2C) 8.34
Human Rights Act 1998 .... 3.38
  s 7 .... 3.42

Insolvency Act 1986
  s 291 .... 3.54
  s 354 .... 3.54
  s 433 .... 3.54

Judicature (Northern Ireland)
  Act 1978 .... 8.50

Magistrates' Courts Act 1980 .... 8.47
  s 97(1) 8.49
  s 97A(1)(b) 8.50

Offences Against the Person Act
  1861
  s 16 .... 8.03

Parks Regulation Act 1872 .... 8.40

Parks Regulation (Amendment)
  Act 1926
  s 2 .... 8.40
Perjury Act 1911
  s 5 .... 3.39
Police Act 1996
  s 8A 8.30
  s 8A(3) 8.30
  s 8A(4) 8.31
  s 8A(6) 8.30
Police Act 1997
  Part V 8.41, 8.42, 8.46
  ss 113–115 .... 8.42
  s 113A 8.43
  s 113A–F 8.42
  s 113B 8.43
  s 113C 8.43
  s 113C(5) 8.43
  s 113D 8.43
  s 113E 8.43
  s 113F 8.43
  s 118(2A) 8.44
  s 119(3) 8.45
  s 119(6) 8.45
  s 119(7) 8.45
  s 120A 8.45
  s 124A 8.45
Police and Criminal Evidence Act
  1984 .... 3.04, 3.19, 3.20, 3.23, 3.41,
                  6.01, 6.11, 6.28
  Part II 6.31, 6.32
  s 1 .... 6.36
  s 1(8B) 6.36
  s 1(8C) 6.36
  s 4(4)(a)(i) 6.18
  s 8 .... 6.33
  s 8(1)(d) 3.58
  s 8(1)(a) 6.18
  s 8(1A)(a) 6.32
  s 8(1A)(b) 6.32
  s 8(1)(b) 3.58
  s 8(1B)(a) 6.32
  s 8(1B)(b) 6.32
  s 8(1C) 6.32
  s 8(1D) 6.32
  s 8(2A)(a) 6.32
  s 8(2A)(b)(i) 6.32
  s 8(2A)(b)(ii) 6.32

s 8(2A)(b)(iii) 6.32
s 8(2A)(b)(iv) 6.32
s 8(6)(a)(iv) 6.32
s 10(2) 3.31, 3.34
s 11 .... 3.34
ss 12–14 .... 3.34
s 15(2)(a)(iii) 6.32
s 15(5A) 6.32
s 16(3A) 6.32
s 16(3B) 6.32
s 16(9)(b) 6.32
s 16(10) 6.32
s 16(10A) 6.32
s 24 .... 6.03, 6.04, 6.05, 6.07, 6.08,
          6.10, 6.11, 6.13, 6.21, 6.23, 6.26
s 24(1)(c) 6.05
s 24(1)(d) 6.05
s 24(1)(a) 6.05
s 24(1)(b) 6.05
s 24(2) 6.05
s 24(3)(a) 6.05
s 24(3)(b) 6.05
s 24(4) 6.13, 6.22
s 24(5) 6.09, 6.13, 6.22, 6.45
s 24(5)(a) 6.06
s 24(5)(b) 6.06
s 24(5)(c)(i) 6.06
s 24(5)(c)(ii) 6.06
s 24(5)(c)(iii) 6.06
s 24(5)(c)(iv) 6.06
s 24(5)(c)(v) 6.06
s 24(5)(d) 6.06
s 24(5)(e) 6.06, 6.09
s 24(5)(f) 6.06, 6.09
s 24(6) 6.06
s 24A 6.04, 6.22, 6.23
s 24A(1)(a) 6.22
s 24A(1)(b) 6.22
s 24A(2)(a) 6.22
s 24A(2)(b) 6.22
s 24A(3) 6.25
s 24A(3)(a) 6.25
s 24A(3)(b) 6.25
s 24A(4)(a) 6.25
s 24A(4)(b) 6.25
s 24A(4)(c) 6.25
s 24A(4)(d) 6.25
s 25 .... 6.03, 6.04, 6.09, 6.45

s 25(3) 6.09
ss 34–35 .... 3.41
ss 37–40 .... 6.54
s 43(4)(b) 6.18
s 44(3)(b) 6.18
s 45A(2)(a) 6.53
s 45A(4) 6.53
s 56(2)(a) 6.18
s 58(6)(a) 6.18
s 61(3A) 6.47
s 61(3)(b)(ii) 6.47
s 61(6A) 6.14, 6.44, 6.47
s 61(6A)(a) 6.44
s 61(6B)(a) 6.44
s 61(6B)(b) 6.44
s 61(6C) 6.47
s 61A 6.48, 6.49
s 61A(8) 6.49
s 63A 6.48
s 63A(1ZA) 6.46
s 64 .... 6.45, 6.47
s 64(1BA) 6.47
s 64A 6.37, 6.39, 6.40
s 64A(1A) 6.37
s 64A(1B) 6.37, 6.38
s 64A(1B)(a) 6.38
s 64A(1B)(b) 6.38
s 64A(1B)(c) 6.38
s 64A(1B)(d) 6.38
s 64A(1B)(e) 6.38
s 64A(1B)(f) 6.38
s 64A(4) 6.40
s 64A(4)(a) 6.40
s 64A(5) 6.40
s 64A(6A) 6.39
s 65 .... 6.50
ss 71–75 .... 3.47
s 74 .... 3.48
s 76 .... 3.49
s 76A 3.49
s 78 .... 3.46, 3.48, 3.49
ss 82–94 .... 3.46
s 116 .... 6.17
s 116(6) 6.17
Sch 1 .... 6.18, 6.33
Sch 1A 6.08
Police Reform Act 2002 .... 2.18, 6.01,
                          6.28, 6.38, 8.39

Police Reform Act 2002—*contd*
Part 2 .... 8.37
Part 4 .... 6.53, 6.56
s 10(2) 8.37
s 10(2A)–(2D) 8.37
s 20A(7) 8.35
s 20A(8) 8.35
s 122 .... 6.03
s 123 .... 6.03
Sch 3 .... 8.35, 8.36
Sch 4 .... 6.38, 6.53
Sch 5 .... 6.38
Powers of Criminal Courts
    (Sentencing) Act 2000
    s 76 .... 4.15
Prevention of Terrorism Act 2005 .... 1.11
Private Security Industry Act
    2001 .... 8.01, 8.51
Proceeds of Crime Act 2002 .... 5.26, 5.36
Part 2 .... 5.37, 5.38
Part 4 .... 5.37, 5.38
Part 5 .... 4.10, 5.39
s 245(C) 5.40
s 245(C)(5) 5.40
s 245(C)(6) 5.40
s 245A 5.40
s 245A(5) 5.40
s 245A(6) 5.40
s 245B 5.40
s 245C 5.40
s 245C(1)(b) 5.40
s 245C(2) 5.40
s 245D 5.40
s 246(2) 5.39
s 246(7) 5.39
s 298 .... 5.43
s 299 .... 5.42
s 299(1) 5.43, 5.44
s 299(2) 5.44
s 299(3) 5.45
ss 327–329 .... 5.46, 5.49
s 327(1) 5.47
s 327(2A) 5.47
s 327(2B) 5.47
s 327(2C) 5.50
s 328 .... 3.31
s 328(1) 5.47
s 328(2A) 5.47

s 328(2B) 5.47
s 328(5) 5.50
s 329(1) 5.47
s 329(2A) 5.47
s 329(2B) 5.47, 5.50
s 330 .... 5.48, 5.52, 5.53, 5.59,
                                        5.61, 5.64
s 330(1) 5.53
s 330(2) 5.54, 5.56
s 330(2)–(4) 5.53
s 330(3) 5.55, 5.56
s 330(3A) 5.56
s 330(4) 5.57
s 330(5A) 5.56
s 330(7) 5.61
s 330(7A) 5.64
s 330(8) 5.65
s 330(9) 5.58, 5.59
s 330(9)(a) 5.59
s 330(9)(b) 5.59
s 330(10) 5.62, 5.63
s 330(11) 5.63
s 330(13) 5.65
ss 330–332 .... 5.46, 5.51
s 331 .... 5.48, 5.52
s 332 .... 5.48, 5.52
s 339 .... 5.60, 5.66
s 339(1) 5.66
s 339(2) 5.66
s 339(3) 5.66
s 339A 5.49
s 412 .... 3.25
Sch 2 .... 3.08, 5.06
Sch 4 .... 3.08
Protection from Harassment Act
    1997 .... 7.06, 7.15, 8.03
    s 1(1A) 7.08, 7.09
    s 1(3) 7.11
    s 2 .... 7.07
    s 3A 7.09
    s 7(3) 7.07
    s 7(3)(b) 7.08
Public Order Act 1986 .... 7.11, 7.15, 8.03
    Part 1 .... 7.13
    s 5 .... 7.11

Regulation of Investigatory Powers
    Act 2000 .... 2.20, 2.23, 2.28

Part I 2.21
Road Traffic Act 1988 .... 8.11
  s 4 .... 8.24, 8.27
  s 5 .... 8.24, 8.27
  s 6(5) 8.23
  s 6D(1) 8.24
  s 6D(1A) 8.24
  s 6D(2A) 8.24
  s 7 .... 8.24
  s 7(1)(a) 8.26
  s 7(2) 8.23
  s 7(2)(c) 8.23
  s 7(2A)–(2D) 8.23
  s 7(2B) 8.23
  s 7(2D) 8.23
  s 7(3) 8.26
  s 8 .... 8.25
  s 10 .... 8.27
  s 52(2) 8.15
  s 87(1) 8.18
  s 143 .... 8.11, 8.18
  s 163 .... 8.18
  s 164 .... 8.15, 8.16, 8.18
  s 165 .... 8.15, 8.16, 8.18
  s 165A 8.20
  s 165A(1) 8.18
  s 165A(4) 8.18
  s 165A(5)(c) 8.19
  s 165A(6) 8.19
  s 165A(7) 8.19
  s 165A(8) 8.20
  s 165A(9)(d) 8.19
  s 165B 8.20
Road Traffic Offenders Act
  1988 .... 6.38, 8.11
  s 54 .... 6.38
  Sch 3 .... 8.14

Serious Organised Crime and Police
  Act 2005 .... 1.01, 1.08, 1.09, 1.12,
    2.01, 2.27, 3.01, 3.03, 3.06, 3.18, 3.69,
    3.70, 3.72, 4.01, 4.02, 4.07, 4.09, 6.08,
            6.21, 6.32, 6.37, 6.39, 6.40
  Chap 1 .... 2.04, 3.04
  Chap 2 .... 2.04, 2.15, 4.02
  Chap 3 .... 2.04, 2.19, 5.01
  Chap 4 .... 4.02, 4.21, 4.39
  Chap 6 .... 5.36

Part 1 .... 2.04, 2.15
Part 2 .... 3.04, 5.01, 5.36, 8.39
Part 3 .... 6.01, 6.02, 6.16
Part 4 .... 7.01, 7.05
Part 5 .... 8.01
ss 1–7 .... 2.13
ss 1–42 .... 2.04
s 2 .... 1.02, 2.08, 2.20
ss 2–4 .... 2.04
s 2(1) 2.05, 2.08
s 2(1)(a) 2.06
s 2(1)(b) 2.06
s 2(3) 2.06
s 2(4) 2.06
s 2(5) 2.07, 2.37
s 2(6) 2.06
s 3 .... 2.08, 2.20
s 3(1) 2.08, 2.28
s 3(1)(a) 2.09
s 3(1)(b) 2.09
s 3(2) 2.09
s 3(3) 2.11
s 3(4) 2.09
s 3(5) 2.09
s 4 .... 2.10
s 4(3) 2.10
s 5 .... 2.04, 2.11, 2.20
s 5(2) 2.11
s 5(3) 1.02, 2.08, 3.11
s 5(5) 2.12
s 5(6) 2.12
s 8 .... 2.13
ss 8–16 .... 2.04
s 9 .... 2.17
s 10 .... 2.17
s 11 .... 2.17
s 12 .... 2.13, 2.17
s 13 .... 2.13
ss 15–19 .... 2.13
s 16 .... 2.17
s 21 .... 2.13
s 21(2) 2.13
ss 21–27 .... 2.04
s 23(1) 2.32
s 23(2) 2.32
s 23(3) 2.32
s 23(4) 2.32
s 24 .... 2.32

Serious Organised Crime and Police Act
    2005—*contd*
s 26(1) 2.33
s 26(2) 2.33
s 26(6) 2.33
s 28 .... 2.33
ss 28–31 .... 2.04
s 31 .... 2.33
ss 31–34 .... 2.28
s 32 .... 2.20
ss 32–35 .... 2.04, 2.09
s 33 .... 2.20, 2.21, 2.24
ss 33–35 .... 2.19
s 33(2) 2.20, 2.24
s 33(2)(b) 2.22
s 33(3) 2.21, 2.22
s 33(4)(a) 2.21
s 33(4)(b) 2.21
s 34(1) 2.23
s 35(1) 2.24
s 35(2) 2.25
s 35(4) 2.24
s 36 .... 2.04
s 36(1) 2.31
s 37 .... 2.04, 2.31
s 37(2)(b) 2.31
s 37(2)(c) 2.31
s 38 .... 2.37
ss 38–40 .... 2.04
s 39 .... 2.36
s 39(1) 2.36
s 39(2) 2.36
s 39(3) 2.36
s 39(4) 2.36
s 39(7) 2.36
s 39(8) 2.37
s 43 .... 3.56
s 43(1) 2.15
s 43(1)(a)–(c) 2.15
s 43(4) 2.15
s 43(5) 2.15
ss 43–54 .... 2.04
s 44 .... 2.15
s 46 .... 2.16
s 48 .... 2.16
s 49 .... 2.16
s 51 .... 2.16
s 56 .... 2.04

s 56(2) 3.13
s 57 .... 2.04
s 60 .... 3.04, 3.05
s 60(3) 3.36
ss 60–70 .... 3.04
s 61 .... 3.04, 3.07, 3.11, 3.12
s 61(1) 3.60
s 61(1)(c) 3.07
s 61(1)(d) 3.09
s 61(1)(e) 3.09
s 61(1)(f)–(g) 3.10
s 61(2) 3.09, 3.11
s 61(4)(a) 3.08
s 61(4)(b)(ii) 3.09
s 62 .... 3.04, 3.17, 3.23, 3.24, 3.32,
                3.34, 3.35, 3.39, 3.41, 3.44,
                3.49, 3.60, 3.63
s 62(1) 3.12, 3.58
s 62(2) 3.14
s 62(3)(b) 3.16
s 62(3)(c) 3.16
s 62(4) 3.19
s 62(5) 3.14
s 63 .... 3.04, 3.21, 3.23, 3.24, 3.32,
                3.35, 3.39, 3.49, 3.60, 3.63
s 63(2)(a) 3.21
s 63(2)(b) 3.22
s 63(4) 3.21
s 63(5) 3.22, 3.56
s 64 .... 3.04, 3.32, 3.36, 3.58
s 64(1) 3.24
s 64(2)–(4) 3.25
s 64(6)–(7) 3.25
s 64(8) 3.35, 3.36
s 64(9) 3.32
s 65 .... 3.04, 3.13, 3.20, 3.39, 3.40,
                3.41, 3.43, 3.51, 3.61, 3.65
s 65(1) 3.49, 3.61
s 65(2)(a) 3.39, 3.65
s 65(2)(b) 3.39
s 65(3) 3.39
s 65(5) 3.34
s 66 .... 3.04, 3.33, 3.55, 3.64
s 66(1)–(2) 3.55
s 66(3) 3.56
s 66(3)(e) 3.56, 3.64
s 66(4) 3.57
s 66(5) 3.57

s 66(6) 3.57
s 66(7)–(8) 3.57
s 66(9) 3.58
s 67 .... 3.04, 3.19, 3.39, 3.59, 3.65
s 67(1) 3.64
s 67(2) 3.45, 3.63, 3.65
s 67(3) 3.64
s 67(4) 3.60, 3.64
s 67(5)(a) 3.63
s 67(5)(b) 3.63
s 68 .... 3.33
s 69 .... 3.66
s 69(2) 3.66
s 69(3) 3.42, 3.66
s 69(4) 3.66
s 71 .... 3.80, 4.05
s 71(2) 4.06
s 71(3) 4.06
s 71(4) 4.05, 4.10
s 71(5) 4.05
s 71(6) 4.05
s 71(7) 4.05
s 72 .... 3.80, 4.10
s 72(2) 4.10
s 72(3) 4.10
s 72(4) 4.10
s 72(5) 4.05
s 72(6) 4.05
s 73 .... 4.14
s 73(1)(b) 4.14
s 73(2) 4.15
s 73(3) 4.15
s 73(3)–(9) 4.19
s 73(4) 4.15
s 73(5) 4.15
s 73(6) 4.15
s 73(7) 4.15
s 73(8) 4.15
s 73(8)(b) 4.15
s 73(9) 4.14
s 74 .... 4.16, 4.19
s 74(2) 4.16
s 74(3) 4.17
s 74(4) 4.17
s 74(5) 4.18, 4.19
s 74(6) 4.18
s 74(7) 4.18
s 74(8) 4.18

s 74(9) 4.18
s 74(13) 4.17
s 74(14) 4.19
s 74(15) 4.19
s 75 .... 4.20
s 75(2)(b) 4.20
s 75(3) 4.20
s 75(4) 4.20
s 75(5) 4.20
s 76(2) 5.01, 5.08
s 76(3) 5.01, 5.05, 5.06, 5.07, 5.08
s 76(4) 5.07
s 76(5) 5.09
s 77 .... 5.10
s 77(3) 5.01
s 78 .... 5.10
s 78(3) 5.01
s 79 .... 5.14, 5.16
s 79(2) 5.11
s 79(3) 5.13
s 79(4) 5.13
s 79(5) 5.12
s 79(6) 5.14
s 79(7) 5.12
s 79(9) 5.14
s 79(10) 5.02, 5.15
s 80(1) 5.21
s 80(2) 5.21
s 80(4) 5.22
s 81 .... 5.16, 5.20
s 81(2) 5.17
s 81(3) 5.17
s 81(4) 5.17, 5.18
s 81(5) 5.19
s 82 .... 4.23, 4.30, 4.36
s 82(1) 4.31, 4.34, 4.36
s 82(1)(a) 4.24
s 82(1)(b) 4.24
s 82(2) 4.25
s 82(3) 4.25
s 82(4) 4.25
s 82(5) 4.23
s 82(6) 4.24
s 82(7) 4.23
s 83 .... 4.26
s 84 .... 4.27
s 84(2) 4.27
s 84(4) 4.27

Serious Organised Crime and Police Act
2005—*contd*

s 85 .... 4.28
s 85(3) 4.28
s 86 .... 4.29, 4.30, 4.31, 4.37
s 86(2) 4.29
s 86(3) 4.29
ss 86–89 .... 4.35
s 87 .... 4.31, 4.33
s 87(1) 4.31
s 87(2) 4.31
s 87(3) 4.31
s 87(4) 4.31
s 87(5) 4.33
s 87(6) 4.33
s 87(7) 4.33
s 88 .... 4.29, 4.32, 4.33, 4.37
s 88(1) 4.32
s 88(2) 4.32
s 88(3) 4.29
s 88(4) 4.29
s 89 .... 4.33
s 89(5) 4.33
s 89(6) 4.33
s 89(7) 4.33
s 90 .... 4.34
s 90(2) 4.34
s 90(3) 4.34
s 91 .... 4.35
s 91(2)–(5) 4.36
s 91(6) 4.34, 4.36
s 91(7) 4.36
s 91(8)–(11) 4.35
s 92 .... 4.35, 4.37
s 92(2) 4.37
s 92(3) 4.37
s 93 .... 4.38
s 93(2)–(3) 4.38
s 93(4) 4.38
s 94 .... 4.25, 4.39
s 94(7) 4.39
s 95 .... 5.24, 5.26
s 96 .... 5.35
s 96(1) 5.35
s 97 .... 5.37
s 97(1) 5.37, 5.38
s 97(2) 5.37
s 97(3) 5.38

s 98 .... 5.39
s 98(1) 5.40
s 98(2) 5.41
s 101 .... 5.42
s 102 .... 5.46
s 103 .... 5.49
s 103(2) 5.50
s 103(3) 5.50
s 103(4) 5.50
s 104 .... 5.51, 5.52, 5.53
s 105 .... 5.66
s 110 .... 6.04, 6.45, 7.24
s 110(1) 6.04
s 110(2) 6.04
s 110(4) 6.04
ss 110–111 .... 6.03
ss 110–124 .... 6.03
s 112 .... 6.03, 6.28, 6.30
s 112(2)(a) 6.29
s 112(2)(b) 6.29
s 112(3)(a) 6.29
s 112(3)(b) 6.29
s 112(4) 6.30
s 112(5) 6.30
s 112(10) 6.30
s 113 .... 6.33
s 113(4) 6.32
s 113(7) 6.32
s 113(8) 6.32
s 113(9)(a) 6.32
s 113(9)(b) 6.32
s 113(10)–(15) 6.33
ss 113–114 .... 6.03
s 114 .... 6.32
s 114(2) 6.32, 6.33
s 114(4)(c) 6.32
s 114(6) 6.32
s 114(8)(b) 6.32
s 114(8)(c) 6.33
s 115 .... 6.03, 6.36
s 115(1)–(4) 6.36
s 115(5) 6.36
s 116 .... 6.03
s 116(2) 6.37, 6.38
s 116(3) 6.40
s 116(5) 6.39
s 117 .... 6.14, 6.44
s 117(2) 6.44, 6.47

s 117(5) 6.46
s 117(8) 6.47
ss 117–118 .... 6.03
s 118 .... 6.48
s 118(2) 6.48, 6.49
s 119 .... 6.03
s 119(2) 6.50
s 119(3) 6.50
s 120 .... 6.52, 6.53
s 120(5) 6.53
ss 120–121 .... 6.03
s 121 .... 6.53
s 122 .... 6.56
s 125 .... 7.07
s 125(1) 7.08
s 125(2)(c) 7.11
s 125(5) 7.09
s 125(7) 7.08
ss 125–127 .... 7.02, 7.06
ss 125–138 .... 7.03
ss 125–144 .... 7.01
s 126 .... 7.13
s 127 .... 7.17
s 127(2) 7.17
s 128 .... 7.24
s 128(1) 7.19
s 128(4) 7.21
ss 128–131 .... 7.02, 7.18
s 129 .... 7.23
s 130(1) 7.24
s 130(2) 7.21
s 131(1) 7.21
s 131(3) 7.21
s 131(4) 7.21
s 132(1) 7.26, 7.26A
s 132(7) 7.26
s 132(7)(e) 7.26
ss 132–138 .... 7.01, 7.02, 7.25, 7.26A
s 133 .... 7.27
s 133(2) 7.27
s 134(2) 7.28
s 134(3) 7.28
s 134(4) 7.28
s 134(7) 7.30
s 136(1) 7.26
s 136(3) 7.30
s 137 .... 7.29
s 137(2) 7.29

s 138 .... 7.26
s 139 .... 7.32
s 139(1) 7.32
s 139(4) 7.32
s 139(5) 7.32
s 140 .... 7.33
s 140(4) 7.33
s 141 .... 7.34
s 142 .... 7.36
s 143 .... 7.37
s 144 .... 7.38
s 145 .... 8.03, 8.04, 8.07, 8.08,
                                                8.09
s 145(2) 8.04
s 145(3) 8.04, 8.07
s 145(4) 8.04
s 145(5) 8.04
ss 145–149 .... 8.02
s 146 .... 8.03, 8.05, 8.07, 8.08
s 146(2) 8.06
s 146(6) 8.06
s 147 .... 8.08, 8.09
s 148 .... 8.04
s 149 .... 8.09
s 150(1) 8.11
s 150(2) 8.14
s 151 .... 8.15
s 152 .... 8.17, 8.18, 8.20
s 153 .... 8.17
s 154 .... 8.22
s 154(1)–(3) 8.24
s 154(4)–(6) 8.23
s 154(6) 8.26
s 154(7) 8.25
s 154(9)–(12) 8.27
s 155 .... 8.28
s 155(3) 8.28
s 156 .... 8.28
s 157 .... 8.29, 8.30
s 158 .... 8.33
s 158(5) 8.34
s 158(6) 8.34
s 159 .... 8.35
s 160 .... 8.37
s 161 .... 8.38
s 162 .... 8.40
s 162(3) 8.40
s 163 .... 8.42

Serious Organised Crime and Police Act
    2005—*contd*
  ss 163–168 .... 8.42
  s 164 .... 8.44
  s 165 .... 8.45
  s 165(1)(a) 8.45
  s 165(1)(b) 8.45
  s 165(2) 8.45
  s 165(3) 8.45
  s 166 .... 8.46
  s 167 .... 8.46
  s 168 .... 8.46
  s 169 .... 8.49
  s 169(3) 8.50
  s 169(4) 8.50
  s 169(5) 8.50
  s 170 .... 8.50
  s 171 .... 8.51
  Sch 1 .... 2.04, 2.13
  Sch 2 .... 2.04, 2.18
  Sch 3 .... 2.04
  Sch 5 .... 4.24
  Sch 6 .... 5.36
  Sch 7 .... 6.02, 6.16, 6.17, 6.32
  Sch 8 .... 6.02, 6.56
  Sch 9 .... 6.02
  Sch 10 .... 7.01, 7.38
  Sch 11 .... 8.35
  Sch 12 .... 8.37
  Sch 13 .... 8.38, 8.39
  Sch 14 .... 8.42
  Sch 15 .... 8.51

Terrorism Act 2000
  ss 15–18 .... 3.07
Theft Act 1968
  s 15 .... 5.06
  s 15A 5.06

  s 16 .... 5.06
  s 20(2) 5.06
Theft Act 1978
  s 1 .... 5.06
  s 2 .... 5.06
Trade Union and Labour Relations
    (Consolidation) Act 1992 .... 8.07

Vehicle Excise and Registration
    Act 1994
  s 28A 8.15, 8.16
  s 28A(1) 8.15
  s 28A(2) 8.15
  s 28A(3) 8.16
  s 28A(4) 8.16
  s 28A(5) 8.16
  s 28A(6) 8.16
  s 28A(7) 8.16
  s 28A(8) 8.16
  s 28A(9) 8.15
  s 28A(10) 8.16
  s 28A(11) 8.16
  s 43C 8.11
  s 43C(1) 8.12
  s 43C(2)(a) 8.12
  s 43C(2)(b) 8.12
  s 43C(3) 8.13
  s 43C(4) 8.13
  s 43C(5) 8.14
  s 43C(7) 8.12

Youth Justice and Criminal Evidence
    Act 1999
  Chap 1 .... 7.37
  Part 2 .... 7.37
  s 45 .... 7.34
  Sch 3 .... 3.39

Table of Abbreviations

ACC	Australian Crime Commission
ARA	Assets Recovery Agency
ASBO	anti-social behaviour orders
CJA 1987	Criminal Justice Act 1987
CRB	Criminal Records Bureau
DPP	Director of Public Prosecutions
DRCP	Director of Revenue and Customs Prosecutions
DTI	Department of Trade and Industry
ECHR	European Convention on Human Rights
ECtHR	European Court of Human Rights
FRO	financial reporting order
IPCC	Independent Police Complaints Commission
OFT	Office of Fair Trading
PACE	Police and Criminal Evidence Act 1984
PITO	Police Information Technology Organisation
PRA	Police Reform Act 2002
RIPA	Regulation of Investigatory Powers Act
RPC	Royal Parks Constabulary
RTA	Road Traffic Act 1988
RTOA	Road Traffic Offenders Act 1988
SFO	Serious Fraud Office
SOCA	Serious Organised Crime Agency
SOCPA	Serious Organised Crime and Police Act
UNCAC	United Nations Convention against Corruption
UNTOC	United Nations Convention against Transnational Organised Crime

1
INTRODUCTION

A. Overview	1.01
B. New Powers of Investigation	1.06
C. Cooperating Criminals	1.07
D. The Need for Change?	1.09
E. Conclusions	1.12

A. OVERVIEW

The Serious Organised Crime and Police Act (SOCPA) was one of the key pieces **1.01** of legislation rushed through Parliament during the final, frantic pre-election week in April 2005. Although much of the debate focused on the 'faith hate' provisions (in the end jettisoned at the eleventh hour to enable the Bill to be passed) there were other even more controversial proposals which received little detailed scrutiny.

It is important to stress that SOCPA is not merely an administrative statute **1.02** which restructures law enforcement agencies with an overseeing body (reported in the media as an 'FBI for the UK'). One purpose of SOCPA is to establish 'a single powerful agency . . . that will bring together the National Crime Squad, the National Criminal Intelligence Service and the investigative and intelligence work of Her Majesty's Customs and Excise'—the Serious Organised Crime Agency (SOCA). However, SOCPA's wider aim is to give effect to Government proposals in the White Paper, *One Step Ahead: A 21st Century Strategy to Defeat Organised Crime* (Cm 6167): 'reducing the profit incentive, disrupting . . . criminal enterprises, and increasing the risk to the major players of being caught and convicted'. Despite SOCPA's title, many of its provisions will be equally relevant to minor offenders whose crimes lack any elaborate planning. Although s 2 describes the general function of SOCA as 'preventing and detecting serious organised crime', the Act deliberately avoids defining 'organised crime'. While asserting that organised crime groups are essentially businesses, the Government contended that 'there is no clear cut-off point at which any group should be

1

categorised as being involved in organised crime. But those at the top end of the spectrum pose a unique threat'. It considered that even lone operators, who are not motivated by profit, could inflict considerable damage to persons and institutions and it was therefore left to SOCA to decide for itself which areas of criminal activity warrant its attention, whether or not the conduct in question would ordinarily be regarded as organised. Indeed, s 5(3) provides: 'despite the references to serious organised crime in s 2(1), SOCA may carry on activities in relation to other crime'. SOCA's remit could hardly be broader.

1.03   Other new provisions in the Act range from giving community support officers additional powers and rewriting money laundering offences, to extending harassment laws and creating new offences of interference with business contracts which damage animal research organisations. In short, the Act is a criminal justice measure relevant to all offenders; creating new powers, offences, and defences while altering a number of pre-existing rules relating to police powers.

1.04   The 179 sections and 17 Schedules of the Act come soon after the 340 sections and 37 Schedules of the Criminal Justice Act 2003. The strain on the parliamentary draftsman is beginning to show and there is an unprecedented number of errors in the numbering of the Schedules to the Act.

1.05   The headline measure is the establishment of SOCA which has responsibility for work currently undertaken by the National Criminal Intelligence Service and National Crime Squad (established less than 10 years ago), the Home Office immigration crime unit and HM Customs and Excise serious drug trafficking and asset recovery team. SOCA will be run by 4,500 civilian support staff (including economists, engineers, linguists, and forensic experts) with designated powers equivalent to police officers. Contrary to the media reports, SOCA lacks any formal 'federal powers' but it does have statutory powers that distinguish it from other agencies, and the police are under a duty to cooperate with it. In practice, SOCA will serve as a clearing house for criminal intelligence, collating data, and then passing it on to agencies best placed to take the appropriate action (including SOCA itself). The Government's stated intention is that SOCA should be 'lawfully audacious'.

B. NEW POWERS OF INVESTIGATION

1.06   Controversially, the Act gives SOCA compulsory powers of investigation. In designated cases, SOCA can force witnesses to answer questions or to provide documents or other information. It is an imprisonable criminal offence not to comply with these powers. Coercive powers of investigation are already available in serious fraud cases. The Government's main justification for extending them to organised crime cases was that witnesses in such cases were too afraid of reprisals from crime gangs to cooperate voluntarily with the police. It also claimed that many of these witnesses would themselves be on the fringes of criminality and there would be little incentive for them to come forward of their own volition. It did not acknowledge, however, the invidious position that prosecution witnesses in organised crime investigations will now be in: facing prison if they do not cooperate with the prosecution, or recriminations from an avowedly violent criminal gang if they do. They may feel that the safest option will be to mislead or lie to the authorities. The Home Office has said it envisages the prosecution forcing a junior member of a criminal group to provide evidence against the 'big fish' and that the benefit of that would outweigh not being able to use the coerced statement made by the junior member against him. While this is superficially attractive, the real risk that convictions based upon such evidence will be unsafe is not one to be taken lightly.

C. COOPERATING CRIMINALS

The move away from the system of voluntary witness cooperation which **1.07** underpins our whole criminal justice system is obviously a radical one, yet the Government provided no evidence of prosecutions collapsing in organised crime cases because witnesses have refused to come forward voluntarily. At the very least, MPs should have had a chance properly to debate the need for such a momentous change.

The increased reliance on witnesses who are acknowledged to have been **1.08** involved in crime is a central theme of SOCPA which seems to have gone largely unnoticed. There are new 'conditional immunity' measures whereby it can be agreed in advance that if a criminal provides the evidence required by the authorities he will not be prosecuted. There are also statutory plea bargains, where the prosecution, defence, and the judge agree what the sentence will be if a particular course is followed and the agreement is enforceable in a court. Although providing a greater degree of transparency than previously available, the real danger is that culpability lines will be decided by the prosecution and judge rather than the jury, and that the defendant is under too much pressure not to accede. The White Paper suggested that the primary reasons for an increased reluctance by defendants to cooperate with the police are juries' suspicions of cooperating defendants' motives and defendants' perceived lack of incentives to cooperate. It also claimed that cooperation in UK courts used to be commonplace, although no evidence is offered to support this. There was no consideration of the increased possibility of miscarriages of justice associated with defendants who cooperate with the prosecution, and a comparison with the many recent successful appeals based on inadequate disclosure where participating informants were involved was also notably absent.

D. THE NEED FOR CHANGE?

1.09   Police powers of arrest are also significantly expanded in SOCPA and civilians can hold very important police roles such as custody officers with little explanation of the need for such widened powers. The anti-social behaviour legislation was once again amended and yet more harassment offences created at a time when there is widespread criticism of the efficacy, propriety, and need for such preventative legislation. There is even a new offence of demonstrating in the vicinity of Parliament which appears to have been enacted just to deal with one particular anti-war placard holder who has taken up permanent residence in Parliament Square.

1.10   Worryingly, many of the changes reflect the Government's openly stated desire in the White Paper of shifting the balance of the criminal law away from defendants—apparently with the aim of securing more convictions by further eroding fundamental rights. As the Government sees it:

> There has been a growing belief over recent years that the law has emerged in a way that has tilted the balance excessively towards the defence. No category of defendant is able to make better use of this than organised criminals, with access often to the best legal advice.

The White Paper went on to single out defence tactics as an aggravating feature of organised crime:

> Organised criminals become particularly adept at frustrating the trial process in their attempts to evade justice. Examples include, the systematic use of the pre-trial process to seek to undermine prosecution evidence and ideally have it rendered inadmissible. Tactics here have included extensive *voire dire* hearings, challenging every aspect of the prosecution case, and looking for every reason to exclude prosecution evidence.

No evidence was given to support these assertions but the suggestion appeared to be that sentences should be heavier where there have been extensive but unsuccessful defence-instigated legal arguments. No doubt we could each think of appropriate sanctions against prolix lawyers who take unarguable points, but punishing their clients does not immediately spring to mind. In the end, the Act did not contain any such measures but the intention may have been to test public reaction to such proposals.

1.11   Encouragingly, the White Paper professed a willingness (despite opposition from the Intelligence Services) to repeal the self-imposed prohibition on the admissibility of intercept material in criminal cases—a move supported by civil liberties groups who have emphasised that the prohibition has persistently been used in partial justification of the detention without trial of suspected foreign terrorists. However the new, equally controversial, control order regime in the Prevention of Terrorism Act 2005 did not repeal the ban.

E. CONCLUSIONS

The raft of measures in SOCPA have far-reaching consequences for organised   **1.12**
crime and serious implications for crime in general. It is therefore particularly
disappointing that a more careful review was not undertaken in the White
Paper, that no detailed justification was advanced for the need substantially to
increase prosecution powers in one particular area of crime, and that the legislative scrutiny of the Act focused almost exclusively on one provision. The
self-professed desire to tilt the balance away from defendants does not suggest
that an objective assessment of needs was carried out. A Government which
was genuinely interested in views concerning the need for special prosecutorial
powers to tackle organised crime would surely have published a Green Paper not
a White one.

2

SERIOUS ORGANISED CRIME AGENCY: ESTABLISHMENT AND POWERS

A.	Introduction and Overview	2.01
B.	SOCA's Functions	2.05
C.	Powers of SOCA	2.11
D.	Structure and Supervision of SOCA	2.13
E.	Use and Disclosure of Information	2.19
F.	SOCA's Relationship with the Police	2.30
G.	Prosecutions Arising out of SOCA Investigations	2.34

A. INTRODUCTION AND OVERVIEW

The establishment of the Serious Organised Crime Agency (SOCA)[1] is the centrepiece of SOCPA. When it begins to function on 1 April 2006, it is intended to be a 'major player in international law enforcement'.[2] It will have responsibility for the work currently done by the National Criminal Intelligence Service, the National Crime Squad, the investigative and intelligence work of Customs and Excise on serious drug trafficking and the recovery of related criminal assets, and the Home Office's responsibilities for organised immigration crime.[3] It will have around 4,500 staff. Its remit is to be 'lawfully audacious' in tackling

2.01

---

[1] For the sake of clarity this book refers to the Act as SOCPA and the Serious Organised Crime Agency as SOCA.

[2] *One Step Ahead: A 21st Century Strategy to Defeat Organised Crime* (Cm 6167) ('White Paper') p 22.

[3] The White Paper states that SOCA 'will need to establish close links with our UK border agencies (HM Customs and Excise, National Ports Police, and the UK Immigration Service). But as border controls are exercised for a wide variety of reasons, many of them distinct from organised crime, they will not be subsumed within the new organisation' (p 23).

serious crime, 'acting firmly within the powers granted by Parliament, but ensuring that these powers are also fully understood and exploited'.[4]

2.02   The rationale for the establishment of SOCA was set out as follows in the White Paper:[5]

To get the better of highly organised criminal enterprises, we need to organise ourselves so that we create the critical mass we need in the key areas of competence and focus our efforts on front-line intelligence and investigation. That is why the Government launched a review of the organisational structure for tackling organised crime.

. . .

The review found that the UK's law enforcement agencies are effective and well respected amongst their international peers. Cooperation has improved immeasurably over recent years, with coordinating groups like CIDA on drugs and REFLEX on immigration crime, while the cooperation between intelligence and law enforcement agencies is almost unique internationally. There are frequent accounts from other jurisdictions of overlapping investigations leading to obstruction and even 'blue on blue' clashes between rival enforcement bodies. It is much to our agencies' credit that these problems are rare in the UK.

Nevertheless, the dividing line between institutional responsibilities remains unclear in several areas . . .

Coupled with what appears to be duplication in some areas, the current fragmented effort against organised crime can make coordination difficult, and lead to a lack of critical mass in some less traditional but important skill areas. This has proved a particular problem in tackling financial crime.

. . .

The new agency will be much more than the sum of its parts. Its creation should lead to greater consistency of approach; a critical mass in key skill areas, address current problems of duplication and coordination, limit bureaucracy, provide opportunities for economies of scale, and represent a 'one stop shop' for our international partners. In particular, it should address some of the key weaknesses in the generation, dissemination and use of intelligence material.

2.03   The announcement of the new agency led to immediate descriptions of the 'British FBI'. This was played down by SOCA's special adviser on communications:

It is not the UK Federal Bureau of Investigation. It does not have the same remit, but it is a fact that the FBI has a reputation for trampling over local concerns. We want to forge links with local policing and not be elitist and a cavalier organisation.[6]

2.04   Part 1 of SOCPA deals with SOCA. Chapter 1 (ss 1–42) deals with SOCA's 'establishment and activities'. This includes defining SOCA's functions (ss 2–4), powers (s 5), supervision and direction (ss 8–16), operational issues and relationship with the police (ss 21–27 and 36–37), liability for unlawful conduct

---

[4] White Paper, p 4.
[5] ibid, pp 21–22.
[6] *Police Review* 19 November 2004, 'SOCA will not "trample over local concerns" '.

(ss 28–31), powers to use and disclose information (ss 32–35), and dealing with prosecutions arising out of SOCA investigations (ss 38–40). Chapter 2 (ss 43–54) deals with 'special powers of designated staff'. Chapter 3 deals with miscellaneous and supplementary matters, including the application of discrimination legislation to staff seconded to SOCA (s 56), and assaults or obstruction in connection with joint investigation teams (s 57). Schedule 1 deals with the staffing of SOCA, Schedule 2 with the functions of the Independent Police Complaints Commission in respect of SOCA, and Schedule 3 with transfers of staff to the new Agency.

B. SOCA'S FUNCTIONS

1. Serious Organised Crime

Section 2(1) of SOCPA defines SOCA's functions in the field of 'serious organised crime' as '(a) preventing and detecting serious organised crime, and (b) contributing to the reduction of such crime in other ways and to the mitigation of its consequences'.   **2.05**

This is clearly a very broadly defined remit. There are certain qualifications in respect of other agencies: if, in exercising its s 2(1)(a) function, SOCA 'becomes aware of conduct appearing to SOCA to involve serious or complex fraud', SOCA can only continue to exercise that function in relation to the fraud in question either with the agreement of the Director of the Serious Fraud Office (SFO) (or an authorised officer), or if the SFO declines to act in relation to it.[7] The same applies to revenue fraud, where the consent of the Customs Commissioners must be obtained.[8] SOCPA cannot exercise its s 2(1)(b) function in respect of revenue fraud *at all* without the consent of the Commissioners.[9]   **2.06**

However, to ensure that defendants who may end up being prosecuted by SOCA in either of these two areas cannot benefit from any lack of clarity in the demarcation of the different agencies' functions, s 2(5) provides that the issue of whether or not SOCA's powers continued to be exercisable in a serious fraud or revenue case 'may not be raised in any criminal proceedings'.   **2.07**

2. Information Relating to Crime

Section 3 of SOCPA sets out the other part of SOCA's functions, in respect of 'information relating to crime'. Section 3(1) provides that SOCA has the function of 'gathering, storing, analysing and disseminating information relevant to (a) the prevention, detection, investigation or prosecution of   **2.08**

---

[7] SOCPA, s 2(3).
[8] SOCPA, s 2(4).
[9] SOCPA, s 2(6).

offences, or (b) the reduction of crime in other ways or the mitigation of its consequences'. These functions are even broader than those in s 2(1), since they are not limited to 'serious organised crime':[10] despite its name,[11] SOCA's work is not in fact restricted to crime which is either serious or organised.

2.09   SOCA has broad powers to disclose information. Section 3(2) provides that it can disclose to police forces in the UK (plus Jersey, Guernsey, and the Isle of Man), 'special police forces',[12] 'law enforcement agencies', and, broadest of all, 'such other persons as it considers appropriate in connection with any of the matters mentioned in subsection 1(a) or (b)'. Law enforcement agencies are also defined extremely broadly in subsection (4): they include the Customs Commissioners or any other government department, the Scottish Administration, 'any other person who is charged with the duty of investigating offences or charging offenders', and 'any other person who is engaged outside the United Kingdom in the carrying on of activities similar to any carried on by SOCA or a police force'. Concerns have been raised about the breadth and vagueness of this disclosure power: they are considered further below, in the discussion of ss 32 to 35 of SOCPA.

3. General Considerations

2.10   Some guidance is given to SOCA on the exercise of its broad powers by s 4, which provides that in exercising its functions it must have regard to its annual plan, current strategic priorities as determined by the Secretary of State, and current performance targets. More importantly from the point of view of those who may come under investigation by SOCA, s 4(3) provides that 'In exercising any function to which a code of practice under section 10 relates, SOCA must have regard to the code.'

C. POWERS OF SOCA

2.11   SOCA's 'general powers' are defined in s 5. Section 5(2) provides that it may:

(a) institute criminal proceedings in England and Wales or Northern Ireland;

(b) at the request of a chief officer of a police force within section 3(3) or of a special police force, act in support of any activities of that force;

---

[10] This is underlined by s 5(3), which provides that: 'Despite the reference to serious organised crime in section 2(1), SOCA may carry on activities in relation to other crime if they are carried on for the purposes of any of the functions conferred on SOCA by section 2 or 3.'

[11] And despite the emphasis on organised crime in the White Paper *One Step Ahead: A 21st Century Strategy to Defeat Organised Crime* (Cm 6167), which stated that: 'Organised crime reaches into every community, ruining lives, driving other crime and instilling fear. At its worst, it can blight our most vulnerable communities driving out innocent residents and legitimate businesses' (p 1).

[12] Defined in s 3(5) as the Ministry of Defence Police, the British Transport Police Force, the Civil Nuclear Constabulary, and the Scottish Drug Enforcement Agency.

(c) at the request of any law enforcement agency, act in support of any activities of that agency;

(d) enter into other arrangements for cooperating with bodies or persons (in the United Kingdom or elsewhere) which it considers appropriate in connection with the exercise of any of SOCA's functions . . .

Section 5(5) empowers SOCA to 'furnish such assistance as it considers appropriate in response to requests made by any government or other body exercising functions of a public nature in any country or territory outside the United Kingdom', subject to certain exceptions which are considered below in the context of mutual assistance.[13] **2.12**

D. STRUCTURE AND SUPERVISION OF SOCA

1. Structure of SOCA

Under s 21 of SOCPA, the Director General of SOCA has 'general operational control' over SOCA's work. This includes deciding 'which particular operations are to be mounted' and 'how such operations are to be conducted.'[14] The management structure of SOCA is dealt with in more detail in Schedule 1 of SOCPA, which provides for SOCA to have a Board, made up of a chairman and ordinary members appointed by the Secretary of State,[15] and staff,[16] and empowers SOCA to form committees and sub-committees.[17] **2.13**

2. Powers of SOCA Staff

In terms of the type of staff to be employed by SOCA, the White Paper states that: **2.14**

Intelligence officers are likely to be the largest single group within the new agency . . . We must ensure that law enforcement have the right resources and skills to conduct financial investigations, not just into criminals' assets and money laundering, but also as a technique for fighting any acquisitive crime. The Assets Recovery Agency's Centre of Excellence has already trained 1,400 financial investigators since its launch in autumn 2002 . . . These intelligence analysts and financial investigators are signs of the new face of law enforcement.[18]

---

[13] See SOCPA, s 5(6).
[14] SOCPA, s 21(2). The first Director General of SOCA, William Hughes (former Director of the National Crime Squad) took up his post in September 2004.
[15] SOCPA, Sch 1, ss 1–7. The first Chairman of SOCA, Sir Stephen Lander (former Director General of MI5) took up his post in September 2004.
[16] SOCPA, Sch 1, ss 8, 12 and 13.
[17] SOCPA, Sch 1, ss 15–19.
[18] White Paper, pp 31–32.

2.15   Chapter 2 of Part 1 of SOCPA is headed 'special powers of designated staff'. The fundamental provision is s 43(1), which empowers SOCA's Director General[19] to confer on any member of SOCA staff the powers of a constable, an officer of Revenue and Customs, or an immigration officer.[20] The Director General may limit a designation, both in terms of functions and duration, and may not make a designation unless he is satisfied that the person is capable of exercising those powers effectively, has received adequate training in the exercise of those powers, and is otherwise suitable.[21]

2.16   Sections 46, 48, and 49 emphasise that persons designated as having the powers of a constable, customs officer, or immigration officer have exactly the same powers as such officers have, and s 51 makes it an offence (punishable, on summary conviction, to a prison sentence of up to 51 weeks or a level 3 fine, or both) to assault, obstruct, or deceive a person acting in the exercise of delegated powers.

3. Supervision of SOCA

2.17   The Secretary of State is to determine SOCA's strategic priorities, in consultation with SOCA and the Scottish Ministers and 'such other persons as he considers appropriate'.[22] He may issue codes of practice relating to the exercise of any of SOCA's functions, and must lay these before Parliament, excluding material which 'would be against the interests of national security', 'could prejudice the prevention or detection of crime or the apprehension or the prosecution of offenders', or 'could jeopardise the safety of any person'.[23] SOCA must report back to the Secretary of State on its work,[24] and may be inspected by Her Majesty's Inspectors of Constabulary, either of their own motion or if the Secretary of State asks them to do so.[25] If an inspection report reveals that all or part of SOCA is 'not efficient or not effective', or is liable to become so, then the Secretary of State can direct SOCA to submit an action plan.[26]

2.18   An important element of independent scrutiny is introduced by Schedule 2 of SOCPA, which amends the Police Reform Act 2002 to bring SOCA within the remit of the Independent Police Complaints Commission.

---

[19] Or a person delegated by him: SOCPA, s 44.

[20] It appears, from the lack of any 'and' or 'or' in the list at s 43(1)(a) to (c), and from the wording of s 43(4), that the same member of staff may be designated as having more than one of these sets of powers.

[21] SOCPA, s 43(5).

[22] SOCPA, s 9.

[23] SOCPA, s 10.

[24] SOCPA, s 11.

[25] SOCPA, s 16.

[26] SOCPA, s 12.

E. USE AND DISCLOSURE OF INFORMATION

Given the vast amount of information which SOCA is bound to gather while **2.19** carrying out its very broad functions, it is important to understand the circumstances in which (a) SOCA can disclose information to other people or agencies, and (b) individuals can, or must, disclose information to SOCA. The powers of compulsory disclosure created by SOCPA are considered in Chapter 3. This section deals with the non-compulsory disclosure provisions of ss 33 to 35 of SOCPA.

1. Disclosure by SOCA

SOCA has a broad power to use information internally: information obtained **2.20** 'in connection with the exercise of any of its functions' may be used 'in connection with any of its other functions.'[27] More interesting is the question of disclosure to external persons or agencies. This is dealt with in s 33, which provides that SOCA can disclose for any of the 'permitted purposes' listed in s 33(2). Accordingly, its powers to disclose are not limited to a list of agencies, but are defined rather by the purpose of disclosure (which must, presumably, be interpreted objectively and not with reference to SOCA's view of the purpose of disclosure). The permitted purposes are as follows:

(a) the prevention, detection, investigation or prosecution of criminal offences, whether in the UK or elsewhere;

(b) the prevention, detection or investigation of conduct for which penalties other than criminal penalties are provided under the law of any part of the UK or of any country or territory outside the UK;

(c) the exercise of any function conferred on SOCPA by ss 2, 3, or 5 (so far as not falling within paragraph (a) or (b));

(d) the exercise of any functions of any intelligence service within the meaning of the Regulation of Investigatory Powers Act 2000;

(e) the exercise of any functions under Part 2 of the Football Spectators Act 1989;

(f) the exercise of any function which appears to the Secretary of State to be a function of a public nature and which he designates by order.

Such disclosure will not breach 'any obligation of confidence owed by the **2.21** person making the disclosure', or 'any other restriction on the disclosure of

---

[27] SOCPA, s 32.

information (however imposed)'.[28] However, s 33 does not authorise the disclosure of personal data protected by the Data Protection Act 1998,[29] or any disclosure prohibited by Part 1 of the Regulation of Investigatory Powers Act (RIPA).[30]

2.22 It is immediately apparent from the list of 'permitted purposes' that SOCA's powers of disclosure are extremely broad. It can disclose information for purposes to do with criminal offences which need not be serious and need not have any connection with the UK. Strikingly, under s 33(2)(b) it can also disclose for purposes to do with conduct 'for which penalties other than criminal penalties are provided', either in UK law or anywhere else. This is extremely broad: in the UK it would include, for example, penalties imposed on those who smuggle people into the country, and in the legal systems of other countries it could encompass conduct for which no penalty at all—either civil or criminal—is imposed in the UK. Section 33(3) also purports to override the common law concerning breach of confidence.

2. Disclosure to SOCA

2.23 Section 34(1) provides that 'Any person may disclose information to SOCA if the disclosure is made for the purposes of the exercise by SOCA of any of its functions'. Again, such disclosure is said not to breach any obligation of confidence, or any other restriction on disclosure, other than under the Data Protection Act or RIPA.

3. Restrictions on the Use of Information Disclosed by or to SOCA

2.24 Section 35(1) provides that, where SOCA has disclosed information under s 33, that information must not be further disclosed except:

(a) for a purpose connected with any function of that person or body for the purposes of which the information was disclosed by SOCA, or otherwise for any permitted purposes (ie the purposes set out in s 33(2)[31]); and

(b) with the consent of SOCA.[32]

2.25 Section 35(2) provides that information disclosed to SOCA 'by the Commissioners or a person acting on their behalf' may not be further disclosed except for any permitted purposes, and with the consent of the Commissioners or an authorised officer of Revenue and Customs. Information disclosed by

---

[28] SOCPA, s 33(3).
[29] SOCPA, s 33(4)(a).
[30] SOCPA, s 33(4)(b).
[31] SOCPA, s 35(4).
[32] SOCPA, s 35(1).

the Commissioners is therefore in a privileged position: no other information disclosed to SOCA is protected by any restriction on further disclosure.

4. Compatibility of these Provisions with the ECHR

Clearly much of the information gathered and potentially disclosed by SOCA may relate to the private lives of individuals, thus engaging Article 8 of the European Convention on Human Rights (ECHR). The Explanatory Notes to SOCPA state that, since Article 8(2) permits interference with the right to respect for private life 'for the prevention of disorder or crime', and since disclosures by SOCA would be for the purposes of the prevention and detection of crime, 'accordingly, these provisions are regarded as compatible with ECHR Article 8.1.'[33]   2.26

The Joint Committee on Human Rights expressed serious concerns about these provisions when SOCPA was passing through Parliament. In order to comply with Article 8:   2.27

There must be a positive framework of legal rules limiting the exercise of any power to interfere with private life, and incorporating legally binding safeguards against abuse . . . On their face, these provisions confer extremely broad discretions on SOCA and others to interfere with an individual's right to respect for their private life. We have therefore looked carefully at the limits on the exercise of those broad discretions in the Bill to determine whether they are 'in accordance with the law' within the meaning of Article 8 ECHR.[34]

Having carried out this scrutiny, the Joint Committee raised the following concerns:[35]   2.28

(a) The fact that SOCA's powers 'in relation to information relating to crime generally go well beyond a power to pass on to other relevant agencies information which it has obtained in the exercise of its functions in relation to serious crime. They include the power to carry on activities for the purposes of gathering, storing and analysing information relating to crime generally'.

(b) The fact that 'information relating to crime' in s 3(1) includes information relevant to 'the reduction of crime in other ways' or 'the mitigation of its consequences', both extremely vague and open-ended concepts.

(c) The fact that disclosure in ss 31–34 relates to the exercise of any of SOCA's functions, a reference to functions which are in themselves extremely broadly defined.

---

[33] Explanatory Notes, para 451.
[34] Joint Committee on Human Rights, *Fourth Report of Session 2004–2005*, HL Paper 26, HC 224, p 13.
[35] ibid, pp 12–16.

(d) The extremely broad range of potential recipients of SOCA information.

(e) The fact that protection from disclosure is limited to information protected by the Data Protection Act and RIPA, both of which themselves have broad exceptions for policing and crime prevention purposes.

(f) The lack of other safeguards against excessive or unnecessary disclosure.

2.29   The provisions criticised by the Joint Committee made it into the final Act with no significant alteration, meaning that these concerns still stand, and that SOCA's disclosure powers may have to be tested through the courts, either by way of judicial review or in criminal proceedings.

F. SOCA'S RELATIONSHIP WITH THE POLICE

2.30   The White Paper stated that:

The Serious Organised Crime Agency and, until it is established, the existing agencies dealing with organised crime will continue to need to work in partnership with individual police forces, other law enforcement agencies, other arms of Government, and with international partners.
Of these, the relationship with individual forces will be particularly important. At the most basic level, there will need to be regular interchange between agencies dealing with organised crime and forces.'[36]

2.31   Clearly the relationship between SOCA and the police is potentially sensitive.[37] This relationship is dealt with in a number of sections of SOCPA. Section 36(1) provides that a chief officer of police must keep SOCA informed of 'any information relating to crime in his police area that appears to him to be likely to be relevant to the exercise by SOCA of any of its functions': a very broad duty. Section 37 imposes on 'any constable'[38] a duty to assist SOCA 'in the exercise of its functions in relation to serious organised crime'.

2.32   SOCPA provides for SOCA to assist UK police forces under either 'voluntary arrangements' or 'directed arrangements'. 'Voluntary arrangements' can be made by SOCA in response to a request from a chief police officer stating that the force has 'a special need for assistance' from SOCA, in which case the Director of SOCA can provide the force with members of SOCA staff or other appropriate assistance.[39] Equally, a police force can provide SOCA with

---

[36] White Paper, p 26.

[37] See discussion in House of Commons Research Paper 04/88, 'The *Serious Organised Crime and Police Bill*—the new Agency; and new powers in criminal proceedings', pp 12–15. The Police Federation has emphasised the need for SOCA to cooperate with local forces and avoid elitism: 'Federation warns stand alone SOCA is a recipe for disaster', <www.polfed.org/default_6A48255730DA4E6193A4A5F4A736036.asp>.

[38] As well as any officer of Revenue and Customs, and any member of Her Majesty's armed forces or Her Majesty's coastguard: s 37(2)(b) and (c).

[39] SOCPA, s 23(1) and (2).

constables or other members of staff in response to a similar request.[40] The Secretary of State can direct similar arrangements to be made in either direction.[41]

SOCA can make arrangements with a police authority to use that police 2.33 force's 'premises, equipment or other material, facilities or services',[42] and in an emergency the Secretary of State can direct SOCA and a police force to make this type of arrangement.[43] SOCA has to contribute to the costs of its use of the force's facilities.[44] SOCA is liable for the unlawful acts of any police officers (or indeed other individuals) who may be seconded to it, in the same way as it is liable for its own employees.[45] Likewise, special police forces and law enforcement agencies are to be liable for the unlawful acts of seconded SOCA staff.[46]

G. PROSECUTIONS ARISING OUT OF SOCA INVESTIGATIONS

Of course, it is the Government's hope that the extensive investigatory powers 2.34 outlined above will lead to prosecutions. The White Paper states:

Agencies tackling organised crime are often operating in areas of considerable legal complexity, against targets who are aware of the law and are adept at exploiting it to thwart enforcement action. More needs to be done, therefore, to build on the recent successes in strengthening the relationship between those conducting investigations and prosecutions.[47]

SOCA itself has no prosecutorial functions. The Government considered giving SOCA the power to carry out prosecutions itself, but, perhaps chastened by the recent failures of Customs prosecutions, it decided that 'separation is essential in order to ensure the independence of both groups'.[48] Accordingly, SOCA cases will be prosecuted either by the Director of Public Prosecutions (DPP) or by the Director of Revenue and Customs Prosecutions (DRCP). Building on the 'lawfully audacious' model, the Government has emphasised that both prosecution agencies are expected to give early legal advice to SOCA, to prevent 'an over-defensive interpretation of the law' and 'shying away from fully using powers which Parliament has given'.[49]

The dividing line between the two prosecution authorities is drawn in SOCA 2.35 cases by SOCPA references to 'designated offences', which are to be prosecuted

---

[40] SOCPA, s 23(3) and (4).
[41] SOCPA, s 24.
[42] SOCPA, s 26(1).
[43] SOCPA, s 26(2).
[44] SOCPA, s 26(6).
[45] SOCPA, s 28.
[46] SOCPA, s 31.
[47] White Paper, p 32.
[48] White Paper, p 33.
[49] White Paper, p 33.

by the DRCP, and 'non-designated offences', which are to be prosecuted by the DPP.

2.36   Interestingly, SOCPA does not designate offences for the purposes of this division of prosecutorial responsibility, but leaves this to the DPP and DRCP themselves. Section 39 empowers them to give directions to SOCA informing them of which offences should be referred to which prosecutorial authority, and how referrals should be made.[50] These directions may divide cases up by reference to categories of offence, criteria, or 'such other matters as the Directors think fit',[51] and can deal with 'different cases, circumstances or areas'.[52] These directions can be revised,[53] and must be published.[54]

2.37   As with the boundary between the investigatory functions of different agencies,[55] a failure to comply with the directions does not make the reference, or anything subsequently done, invalid 'by reason of anything in the directions or in section 38'[56] (leaving open the possibility of challenging the validity of the reference or subsequent prosecution for other reasons).

---

[50] SOCPA, s 39(1).
[51] SOCPA, s 39(2).
[52] SOCPA, s 39(7).
[53] SOCPA, s 39(3).
[54] SOCPA, s 39(4).
[55] SOCPA, s 2(5).
[56] SOCPA, s 39(8).

3

ORGANISED CRIME: NEW INVESTIGATORY POWERS

A. Investigatory Powers Created by SOCPA   3.01
B. Overview   3.04
C. Who can Exercise the New Investigatory Powers?   3.05
D. Offences to which the New Investigatory Powers Apply   3.07
E. Disclosure Notices   3.12
F. Production of Documents   3.21
G. Restrictions on Requiring Information   3.23
H. Restrictions on Use of Statements   3.37
I. Enforcement   3.55
J. Procedural Issues   3.66
K. The Approach in Other Jurisdictions   3.68

A. INVESTIGATORY POWERS CREATED BY SOCPA

'Compulsory powers' denote investigatory powers to require an individual to **3.01** answer questions, provide information, or produce documents. Failure to comply with such powers is typically a criminal offence or a contempt of court, with the possibility of imprisonment. Prior to SOCPA, compulsory powers were available primarily in the regulatory sphere and in the investigation of serious fraud.[1] The rationale was that serious fraud, by its very nature, is necessarily elaborately concealed thereby rendering investigation particularly difficult— hence the need for far-reaching powers elsewhere unavailable.[2] Furthermore, those who operate in the regulatory field do so voluntarily and are

---

[1] eg Powers of the Serious Fraud Office, Office of Fair Trading, Financial Services Authority, Department of Trade and Industry, Inland Revenue, and Asset Recovery Agency.
[2] See eg *Legislating the Criminal Code: Corruption* (March 1997) Law. Comm CP145 at [12.7] and the Government's submissions in *Saunders v UK* (1996) 23 EHRR 313 at [64].

therefore choosing to subject themselves to greater scrutiny and heightened investigation.

3.02 The Government's reasons for extending compulsory powers to combat general, organised crime were set out in the White Paper:[3]

Organised crime investigations rarely affect individuals who are not involved in one way or other in the crime. If the conspirators themselves or those who aid them are not willing to talk, the burden of proof is entirely on the investigators to find the necessary evidence. This obviously means prosecutions will rely heavily on catching criminals red-handed, or the use of highly intrusive and expensive surveillance techniques. But in every case, the authorities are likely to know of individuals who could assist them in their investigations. The sophistication and breadth of much organised crime activity mean it is often surrounded by a wider circle of people with some knowledge of the group's activities. There are often professional facilitators, particularly those involved in money laundering and fraud (including excise fraud) cases or where illegitimate business is mixed with legitimate business. There is seldom likely to be enough evidence to charge these individuals on the fringes. Nor is there any incentive on them to share with the police information on criminal activity.

. . .

In Australia, so-called 'Royal Commission' powers have been steadily expanded since the 1980s. Under the Australian Crime Commission Act 2002, the Australian Crime Commission now runs a system of 'Examiners' who are appointed for a maximum period of five years. These are legal practitioners appointed by the Governor General on the recommendation of the Cabinet. The Examiners have access to a number of special powers which include the power to require individuals to produce documents and to appear and answer questions. In both cases, refusal to comply is an offence, as is disclosing the existence of the order to anyone other than legal representatives.

. . .

In the US, a similar role is played by the Grand Jury system, where the powers to subpoena individuals and documents, exercised by prosecutors, have developed to become a powerful tool in the investigative process, particularly in organised crime cases. All organised crime cases will be brought before a Grand Jury to secure a Federal indictment. Here too, the existence of an offence of refusing to testify seems to have been powerful in ensuring cooperation.

3.03 The White Paper proposed that the compulsory powers in SOCPA follow the Australian approach.

B. OVERVIEW

3.04 Chapter 1 of Part 2 of SOCPA (ie ss 60–70) creates a scheme of compulsory powers broadly similar to those already contained in the Criminal Justice Act 1987 (CJA 1987). Section 60 grants compulsory powers to the Director of Public

---

[3] *One Step Ahead: A 21st Century Strategy to Defeat Organised Crime* (March 2004, Cm 6167) at [6.2.1].

Prosecutions (DPP) and other senior prosecutors with provision for delegation of the powers. Section 61 details the offences to which the new compulsory powers apply. These include lifestyle offences, terrorist fund-raising and money laundering offences, fraudulent evasion of duty, false accounting, and the corresponding inchoate offences. Section 62 creates a power to issue a 'disclosure notice' in certain circumstances. A disclosure notice can require any person (suspect or not) to answer questions relevant to the investigation, to provide information, or to produce documents specified in the notice. Section 63 regulates the retention of documents produced pursuant to a disclosure notice and includes powers to require the producer to explain documents or to give information as to their likely location. Section 64 exempts material covered by legal professional privilege as well as the Police and Criminal Evidence Act 1984 (PACE) excluded material and regulates requests concerning confidential banking material. Section 65 prohibits the use of material obtained under compulsory powers against the person under compulsion in any criminal proceedings save in limited circumstances. These include proceedings for offences of failing to comply with the compulsory powers and perjury offences. A further exception is where the person under compulsion is prosecuted for some other offence and himself refers to a statement obtained under compulsion and gives evidence inconsistent with it. Section 66 creates enforcement powers, including search warrants permitting entry and seizure of documents which have not been provided in accordance with a disclosure notice, or where giving a disclosure notice was impracticable or might seriously prejudice the investigation. Section 67 creates criminal offences in connection with disclosure notices or search warrants.

C. WHO CAN EXERCISE THE NEW INVESTIGATORY POWERS?

Section 60 confers the new compulsory powers relating to the investigation 3.05 of particular crimes on investigating authorities, which are the DPP, the (newly created) Director of Revenue and Customs Prosecutions, and the Lord Advocate. Delegation is, however, possible to Crown or Revenue and Customs prosecutors and procurators fiscal. Thus more than 2,500 Crown prosecutors, for example, will be able to authorise compulsory questioning. This broadly corresponds to the wide delegability of powers under s 2(11) CJA 1987, which can be exercised by a 'competent investigator (other than a constable)', even one who is not a member of the Serious Fraud Office (SFO). In other jurisdictions (eg Australia), however, a *senior* legally qualified lawyer must authorise the compulsory questioning.

Despite the difficult privilege issues involved, SOCPA has no additional 3.06 requirement of judicial authorisation for compulsory questioning of a person's lawyer, accountant, banker, or other professional adviser. There are no overarching safeguards, such as annual reports to Parliament concerning the frequency, efficacy, and any complaints concerning the use of the new compulsory powers. The Act creates no statutory right of appeal against an authorisation to use compulsory powers but such decisions will be amenable to judicial review.[4]

D. OFFENCES TO WHICH THE NEW INVESTIGATORY POWERS APPLY

3.07 Section 61 permits the use of the compulsory powers only in connection with the investigation of specified offences set out in that section. Serious crimes such as terrorist fund-raising offences and terrorist money laundering offences under ss 15–18 Terrorism Act 2000 are included (s 61(1)(c)).

3.08 However, the list is extensive and includes any 'lifestyle offence' in Schedules 2 and 4 of the Proceeds of Crime Act 2002. The list of lifestyle offences currently extends to more than 30 statutory provisions and includes comparatively minor offences such as possessing counterfeit coins, keeping a brothel, trademark, and copyright offences. Under s 61(4)(a) the list of offences can be amended by order of the Home Secretary subject to the affirmative resolution procedure.

3.09 Section 61(1)(d) and (e) permits coercive investigations in relation to offences of fraudulent evasion of duty of VAT, false accounting, or cheating the public revenue. For each of these offences, however, the (potential) loss involved must be at least £5,000 (s 61(2)). This sum can be amended by order of the Home Secretary subject to the affirmative resolution procedure (s 61(4)(b)(ii)).

3.10 Attempts and conspiracies to commit the specified offences are also included within the list (s 61(1)(f)–(g)).

3.11 The breadth of the list of specified offences was widely criticised during the pre-legislative consultation. JUSTICE felt such a draconian power should be limited to 'serious offences'.[5] The Police Federation thought that the powers should apply only to the most serious types of offences, for example, terrorism, murder and conspiracy to kill, and offences 'likely to affect the public interest', such as paedophilia and human trafficking.[6] The Institute of Chartered Accountants had concerns over the unrestricted inclusion of money laundering offences.[7] The use of coercive powers in the investigation of minor offences is open to challenge on proportionality grounds. Moreover, s 61 must be read together with the core definition in s 2(1)(a) of the Act, which provides that SOCA functions are to prevent and detect *serious* organised crime.[8]

---

[4] Cf *R v Director of the Serious Fraud Office ex p Evans* [2003] 1 WLR 299.

[5] JUSTICE Response to White Paper <www.justice.org.uk./images/pdfs/orgcr.pdf>.

[6] <www.polfed.org/fbi-styleagencytobelaunched.pdf>.

[7] <www.icaew.co.uk/viewer/index.cfm/aub/tb2i_68333>. This prompted the inclusion of the minimum threshold in s 61(2).

[8] Note that the Act deliberately makes no attempt to define what *organised* crime is. However, s 5(3) provides: 'Despite the references to serious organised crime in s 2(1), SOCA may carry on activities in relation to other crime.'

E. DISCLOSURE NOTICES

The primary mechanism for exercising the new investigatory powers is by the   3.12
service of a 'disclosure notice' upon a person. Under s 62(1), the power to give a
disclosure notice is exercisable when 'it appears to the Investigating Authority'
that three conditions are met:

(a) there are reasonable grounds for suspecting that a qualifying offence has
    been committed (ie an offence specified in s 61);

(b) a person has information (in a document or otherwise) relating to a matter
    relevant to the investigation of that offence;

(c) there are reasonable grounds for believing that information which may be
    provided by that person in compliance with a disclosure notice is likely to
    be of substantial value (whether or not by itself) to that investigation.

A disclosure notice may then be given to that person. As with s 2(3) CJA 1987,   3.13
no distinction at all is made between persons under investigation and non-
suspects. The original requirement in clause 56(2) of the Bill that a disclosure
notice could only be served on a person under investigation if there were also
exceptional circumstances making it expedient to do so, was removed from the
Act.[9] Suspects and non-suspects are therefore treated alike during the compulsory investigation phase, but are treated differently as concerns the use of
any material obtained under compulsion (s 65).[10]

The disclosure notice is authorised by the relevant investigating authority   3.14
(delegated, for example, to a Crown prosecutor) but may be given by a constable,
a designated member of SOCA staff, or a Customs officer (s 62(2)). The notice
must be (counter-)signed by the relevant investigating authority (s 62(5)).

The disclosure notice may require the recipient to answer questions, pro-   3.15
vide information, and/or produce documents relevant to an investigation. It is

---

[9] When the amendment removing clause 56(2) was introduced, the Home Office Under-Secretary
said the clause created 'a bit of an artificial distinction' between suspects and others. She continued:
'our intention is that notices will usually be given to people other than the primary suspects, partly as
they are more likely to cooperate and partly because of the protections against self-incrimination
for the subject of the notice . . . Also, in certain circumstances the prosecutor may decide to give a
notice to someone suspected of one of the offences anyway. For example, a junior member of a
criminal group may be suspected of one of the specified offences, but the prosecutor may believe that
serving a notice on him would provide information of substantial value to the wider investigation,
and that the benefit of that would outweigh not being able to use a self-incriminatory statement
made by the junior member' (HC Standing Committee Debate on Serious Organised Crime Bill,
13 January 2005, col. 132).

[10] The distinction between the treatment of suspects and non-suspects in the DTI's powers under
the Companies Act (coercive powers usable against a person who does not know whether or not they
are subject to criminal proceedings) as compared with the SFO's powers under the CJA 1987 (person
knows if they are a suspect and is protected by s 2(8)) was critical in *Saunders v UK* (n 2 above)—see
[74] thereof.

well established that under s 2 CJA 1987, similar requests cannot be vague and speculative, but must be as precise and focused as possible.[11] Although a prosecution 'fishing expedition' is not possible, the fact that proceedings are only at the investigative stage allows a greater latitude in the disclosure notice than otherwise.

3.16   When requesting documents relevant to an investigation, the notice itself must specify or describe the documents in question (s 62(3)(c)). A similar requirement applies when information is requested (s 62(3)(b)). When requiring a person to answer questions, however, there is no requirement to specify, describe, or outline the questions in the notice itself.

3.17   It is likely that a notice under s 62 will be drafted as follows. It will be headed 'Notice requiring attendance to answer questions, provide information and produce documents'. It will recite the coercive powers of the investigating authority and the delegation to carry out the powers on behalf of the authority. It will set out that the pre-conditions for the exercise of the powers are made out and that a requirement is made that the individual should answer questions or otherwise provide information or documents at a specified time or place or immediately. It will state that the constable etc who is giving the notice is empowered to take copies or extracts from the specified documents or require the recipient to explain the documents or where any unavailable documents are. It ought to remind the recipient that he is entitled to legal representation during any questioning and will be provided with a transcript of any answers which he can correct or expand.[12] It will include the warning that failure without reasonable excuse to comply with these requirements is a criminal offence, punishable with imprisonment.

3.18   The notice should also state who is under investigation (persons and/or companies) and therefore whether the recipient is merely a witness or is himself a suspect. But is the investigating authority also under any obligation to disclose to the recipient of a notice, in particular to a person under investigation, the nature of the inquiry being conducted? Comparison with the s 2 CJA 1987 powers suggests that, for non-suspects, the only duty is to identify the existence of the investigation. There is no duty to disclose the reasons for, or the areas of, the inquiry. In practice, however, the SFO usually willingly gives details of the areas of interest in its inquiries, in advance of an interview, to a witness. A critical difference between the use of compulsory powers under SOCPA and under s 2 CJA 1987, however, is that the investigating authorities are more likely to regard mere witnesses in organised crime cases as being 'on the fringes' of criminality. Accordingly, under SOCPA, it seems likely that the investigating authorities will be more guarded than the SFO in revealing in advance the areas

---

[11] See eg *R v Home Secretary ex p Finivest SpA* [1997] 1 All ER 942, and [2.3.2] Kirk and Woodcock *Serious Fraud: Investigation and Trial* (Butterworths, 3rd edn, 2003).
[12] Cf the safeguards during the investigative phase relied on by the Government at [63] of *Saunders v UK* (n 2 above).

of inquiry to witnesses who are not formally suspects, for fear of contaminating the investigation.

For a person under investigation, however, is there a valid analogy with the PACE and Article 5 European Convention on Human Rights (ECHR) requirements for arrested persons? Section 62(4) of the Act permits the disclosure notice to specify the time at or by which, the place at which, or the manner in which the recipient is to do the requests in the notice. Therefore, the recipient of a notice who is required to do something immediately (permissible under s 62(4)) would theoretically be in the same position as a person attending voluntarily at a police station and then not allowed to leave. In those circumstances, the recipient would commit a criminal offence under s 67 of the Act (detailed below) unless he complied immediately and might therefore be technically or actually arrested. However, even in such circumstances, the PACE and ECHR requirements have been narrowly interpreted and would not extend to any duty to detail the precise areas under investigation.[13]

For a person under investigation, careful thought will need to be given as to whether to agree to an interview under caution or to force the investigating authority to use its compulsory powers. In deciding this, the procedural protections offered by PACE, the right to silence (qualified by the possibility of adverse inferences), must be weighed against the more limited admissibility of answers obtained under compulsion (s 65). Obtaining statements by compulsion from people who are themselves under suspicion has the potential to cause significant complications, particularly in a trial involving multiple defendants. In making the decision, it should also be borne in mind that compulsory powers can be used after charge, although this is rarely done in practice.[14] By comparison, it is in fact now standard practice for the SFO to conduct most interviews under caution with the familiar PACE safeguards.[15] The SFO has also agreed not to use any material gathered under compulsory powers in the Insolvency or Companies Acts.

F. PRODUCTION OF DOCUMENTS

Section 63 further regulates what may be done in connection with documents specified in a disclosure notice. A person authorised by the investigating authority (eg the constable who served the notice) can take copies of any documents produced in compliance with the notice (s 63(2)(a)). Original documents

---

[13] Cf *R v SFO ex p Maxwell (Kevin)* The Times, 9 October 1992.
[14] *R v Director of SFO ex p Smith* [1993] AC 1; *R v Metropolitan Stipendiary Magistrate ex p SFO* The Independent, 24 June 1994, DC.
[15] This may now be partly motivated by a fear of the cross-use of s 2 statements subsequently forcing severance. (See discussion of *Wickes* case below and Hood, 'Compulsory Questions' [2003] NLJ 1140.)

provided may be retained by the investigating authority for as long as is necessary. Originals will normally be retained until proceedings have concluded (see s 63(4)).

3.22   There is also a power to require the person producing documents in compliance with a disclosure notice to provide an explanation of any of them (s 63(2)(b)), or if they are not produced, to state, to the best of his knowledge and belief, where they are (s 63(5)). These requirements derive from the SFO powers in s 2(3) CJA 1987 and the Department of Trade and Industry (DTI) powers in s 447(5) Companies Act 1985. Although the requirement to provide an explanation will normally take place at the time of seizure, there is no express restriction on the nature and extent of questioning which can take place. Clearly, any attempt to use this as a device to perform a coercive interview would be open to challenge.[16]

G. RESTRICTIONS ON REQUIRING INFORMATION

3.23   There are three categories of restrictions on the use of the powers in ss 62 and 63: material covered by legal professional privilege, 'excluded material' defined by PACE, and confidential banking material.

1. Privilege

3.24   Section 64(1) provides that:[17]

A person may not be required under section 62 or 63—
(a) to answer any privileged question,
(b) to provide any privileged information, or
(c) to produce any privileged document,
except that a lawyer may be required to provide the name and address of a client of his.

3.25   Privileged questions, information, and documents are defined as those which a person would be entitled to refuse to answer, provide, or produce on (common-law) grounds of legal professional privilege in proceedings in the High Court (s 64(2)–(4)). In Scotland, however, legal privilege is deemed to have the statutory meaning given by s 412 Proceeds of Crime Act 2002 (s 64(6)–(7)).

3.26   Claiming legal professional privilege raises a number of difficult legal and practical issues.[18] Legal professional privilege remains a critical feature of the

---

[16] Cf PACE Code of Practice: Code B: [6.12]–[6.12A] and Code C: [10.1] eg questions necessary for the purpose of furthering the proper and effective conduct of a search do not constitute an interview and a caution need not been given. However, questions going further, regarding a person's suspected involvement in an offence, constitute an interview, must be under caution, and attract the familiar PACE safeguards Code C: [11.1A].

[17] The section is similar to s 2(9) CJA 1987.

[18] See further Chapter 3 of Kirk and Woodcock (n 11 above).

UK legal system. Its high constitutional status has recently been reaffirmed by the House of Lords in *Three Rivers DC v Bank of England (No 6)*.[19] Lord Scott noted that good policy reasons underpinned the law affording a special privilege to communications between lawyers and their clients which it denies to all other confidential communications, and considered that the rationale underlying the privilege was 'the rule of law rationale'.[20] In *R (Morgan Grenfell & Co Ltd) v Special Commissioner for Income Tax*[21] Lord Hoffmann described the privilege as a 'fundamental human right long established in the common law'. Lord Taylor CJ in *R v Derby Magistrates' Court ex p B*[22] said 'it is a fundamental condition on which the administration of justice as a whole rests'.

Obviously, claiming legal professional privilege in respect of unspecified **3.27** documents somewhere on a hard drive from a number of seized computers, for example, has the potential to frustrate the investigation of serious crime by causing serious delay. Nevertheless, in deciding whether to claim or waive privilege in any particular case, it should be remembered that it is a fundamental human right, specifically preserved in the Act. A number of important factors need to be assessed when deciding whether to claim privilege. It should not be seen or used as a tactical ploy but, rather, as the exercise of a basic right; once waived it cannot be reasserted (so early decisions on it are significant); it is the *client's* privilege to waive (not the lawyer's).

The basic rule is that when a lawyer is advising a client or acting for him in **3.28** litigation, he may not disclose to a third party any information about his client's affairs without his express or implied consent. Specifically, in civil and criminal cases, confidential communications between a client and his legal adviser are privileged in that such communications need not be given in evidence by the client and may not be given in evidence by the lawyer without the client's consent if such communications were made:

(a) to enable the client to obtain, or the adviser to give, legal advice; and

(b) with reference to litigation that is actively taking place, or was in the contemplation of the client.

Communications between the legal adviser or client and third parties are **3.29** also privileged, if made for the purpose or pending or contemplated litigation. Communications relating to the preparation of witness statements are privileged.

The House of Lords in *Three Rivers* held that 'legal advice privilege' was **3.30** also just as important as litigation privilege. Presentational advice sought from

---

[19] [2004] UKHL 48, [2004] 3 WLR 1274.
[20] [23] to [28]; [34].
[21] [2002] UKHL 21, [2003] 1 AC 563 at [7] to [9].
[22] [1996] 1 AC 487 at pp 503–508.

lawyers by any individual or company who believed himself, herself, or itself to be at risk of criticism by an inquiry, whether a coroner's inquest, a statutory inquiry, or an *ad hoc* inquiry, was privileged.

3.31   Obviously privilege no longer continues after the client has waived it. It is virtually impossible to waive privilege partially. The only true exception to privilege is therefore where the communication between client and lawyer has been made in order to facilitate crime or fraud. Thus, if a client seeks guidance concerning the facilitation of a crime, the lawyer may be compelled to disclose the contents of the communication. The crime/fraud exception is preserved by the common law[23] and in s 10(2) PACE.[24] The Court of Appeal in *Bowman v Fels*[25] recently held that money laundering requirements on lawyers in s 328 Proceeds of Crime Act 2002 are not intended to cover or affect the ordinary conduct of litigation by legal professionals. There is no longer any exception to the privilege where the material 'tends to establish the innocence of the defendant in criminal proceedings'.[26]

3.32   Further complexities arise if the disclosure notice is directed at a client's lawyer. The SFO extensively uses its compulsory powers against lawyers, accountants, and bankers. The Guide to the Professional Conduct of Solicitors makes it clear that a solicitor will be in breach of his contractual duty to his client if he cooperates with the police without the coercion of a disclosure notice. There are further issues concerning the duty to challenge a notice on behalf of a client and the duty (or prohibition) to inform the client of the issue of a notice against his lawyer.[27] Although s 64 respects legally privileged and certain types of confidential material, a requirement under ss 62 and 63 takes precedence over any other restrictions that may limit disclosure of the material/ information in question (s 64(9)).

3.33   Part 2 of the Criminal Justice and Police Act 2001 (as amended by s 68 SOCPA) provides that where an investigating authority is proposing to remove a mass of material in a s 66 SOCPA warrant case, in which it is believed that there are documents which would be protected by legal professional privilege, it should be possible to agree that all the material taken should be sealed, pending an examination of it by lawyers representing the person claiming privilege, and the removal of privileged material. The situation is similar to that envisaged under paragraph 9 of the Attorney-General's *Guidelines on the Disclosure of Information in Criminal Proceedings*[28] which exempts prosecutors from

---

[23] *R v Cox and Railton* (1884) 14 QBD 153.

[24] Which permits (with judicial authorisation) the seizure of otherwise privileged documents which 'further a criminal purpose'. See also *R v Central Criminal Court ex p Francis and Francis (a Firm)* [1989] AC 346.

[25] [2005] EWCA Civ 226.

[26] *R v Derby Magistrates ex p B* (n 22 above).

[27] Cf *Barclays Bank v Taylor* [1989] 1 WLR 1066 and *Bowman v Fels* (n 25 above).

[28] Issued on 29 November 2000: Archbold 2005 supplement at [A-245].

examining large volumes of material which have been seized 'out of an abundance of caution' by investigators.

2. Excluded Material

By s 65(5), a s 62 disclosure notice may not, in any circumstances, include a request for 'excluded material' as defined by s 11 PACE. Section 11 PACE defines such material as: personal records which a person has acquired or created in the course of any trade, business, profession, or other occupation or for the purposes of any paid or unpaid office and which he holds in confidence; human tissue or tissue fluid which has been taken for the purposes of diagnosis or medical treatment and which a person holds in confidence; journalistic material which a person holds in confidence. These terms are further defined by ss 12–14 PACE. Excluded material remains, therefore, subject to the existing protections in PACE: eg circuit judge authorisation and preservation of crime/fraud exception in s 10(2).[29]

3.34

3. Banking Confidentiality

Section 64(8) provides that:

3.35

A person may not be required under section 62 or 63 to disclose any information or produce any document in respect of which he owes an obligation of confidence by virtue of carrying on any banking business, unless—
(a) the person to whom the obligation of confidence is owed consents to the disclosure or production, or
(b) the requirement is made by, or in accordance with a specific authorisation given by, the Investigating Authority.

This is materially identical to the exception in s 2(10) CJA 1987 save in one important respect. Under the 1987 Act, ordinarily, only the Director of the SFO can authorise such a request. However, by the general power of delegation in s 60(3) SOCPA, any Crown prosecutor, for example, could authorise a coercive request for production of banking records under s 64(8). The position contrasts sharply with the special procedure material protected by PACE, which requires an application to a circuit judge on stringent criteria before banking records can be sought. The breadth of the power under s 64 is particularly troubling when noting, for example, that the SFO directed 50 per cent of its s 2 notices at banks in 2001/02.[30]

3.36

---

[29] See further Archbold 2005 at [15-74] to [15-79]; [15-90] to [15-100] for a detailed consideration of excluded and special procedure material.
[30] Kirk and Woodcock at [2.3.5(a)] (n 11 above).

H. RESTRICTIONS ON USE OF STATEMENTS

1. Protection Against Self-incrimination

3.37 The right to a fair trial includes 'the right of anyone charged with a criminal offence . . . to remain silent and not to contribute to incriminating himself'[31]. In *Saunders v UK*[32] the European Court described these rights as generally recognised international standards which lay at the heart of the notion of a fair procedure under Article 6. The right not to incriminate oneself presupposed that the prosecution in a criminal case must prove its case without resort to evidence obtained through methods of coercion and oppression in defiance of the will of the accused. In this sense the privilege against self-incrimination was closely linked to the presumption of innocence. The common law also excludes involuntary confessions by prophylactic rules designed to inhibit abuse of power by investigatory authorities and to preserve the fairness of the trial by preventing the eliciting of confessions which may have doubtful probative value.[33]

3.38 The House of Lords considered the Strasbourg and domestic authorities on the issue in *R v Hertfordshire CC ex p Green Environmental Industries Ltd*.[34] It was held that the protection against self-incrimination, as understood in *Saunders*, was relevant only where the prosecution sought to introduce evidence obtained by powers of compulsory questioning in the course of a criminal trial. Under the Human Rights Act 1998, it would be incumbent on a judge to consider whether Article 6 required the exclusion of such evidence. Article 6 did not, however, prevent the use of compulsory questioning powers during the *investigative* phase of an inquiry.[35] Notwithstanding the decision in *Funke*, the House of Lords held that the European Court of Human Rights (ECtHR) had drawn a clear distinction in *Saunders* between questioning during the course of 'extra-judicial inquiries' and the *use* of the material thereby obtained in a subsequent criminal prosecution.

3.39 Accordingly, s 65 prohibits the use in evidence in criminal proceedings of statements made by a person in response to a s 62 disclosure notice or a s 63 requirement, save in specified circumstances. This broadly reflects the decision in *Saunders v UK* on the scope of the protection against self-incrimination in criminal proceedings.[36] Section 65 closely resembles, for example, s 2(8) and

---

[31] *Funke v France* 16 EHRR 297.
[32] (1996) 23 EHRR 313 at [68]–[69]. See also *IJL, GMR and AKP v UK* (2001) 33 EHRR 11 and *Serves v France* 28 EHRR 265.
[33] See Lord Templeman in *AT & T Istel Ltd v Tully* [1993] AC 45, 53.
[34] [2000] 2 AC 412.
[35] *Saunders v UK* (n 2 above) [67]; *Fayed v UK* (1994) 18 EHRR 393 at [61].
[36] At [71]–[76]. Sedley LJ in 'Wringing Out the Fault: Self-Incrimination in the 21st Century' NILQ 52 (No 2) 107 thought the result that *Saunders v UK* produced had 'more in common with snakes and ladders than with a serious legal system'.

s 2(8AA) CJA 1987.[37] Statements made in response to s 62 and s 63 requirements may be used in evidence against the maker in criminal proceedings in only
three distinct situations:

(a) where the maker is being prosecuted for an offence under s 67 (eg failing to
comply with a disclosure notice);[38]

(b) where the maker is being prosecuted for a perjury offence under s 5
Perjury Act 1911 (false statements made on oath otherwise than in judicial
proceedings or made otherwise than on oath);[39]

(c) where the maker is being prosecuted for some other offence[40] and
(i) when giving evidence in the proceedings, makes a statement inconsistent
with the statement obtained under compulsion and
(ii) the maker himself adduces evidence relating to, or asks a question
about, the statement obtained under compulsion.

While s 65 protects a defendant from self-incrimination in the strict sense, the   **3.40**
material obtained under compulsion can still be used by investigators to assist
them in convicting the suspect. It can, for example, shape the investigation,
influence which witnesses are interviewed, and direct the line of future questioning. It can also help formulate cross-examination at trial. Moreover, there is no
express prohibition on statements obtained under compulsory powers being
passed from one law enforcement authority to another.[41] Neither is there any
obligation to provide the maker of the statement with notice that this has been
done.[42] Nor is there is any express prohibition on the use of the compelled
material being passed to overseas authorities. Many European jurisdictions
(eg Belgium, France, Germany, and the Netherlands) permit the direct use of
UK coercive interview answers in their own domestic criminal proceedings.[43]

Although s 65 represents a considerable erosion of the right to silence, the   **3.41**
adverse inferences which a court can draw from a suspect's failure to answer
questions in a PACE interview[44] may somewhat diminish the significance of the
compulsory powers as against suspects. In effect, the adverse inference is a form
of compulsion/coercion. It is unclear, however, whether adverse inferences could

---

[37] This and many other statutes were amended by Sch 3 of the Youth Justice and Criminal Evidence
Act 1999 which gave effect to *Saunders v UK* and superseded the Attorney-General's 'General Note
for Prosecutors' [1998] NLJ 208.

[38] Section 65(2)(a).

[39] Section 65(2)(b).

[40] Section 65(3).

[41] Cf the restrictions in s 242 Enterprise Act 2002 on Office of Fair Trading investigators passing
information to prosecutors.

[42] *R v Brady* [2004] 3 All ER 520.

[43] It is unclear how this remains possible in the light of *Saunders v UK* and the Draft EU Framework
Decision on Procedural Rights in Criminal Proceedings.

[44] Criminal Justice and Public Order Act 1994, s 34.

be drawn if a defendant gave a full account in his s 62 compulsory interview but refused to answer questions in a subsequent PACE interview.[45]

3.42　The self incrimination protection may be relied upon by a corporation in the same way as it applies to an individual,[46] which is particularly significant given that the Act makes specific provision for service of disclosure notices upon corporate bodies (s 69(3)). Note, however, that a public authority cannot be a victim within the meaning of s 7 of the Human Rights Act.[47] By contrast, in Canada, the United States, and Australia, corporations cannot rely on the protection.[48]

2. Limits of the Protection against Self-incrimination

3.43　The White Paper emphasised, however, that a key motivation for extending compulsory powers to organised crime cases was to coerce non-participants and those on the periphery of criminality to give evidence in compelled statements which could shape the investigation or be *used against other persons*. Section 65 does not explicitly restrict the use by the prosecution of compelled statements against persons other than the maker—even where both the maker and the person against whom they are used are both co-defendants in a joint trial. Nor is there any express prohibition on the use of evidence obtained under compulsion in civil proceedings against the maker.[49]

3.44　Absent express prohibition in the Act, the prosecution may adduce the compelled answers of a witness obtained under s 62 against another person in the latter's trial via a number of routes. The prosecution could use the standard witness summons procedure to secure the attendance at trial of a reluctant witness (with a power of arrest if required) who had previously made a compelled statement. If the witness remained uncooperative, assuming the prosecution were permitted to treat them as hostile, the answers given under compulsion could form the basis of the prosecution's questioning. This, coupled with the usual contempt of court sanction for failing to answer questions on oath, would be a powerful incentive for a witness to give evidence consistent with their answers obtained under compulsion.

---

[45] Criminal Justice and Public Order Act 1994, ss 34–35. Cf [73]–[74] *Saunders v UK* (n 2 above).

[46] *Triplex Safety Glass Co v Lancegaye Safety Glass (1934) Ltd* [1939] 2 KB 395; *Rio Tinto Zinc Corp v Westinghouse Electric Corp* [1978] AC 547 and *R v Hertfordshire CC ex p Green Environmental Industries Ltd* (n 34 above). Cf Lord Templeman in *AT & Istel v Tully* [1993] AC 45 at 53B.

[47] *Aston Cantlow Parochial Church Council v Wallbank* [2003] UKHL 37 at [10], [59], [87], and [166].

[48] See the cases set out in [12.59] to [12.62] of Pinto and Evans *Corporate Criminal Liability* (Sweet & Maxwell, 2003).

[49] Cf *R (Kent Pharmaceuticals Ltd) v Director of Serious Fraud Office (Secretary of State for the Home Department)* [2004] EWCA Civ 1494, [2005] 1 All ER 449. An application to the ECtHR has been made.

In any event, the coerced witness might feel under pressure to give evidence **3.45** consistent with their answers obtained under compulsion. Although in a prosecution for perjury on oath their compelled evidence is inadmissible, evidence given in another's trial which is inconsistent with the compelled answers is admissible on a charge of making false or misleading statements in response to a disclosure notice (s 67(2)). Alternatively a witness's compelled answers might be potentially directly admissible against a defendant under the new hearsay rules in Chapter 2 of the Criminal Justice Act 2003: eg previous inconsistent statements (s 119 CJA 2003); previous consistent statements (s 120 CJA 2003).

The only method of excluding such evidence would be on unfairness grounds **3.46** under s 78 PACE (which is expressly preserved by s 126 CJA 2003). The problem is heightened in organised crime cases as compared with business crime or fraud trials. The Government accepts that witnesses who are not formally suspects in organised crime cases, because of the nature of the criminality in question, may nevertheless be on the periphery of criminality. These are among the witnesses most likely to give false, misleading or partial evidence. Moreover, a witness who is not a suspect may be faced with an invidious choice: statutory coercion to answer questions or retribution from an avowedly violent criminal gang if cooperation with the authorities is forthcoming. There is not a great deal of public confidence in current witness protection schemes.[50] Admittedly, there are new enhanced witness protection measures in Chapter 4 of Part 2 of the Act (ss 82 to 94) which aim to address some of these concerns (and which are dealt with in Chapter 4 below). Nevertheless, it remains the case that a witness who, in effect, has to say something or face criminal penalties for their silence, is not one whose reliability can be assured.[51] These factors are likely seriously to affect the reliability of compelled answers and form the basis of an exclusionary challenge.

There are also wider consequential issues involved in departing from the **3.47** voluntary scheme of witness cooperation which currently underpins the investigation and prosecution of crimes in English law, eg discouraging witnesses from coming forward for fear of subsequent compulsion. The White Paper did not provide any actual examples of an inability to prosecute organised crime cases because of the failure of witnesses to come forward voluntarily. However, the increased use of witnesses on the fringes of criminality is consistent with the other measures in the Act designed to further encourage cooperation by those who have themselves participated in criminal conduct (eg conditional immunities and enforceable plea bargains in ss 71 to 75).

The position is further complicated when the compelled answers emanate **3.48** from a co-defendant. A defendant's compelled answers are not directly admissible

---

[50] Cf the complaints about inadequate protection made in *R (D) v Central Criminal Court* [2004] 1 Cr App R 41.

[51] The concerns of Liberty, JUSTICE and the Law Society in this regard are summarised in the House of Commons Research Paper on the Bill (2 December 2004, HC 04/88) at p 20.

against a co-defendant (unless they are an exception to the hearsay rule) and this is preserved by s 118 CJA 2003. However, a common-law extension to the exception to the hearsay rule contained in s 74 PACE was recently identified by the House of Lords in *R v Hayter*,[52] where one defendant's guilt, even where exclusively based on his confession, can be used to establish a co-defendant's guilt. There is no obvious reason why this should not apply even where the confession relied upon flows from compelled answers. However, in those circumstances, it will be critical to determine whether the PACE confession is tainted by the compelled answers—eg is there some causative link between them?[53]

3.49   In the recent *Wickes* fraud case,[54] the defendant C successfully sought to admit, as part of his case, an extract from his co-defendant R's s 2 CJA 1987 interview (pursuant to *R v Myers*[55]). At the time, ss 76 and 78 had no application in relation to co-defendants, and therefore the trial judge allowed R's application for severance because of the potential unfairness caused to R as a result of being forced to give evidence to explain the circumstances of the interview and his answers.[56] The drafting of s 65(1) ('A statement made by a person in response to a requirement imposed under s 62 or 63 . . . *may not be used in evidence against him* in any criminal proceedings') is sufficiently broad to prohibit any party, not only the prosecution, from adducing evidence obtained under compulsion against the maker in criminal proceedings.[57] The position is now somewhat simplified by s 76A PACE[58] (which is apt to exclude involuntary confessions) which extends s 76 PACE to confessions adduced by a co-defendant.[59]

3.50   Additional difficulties may remain, however, if, at the time of the compulsory questioning, the witness is not a suspect but as the investigation progresses he becomes a suspect or defendant.

3. Derivative Use

3.51   The s 65 restriction applies only to *statements* obtained under compulsion. There is no express statutory prohibition on the use in evidence of documents obtained under compulsion or of information obtained as a result of compelled testimony against the coerced person in criminal proceedings against him. This

---

[52] [2005] UKHL 6.

[53] Although, in general, the breadth of s 78 ensures that the use of confession evidence will not violate Article 6, s 78 did not *in itself* provide an adequate substitute for the self-incrimination protection in relation to evidence obtained under compulsion: *Saunders v UK* (n 2 above) at [63], [71], and [75]; *R v Hasan* [2005] UKHL 22.

[54] *R v Rosenthal; R v Sweetbaum & ors* (unreported, Southwark Crown Court, Mitting J).

[55] [1998] AC 124: an out of court statement by one defendant admissible in the case of another defendant as an exception to the rule against hearsay provided it was a confession and was relevant.

[56] Cf *Saunders v UK* (n 2 above) at [32] and [72]; *R v Blastland* [1985] AC 41.

[57] Cf Mitting J's ruling on the width of s 2(8) CJA 1987 (drafted pre-*Myers*).

[58] Amended by s 128 CJA 2003.

[59] This was previously governed by common law: *R v Myers* (n 55 above).

reflects the prevailing interpretation of the self-incrimination protection; that it does not extend to documents or other information which have an existence 'independent of the will of the accused'.[60] Although, in principle, there is a clear difference between compelled testimony and evidence derived from it, the domestic and Strasbourg case law on the issue remains unclear.[61]

The protection against self-incrimination (at common law and in Article 6) **3.52** prevents the use in a criminal trial of compelled statements incriminating the maker but does not prohibit the use of documents (or other items/information) produced under compulsion which may have that effect. The rationale for this distinction is that the compulsion might produce unreliable confessions, whereas it could not affect pre-existing documents (or other items/information). The decision in *Saunders v UK* established a 'use immunity'—ie a protection against the *use* by the prosecution in criminal proceedings of answers obtained under compulsion. But is there any 'derivative use' immunity—ie protection against the use of any revelations made during compulsory questioning or other items/ information derived from it?[62]

The absence of any English 'fruit of the poisoned tree' doctrine operates at **3.53** common law to permit adduction of evidence of facts discovered as a result of, or in the course of, an inadmissible confession. This was preserved by s 76 PACE. However, adduction of such evidence is only possible if there is some independent link between the defendant and the material in question— otherwise the discovery and existence of the material would be irrelevant or its relevance only referable to the inadmissible confession.[63]

The House of Lords in *R v Hertfordshire CC ex p Green Environment* **3.54** *Industries Ltd*[64] recognised that the Strasbourg case law on derivative use was unclear. In *Attorney-General's Reference (No 7 of 2000)* the Court of Appeal held that Article 6 did not prohibit the admission of documents delivered up to the Official Receiver produced under compulsion pursuant to s 291 of the Insolvency Act 1986, but rendered answers obtained under the s 433 compulsory powers inadmissible. It held that, in so far as *Funke* supported the proposition that the protection against self-incrimination extended to documents which had an existence independent of the will of the accused, it was inconsistent with *Saunders*, and the latter was to be preferred.[65] Two months, later, however, the

---

[60] See eg *Attorney-General's (No 7 of 2000)* [2001] 2 Cr App R 19 and *Saunders v UK* (n 2 above) at [69].

[61] This distinction was also severely criticised by Sedley LJ in 'Wringing Out the Fault: Self-Incrimination in the 21st Century' (n 36 above). See eg the example given by the Supreme Court in *Doe v United States* (1988) 487 US 201 *(Doe II)* at 210; discussed at para 3.77 below.

[62] [69] of *Saunders v UK* (n 2 above) gave documents, breath, blood, and urine samples and bodily tissue as *examples* of such material whose existence was independent of the will of the accused. The list was not intended to be exhaustive.

[63] Cf *R v Lam Chi-Wing* [1991] 2 AC 212, PC.

[64] n 34 above, at 426 *per* Lord Cooke.

[65] See also *R v Hundal and Dhaliwal* The Times, 13 February 2004.

ECtHR in *JB v Switzerland*[66] followed *Funke* and found a violation of Article 6 where the applicant had been fined for failing to produce documents to the tax authorities. These conflicting authorities were reconsidered by the House of Lords in *R v Allen*[67] (compulsory tax 'Hansard procedure') and by the Court of Appeal in *R v Kearns*[68] (bankruptcy compulsory requirements under s 354 Insolvency Act 1986). Neither Court found any violation of Article 6, and preferred *Saunders* to *JB v Switzerland*. Part of their reasoning was endorsed by the European Court in *Allen v UK*[69] on the basis that the prosecution for making a false declaration 'was not an example of forced self-incrimination about an offence which he had previously been committed; it was the offence itself'.[70] Nevertheless, the key Strasbourg ruling in *Heaney and McGuiness v Ireland*,[71] that Article 6 was violated where the offence in question destroyed the 'very essence' of the privilege against self-incrimination, remains on the face of it irreconcilable with the Privy Council decision in *Brown v Stott*.[72] Until this conflict is definitively resolved by the House of Lords, the precise ambit of the protection against self-incrimination and the status of derivative use immunity will remain unclear.[73]

I. ENFORCEMENT

1. Power to Enter and Seize Documents

3.55 Section 66 gives a justice of the peace the power to issue a warrant to enter premises and seize documents. The justice of the peace may issue a warrant under the section if, on an information on oath, he is satisfied that any of the following three conditions are met and that the documents in question are on the premises in question:[74]

(a) that the recipient of a disclosure notice who is required to produce documents has not done so;

(b) that it is not practicable to give a disclosure notice requiring their production;

(c) that giving such a notice might seriously prejudice the investigation of a qualifying offence.

---

[66] [2001] Crim LR 748.
[67] [2002] 1 AC 509.
[68] [2003] 1 Cr App R 111.
[69] [2003] Crim LR 280.
[70] See also *R v Gill* [2004] 1 Cr App R 20.
[71] (2001) 33 EHRR 12 at [56].
[72] [2003] 1 AC 681.
[73] The position in other jurisdictions is considered at para 3.68 below.
[74] Section 66(1) to (2).

The warrant may empower an authorised person (ie constable, SOCA staff 3.56 designated under s 43, or a Revenue and Customs officer) to do any of the following (s 66(3)):[75]

(a) to enter and search the premises, using such force as is reasonably necessary;

(b) to take possession of any documents appearing to be documents of a description specified in the information, or to take any other steps which appear to be necessary for preserving, or preventing interference with, any such documents;

(c) in the case of any such documents consisting of information recorded otherwise than in legible form, to take possession of any computer disk or other electronic storage device which appears to contain the information in question, or to take any other steps which appear to be necessary for preserving, or preventing interference with, that information;

(d) to take copies of or extracts from any documents or information falling within paragraph (b) or (c);

(e) to require any person on the premises to provide an explanation of any such documents or information, or to state where any such documents or information may be found;[76]

(f) to require any such person to give the appropriate person such assistance as he may reasonably require for the taking of copies or extracts as mentioned in paragraph (d).

Persons executing a warrant can take any other persons with them if necessary 3.57 (s 66(4)). The warrant must be available for inspection (s 66(5)). Unoccupied searched premises must be left secured (s 66(6)). Documents or devices seized may be retained for as long as the investigating authority considers necessary and until the conclusion of any legal proceedings (s 66(7)–(8)).

Section 8(1)(d) PACE expressly prevents the granting of a warrant relating 3.58 to legally privileged, excluded, or special procedure material. By contrast, s 66(9) prevents only the *seizure* of any such material which falls within s 64. There is no requirement for the justice of the peace to be satisfied that the material in question does not include any privileged or similar material although it is arguable that this is implicit given that a disclosure notice cannot include a requirement to provide privileged or similar material. If not, the difference may be important because seized material which subsequently turns out to be legally privileged is not unlawfully seized (*R v Chesterfield JJ ex p Bramley*[77]).

---

[75] A helpful checklist of practical steps to be taken during and after a raid by OFT investigators using compulsory powers is set out by C Whiddington in 'Dawn Raids under UK Competition Law' [2002] Finance & Credit Law 4.10(1).

[76] This requirement is similar to that imposed by s 63(5) relating to the production of documents specified in a disclosure notice (see above). As with s 63(5), any attempt to use the s 66(3)(e) power as a device to perform a coercive interview would be open to challenge.

[77] [2000] QB 576.

Moreover, the widespread use by the SFO of compulsory powers against professional advisers may indicate a high likelihood of SOCA's warrant requests inadvertently including privileged material. Unlike s 8(1)(b) PACE there is no express requirement that the material sought in a warrant be of substantial value to the investigation. However, given that material requested in a warrant can only be material which itself could have formed the subject matter of a disclosure notice, this requirement is implicit by s 62(1).

2. Offences in Connection with Disclosure Notices or Search Warrants

3.59 Section 67 creates criminal offences connected to non-compliance with disclosure notices and search warrants. These give the new investigatory powers their compulsory and coercive force.

3.60 An offence is committed under s 61(1) if a person, without reasonable excuse, fails to comply with any requirement imposed on him under s 62 (disclosure notice) or s 63 (production of documents). This is a summary only offence and is punishable with a fine not exceeding level 5 on the standard scale and/or imprisonment not exceeding 51 weeks (s 67(4)).

3.61 It should be emphasised, however, that a refusal to comment will not necessarily constitute a refusal to answer a question without reasonable excuse. For example, a witness is entitled not to comment on documents he has not seen before, on speculation, or on comments by other witnesses. However, the s 65 protection on the use of compulsory answers does not automatically entitle the recipient of a disclosure notice completely to refuse to answer questions on the basis of self-incrimination. The (statutory and Convention) self-incrimination protections prevent subsequent use of answers obtained under compulsion at trial—it is does not completely defeat the compulsory powers themselves.[78] The common law privilege against self-incrimination, however, entitles the recipient to refuse to answer questions on the basis that there is a reasonable prospect that he might incriminate himself.[79] But, as noted above, the wide drafting of s 65(1), prohibiting the use in criminal proceedings (by any party) of compulsorily obtained evidence against the maker, makes it extremely difficult to envisage how the recipient of a disclosure notice could reasonably contend that his answers might incriminate himself. This applies equally to suspects or witnesses who later become suspects (for whom the dividing line between the investigatory and trial phases is easily blurred).

3.62 There is no statutory definition of 'reasonable excuse'. The width of the identical exception in s 2 CJA 1987 was recently considered by the Court of Appeal in *Marlwood Commercial Inc v Kozeny*.[80] The Court rejected the submission that reasonable excuse was confined to rare cases described as 'national security,

---

[78] See eg *Saunders v UK* (n 2 above) at [70].
[79] See eg *R v Hertfordshire CC ex p Green Environmental Industries Ltd* (n 34 above) at 422.
[80] [2004] 3 All ER 648.

diplomatic relations and the administration of local government'. Without defining the term, the Court held that it went wider than the three examples given. The decision in *Re Arrows Ltd*[81] was one example of a reasonable excuse (direction not to disclose under rule 9.5(4) Insolvency Rules 1986). But on the facts of *Marlwood* itself, the fact that the documents in question had been brought within the jurisdiction for the purposes of disclosure by a foreign litigant himself brought compulsorily before the English court was not a reasonable excuse.

A second, more serious, offence is committed under s 67(2) where a person, in purported compliance with any s 62 or s 63 requirement, knowingly or recklessly makes a false or misleading statement. 'False or misleading' means false or misleading in a material particular. This offence is triable either-way. On conviction on indictment, it is punishable with up to two years' imprisonment and/or an unlimited fine (s 67(5)(a)). On summary conviction, the maximum penalty is the statutory maximum and/or imprisonment not exceeding 12 months (s 67(5)(b)). **3.63**

A third offence is committed under s 67(3) where a person wilfully obstructs any person in the exercise of any of the warrant powers conferred by s 66. Cases on the obstruction of police officers will be relevant in determining the degree of obstruction required and the necessary mental element.[82] The offence is summary only and the maximum penalties are as for the s 67(1) offence (s 67(4)). There is no specific offence of knowingly or recklessly making a false or misleading statement in response to a s 66(3)(e) question during the execution of a search warrant—an offence is only committed if the untruthful answer also amounts to obstruction. **3.64**

For all three s 67 offences the usual s 65 restriction on the use of the compelled statements in evidence against the maker in criminal proceedings does not apply (s 65(2)(a)). Moreover, a witness who gives a compelled statement and then gives evidence for the prosecution at trial can himself subsequently be prosecuted under s 67(2). In the trial of the s 67 offence, the evidence from the previous criminal trial would be admissible potentially to prove that the compelled evidence was false or misleading. **3.65**

J. PROCEDURAL ISSUES

Section 69 prescribes the methods of service for disclosure notices. Service may be in person or by leaving it, or by posting it to a person's proper address (s 69(2)). Proper address is defined in the usual way in s 69(4). The notice may be served **3.66**

---

[81] [1992] Ch 545.

[82] eg *Attorney-General's Reference (No 3 of 2003)* [2004] Cr App R 23: 'wilful' misconduct means deliberately doing something that is wrong, knowing it to be wrong, or with reckless indifference as to whether it is wrong or not. See also *Willmott v Atack* [1977] QB 498.

on the secretary or clerk of a body corporate, on a partner or equivalent in a partnership, or on the officer of an unincorporated association (s 69(3)).

3.67   It is becoming increasingly commonplace for investigators exercising compulsory powers to seek an undertaking from the interviewee not to disclose information put to him in the course of their questioning. Typically, inspectors exercising compulsory powers are not under a duty to insist on the interviewee giving a confidentiality undertaking, although they are entitled to request this as a matter of discretion. In *re An Inquiry Into Mirror Group Newspapers plc*[83] Sir Richard Scott V-C held that the respondent's refusal to sign such an undertaking, in circumstances where the undertaking went further than was reasonable or necessary, did not represent a failure on his part to give the inspectors any assistance he was reasonably able to give and that, accordingly, he could not be guilty of any contempt. Under the Act, the use of undertakings may be of critical importance in circumstances where the recipient is believed to be on the fringes of criminality and the authorities may be most reluctant for information revealed during the compulsory questioning to be disseminated by the interviewee.

K. THE APPROACH IN OTHER JURISDICTIONS

3.68   Many other jurisdictions (eg Norway, Canada, Australia, New Zealand, and the United States) permit the compulsory taking of statements during investigations into corporate and financial frauds and their subsequent use in a criminal trial in order to confront the accused's and witnesses' oral testimony. In addition to self-incrimination protections relating to coerced testimony, some jurisdictions impose limits on the use of evidence derived from compelled statements. Canada and South Africa, for example, have a limited form of derivative use immunity, whereas the Hong Kong Court of Appeal rejected the existence of the concept.[84]

3.69   It was the Australian approach to compulsory powers which was heavily relied upon in the White Paper to justify the extension of coercive investigatory techniques to organised crime in England. However, a number of key safeguards in the Australian model are notably absent from SOCPA.

3.70   The Australian Crime Commission (ACC) combines the National Crime Authority, Bureau of Criminal Intelligence, and Office of Strategic Crime Assessments. It also draws on the resources of the State and Territory police forces and uses Commonwealth agencies such as the Federal Police, Customs, and the Securities and Investments Commission. The ACC is overseen by an

---

[83] [2000] Ch 194.
[84] See *RJS v The Queen* (1995) 121 DLR 589; *Ferreira v Levin* (1996) 1 BCLR 1(CC)1; *HKSAR v Lee Ming Tee* [2001] 1 HKLRD 599 (resp.). See further Caplan, 'The Coming of Derivative Use Immunity?' (2002) JoCL 65 (273); Pinto and Evans, n 48 above, at [12.49].

Inter-Governmental Committee and a Parliamentary Joint Committee and there is a far greater degree of accountability present than SOCPA provides. The ACC's aim is to deal with nationally significant crime and it investigates crimes with a federal aspect (as defined in the ACC Act 2002). The class of qualifying crimes is considerably narrower than under SOCPA.

Unlike SOCA, before the ACC can deploy its compulsory powers, the ACC Board must consider whether ordinary methods of investigation, not involving the use of powers in the Act, have been or are likely to be as effective. At least nine Board members' votes are required to authorise the use of the coercive powers. **3.71**

ACC examiners who are authorised to use the compulsory powers are appointed by the Governor General and must have been legal practitioners for at least five years and are, in practice, senior lawyers. By contrast, SOCPA permits any Crown prosecutor (or equivalent) to authorise the use of compulsory powers and the powers can be exercised by *any* designated member of SOCA staff. Attendance at ACC examinations is compulsory, and questions must be answered. Individuals required to attend may be prevented from disclosing to a third party that they have been summonsed to the ACC but, unlike the SOCPA equivalent, have a *statutory* right to legal representation during examinations. **3.72**

In Australia the common-law privilege against self-incrimination entitles a person to refuse to answer any question or produce any document if the answer or production would tend to incriminate that person.[85] The privilege originally applied only to testimonial evidence but has since been extended to documentary evidence.[86] However, a distinction is drawn between protecting people from testifying to their own guilt and producing existing documents that speak for themselves.[87] The privilege does not, however, prevent the compulsory, direct seizure of documents in administrative investigations. **3.73**

In addition, s 128 Australian Evidence Act 1995 enables a witness claiming the privilege on 'reasonable grounds' to refuse to provide the required evidence unless the court considers it is in the 'interests of justice' to do so. If the witness does give evidence, the court must give the witness a certificate granting both use and derivative use immunity in relation to the evidence (except in criminal proceedings in respect of the falsity of the evidence). **3.74**

However, the Australian courts have recently held that the privilege against self-incrimination has been abrogated during the investigatory phase by the compulsory powers legislation (eg ACC Act 2002), but a 'compensatory protection' clause prevents the admissibility of answers and documents in criminal **3.75**

---

[85] *Pyneboard Pty Ltd v Trade Practices Commission* (1983) 152 CLR 328, 335.

[86] *Australian Competition and Consumer Commission v Amcor Printing Papers Group Ltd* (1999) 163 ALR 465.

[87] *Trade Practices Commission v Abbco Ice Works Pty Ltd* (1994) 52 FCR 96, 540; *Sorby v The Commonwealth* (1983) 152 CLR 281 at 316.

proceedings against the maker/producer. This 'direct use immunity' does not extend to derivative use.[88]

3.76　The White Paper also drew an analogy with the American system, despite the vast differences in the two legal systems. In the United States, compulsory powers are available via the grand jury system, in which a preliminary jury assesses (in secret) whether there is sufficient evidence for a defendant to be tried on indictment. As part of their ability to prefer criminal charges, grand juries also have the power to investigate. In particular, a grand jury has the power to subpoena witnesses and physical evidence. A failure to comply with a grand jury subpoena is a civil contempt and punishable with imprisonment. The Miranda rule (evidence without caution is inadmissible) does not apply in grand jury proceedings: in particular there is no right to counsel and no full right to silence under subpoena from a grand jury. Witnesses can invoke their Fifth Amendment privilege against self-incrimination (which is significantly narrower than the Miranda rule) and any applicable evidentiary privileges as the basis for refusing to testify or otherwise comply with a grand jury's demands.

3.77　The Fifth Amendment provides that 'no person . . . shall be compelled in any criminal case to be a witness against himself'. The purpose underlying the Fifth Amendment was to compel the prosecution to procure independent evidence of the facts and proof of a crime other than through the mouth of the accused. This self-incrimination protection clause is concerned directly with testimony; it does offer protection from being required to provide non-testimonial incriminating evidentiary materials.[89] The Fifth Amendment has been interpreted so as only to bar the production of 'testimonial information'[90] but this extends to an incriminating communication that might 'itself, explicitly or implicitly, relate a factual assertion or disclose information'.[91] However, the Supreme Court in *Doe v United States (Doe II)* highlighted the difficulty in distinguishing between testimonial and non-testimonial compulsion. It suggested, for example, that being compelled to reveal the combination to a wall safe would be testimonial compulsion, whereas being forced to provide the key to a strongbox containing incriminating documents would not.[92]

3.78　If it is established that the evidence in question falls within the protection of the Fifth Amendment, then it may only be compelled if an associated immunity is granted to the individual.[93] The immunity given may be a 'transactional immunity', where the witness is immune from prosecution for offences related to the testimony, or a 'use immunity', where the witness may be prosecuted but his

---

[88] *A v Boulton* [2004] FCA 56; affirmed by the full Federal Court in [2004] FCAFC 101.

[89] *United States v Hubbell* 530 US 27, 34–35 (2000) applying *Schmerber v California* 384 US 757 (1966).

[90] *Doe v United States* 487 US 201 (1988) (*Doe II*) (stating that a directive to disclose bank records was not testimonial).

[91] *Doe II* at 210.

[92] *Doe II* at 210 n 9.

[93] See Department of Justice Criminal Resources Manual 718.

testimony may not be used against him. The Supreme Court has held that the government need only grant a use immunity in order to compel testimony. The use immunity must not only extend to the testimony made by the witness but also include derivative use immunity, ie immunity from 'any use, direct or indirect, of the compelled testimony and any information derived therefrom'.[94] Use immunity therefore prohibits the use of compulsory testimony as an 'investigatory lead' or using 'any evidence obtained by focusing investigation on a witness as a result of his compelled disclosures'.[95]

Granting immunity to a grand jury witness will therefore partially circumvent their privilege against self-incrimination. An immunised witness can be required to testify but the prosecutor is prohibited from using that testimony or leads from it to bring charges against the witness. If a subsequent prosecution is brought, the prosecutor must prove that all of the prosecution evidence was obtained independently of the immunised testimony.   **3.79**

The English courts may find the American concept of derivative use immunity attractive, particularly when the granting of conditional immunity and undertakings to prosecution witnesses have been codified in ss 71 and 72 of the Act. However, the secrecy and the apparent lack of proper judicial supervision of the grand jury process has drawn widespread and fierce criticism of the system as a whole and this may inhibit the adoption of the protections which have evolved within it as a template.   **3.80**

---

[94] *Kastigar v United States* 406 US 441, 460 (1972).
[95] ibid at 461.

4

OFFENDERS ASSISTING INVESTIGATIONS AND PROSECUTIONS, AND THE PROTECTION OF WITNESSES

A. Overview	4.01
B. Offenders Assisting Investigations and Prosecutions	4.03
C. Protection of Witnesses and Other Persons	4.21

A. OVERVIEW

The White Paper *One Step Ahead: A 21st Century Strategy to Defeat Organised* **4.01**
Crime (the White Paper) confirmed that one thrust of the Government's fight
against organised crime was to encourage cooperation by increasing the
incentives open to those who assist the investigation and prosecution of
crimes. It claimed that the 'real prize' was 'to encourage defendants not only
to plead guilty, where they are indeed guilty, but to cooperate with the
prosecution'.[1] The Serious Organised Crime and Police Act (SOCPA) aims to
achieve this by putting Queen's evidence[2] and witness protection on a statutory
footing and by increasing the incentives for convicted offenders to give evidence. Prior to SOCPA, the common law provided for a defendant to be
rewarded for cooperating.[3] However, these provisions were widely seen as
lacking in transparency and consistency. Further, the White Paper also

---

[1] White Paper *One Step Ahead: A 21st Century Strategy to Defeat Organised Crime*, p 47
<www.homeoffice.gov.uk/docs3/wp_organised_crime.pdf>.
[2] This is evidence given for the prosecution by an accomplice against former criminal
associates.
[3] See *R v King* (1985) 7 Cr App R (S) 227. See also *R v Sivan* (1988) 10 Cr App R (S) 282; *R v
Debbag and Izzet* (1991) 12 Cr App R (S) 733; *R v Wood* (1997) 9 Cr App R (S) 238; and *R v A and B*
(1999) 1 Cr App R (S) 52.

suggested that the mechanism for 'turning Queen's Evidence' was being under-used because juries were suspicious of defendants who cooperated in this way. It also claimed that potential witnesses were unwilling to give evidence because the incentives were not significant enough, with the result that 'the additional discount from cooperating does not look attractive compared to the risks involved'.[4]

4.02   The result of the debate around these provisions is Chapter 2 (offenders assisting investigations and prosecutions) and Chapter 4 (protection of witnesses and other persons) in Part 2 of SOCPA. Chapter 2 establishes statutory powers to grant immunity, to provide prosecution undertakings in relation to evidence, and to request sentence reductions and reviews following the provision of assistance by the defendant. These powers are to be based on binding cooperation agreements between the prospective witness and the prosecution. Similar systems operate in the United States and Australia. In other European Union countries, such as Italy and Spain, sentence reductions are also granted for cooperation.[5] Chapter 4 puts existing provisions for witness protection into statutory form and creates criminal offences for disclosure of information in relation to witness protection arrangements and the provision of new identities. The two chapters thus present a package of measures aimed at increasing the possibility that individuals involved in organised crime may be prepared to supply evidence to the prosecution, particularly against those further up the criminal hierarchy.

B. OFFENDERS ASSISTING INVESTIGATIONS AND PROSECUTIONS

4.03   Before considering the detail of these provisions, it is important to note that any guidelines for the use of these powers will be vital in establishing how they will work in practice.[6] The use of accomplice evidence has long been considered a possible source of miscarriages of justice because witnesses with their own 'axe to grind' may give unreliable evidence. In the first half of the 1980s, a series of high profile controversial trials took place in Northern Ireland on the evidence of 'supergrasses' prepared to betray large numbers of their alleged accomplices in return for various rewards. These trials were widely condemned

---

[4] White Paper, n 1 above, p 48.

[5] In Italy, one example of sentence reduction in return for cooperation (*misure a favore di chi si dissocia dal terrorismo*) is the Law of 18 February 1987, no 34. This provides for substantial reductions in sentence for criminals who dissociate themselves from terrorist organisations and who give evidence to support a prosecution and cooperate with judicial inquiries. Article 579 of the Spanish Penal Code similarly provides for sentence reductions in return for cooperation (see the Joint Committee on Human Rights, *Eighteenth Report*, 21 July 2004, paras 61 and 69).

[6] No such guidelines were available at the time of writing.

by independent observers[7] and resulted in many successful appeals. Thus, any encouragement of the increased use of such techniques will require substantial protections against abuse, unreliability, and the corruption fostered by secret 'deals'. For example, JUSTICE has warned that 'encouraging the more wide-spread use of "Queen's Evidence" means that the decision as to the relative roles of the criminal participants is taken away from the court and put into hands of the prosecution advised by the police. One may question whether this is right.'[8] JUSTICE suggested that protections against abuse should include carefully drawn prosecution guidelines, sentence being passed before cooperation is given wherever possible, full immunity being granted only in exceptional cases (where the public interest outweighs gravity of offence), and the restoration of cor-roboration warnings.[9] These types of safeguards have not been drafted into the legislation but may be contained within prosecution guidelines. Any guidelines should also address the difficulty of deciding on the relative culpability of offenders.

1. Immunity from Prosecution

The existing common law criteria to be applied in deciding whether to grant **4.04** witness immunity are set out in the Attorney-General's Written Answer to the House of Commons on 9 November 1981. They include, whether, 'in the inter-ests of justice, it is of more value to have a suspected person as a witness for the Crown rather than as a possible defendant' and whether, 'in the interests of public safety and security, the obtaining of information about the extent and nature of criminal activities is of greater importance than the possible convic-tion of an individual'.[10]

Section 71 creates a statutory mechanism to enable a 'specified prosecutor' **4.05** to grant immunity in writing against prosecution for any offence.[11] The only condition to be met is that the prosecutor must feel that it is 'appropriate' to grant immunity for the purposes of investigating or prosecuting an offence. A specified prosecutor is defined in s 71(4) to include the Director of Public

---

[7] See Amnesty International, *United Kingdom: Killings by Security Forces and 'Supergrass' Trials* (Amnesty International, 1988).

[8] JUSTICE 'Response to White Paper, "One Step Ahead: A 21st century strategy to defeat organised crime" ' <www.justice.org.uk/images/pdfs/orgcr.pdf>, para 29.

[9] ibid, para 33. It is no longer obligatory for a court to give a warning in respect of convicting a defendant on the uncorroborated evidence of an accomplice, but a judge has discretion to decide what, if any, direction should be given. Archbold 4-404 j–l.

[10] <www.publications.parliament.uk/pa/cm/cmpubns.htm>. See also 'Witness Immunities and Undertakings Guidance on Decisions to Prosecute' <www.cps.gov.uk/legal/section3/chapter_i.html>. The Privy Council has recognised the important role played by formal undertak-ings of immunity where accomplices are called by the Crown, describing the role of such undertak-ings as being 'to remove or minimise the inducement to [accomplices] to give false evidence exonerat-ing themselves and inculpating the accused'—see *R v McDonald* 77 Cr App R 196.

[11] The only exception is an offence under s 188 Enterprise Act 2002—see s 71(7).

Prosecutions (DPP), the Director of Revenue and Customs Prosecutions, the Director of the Serious Fraud Office, the Director of Public Prosecutions for Northern Ireland, or a prosecutor designated by them.[12]

4.06 Immunity is provided in the form of an 'immunity notice' which sets out the offence for which immunity is granted and confirms that no proceedings may be brought against that person in England and Wales or Northern Ireland except in the circumstances specified in the notice.[13] The notice may set out conditions with which the individual must comply for immunity to be granted; however, there is no statutory requirement that it does so. If conditions do exist, and they are not met, then the immunity notice will cease to have effect.[14]

4.07 Although it is suggested that immunity is an incentive to tackle organised crime, there is no confinement of this power to 'serious' offences. The power is a wide one and can be designated to any prosecutor. Liberty declared itself 'uneasy' with the idea of 'total immunity' given that the test is simply that it should appear 'appropriate' to a prosecutor for it to be granted and has called for the power to be used only where essential and for the jury to be told of the consequential implications for credibility.[15]

4.08 It should be noted that this provision follows the precedent set by s 190(4) Enterprise Act 2002 which offers immunity from prosecution for cooperation in cartel offences but which is subject to published guidelines.[16]

2. Undertakings as to Use of Evidence

4.09 Prior to SOCPA, the law allowed the Crown to make a written agreement to refrain from using information, documents, or evidence in criminal proceedings if the person had provided the information, documents, or evidence themselves. Also, known as a 'Salmon undertaking', such an arrangement did not prevent a witness from being prosecuted where other evidence justified a prosecution.[17]

4.10 Section 72 now allows a specified prosecutor (as defined by s 71(4) above) to give a 'restricted use undertaking' in writing to a person to confirm that information he has given will not be used against him in proceedings. Proceedings include criminal proceedings and proceedings under Part 5 of the Proceeds of Crime Act 2002.[18] An undertaking can only be given if 'appropriate' for the purposes of investigating or prosecuting an offence. It can specify the circum-

---

[12] Note ss 71(5) and (6) and 72(5) and (6) which confirm that the DPP may not grant immunity notice or undertaking in relation to Northern Ireland nor may the DPP for Northern Ireland in relation to England and Wales.

[13] Section 71(2).

[14] Section 71(3).

[15] SOCPA, Liberty's briefing for the second reading in the House of Commons, December 2004, para 9.

[16] See pp 5–6, 'The Cartel offence: Guidance on the issue of no-action letters for individuals' <www.oft.gov.uk/NR/rdonlyres/C6B72EDF-EA6A–42F4–9F44-E8FED8268458/0/oft513.pdf>.

[17] See n 10 above, <www.cps.gov.uk/legal/section3/chapter_i.html>.

[18] Section 72(2).

stances in which the information can be used and it might detail conditions which have to be complied with.[19] Failure to comply with any stated conditions will cause the undertaking to cease to have effect.[20]

3. Reduction in Sentence

The White Paper initially proposed two components to the concept of reduced **4.11** sentences—namely plea bargaining (ie advance indication of sentence[21]) and reductions for those turning 'Queen's evidence'. Ultimately, the Government concluded that arrangements for sentence indication (where a defendant would be able to seek an indication of the likely sentence on a guilty plea) did not require legislation but could be 'established by the judiciary'.[22] It was thought, however, that placing the concept of 'Queen's evidence' on a statutory footing would consolidate and strengthen this area of law.

In relation to advance indication of sentence, these judicial guidelines now **4.12** exist. In April 2005, the case of *R v Goodyear*[23] modified existing law (as reflected in *R v Turner*[24]) and effectively introduced a judicially approved system of advance indication of sentence on a guilty plea. The Court in *Turner* had held that a judge should not indicate the sentence he was minded to impose save in the most exceptional circumstances. This was because plea was the defendant's sole responsibility and should not be the subject of 'bargaining' with a judge. A judge's views regarding sentence, expressed to counsel, and communicated to the defendant could represent improper pressure to plead guilty. In *Goodyear*, the court distinguished the facts before them by stating that *Turner* had dealt with an unsolicited indication and not with a situation where the request comes from a defendant personally.

The court issued guidelines for this procedure. These guidelines will only **4.13** apply in the Crown Court.[25] The procedure is as follows:

(i) The defendant must request an indication (it should not be initiated by the Prosecution). This can occur at any stage of proceedings but it is suggested that it should take place at the Plea and Case Management hearing so that the defendant may take advantage of maximum sentence discount.

(ii) The plea must be in writing and must be acceptable to the prosecution. All issues between defence and prosecution should be resolved before the

---

[19] Section 72(3).

[20] Section 72(4).

[21] Initially, recommended by Lord Justice Auld in his 'Review of the Criminal Courts of England and Wales' <www.criminal-courts-review.org.uk/ccr–10.htm> p 91, para 91.

[22] White Paper, n 1 above, p 46.

[23] [2005] EWCA Crim 888.

[24] [1970] 2 QB 321.

[25] Paragraph 20 of Sch 3 to the Criminal Justice Act 2003 introduces an advance indication of sentence procedure in the magistrates' court in respect of the likelihood of a custodial sentence being imposed in the event of summary trial. At the time of writing, these provisions are not yet in force.

hearing. If there is a dispute about facts which the defence believe to be immaterial to sentencing, the difference should be recorded and left to the judge to decide. Where the issues are 'complicated or difficult' the defence must give advance notice of the request in writing.

(iii) This should be at least seven days in advance of the hearing or the defendant's discount is at risk.

(iv) The defence should obtain the defendant's written authority to request the indication and should ensure he understands that he should not plead guilty unless he is guilty and that he understands the consequences of the indication procedure.

(v) The judge may remind the defendant that he can take advantage of this procedure but cannot insist an indication takes place. A judge can also refuse to give an indication (eg if s/he feels the defendant is under pressure or does not understand the nature of his plea) or s/he may decide to postpone the indication until later (eg after pre-sentence reports).

(vi) The judge should not give an indication in a case that appears to be a plea bargain.[26]

(vii) The hearing should be in open court with all parties, including the defendant but reporting restrictions will apply.

(viii) The prosecutor's role at the hearing is set out in paragraph 70 of the judgment and includes ensuring the judge has all relevant information and drawing the judge's attention to mandatory or minimum sentence requirements. The prosecutor should never indicate the Crown's support for the sentence indication.

(ix) If the judge decides to give an indication, it should be confined to the maximum sentence for a plea of guilty at that stage in proceedings. A judge should not indicate the maximum level of sentence following conviction.[27] Any indication will bind the judge and any other judge dealing with the case.

(x) The defendant will be given a 'reasonable opportunity' to decide on his plea following the indication. If he does not enter a plea of guilty after a reasonable period has elapsed, the indication will no longer have effect. Reporting restrictions may be lifted if the defendant pleads guilty.

(xi) The Attorney-General's discretion to refer an unduly lenient sentence remains unaffected by this procedure provided the prosecution have properly discharged their responsibilities. Likewise, the defendant can still apply for leave to appeal against sentence.

---

[26] [2005] EWCA Crim 888, para 67.
[27] ibid, para 54.

In relation to sentence reductions for cooperation, s 73 SOCPA puts into **4.14** statutory form the mechanism for allowing assistance by a defendant to be rewarded by a reduction in sentence. The section bites when a defendant pleads guilty in the Crown Court or he is committed to the Crown Court for sentence and he has (after making an agreement with a specified prosecutor in writing) assisted or offered to assist the investigator or prosecutor in relation to that or any other offence. There need be no connection between the offence for which sentence is reduced and the offence for which assistance is offered. Although the agreement is with a specified prosecutor, the assistance can be given to that prosecutor or another or to an investigator.[28] Assistance is not defined and is, therefore, not limited to those who become prosecution witnesses.

The procedure to be followed is that the prosecution will explain to the court **4.15** the extent and nature of the assistance given or offered.[29] It is then up to the court to decide on sentence. The term 'sentence' includes the minimum period an offender is required to serve under a sentence fixed by law.[30] If the court decides to pass a lower sentence because of the assistance given, it is required to state this in open court and confirm the greater sentence it would have passed but for the assistance.[31] However, it need not do this if it feels that it would not be in the public interest to state this openly. In this case, the court must give written notice of the sentence reduction to the prosecutor and the defendant.[32] These provisions also apply in the case of mandatory minimum sentences and sentences fixed by law.[33] Equally, the court is not prevented from taking into account any other statutory matter which enables it to determine sentence.[34]

4. Review of Sentence

Section 74 provides for a review of sentence to be requested by a specified **4.16** prosecutor on three grounds:

(i) where the defendant received a discounted sentence following an agreement to provide assistance but has 'knowingly' failed to provide assistance in accordance with the agreement;

---

[28] See s 73(1)(b) and s 73(9).

[29] Section 73(2).

[30] Section 73(8). Section 73(8)(b) confirms that a reference to imprisonment includes a reference to any other custodial sentence within the meaning of s 76 Powers of Criminal Courts (Sentencing) Act 2000 (c 6) or Art 2 of the Criminal Justice (Northern Ireland) Order 1996 (SI 1996/ 3160).

[31] Section 73(3).

[32] Section 73(4). Sections 174(1)(a) and 270 Criminal Justice Act 2003 are accordingly disapplied 'to the extent that the explanation will disclose that a sentence has been discounted in pursuance of this section'—see s 73(7).

[33] Section 73(5).

[34] Section 73(6).

(ii) where the defendant did not receive a discounted sentence but offers to provide or provides assistance in pursuance of an agreement after sentence;

(iii) where the defendant did receive a discounted sentence but has provided further assistance in pursuance of a further agreement.[35]

4.17   If a sentence was fixed by law, the defendant must have pleaded guilty for these provisions to apply.[36] A Crown Court sentence must have been passed allowing the prosecutor to refer the case back to the court which passed sentence. The person must still be serving his sentence, and the specified prosecutor must think that it is in the interests of justice to take this action.[37] Where possible, the case should be heard by the judge who passed the sentence.[38]

4.18   The court has the power to vary sentence. For a person who has knowingly failed to comply with the agreement to cooperate, it may substitute such greater sentence as it thinks appropriate, provided this does not exceed a sentence that it would have passed but for the agreement.[39] In the other two situations, the court may substitute such lesser sentence as it deems appropriate after taking into account the extent and nature of the assistance given or offered.[40] Any part of the sentence already served must be taken into account in determining the sentence to be imposed.[41] Any reduced sentence imposed becomes a 'discounted' sentence. Section 74(8) and (9) preserves the right of appeal to the Court of Appeal.

4.19   Section 174(1)(a) or 270 Criminal Justice Act 2003[42] will apply to a sentence substituted under s 74(5) unless the court thinks that it would not be in the public interest to disclose this.[43] Section 73(3) to (9) (relating to the public interest test in disclosing a reduction in sentence and other provisions relating to the process of determining a sentence) apply to s 74.[44]

5. Proceedings under Section 74: Exclusion of Public

4.20   Section 75 allows the court to exclude individuals from proceedings involving a review of sentence (or any other proceedings which arise as a consequence of it) unless they fall within s 75(4). This section refers to members or officers of the court, parties to proceedings, counsel or a solicitor for a party to the proceedings, or a person otherwise directly concerned with the proceedings. The

---

[35] Section 74(2).
[36] Section 74(13).
[37] Section 74(3).
[38] Section 74(4).
[39] Section 74(5).
[40] Section 74(6).
[41] Section 74(7).
[42] The duty to give reasons for, and explain the effect of, sentence; and the duty to give reasons for the determination of minimum term in relation to mandatory life sentence.
[43] Section 74(14).
[44] Section 74(15).

court may also give directions prohibiting the publication of information relating to the proceedings (including the fact that the reference has been made).[45] The court must believe that it is necessary to make such an order to protect the safety of any person and that it is in the interests of justice to do so.[46] This power is additional to any other the court has to exclude people or restrict the publication of information relating to proceedings.[47]

C. PROTECTION OF WITNESSES AND OTHER PERSONS

The consultation following the White Paper resulted in a Government proposal for the 'rationalisation' and 'consolidation' of witness protection. This includes placing protection on a statutory footing.[48] The provisions of Chapter 4 thus create a statutory framework for witness protection, rather than a National Witness Protection Agency. **4.21**

Witness protection is a vital part of a strategy which aims to encourage witnesses to cooperate against fellow criminals. Such action clearly necessitates strong assurances for individual safety. JUSTICE, in their response to the White Paper, pointed out that witness protection was an important but difficult task because lifelong protection is often required and because organised crime groups may have considerable resources. However, they also emphasised that ensuring adequate protection was a matter of legal obligation.[49] **4.22**

1. Protection Arrangements

Section 82 sets out the circumstances in which arrangements for protection may be made by a 'protection provider' but it does not require protection to be given. A protection provider is defined by s 82(5) to include a chief officer of a police force in England and Wales, a chief constable of a police force in Scotland, the Chief Constable of the Police Service of Northern Ireland, the Director General of SOCA, any of the Commissioners for Her Majesty's Revenue and Customs, and the Director of the Scottish Drug Enforcement Agency. The term also includes any person designated by the people mentioned above. The nature of the arrangements made will depend on what the protection provider feels is 'appropriate' for the purposes of protection. Agencies may continue to use any existing powers they have.[50] This includes providing 'lesser levels of protection **4.23**

---

[46] Section 75(3).
[45] Section 75(2)(b).
[47] Section 75(5).
[48] 'Summary of Responses to the White Paper "One Step Ahead: A 21st Century Strategy to Defeat Organised Crime" ', p 15 <www.homeoffice.gov.uk/docs3/organised_crime_responses.pdf>.
[49] See *Osman v UK* [1999] 29 EHRR 245.
[50] Section 82(7).

which fall outside the scope of these provisions, eg security locks, panic alarms etc'.[51]

4.24 Protection arrangements can be made for a person, ordinarily resident in the UK,[52] only if the protection provider believes their safety is at risk because they fall into one of the categories of individuals established by Schedule 5 of SOCPA.[53] This Schedule includes witnesses, jurors, prosecutors, prison officers, those involved in the legal system, informants, and people with a connection to the above such as those who live in the same household or who are family members. Schedule 5 can be amended by order by the Secretary of State, although s/he must consult Scottish Ministers before doing so.[54]

4.25 Under s 82(4), when establishing, cancelling, or varying protection arrangements, a protection provider must have regard to:

(i) the nature and extent of the risk to the person's safety;

(ii) the cost of the arrangements;

(iii) the likelihood that the person, and any person associated with him,[55] will be able to adjust to any change in their circumstances which may arise from the making of the arrangements or from their variation or cancellation (as the case may be); and

(iv) if the person is or might be a witness in legal proceedings (whether or not in the UK), the nature of the proceedings, and the importance of the person being a witness in those proceedings.

Protection arrangements can be varied or cancelled whenever the protection provider considers it appropriate.[56] A record must be made of any arrangements for protection or their cancellation under these powers.[57]

4.26 Section 83 allows joint protection arrangements to be made by two or more protection providers acting together. Such arrangements can be made by jointly by all protection providers, by one, or by some of them acting with the agreement of the others.

4.27 Section 84 enables a protection provider to transfer protection arrangements for an individual to another protection provider, for example where a person relocates. A record of such an agreement must be made and may include provision for costs.[58]

---

[51] Explanatory Note, para 187, <www.publications.parliament.uk/pa/ld200405/ldbills/024/en/05024x--.htm>.
[52] Section 82(1)(b).
[53] Section 82(1)(a).
[54] Section 82(6).
[55] Section 94.
[56] Section 82(2).
[57] Section 82(3).
[58] Section 84(2) and (4).

2. Duty to Assist Protection Providers

Section 85 creates a duty on public authorities to take 'reasonable steps' to **4.28** assist protection providers in making protection arrangements. The aim is to enable the protected person to gain access to public services such as housing, health, or education when they might not have the necessary documentation.[59] A public authority is defined as 'any person certain of whose functions are of a public nature'.[60] This specifically excludes a court or tribunal, the Houses of Parliament, and the Scottish Parliament.

3. Offences of Disclosing Information Relating to Protection Arrangements and new Identities

Sections 86 and 88 establish offences relating to the disclosure of information **4.29** about protected persons which are punishable by a maximum of 12 months on summary conviction or two years on indictment.[61] The offences can be committed by protected persons themselves, those protecting them, or third parties.

An offence under s 86 is committed by a person who discloses information **4.30** about the creation, implementation, variation, or cancellation of protection arrangements under s 82. The person must know or suspect that this information relates to such arrangements.

Section 87 establishes four statutory defences to liability under s 86. They are **4.31** that:

(i) when the information was disclosed the person disclosing it was (or had been) a protected person and that the information related to arrangements for his own protection (or the protection of someone associated with him). In addition, it must be shown that, when the information was disclosed, its disclosure was not likely to endanger anyone's safety;[62]

(ii) the information was disclosed by someone with the agreement of a person who was, or had been at the time of disclosure, a protected person. This information must relate only to arrangements made for the protection of this protected person (or someone associated with him) and its disclosure must not have been likely to endanger anyone's safety;[63]

(iii) if the information was disclosed for the purposes of safeguarding national security or preventing, detecting, or investigating crime;[64]

---

[59] See n 51 above, para 197.

[60] Section 85(3).

[61] Section 86(2) and (3) and s 88(3) and (4). In Scotland and Northern Ireland, on summary conviction, imprisonment is limited to 6 months.

[62] Section 87(1).

[63] Section 87(2).

[64] Section 87(3).

(iv) when the information was disclosed, the person disclosing it was a protection provider (or involved in the making of arrangements under s 82(1) or in the implementation, variation, or cancellation of such arrangements), and the information was disclosed for the purposes of the making, implementation, variation, or cancellation of such arrangements.[65]

4.32 An offence under s 88 concerns the disclosure of information relating to people who have assumed a new identity and can be committed in one of two ways:

(i) By a person who is (or has been) a protected person, and who has assumed a new identity under protection arrangements under SOCPA, who discloses information about these arrangements (which indicate that he has assumed, or might have assumed, a new identity). The person must know or suspect that the information disclosed by him will indicate this.[66]

(ii) By a person who discloses information about another person, who is or has been a protected person who has assumed a new identity as above. The disclosure must indicate that this person has assumed, or might have assumed, a new identity. The person disclosing the information must also know or suspect that the person is (or has been) a protected person, and that the information he has disclosed will indicate that he has assumed, or might have assumed, a new identity.[67]

4.33 Under s 89, the four statutory defences under s 88 are repeated under s 87, although the first two are differently worded.[68] Under ss 87(7) and 89(7), if a defendant adduces sufficient evidence to raise an issue relating to one of the defences, then it is for the prosecution to disprove it beyond reasonable doubt. The statutory defences may be amended by order of the Secretary of State or the Scottish Ministers.[69]

4. Protection from Liability

4.34 Section 90 provides for specified persons, in the case of a person who has assumed a new identity, to be given protection against civil or criminal liability for making a false or misleading representation.[70] The false statement must

---

[65] Section 87(4).

[66] Section 88(1).

[67] Section 88(2).

[68] The protected person is not guilty of an offence if, 'at the time he disclosed the information, it was not likely that its disclosure would endanger the safety of any person' or if the disclosure is made 'with the agreement of the protected person and at the time it was disclosed, it was not likely its disclosure would endanger the safety of any person.'

[69] Sections 87(5) and (6) and 89(5) and (6).

[70] Section 90(3) provides protection for the protected person or person associated with him, the protection provider, and a person involved in the making of arrangements under s 82(1) or in the implementation, variation, or cancellation of such arrangements.

relate to the protected person and must be made 'solely for the purpose of ensuring that the arrangements made for him to assume a new identity are, or continue to be, effective'.[71] This ensures that protected persons (and their family members) are not committing offences if, for example, they claim state benefits under their new identity.[72] Section 91(6) confirms that this only applies if the false or misleading representation is made on or after the 'relevant date' (defined in para 4.37 below).

5. Transitional Provisions

Transitional provisions are set out in ss 91 and 92. Section 91 enables existing protection arrangements to be treated as if they were made under this Act. This means they can attract criminal liability for disclosure of information under ss 86 to 89. Section 91(8) to (11) also enables arrangements made by the National Criminal Intelligence Service, the National Crime Squad, or Her Majesty's Customs and Excise, which have become the responsibility of a protection provider, to be treated as having been made under the new statutory provisions.[73]   **4.35**

Under s 91(2) to (5), three conditions must be satisfied for arrangements to be brought under SOCPA. They are that: **4.36**

(i) the protection provider could have made the arrangements under s 82(1) if it had been in force when the arrangements were made;

(ii) the arrangements were in operation immediately before the commencement of s 82;

(iii) the protection provider determines that it is appropriate to treat the arrangements as having been made under s 82(1). This must be done within six months of the day on which s 82 comes into force.[74] A record of a determination must be made.[75]

Section 92 contains supplemental transitional provisions which confirm the 'relevant date' for liability under ss 86 and 88. This is the date of the record made by the protection provider. This is important because, under s 92(2), a person does not commit an offence by disclosing information relating to the arrangements unless the information is disclosed on or after the relevant date. However, under s 92(3), it does not matter whether the information relates to something done before or after that date.   **4.37**

---

[71] Section 90(2).
[72] See n 51 above, para 202.
[73] See n 51 above, para 203.
[74] Section 91(6).
[75] Section 91(7).

57

6. Duty to Provide Information and the Interpretation of Chapter 4

4.38 Section 93 imposes a duty on the protection provider to supply information about the provisions under this chapter to the protected person or to an appropriate person if the person is unable to understand it himself.[76] If the arrangements are made by joint protection providers, then one must be nominated to do this.[77]

4.39 Section 94 defines some of the terms used in Chapter 4. This includes 'protected persons', 'associated persons', and 'witness'. The term 'witness' includes an accused person who becomes a witness for the prosecution.[78]

---

[76] Section 93(2) to (3).
[77] Section 93(4).
[78] Section 94(7).

5

FINANCIAL REPORTING ORDERS, INTERNATIONAL OBLIGATIONS, AND THE PROCEEDS OF CRIME

A. Financial Reporting Orders	5.01
B. International Obligations	5.23
C. Proceeds of Crime	5.36

A. FINANCIAL REPORTING ORDERS

1. Introduction

Chapter 3 of Part 2 (ss 76–81) introduces a new sentencing disposal known as **5.01** a 'financial reporting order' (FRO). It is to be available on conviction for the wide range of offences specified in ss 76(3) (ss 77(3) and 78(3) in Scotland and Northern Ireland) but only if the court is satisfied that the risk of the offender committing another offence on the list is sufficiently high to justify the making of an order (s 76(2)). The maximum duration when imposed in the magistrates' court is 5 years, and 15 years when imposed in the Crown Court (20 years if the offender is sentenced to life imprisonment).

The effect of an FRO is to require the offender to make reports containing **5.02** specified particulars of his financial affairs. Failure to comply (or inclusion of false or misleading information) is a separate offence punishable with up to 12 months' imprisonment (s 79(10)).

The White Paper which preceded the Act envisaged that FROs would be **5.03** ancillary orders, taking effect after the offender's release from a prison sentence (see *One Step Ahead: A 21st Century Strategy to Defeat Organised Crime*, Cm 6167, March 2004, para 6.6):

This could constitute a requirement to file every six months after release detailed returns setting out income, assets and expenditure. Released offenders would be obliged to report all bank accounts, credit cards etc being used . . . Such an obligation would inevitably impose a considerable burden on the released prisoner but one which is fully compatible with the normal goal of probation to encourage those released to turn away from crime. In the event that offenders returned to unlawful activities, the returns would provide a vein of information for law enforcement, while the criminal offence of non-compliance would offer a valuable tool in pursuing investigations.

5.04   The extent to which an FRO may require an individual to disclose their financial affairs to the state goes far beyond the usual sort of financial disclosure made in other contexts such as taxation. An FRO is made not on the basis of what someone has done, but on a judgement (by its nature speculative and therefore prone to error) of what he may do in the future. The making of an FRO will engage Article 8 of the European Convention on Human Rights and it will therefore need to be proportionate in its scope. The Parliamentary Joint Committee on Human Rights drew attention to the potentially disproportionate impact of FROs in its Fourth Report of Session 2004–2005, paras 1.57 to 1.58; however, its request for more specific criteria to be inserted into the Bill was ignored by the Government.

2. Making a Financial Reporting Order

5.05   FROs may be made by either the magistrates' court or the Crown Court. A court sentencing or otherwise dealing with a person convicted of an offence mentioned in s 76(3) may also make a financial reporting order in respect of him. 'Dealing with' includes making a confiscation order or hearing an appeal.

5.06   The offences in s 76(3) are the following offences contrary to the Theft Act 1968: s 15 (obtaining property by deception), s 15A (obtaining a money transfer by deception), s 16 (obtaining a pecuniary advantage by deception), s 20(2) (procuring execution of valuable security, etc); the offence contrary to s 1 of the Theft Act 1978 (obtaining services by deception); the offence contrary to s 2 of the Theft Act 1978 (evasion of liability by deception); and any offence specified in Schedule 2 to the Proceeds of Crime Act 2002 (lifestyle offences).

5.07   The Secretary of State may amend the list in s 76(3) by order so as to remove an offence from it or add an offence to it (s 76(4)).

5.08   The court may make an FRO only if it is satisfied that the risk of the person's committing another offence mentioned in s 76(3) is sufficiently high to justify the making of an FRO (s 76(2)). The circularity inherent in this test is bound to make the proper assessment of whether an FRO ought to be made difficult. The need to look into the future in order to judge whether a person is at risk of committing a further specific offence is also likely to be difficult. The court will obviously have to look at the nature and extent of the defendant's previous convictions as well as those of his most recent offence in order to see whether the risk is sufficiently high.

5.09   An FRO comes into force when it is made, and has effect for the period specified in the order, beginning with the date on which it is made (s 76(5)). If the order is made by a magistrates' court the maximum length of the order is 5 years. Otherwise, that period must not exceed 20 years if the person is sentenced to imprisonment for life, and 15 years in any other case.

Sections 77 and 78 contain equivalent provisions for Scotland and Northern Ireland. 5.10

3. The Effect of a Financial Reporting Order

A person in relation to whom an FRO has effect must make a report, in respect of the period of a specified length beginning with the date on which the order comes into force, and subsequent periods of specified lengths, each period beginning immediately after the end of the previous one (s 79(2)). 5.11

Rules of court may provide for the maximum length of the periods which may be specified (s 79(7)). The FRO must indicate within how many days after the end of each period the report is to be submitted (s 79(5)). The Bill in its original form proposed that reports should be at fixed intervals throughout the course of the order; however, the Bill was amended to allow the sentencer to direct when reports are to be served at the suggestion of the Lord Chief Justice (*Hansard*, 7 April 2005, col. 1585). 5.12

In each report the defendant must set out, in the manner specified in the order, such particulars of his financial affairs relating to the period in question as may be specified. He must also include any specified documents with each report (s 79(3) and (4)). 5.13

The report must be addressed to the person specified in the FRO (s 79(6)). In Scotland the specified person must be selected by the court from a list set out in an order made for the purposes of s 79 by the Scottish Ministers (s 79(9)). 5.14

4. Failure to Comply with a Financial Reporting Order

Section 79(10) makes it an offence to fail to comply with an FRO and to include false information in a report made pursuant to it. A person who without reasonable excuse includes false or misleading information in a report, or otherwise fails to comply with any requirement of this section, is guilty of an offence and is liable on summary conviction to imprisonment for a term not exceeding 51 weeks (12 months in Scotland, and 6 months in Northern Ireland), or a fine not exceeding level 5 on the standard scale, or to both. 5.15

5. Verifying the Information in a Financial Reporting Order Report

Section 81 confers powers on the person to whom a report is made under s 79 (the specified person) so that he can verify the accuracy of the information in it (including any documents included with the report). 5.16

The specified person may, for the purpose of doing either of the things mentioned in s 81(4), disclose a report to any person who he reasonably believes may 5.17

be able to contribute to doing either of those things (s 81(2)). Any other person may disclose information to the specified person, or a person to whom the specified person has disclosed a report, for the purpose of contributing to doing either of the things mentioned in s 81(4) (s 81(3)).

5.18   The things mentioned in s 81(4) are checking the accuracy of the report or of any other report made pursuant to the same order, and discovering the true position.

5.19   The specified person may also disclose a report for the purposes of the prevention, detection, investigation, or prosecution of criminal offences, whether in the UK or elsewhere, and the prevention, detection, or investigation of conduct for which penalties other than criminal penalties are provided under the law of any part of the UK or of any country or territory outside the UK (s 81(5)).

5.20   A disclosure under s 81 does not breach any obligation of confidence owed by the person making the disclosure, or any other restriction on the disclosure of information (however imposed). However, nothing in s 81 authorises a disclosure, in contravention of any provisions of the Data Protection Act 1998, of personal data which are not exempt from those provisions.

6. Variation and Revocation

5.21   An application for variation or revocation of an FRO may be made to the court which made the order either by the person in respect of whom it has been made or by the person to whom reports are to be made under it (s 80(1), (2)). If the FRO was made on appeal, the application must be made to the court which originally sentenced the person in respect of whom the order was made.

5.22   If the court to which the application is to be made is a magistrates' court the application may be made to any magistrates' court acting in the same local justice area (or in Northern Ireland for the same county court division) as that court (s 80(4)).

B. INTERNATIONAL OBLIGATIONS

1. Enforcement of Overseas Forfeiture Orders

5.23   Section 9(1) of the Criminal Justice (International Cooperation) Act 1990 confers the power to make an Order in Council to provide for the enforcement in the UK of an order made by a court in a country or territory outside the UK designated in the Order in Council which is for the forfeiture and destruction or other disposal of anything in respect of which an offence as specified in s 9(6) has been committed or which was used or intended for use in connection with the commission of such an offence. Such items are known as 'instrumentalities of crime'.

In its original form s 9(6) included only drugs offences and the offences in   **5.24**
Part VI of the Criminal Justice Act 1988 (and the Scottish equivalents). Section
95 SOCPA inserts a new s 9(6) into the Criminal Justice (International Cooperation) Act 1990. Section 9(6) now provides that s 9 applies to any offence
that corresponds to or is similar to an offence under the law of England and
Wales, an offence under the law of Scotland, or an offence under the law of
Northern Ireland.

The amendment will enable the UK to give effect to international conventions   **5.25**
requiring the enforcement of foreign orders for the forfeiture of instrumentalities in relevant offences. These conventions are the United Nations Convention
Against Transnational Organised Crime (UNTOC), which was agreed in 2000,
and the United Nations Convention Against Corruption (UNCAC), which was
agreed in 2003.

The Criminal Justice (International Cooperation) Act 1990 (Enforcement of   **5.26**
Overseas Forfeiture Orders) Order 1991 (SI 1991/1463) made under s 9(1) permits forfeiture orders made by foreign courts to be enforced in the UK for drugs
offences. It also permits restraint orders to be made in support of forfeiture
orders. It also originally included offences under Part VI of the Criminal Justice
Act 1988; however this was repealed by the Proceeds of Crime Act 2002. This
limitation of s 9 came to light when the requirements of the UN Conventions
were reviewed for the purposes of assessing the UK's legislative compliance. The
amendments made by s 95 will enable the UK to ratify the UN Conventions.

For further details on the operation of the Criminal Justice (International Co-   **5.27**
operation) Act 1990 (Enforcement of Overseas Forfeiture Orders) Order 1991
see Nicholls, Montgomery, and Knowles, *The Law of Extradition and Mutual
Assistance* (2002), para 19.25.

2. Mutual Assistance in Freezing Property or Evidence

At its meeting in Tampere in October 1999 the European Council endorsed the   **5.28**
principle of mutual recognition in both civil and criminal matters within the
European Union. It concluded that the principle of mutual recognition should
also apply to pre-trial orders, in particular to those which would enable competent judicial and prosecuting authorities quickly to secure evidence and to
seize property which are easily movable.

On 29 November 2000 the Council, in accordance with the Tampere   **5.29**
conclusions, adopted a programme of measures to implement the principle of
mutual recognition in criminal matters, giving first priority to the adoption
of an instrument applying the principle of mutual recognition to the freezing of
evidence and property.

On 22 July 2003 the Council adopted Framework Decision 2003/577/JHA on   **5.30**
the execution in the European Union of orders freezing property or evidence
(available   at   <europa.eu.int/eur-lex/pri/en/oj/dat/2003/l_196/l_19620030802
en00450055.pdf>).

5.31   The purpose of the Framework Decision is to establish the rules under which a Member State shall recognise and execute in its territory a freezing order issued by a judicial authority of another Member State in criminal proceedings. The purpose of such an order is to secure property for use as evidence or for the purposes of confiscation.

5.32   Article 5(1) provides for the recognition and immediate execution in one state of freezing orders made in another state. It provides that the competent judicial authorities of the executing state shall recognise a freezing order, transmitted in accordance with Article 4, without any further formality being required. It requires the executing state to take measures necessary for its immediate execution in the same way as a domestic freezing order, unless that authority decides to invoke one of the grounds for non-recognition or non-execution provided for in Article 7 or one of the grounds for postponement provided for in Article 8.

5.33   These grounds include where execution would jeopardise a criminal investigation, or where it would infringe the principle of *non bis in idem*, or where the offence is not an offence under the law of the executing state.

5.34   However, this dual criminality requirement is limited by Article 3(2) which provides a generic list of offences for which dual criminality shall not be required. These offences are: participation in a criminal organisation; terrorism; trafficking in human beings; sexual exploitation of children and child pornography; illicit trafficking in narcotic drugs and psychotropic substances; illicit trafficking in weapons, munitions, and explosives; corruption; fraud, including that affecting the financial interests of the European Communities within the meaning of the Convention of 26 July 1995 on the Protection of the European Communities' Financial Interests; laundering of the proceeds of crime; counterfeiting currency, including of the euro; computer-related crime; environmental crime, including illicit trafficking in endangered animal species and in endangered plant species and varieties; facilitation of unauthorised entry and residence; murder; grievous bodily injury; illicit trade in human organs and tissue; kidnapping; illegal restraint and hostage-taking; racism and xenophobia; organised or armed robbery; illicit trafficking in cultural goods, including antiques and works of art; swindling; racketeering and extortion; counterfeiting and piracy of products; forgery of administrative documents and trafficking therein; forgery of means of payment; illicit trafficking in hormonal substances and other growth promoters; illicit trafficking in nuclear or radioactive materials; trafficking in stolen vehicles; rape; arson; crimes within the jurisdiction of the International Criminal Tribunal; unlawful seizure of aircraft/ships; sabotage.

5.35   Implementation of the Framework Decision requires legislation, and the machinery for implementation is contained in s 96. Section 96(1) provides that the Secretary of State or the Scottish Ministers may by order make provision for the purpose of implementing any obligation of the UK created or arising by or under the Decision or enabling any such obligation to be implemented.

C. PROCEEDS OF CRIME

Chapter 6 of Part 2 and Schedule 6 contain a collection of provisions relating to **5.36** the proceeds of crime, money laundering, and related matters. Some of these provisions amend the Proceeds of Crime Act 2002, and the provisions of that Act will not be dealt with in detail here. For a detailed treatment of the Act see Smith and Owen (eds), *Asset Recovery: Criminal Confiscation and Civil Recovery* (Butterworths, 2003).

1. Confiscation Orders in Magistrates' Courts

Section 97 provides that the Secretary of State may by order make such pro- **5.37** vision as he considers appropriate to enable confiscation orders under Part 2 of the Proceeds of Crime Act 2002 (confiscation: England and Wales), or Part 4 of that Act (confiscation: Northern Ireland), to be made by magistrates' courts in England and Wales or Northern Ireland. An order under s 97(1) may not enable such a confiscation order to be made by any magistrates' court in respect of an amount exceeding £10,000 (s 97(2)).

An order under s 97(1) may amend, repeal, revoke, or otherwise modify any **5.38** provision of Part 2 or 4 of the 2002 Act or any other enactment relating to, or to things done under or for the purposes of, either (or any provision) of those Parts (s 97(3)).

2. Civil Recovery: Freezing Orders

The Proceeds of Crime Act 2002 makes provision for the Director of the Assets **5.39** Recovery Agency (ARA) to be able to apply to the High Court for a property freezing order in civil recovery cases under Part 5 of the Act. The effect of s 246(2) and (7) of the 2002 Act was that an interim receiver had to be appointed in every case. Section 98 inserts a number of new sections into the 2002 Act that have the effect of allowing the Director of the ARA in England, Wales, and Northern Ireland to be able to apply for a property freezing order as an alternative to an order appointing a receiver, and makes similar provision for property freezing orders to be made in Scotland.

Section 98(1) inserts ss 245A to 245D into the Proceeds of Crime Act 2002. **5.40** The effect of these sections in summary is as follows:

(a) Section 245A provides that where the enforcement authority may take proceedings for a recovery order in the High Court, the authority may apply to the court for a property freezing order. A property freezing order is an order that specifies or describes the property to which it applies, and subject to any exclusions (see s 245C(1)(b) and (2)), prohibits any person to whose property the order applies from in any way dealing with the property.

The court may make a property freezing order if it is satisfied that the condition in s 245A(5) is met and, where applicable, that the condition in s 245A(6) is met. The condition in s 245A(5) is that there is a good arguable case that the property to which the application for the order relates is, or includes, recoverable property, and that, if any of it is not recoverable property, it is associated property. The condition in s 245A(6) is that if the property to which the application for the order relates includes property alleged to be associated property, and the enforcement authority has not established the identity of the person who holds it, the authority has taken all reasonable steps to do so.

(b) Section 245B contains provisions allowing for the variation and setting aside of a property freezing order.

(c) Section 245C provides that the power to vary a property freezing order includes (in particular) power to make exclusions as follows: power to exclude property from the order; and power, otherwise than by excluding property from the order, to make exclusions from the prohibition on dealing with the property to which the order applies. Exclusions from the prohibition on dealing with the property to which the order applies (other than exclusions of property from the order) may also be made when the order is made. Section 245(C) provides that an exclusion may, in particular, make provision for the purpose of enabling any person to meet his reasonable living expenses, or to carry on any trade, business, profession, or occupation. Section 245(C)(5) and (6) contains provisions relating to exclusions for the purposes of enabling a person to meet legal expenses. Previously there was no provision to allow for payment of legal expenses out of restrained funds in civil cases, in contrast to criminal cases (*S v Customs & Excise Commissioners*).[1]

(d) Section 245D contains provisions restricting proceedings and remedies in relation to property subject to a property freezing order.

5.41 Section 98(2) contains provisions relating to Scotland, where property freezing orders are known as prohibitory property orders.

3. Appeal in Proceedings for Forfeiture of Cash

5.42 Section 101 has the effect, by inserting a new s 299 into the Proceeds of Crime Act 2002, of giving a right of appeal to police and customs officers in all cash forfeiture applications where a court dismisses an application for cash forfeiture. This is in addition to the right of appeal given to a person aggrieved by the making of an order for the forfeiture of cash.

---

[1] [2004] EWCA Crim 2374.

Section 299(1) of the 2002 Act now provides that any party to proceedings for **5.43** an order for the forfeiture of cash under s 298 who is aggrieved by an order under that section or by the decision of the court not to make such an order may appeal in relation to England and Wales, to the Crown Court; in relation to Scotland, to the Sheriff Principal; in relation to Northern Ireland, to a county court.

An appeal under s 299(1) must be made before the end of the period of 30 **5.44** days starting with the day on which the court makes the order or decision (s 299(2)).

The court hearing the appeal may make any order it thinks appropriate **5.45** (s 299(3)). If the court upholds an appeal against an order forfeiting the cash, it may order the release of the cash.

4. Money Laundering: Defence where Overseas Conduct is Legal under Local Law

Section 102 amends the three principal money laundering offences in ss 327 to **5.46** 329 Proceeds of Crime Act 2002 and the related offences of failure to report money laundering in ss 330 to 332. The amendments provide a defence to the offences where the person knows, or believes on reasonable grounds, that the relevant criminal conduct occurred overseas, and where the conduct is legal under local law. The defence does not apply where the relevant conduct is of a type described by order.

The defence in relation to each offence is introduced by the insertion of **5.47** s 327(2A) and (2B) in relation to the offence of concealing, etc; s 328(2A) and (2B) in relation to the offence of arrangements; and s 329(2A) and (2B) in relation to acquisition, use, and possession. Each defence is in similar form. A person does not commit an offence under ss 327(1), 328(1), 329(1) if:

(a) he knows, or believes on reasonable grounds, that the relevant criminal conduct occurred in a particular country or territory outside the UK, and

(b) the relevant criminal conduct:
   (i) was not, at the time it occurred, unlawful under the criminal law then applying in that country or territory, and
   (ii) is not of a description prescribed by an order made by the Secretary of State.

'The relevant criminal conduct' means the criminal conduct by reference to which the property concerned is criminal property.

A person does not commit an offence under s 330 (failure to disclose: **5.48** regulated sector); s 331 (failure to disclose: nominated officers in the regulated sector); or s 332 (failure to disclose: other nominated officers) if:

(a) he knows, or believes on reasonable grounds, that the money laundering is occurring in a particular country or territory outside the UK, and

(b) the money laundering:
  (i) is not unlawful under the criminal law applying in that country or territory, and
  (ii) is not of a description prescribed in an order made by the Secretary of State.

5. Money Laundering: Threshold Amounts

5.49   Section 103 amends the three principal money laundering offences in ss 327 to 329 Proceeds of Crime Act 2002, and inserts a new s 339A on threshold amounts.

5.50   Sections 327(2C), 328(5), and 329(2B), introduced by s 103(2), (3), and (4), mean that it is not an offence for a bank or other deposit-taking body to carry out transactions in circumstances where formerly they would have had to seek consent when the amount of money concerned in the transaction is below £250 or such higher threshold amount as may be specified by a constable or customs officer in accordance with s 339A.

6. Money Laundering: Disclosures to Identify Persons and Property

5.51   Section 104 amends the failure-to-report provisions in ss 330 to 332 Proceeds of Crime Act 2002. The amendments mean that the obligation to report suspicions of money laundering will apply only if: the person required to make a report knows the identity of the person engaged in the money-laundering offence or the whereabouts of any of the laundered property; or the information which would have to be reported discloses, or may assist in uncovering, the identity of the person engaged in that offence or the whereabouts of any of the laundered property.

5.52   Section 104 makes similar changes in each of ss 330, 331, and 332. Here only s 330 will be discussed in detail.

5.53   Section 330 of the 2002 Act is entitled 'failure to disclose: regulated sector'. Following the amendments made by s 104, by s 330(1), a person commits an offence if the conditions in s 330(2) to (4) are satisfied.

5.54   The first of these conditions (s 330(2)) is that he:

(a) knows or suspects, or
(b) has reasonable grounds for knowing or suspecting, that another person is engaged in money laundering.

5.55   The second condition (s 330(3)) is that the information or other matter on which his knowledge or suspicion is based, or which gives reasonable grounds for such knowledge or suspicion:

came to him in the course of a business in the regulated sector.

The third condition (s 330(3A)) is that he can identify the other person men- **5.56** tioned in subsection (2) or the whereabouts of any of the laundered property, or that he believes, or it is reasonable to expect him to believe, that the information or other matter mentioned in s 330(3) will or may assist in identifying that other person or the whereabouts of any of the laundered property. The laundered property is the property forming the subject-matter of the money laundering that he knows or suspects, or has reasonable grounds for knowing or suspecting, that other person to be engaged in (s 330(5A)).

The fourth condition (s 330(4)) is that he does not make the required **5.57** disclosure to:

a nominated officer, or person authorised by the Director General of the Serious Organised Crime Agency.

A disclosure to a nominated officer is a disclosure which is made to a person **5.58** nominated by the alleged offender's employer to receive disclosures under this section, and is made in the course of the alleged offender's employment and in accordance with the procedure established by the employer for the purpose (s 330(9)).

However, a disclosure which satisfies paragraphs (a) and (b) of s 330(9) is **5.59** not to be taken as a disclosure to a nominated officer if the person making the disclosures is a professional legal adviser, he makes it for the purpose of obtaining advice about making a disclosure under this section, and he does not intend it to be a disclosure under s 330.

The required disclosure is a disclosure of the information or other matter to a **5.60** nominated officer or a person authorised by the Director General of SOCA, in the form and manner (if any) prescribed for the purposes of this subsection by order under s 339.

However a person does not commit an offence under s 330 if: **5.61**

(a) he has a reasonable excuse for not disclosing the information or other matter;

(b) he is a professional legal adviser and the information or other matter came to him in privileged circumstances; or

(c) s 330(7) applies to him—s 330(7) applies to a person if he does not know or suspect that another person is engaged in money laundering; and

(d) he has not been provided by his employer with such training as is specified by the Secretary of State by order for the purposes of this section.

Information or other matter comes to a professional legal adviser in privil- **5.62** eged circumstances if it is communicated or given to him by (or by a representa- tive of) a client of his in connection with the giving by the adviser of legal advice to the client, by (or by a representative of) a person seeking legal advice from the adviser, or by a person in connection with legal proceedings or contemplated legal proceedings (s 330(10)).

5.63   By s 330(11), s 330(10) does not apply to information or other matter which is communicated or given with the intention of furthering a criminal purpose.

5.64   By s 330(7A):

(a) a person does not commit an offence under s 330 if he knows, or believes on reasonable grounds, that the money laundering is occurring in a particular country or territory outside the UK; and

(b) the money laundering is not unlawful under the criminal law applying in that country or territory, and is not of a description prescribed in an order made by the Secretary of State.

5.65   In deciding whether a person committed an offence under this section the court must consider whether he followed any relevant guidance issued by a supervisory authority or any other appropriate body (s 330(8)). An appropriate body is any body which regulates or is representative of any trade, profession, business, or employment carried on by the alleged offender (s 330(13)).

7. Money Laundering: Form and Manner of Disclosures

5.66   Section 105 inserts new provisions into s 339 Proceeds of Crime Act 2002 concerning the form and manner of disclosure. These replace s 339(2) and (3) Proceeds of Crime Act 2002, under subsection (1) of which the Secretary of State has the power to prescribe by order the form and manner in which disclosures of money laundering should be made.

6

POLICE POWERS

A.	Overview of Part 3 of SOCPA	6.01
B.	Powers of Arrest without Warrant by Constables	6.04
C.	Powers of Arrest without Warrant by Other Persons	6.22
D.	Exclusion Zones	6.28
E.	Search Warrants	6.31
F.	Stop and Search for Prohibited Fireworks	6.36
G.	Photographing of Suspects	6.37
H.	Fingerprints	6.44
I.	Footwear Impressions	6.48
J.	Intimate Samples	6.50
K.	Staff Custody Officers	6.52
L.	Additional Matters in Part 3 of SOCPA	6.56

A. OVERVIEW OF PART 3 OF SOCPA

Part 3 of SOCPA makes changes to police powers at a fundamental level, **6.01** amending the two most significant existing statutes in this area, the Police and Criminal Evidence Act 1984 (PACE) and the Police Reform Act 2002 (PRA), in important respects. The provisions enacted were foreshadowed in two Government initiatives. The first was the comprehensive review of PACE in 2002, *Report of the Joint Home Office/Cabinet Office Review of PACE* (2002)[1] (the PACE Review), and the second was the Home Office Consultation in 2004, 'Policing: Modernising Police Powers to Meet Community Needs'[2] (the Consultation Paper). The latter discussed most of the changes which now appear in Part 3. Virtually all of the significant Part 3 proposals met strong opposition

---

[1] Available at <www.homeoffice.gov.uk/docs/pacereview2002.pdf>.
[2] Available at <www.homeoffice.gov.uk/docs3/PolicingConsultation.pdf>.

from civil liberties groups[3] and the Law Society,[4] and drew mixed responses from the Police Federation, the Association of Chief Police Officers, and the Parliamentary Joint Committee on Human Rights.[5] There has also been forceful criticism from legal academics.[6]

6.02   Although nominally part of SOCPA, Part 3 is not limited to serious organised crime. It affects the exercise of police powers for all criminal investigations, no matter how minor. It also extends the role of civilian police staff, creating a new position of 'staff custody officer', allowing custody officer functions to be carried out by a person who is not a police officer. The changes are far-reaching and have necessitated numerous consequential amendments to other Acts, which are contained in Part 3 and in Schedules 7, 8, and 9 of SOCPA.

6.03   The 15 sections (ss 110–124) deal with the following: new powers of arrest without warrant (ss 110–111), which replace the powers previously contained in ss 24 and 25 of PACE; exclusion zones (s 112); search warrants (s 113–114); stop and search for fireworks (s 115); photographing of suspects (s 116); fingerprint and footwear impressions (ss 117–118); intimate samples (s 119); 'staff custody officers' (ss 120–121); powers of persons 'designated' or 'accredited' under the PRA (s 122); and provision of access to information by police staff (s 123).

B. POWERS OF ARREST WITHOUT WARRANT BY CONSTABLES

6.04   Section 110 creates two new sections in PACE, relating to arrest without warrant. Section 24 of PACE is replaced by a new s 24, relating to the powers of constables, and a new s 24A, relating to arrests made by other persons.[7] Section 25 of PACE ceases to have effect.[8] The new powers apply to arrests after commencement of the Act, regardless of when the relevant offence was committed.[9]

6.05   Under the new s 24 of PACE a constable may, without a warrant, arrest a person for **any** offence, provided that two sets of criteria are met. Firstly, the person who is to be arrested must fall into one of the following categories:

(a) the person is about to commit an offence;[10]

---

[3] See, in particular, the submissions by Liberty (*Serious Organised Crime and Police Bill: Liberty's Briefing for the Second Reading in the House of Commons*, December 2004) and JUSTICE (*Serious Organised Crime and Police Bill, Parts 1 and 2, Briefing for House of Lords Second Reading*, March 2005).

[4] See Law Society, *Parliamentary Brief, Serious Organised Crime and Police Bill, House of Commons Second Reading*, 7 December 2004.

[5] See *Scrutiny: First Progress Report, Fourth Report of Session 2004–2005* available at <www.publications.parliament.uk/pa/jt200405/jtselect/jtrights/26/2602.htm>.

[6] See, for example, Prof J R Spencer QC 'Extending the Police State' (2005) 155 NLJ 477.

[7] SOCPA, s 110(1).

[8] SOCPA, s 110(2).

[9] SOCPA, s 110(4).

[10] Section 24(1)(a).

(b) the person is in the act of committing an offence;[11]

(c) the constable has reasonable grounds to suspect that the person is about to commit an offence;[12]

(d) the constable has reasonable grounds to suspect the person is committing an offence;[13]

(e) the constable has reasonable grounds to suspect that an offence has been committed and has reasonable grounds to suspect that the person is guilty of it;[14]

(f) an offence has, in fact, been committed and the person is guilty of that offence;[15]

(g) an offence has, in fact, been committed and the constable has reasonable grounds to suspect that the person is guilty of it.[16]

Secondly, even if the person falls into one of those categories, the power of arrest is exercisable only if the constable has reasonable grounds for believing that, for one of the following reasons, it is 'necessary to arrest the person in question': **6.06**

(a) to enable the name of the person in question to be ascertained;[17]

(b) to enable the address of the person in question to be ascertained;[18]

(c) to prevent the person in question:
  (i) causing physical injury to himself or any other person,[19]
  (ii) suffering physical injury,[20]
  (iii) causing loss or damage to property,[21]
  (iv) committing an offence against public decency—where members of the public going about their normal business cannot reasonably be expected to avoid the person,[22]
  (v) causing an unlawful obstruction of the highway;[23]

(d) to protect a child or other vulnerable person from the person in question;[24]

(e) to allow prompt and effective investigation of the offence or of the conduct of the person in question;[25]

---

[11] Section 24(1)(b).
[12] Section 24(1)(c).
[13] Section 24(1)(d).
[14] Section 24(2).
[15] Section 24(3)(a).
[16] Section 24(3)(b).
[17] Section 24(5)(a).
[18] Section 24(5)(b).
[19] Section 24(5)(c)(i).
[20] Section 24(5)(c)(ii).
[21] Section 24(5)(c)(iii).
[22] Section 24(5)(c)(iv) and s 24(6).
[23] Section 24(5)(c)(v).
[24] Section 24(5)(d)).
[25] Section 24(5)(e).

(f) to prevent the prosecution of the offence from being hindered by the disappearance of the person in question.[26]

6.07 This fundamental change in the nature of arrest powers has been controversial. The concerns expressed are not of purely political or academic interest, since they relate to the effectiveness and legality of the new provisions. Accordingly, they merit some consideration here and are best understood by comparing the new s 24 with its repealed predecessor.

6.08 Prior to SOCPA, arrest without warrant was usually impermissible, unless the offence was a serious one.[27] The repealed s 24 had defined such offences as 'arrestable offences'. These were: murder; offences which may have resulted in a sentence of imprisonment for a term of 5 year or more; and those offences contained within a specific list set out in Schedule 1A to PACE.

6.09 The only exception to the seriousness criterion was that s 25 PACE permitted arrest without warrant for offences which were not 'arrestable', if 'general arrest conditions' were met. These were set out in s 25(3) and broadly followed the 'necessary' criteria in the new s 24(5). However, the 'general arrest conditions' of s 25(3) did not include two criteria which are contained within the new s 24(5)(e) and (f): 'to allow prompt and effective investigation of the offence or of the conduct of the person in question', and 'to prevent the prosecution of the offence from being hindered by the disappearance of the person in question'.

6.10 The Government believed that s 24 needed to be amended in order to provide a 'straightforward, universal framework'[28] relating to all offences. There were suggestions that the powers were too complicated and confusing for officers to remember.[29] In an attempt at simplification, the seriousness threshold for the exercise of this important power has been removed. It is this widening of the power to arrest without warrant to include the most minor offences, combined with broad justifications for the exercise of that power, such as 'allowing prompt and effective investigation', that is at the heart of the criticisms of the new sections.

6.11 The principal concern is that the removal of the seriousness criteria is a disproportionate step in fulfilment of the purported aim of clarity.[30] Citizens are

---

[26] Section 24(5)(f).

[27] At common law there was only a power of arrest in relation to 'felonies'; in general those suspected of less serious offences ('misdemeanours') could only be arrested with a warrant.

[28] The Consultation Paper, para 2.5.

[29] The Consultation Paper, para 2.2, '. . . the basis of arrest remains diverse—it is not always straightforward or clear to police officers or members of the public when and if the power of arrest exists for offences at the lower end of seriousness . . .'; and at para. 2.3, '. . . there is a complex and often bewildering array of powers and procedures'.

[30] *Liberty's Briefing for the Second Reading in the House of Commons* (December 2004) at para 17 '[the new section 24 powers are] a move away from consent based policing towards policing by discretion', and continued at para 20, 'The purpose of legislation is to provide parameters of what is permissible. It will not be of any benefit to tell the police 'you can have all the powers you want but you must only use them when necessary'.

now susceptible to arrest and detention for minor offences which previously were considered not to have justified such a fundamental infringement of civil liberties. It is notable that the comprehensive PACE Review did not suggest this approach. It recommended the broadening of arrest powers but proposed enhanced training of officers to ensure greater clarity and understanding of existing powers.[31]

Secondly, the only check on the use of such a broad new power is the arresting officer's discretion as to whether the arrest is necessary, with such necessity being defined in wide terms, such as 'allowing prompt and effective investigation'. This heavy reliance on the individual officer's discretion arguably increases the risk of arbitrary, inconsistent, and disproportionate use of arrest powers.   **6.12**

The broader police powers under the new s 24 are welcomed by both the Police Federation and the Association of Chief Police Officers.[32] However, wider discretion in the use of such an important power is not always a benefit to officers, who have to make complicated arrest decisions under pressure. In a difficult area, where mistakes can result in significant loss to individuals and civil liability for wrongful arrest, it is arguable that clear parameters in primary legislation are of more assistance than open-ended discretion. It is well established in English law that where a power to arrest is available, an officer retains a discretion as to the exercise of that power. He must exercise it reasonably and proportionately in order for the arrest to be lawful.[33] When such a power was available only in relation to more serious offences, a constable could proceed with the confidence that in most cases arrest would be a proportionate measure in the investigation of that offence. But when such powers are extended to more minor offences, the proportionality exercise becomes more nuanced and more difficult. This difficulty is increased by the greater scrutiny that the new provisions place on an officer's use of his discretion. An officer's assessment of the necessity of making the arrest will now be examined by a court under the terms of the new s 24(4): did the officer have 'reasonable grounds for believing' that one of the criterion set out in s 24(5) was fulfilled? This is certainly a more stringent test than that of *Wednesbury* reasonableness, proportionality, or even 'reasonable grounds to suspect' against which arrest decisions were previously assessed—'belief' denoting a higher requirement of certainty than 'suspicion'.[34]   **6.13**

---

[31] Paragraph 2, p 9.

[32] See p 4 of the *Summary of Response to the Consultation Paper, January 2005*, available at <www.homeoffice.gov.uk/docs4/summary_of_responses.pdf>.

[33] See *Mohammed-Holgate v Duke* [1984] AC 437. Lord Diplock's view in that case, that the lawfulness of a discretion to exercise arrest powers should be assessed on *Wednesbury* principles is no longer an adequate analysis. The *Wednesbury* test, traditionally generous to the decision maker, now needs to be narrowed depending on the engagement of the rights involved (see *Al-Fayed and others v Commissioner of Police for the Metropolis and others* (CA, 25 November 2004), Auld LJ at paras 81–84.

[34] The House of Lords have described the distinction as 'a fine one'. For an analysis of this distinction see R Clayton and H Tomlinson, *Civil Actions Against The Police* (Sweet & Maxwell, 3rd edn, 2005), pp 204–205.

Accordingly, the notion that this enhanced power will make arrest without warrant a simpler and clearer process for either the officer, or the suspected person, is questionable.

6.14   When considering whether an arrest is 'necessary', it is worth noting that the power to make an arrest when a person's identity is unclear now sits alongside the new power to take fingerprints and use mobile fingerprint checks in public.[35] All persons considering using powers of arrest for confirmation of identity will have to consider whether the use of the power to take and check fingerprints is a less intrusive, and therefore more appropriate, means by which to confirm a suspect's identity, rather than arrest followed by detention at a police station.

6.15   Thirdly, there is considerable concern over the abolition of the 'arrestable offence' seriousness standard when it comes to the consequential police powers triggered by arrest. By eliminating the seriousness standard for making an arrest, ancillary powers such as the search of a person's home, or the taking of fingerprints and DNA samples are also exercisable on a lower standard of seriousness.

6.16   This problem was identified by the Government at an early stage. Even in proposing the abolition of the 'arrestable offence' criteria, the Government acknowledged that the reliance of that framework on 'seriousness is an important concept which provides a focus on proportionality and appropriateness' in relation to ancillary powers triggered by arrest.[36] To overcome this problem, SOCPA makes many post-arrest powers exercisable only in relation to 'indictable' offences.[37] While this reintroduces a seriousness criterion as a trigger for ancillary powers, it is important to note that 'indictable offences' is a lower standard of seriousness than 'arrestable offences' since it includes offences that may be triable both summarily and on indictment.

6.17   Similarly, it automatically follows that another definition contained in PACE—'serious arrestable offence'—also disappears. This definition acted as an even higher seriousness threshold before the most intrusive police powers were triggered. Section 116 of PACE previously set out a list of those offences defined as 'serious arrestable offences'. The definition included any arrestable offences, but only if they would be likely to lead to any of the following consequences: serious harm to the security of the state or to public order; serious interference with the administration of justice or with the investigation of offences or of a particular offence; the death of any person; serious injury to any person; substantial financial gain to any person; and serious financial loss to any person.[38]

---

[35] SOCPA, s 117, creating a new s 61(6A) of PACE. See below for further discussion on this provision.

[36] The Consultation Paper, para 2.12.

[37] SOCPA, Sch 7, Part 3.

[38] PACE, s 116(6). PACE, s 116, was repealed by SOCPA, Sch 7, para 43(12).

The police powers applicable only to 'serious arrestable offences' had **6.18** included: the power to establish a road check;[39] powers to obtain search warrants;[40] the power to obtain an order for access to or production of confidential or journalistic material;[41] the power to detain an arrested person without charge for longer than 24 hours, up to 96 hours;[42] the power to delay the right of an arrested person to have someone informed of his arrest;[43] and the power to delay the right of an arrested person to legal advice.[44]

These enhanced police powers will now be exercisable on arrest for any indict- **6.19** able offence, with the only check on their use being the level of authorisation required and, in the case of search warrants, the oversight of a judge, relying on information given to him by the investigating officers.

The broadening of the applicability of intrusive powers will require officers **6.20** to have greater sensitivity as to whether those available powers should be used in any given situation. It is, on one view, a more complicated decision-making process for the officer than under the previous framework.

The Parliamentary Joint Committee on Human Rights (*Scrutiny: First Pro-* **6.21** *gress Report, Fourth Report of Session 2004–2005*) (the JCHR Report) reported on the Bill that became SOCPA. It pointed out that the statutory framework for arrest was one which had been carefully arrived at in the drafting of PACE, taking into account the historical origins of this important and intrusive power.[45] The Committee was sufficiently concerned at the potential erosion of rights under the new s 24, to write to the Government seeking an explanation for the assertion that the section was compatible with Articles 5.1 and 8 of the European Convention on Human Rights.[46] The JCHR Report expressed particular concern over whether the justifications for making arrest, outlined in s 24(5)(c)(i) ('causing physical injury to himself . . .') or s 24(5)(e) ('to allow the prompt and effective investigation of the offence or the conduct of the person in question'), necessarily fell within Article 5.1(c). In response the Government drew attention to its positive obligation under Article 2 to protect life and promised that there would be a new code of practice on the use of this power. The Joint Committee accepted that the proposed provisions were likely to be compatible with Article 5.1 and justified under Article 8.2.[47]

---

[39] PACE, s 4(4)(a)(i).
[40] PACE, s 8(1)(a).
[41] PACE, Sch 1, para 2(a)(i).
[42] PACE, s 43(4)(b) and s 44(3)(b).
[43] PACE, s 56(2)(a).
[44] PACE, s 58(6)(a).
[45] JCHR report, para 1.60.
[46] JCHR report, para 1.85.
[47] Joint Committee on Human Rights, *Scrutiny: Fourth Progress Report, 8th Report of Session 2004–2005* (HL Paper 60, HC 388), 23 February 2005, para 2.25.

C. POWERS OF ARREST WITHOUT WARRANT
BY OTHER PERSONS

6.22   The new s 24A of PACE is concerned with arrests by persons other than police officers. It replicates the position that had previously existed under s 24(4) and (5) of PACE, replacing the expression 'arrestable offence' with 'indictable offence'. Accordingly, any person may arrest without a warrant:

(a) anyone who is in the act of committing an indictable offence;[48]

(b) anyone whom he has reasonable grounds for suspecting to be committing an indictable offence;[49]

(c) any person who is guilty of committing an indictable offence;[50]

(d) any person whom he has reasonable grounds for suspecting to be guilty of committing an indictable offence, provided that offence has, in fact, been committed by someone.[51]

6.23   It is noteworthy that the importance of clarifying arrest powers for constables, which necessitated such a comprehensive re-drafting of powers under s 24, was not regarded as appropriate in relation to the new powers of arrest given to other persons under s 24A. By preserving a seriousness threshold ('indictable offences') before such arrests can be effected under s 24A, untrained civilians and community support officers will be required to remember different categories of offences to ensure they are acting lawfully, notwithstanding that such distinctions were considered too complicated and bewildering for police constables.

6.24   The section preserves the anomaly that while police officers may effect a lawful arrest on reasonable grounds of suspicion that an offence has been committed at some stage in the past, such grounds will not suffice for non-constables. For persons other than constables to arrest for an offence they believe has already been committed, the offence must, in fact, have been committed.[52]

6.25   Section 24A(3) also imposes two new 'necessity' criteria in relation to arrests by person who are not constables, both of which must be fulfilled for the arrest to be lawful:

(1) the person making the arrest must have reasonable grounds for believing it is necessary to arrest the person in questions for any of the following reasons:

---

[48] Section 24A(1)(a).
[49] Section 24A(1)(b).
[50] Section 24A(2)(a).
[51] Section 24A(2)(b).
[52] See *R v Self* [1992] 1 WLR 657.

(a) to prevent the person in question injuring himself or any other person;[53]

(b) to prevent the person in question suffering physical injury;[54]

(c) to prevent the person in question causing loss of or damage to property;[55] or

(d) to prevent the person in question making off before a constable can assume responsibility for him.[56]

(2) it must appear to the person making the arrest that it is not reasonably practicable for a constable to make it instead.[57]

The first criterion is subject to the same concerns expressed in relation to the new s 24, with the added difficulty that the assessment of such complex issues may be even more difficult for those who are not trained police officers. **6.26**

The second criterion is not expressed in the usual terminology of 'reasonable grounds to suspect/believe' and is expressed in 'subjective' terms. It will be sufficient if the person making the arrest in fact thinks that it is not reasonably practicable for a constable to make the arrest, whatever the position is in fact. **6.27**

D. EXCLUSION ZONES

The Consultation Paper did not suggest the new power of 'exclusion zones' provided by s 112 SOCPA, but the zones are relatively uncontroversial. It is a slightly unfortunate piece of drafting, because whereas the other new provisions amend PACE or PRA, maintaining the bulk of police powers in the two main statutes, s 112 stands independently of those two Acts. It creates a power for a constable to facilitate the enforcement of court orders and conditions of release from prison, by giving him the power to direct a person to leave a place if the order or condition so requires. It also makes it an offence for a person knowingly to disobey such a direction. **6.28**

Under s 112 SOCPA, a constable may direct a person to leave a place if he believes, on reasonable grounds, that the person would be prohibited from entering that place as a result of: **6.29**

(a) an order made by virtue of an enactment following the person's conviction for an offence;[58]

(b) a condition imposed by virtue of a person's release from prison in which he was serving a sentence of imprisonment following conviction of an offence;[59]

---

[53] Section 24A(3)(a) read with s 24A(4)(a).
[54] Section 24A(3)(a) read with s 24A(4)(b).
[55] Section 24A(3)(a) read with s 24A(4)(c).
[56] Section 24A(3)(a) read with s 24A(4)(d).
[57] Section 24A(3)(b).
[58] SOCPA, s 112(2)(a).
[59] SOCPA, s 112(3)(a).

(c) an order or condition prohibiting the person from entering the place.[60]

6.30   The direction may be given orally[61] and it is an offence for a person knowingly to contravene such a direction.[62] The offence makes the person liable on summary conviction to a term of imprisonment not exceeding 51 weeks and/or to a fine not exceeding level 4 on the standard scale.[63] The power is exercisable from commencement of s 112, regardless of when the order or condition in relation to which the power is being exercised, was made.[64]

E. SEARCH WARRANTS

6.31   SOCPA amends Part II of PACE to allow officers to apply for search warrants by reference to all the premises attributable to a person, rather than specifying the precise addresses to be searched. The new warrants allow for multiple searches and are valid for up to three months. In proposing the idea, the Consultation Paper stated as follows: 'A "super warrant" as suggested here would undoubtedly raise issues about interference with the basic rights to privacy. However, officers would still need to have justification for entry onto specific premises.'[65] The justification imposed appears to be that of 'reasonable practicability' which is of questionable rigour in relation to such extended powers of search.

6.32   The significant amendments that SOCPA has made to Part II of PACE are as follows.

- An application for a warrant may be made on reasonable grounds for suspecting that an indictable offence has been committed, and not a 'serious arrestable offence'; as was previously required.[66]

- A warrant application may be for premises specified in the application, as was previously the case (now termed a 'specific premises warrant').[67] But it may also be for all premises occupied or controlled by the person specified in the application including, but not limited to, such sets of premises as are so specified (an 'all premises warrant').[68]

- If the application is for an 'all premises warrant', the justice of the peace must also be satisfied of the following requirements:

---

[60] SOCPA, s 112(2)(b) and (3)(b), respectively.
[61] SOCPA, s 112(4).
[62] SOCPA, s 112(5).
[63] SOCPA, s 112(5).
[64] SOCPA, s 112(10).
[65] Consultation Paper, para 3.8.
[66] SOCPA, Sch 7, para. 43(3).
[67] SOCPA, s 113(4), inserting PACE, s 8(1A)(a).
[68] SOCPA, s 113(4), inserting PACE, s 8(1A)(b).

(a) that because of the particulars of the offence specified in the application, there are reasonable grounds for believing that it is necessary to search premises occupied or controlled by the person in question which are not specified in the application in order to find the material which is likely to be of substantial value to the investigation;[69]

(b) that it is not reasonably practicable to specify in the application all the premises which he occupies or controls and which might need to be searched.[70]

- If the application is for a 'specific premises warrant', the application must specify each set of premises which it is desired to enter and search.[71]

- If the application is for an 'all premises warrant', the application must specify:

  (a) as many sets of premises which it is desired to enter and search as is reasonably practicable to specify;[72]

  (b) the person who is in occupation or control of those premises and any others which it is desired to enter and search;[73]

  (c) why it is necessary to search more premises than those that have been specified;[74]

  (d) why it is not reasonably practicable to specify all the premises which it is desired to enter and search.[75]

- Warrant applications must specify each set of premises to be searched, but in the case of 'all premises warrants', the application must specify the person who is in occupation or control of premises to be searched, together with any premises under his occupation or control which can be specified and which are to be searched.[76]

- In relation to all premises warrants, premises not specified may only be entered or searched with the written authorisation of a police officer of at least the rank of inspector.[77]

- The constable making the usual endorsements on a warrant after execution, stating whether articles or persons were found and whether articles other than those sought were seized, must make separate endorsements in relation to each premises searched.[78]

---

[69] SOCPA, s 113(4), inserting PACE, s 8(1B)(a).
[70] SOCPA, s 113(4), inserting PACE, s 8(1B)(b).
[71] SOCPA, s 113(7), inserting PACE, s 8(2A)(a).
[72] SOCPA, s 113(7), inserting PACE, s 8(2A)(b)(i).
[73] SOCPA, s 113(7), inserting PACE, s 8(2A)(b)(ii).
[74] SOCPA, s 113(7), inserting PACE, s 8(2A)(b)(iii).
[75] SOCPA, s 113(7), inserting PACE, s 8(2A)(b)(iv).
[76] SOCPA, s 113(8), amending PACE, s 8(6)(a)(iv).
[77] SOCPA, s 113(9)(a), inserting PACE, s 16(3A).
[78] SOCPA, s 113(9)(b), inserting PACE, s 16(9)(b).

- The warrant may authorise entry to, and search of, premises on more than one occasion if, on the application, the justice of the peace is satisfied that it is necessary to authorise multiple entries in order to achieve the purpose for which he issues the warrant. There is no limit on the amount of entries that may be authorised and the warrant may be granted for an unlimited number of entries.[79]

- If the application is for a warrant authorising entry and search on more than one occasion, the officer must state the ground on which he applies for such a warrant, and whether he seeks a warrant authorising unlimited entries, or (if not) the maximum number of entries he desires.[80]

- If the warrant authorises multiple entries it must specify whether an unlimited number of entries are authorised and (if not) the number of entries authorised.[81]

- No premises may be entered or searched for a second or subsequent time under the same warrant unless a police officer of at least the rank of inspector has given such authorisation in writing.[82]

- Entry and search under a warrant must be within three months from the date of issue.[83] The warrant must be returned after execution or, in the case of warrants authorising multiple entry, within three months or sooner.[84]

6.33   Section 113 of SOCPA also effects similar amendments to PACE in relation to warrants regarding 'special procedure material' and 'excluded material', under Schedule 1 to PACE.[85] However, the new power to order multiple entries under a warrant appears to be limited to warrants issued under s 8—by a justice of the peace—and not warrants issued under Schedule 1 by a High Court judge, Crown Court judge, or Recorder.[86]

6.34   Many of those consulted on these proposals saw them as being useful, particularly to the extent that a single warrant could cover multiple addresses or multiple visits.[87] However, the proposals were strongly opposed by others, and drew the following comments from the Parliamentary Joint Committee on Human Rights:

In short, the clauses give justices of the peace authority to issue a general warrant of a kind that has been anathema to the common law for centuries on account of the very

---

[79] SOCPA, s 114(2), inserting PACE, s 8(1C) and (1D).
[80] SOCPA, s 114(4)(c), amending PACE, s 15(2)(a)(iii).
[81] SOCPA, s 114(6), inserting PACE, s 15(5A).
[82] SOCPA, s 114(8)(b), inserting PACE, s 16(3B).
[83] SOCPA, s 114, amending PACE, s 16(10).
[84] SOCPA, s 114(8)(c), creating PACE, s 16(10A).
[85] SOCPA, s 113(10)–(15).
[86] SOCPA, s 114(2).
[87] See p 6 of the *Summary of Response to the Consultation Paper, January 2005*, available at <www.homeoffice.gov.uk/docs4/summary_of_responses.pdf>.

wide discretion it confers on public officials, and the lack of effective prior judicial control over the decision to enter (if need be, by force) private premises including dwellings . . .[88]

. . . safeguards external to the police are weak, because the justice of the peace is very unlikely to be able to assess properly the proportionality of a request to be allowed to enter and search unspecified premises on an unlimited number of future occasions over the following three months; and decisions of an inspector in relation to particular premises are unlikely to be subject to judicial or public scrutiny.[89]

The Committee wrote to the Government explaining that it was not satisfied 6.35 that the proposals relating to search warrants were compatible with Article 8 of the European Convention on Human Rights and sought more detailed explanation from the Government as to the basis for its assertion of compatibility.[90] The Government's response was that the proposed changes were being made to simplify the process of obtaining warrants, reduce delays to investigations, and to respond to the 'increasing complexity and organisation of criminal activity'.[91] This did not alleviate the Joint Committee's concerns. They concluded that it was

impossible for us to be satisfied that the proposed new powers could be shown to be proportionate to a pressing social need in pursuit of a legitimate aim as required by Article 8.[92]

As a result, they stated that these proposals gave rise to a significant risk of incompatibility with Article 8.

F. STOP AND SEARCH FOR PROHIBITED FIREWORKS

Section 1 of PACE is amended by s 115 of SOCPA, to allow a person to be 6.36 stopped and searched in relation to prohibited fireworks. This is done by simply adding a subsection (8B) to s 1,[93] and making consequential references to that subsection in the rest of s 1,[94] thereby adding prohibited fireworks to the articles that justify an officer exercising stop and search powers.

---

[88] JCHR Report, para 1.91.
[89] JCHR Report, para 1.95.
[90] JCHR Report, para 1.96.
[91] Joint Committee on Human Rights, *Scrutiny: Fourth Progress Report, 8th Report of Session 2004–2005* (HL Paper 60, HC 388), 23 February 2005, para 2.32.
[92] ibid, para 2.38.
[93] SOCPA, s 115(5), creating PACE, s 1(8B) and (8C).
[94] SOCPA, s 115(1)–(4).

G. PHOTOGRAPHING OF SUSPECTS

6.37 SOCPA amends s 64A of PACE by adding new subsections (1A) and (1B).[95] Section 64A now allows photographs of suspects to be taken at places other than police stations.

6.38 If a person falls within subsection (1B), his photograph may be taken and retained, even if his consent is withheld or it is 'not practicable' to obtain his consent. A person falls within subsection (1B) if he has been:

(a) arrested by a constable for an offence;[96]

(b) taken into custody by a constable after being arrested for an offence by a person other than a constable;[97]

(c) made subject to a requirement to wait with a community support officer, under the PRA;[98]

(d) given a penalty notice by a constable in uniform under Chapter 1, Part 1 of the Criminal Justice and Police Act 2001 (an on-the-spot penalty for disorderly behaviour); or given a penalty notice by a constable under s 444A Education Act 1996 (in respect of failure to secure regular attendance at school of registered pupil); or given a fixed penalty notice by a constable in uniform under s 54 Road Traffic Offenders Act 1988;[99]

(e) given a fixed penalty notice by a community support officer, within the meaning of paragraph 1 of Schedule 4 to the PRA;[100]

(f) given a fixed penalty notice by an accredited person, within the meaning of paragraph 1 of Schedule 5 to the PRA.[101]

6.39 SOCPA also extends the meaning of photographs within s 64A, to include moving images.[102]

6.40 As with other images permitted to be taken by s 64A PACE, subsections (4) and (5) permit such images to be used for 'any purpose related to the prevention or detection of crime, the investigation of an offence, or the conduct of a prosecution'.[103] SOCPA amends s 64A(4)(a) by adding to that list the enforcement of a sentence as another potential legitimate use.[104]

---

[95] SOCPA, s 116(2).
[96] SOCPA, s 116(2), creating PACE, s 64A(1B)(a).
[97] SOCPA, s 116(2), inserting PACE, s 64A(1B)(b).
[98] SOCPA, s 116(2), inserting PACE, s 64A(1B)(c).
[99] SOCPA, s 116(2), inserting PACE, s 64A(1B)(d).
[100] SOCPA, s 116(2), inserting PACE, s 64A(1B)(e).
[101] SOCPA, s 116(2), inserting PACE, s 64A(1B)(f).
[102] SOCPA, s 116(5), inserting PACE, s 64A(6A).
[103] PACE, s 64A(4)(a).
[104] SOCPA, s 116(3).

The keeping of photographs does engage significant issues under Article 8 of **6.41** the European Convention on Human Rights,[105] particularly when, as here, there is no time limit on the retention of such photographs. However, English courts have thus far given approval to the Government taking wider powers to increase the quality and quantity of information it retains about individuals for the purposes of law enforcement and the investigation of crime.[106] It is therefore unlikely that these provisions would be considered by the courts to be a disproportionate interference with Article 8 rights.

However, several points are worthy of consideration. Firstly, this provision **6.42** does represent a qualitative further step in the collecting of information by police officers, creating the hitherto unusual sight of law enforcement officials, whether police officers or community support officers, photographing or even filming individual citizens in public. It is obviously a power that requires careful use, carrying with it the real potential to aggravate relationships between the police and the communities they serve. Furthermore, it permits a person who is not a police officer to take photographs of persons who have not been arrested for any offence (eg a person placed under a requirement to wait by a community Support Officer), or have merely been given fixed penalty notices by officers. The scope for error, misuse, or arbitrary use of such a power is increased, particularly since it takes place outside the controlled environment of a police station.

The extension of this power to moving images is clearly to ensure the best **6.43** identification tools are available[107] but it brings concomitant dangers. The use of moving images in these circumstances, particularly when the power may be exercised by non-police officers outside the police station, may begin, even inadvertently, to encroach into the realms of surveillance.

H. FINGERPRINTS

SOCPA also amends the powers of constables to take fingerprints, by extending **6.44** that power to people who are not detained at police stations. Section 117 of SOCPA adds a subsection (6A)[108] to s 61 of PACE, allowing a constable to take a person's fingerprints without their consent, if:

(a) the constable reasonably suspects that the person is committing or attempting to commit an offence, or has committed or attempted to commit an offence;[109] and

(b) either of two additional conditions is met:

---

[105] See eg, *Friedl v Austria* (1995) 21 EHRR 83.
[106] See *R v Chief Constable of South Yorkshire Police ex p Marper* [2004] 1 WLR 2196 in relation to fingerprint and DNA samples.
[107] Consultation Paper, para 6.13.
[108] SOCPA, s 117(2).
[109] SOCPA, s 117(2), inserting PACE, s 61(6A)(a).

(i) the name of the person is unknown to, and cannot be readily ascertained by, the constable;[110]

(ii) the constable has reasonable grounds for doubting whether a name furnished by the person as his name is his real name.[111]

6.45   It is clear that the same conditions would allow a constable to arrest that person.[112] However, the rationale of the extended power appears to obviate the need to arrest when the principal issue is confirmation of the identity of a suspect. The Consultation Paper explained the reasoning for this provision in the following way:

> The power would reduce the need to use arrest powers under section 25 of PACE (general arrest conditions) in relation to those whose identity was not known or whose details were believed to be false. This impacts greatly upon [Automatic Number Plate Recognition] (and general policing operations), as officers have to arrest and take the offender to a police station to carry out appropriate identity checks. The new power would apply in respect of drivers subject to a roadside interception and their identity is in doubt.
>
> There is no general power to request fingerprints from suspected offenders in a public place if identity is not known or believed to be true. But there is significant advantage in extending the power to all areas where a police officer is unable to establish the identity of a suspect other than the police station.
>
> ... the advantages are:
>
> • a quick and direct route to establish identity;
>
> • a more efficient use of officer's time;
>
> • increased opportunity to detect crime;
>
> • early warning access for police for suspected or wanted criminals.
>
> The provisions of section 64 of PACE would apply in relation to the destruction of fingerprints.

6.46   The fingerprints taken may be checked against other fingerprints retained by relevant authorities in the usual way.[113]

6.47   SOCPA has imposed a more stringent obligation to destroy fingerprints taken under the new s 61(6A), than fingerprints taken in other circumstances. While fingerprints do not usually have to be destroyed by the police,[114] fingerprints taken by virtue of s 61(6A) must be destroyed as soon as they have fulfilled the purpose for which they were taken.[115] Similarly, fingerprints taken by virtue of s 61(6A) fall outside the usual fingerprint regime, for the purposes of additional investigation. In particular, they do not count as fingerprints taken 'in the course

---

[110] SOCPA, s 117(2), inserting PACE, s 61(6B)(a).
[111] SOCPA, s 117(2), inserting PACE, s 61(6B)(b).
[112] PACE, s 24(5), as amended by SOCPA, s 110.
[113] SOCPA, s 117(5), creating PACE, s 63A(1ZA).
[114] PACE, s 64.
[115] SOCPA, s 117(8), creating PACE, s 64(1BA).

of investigation of an offence by the police'[116] and accordingly there is no bar to new prints being taken if the person is subsequently arrested and detained at a police station.[117]

I. FOOTWEAR IMPRESSIONS

Section 118 of SOCPA creates a new s 61A of PACE, which effectively applies **6.48** virtually identical provisions relating to the taking of fingerprints to the taking of impressions of footwear. Section 63A of PACE, which sets out supplementary provisions relating to fingerprint impression, is also amended to include footwear impressions.[118]

However, there are two differences. Firstly, footwear impressions cannot be **6.49** taken outside of a police station. Secondly, the new s 61A does not apply to persons arrested or detained under terrorism provisions, or under an extradition arrest power.[119]

J. INTIMATE SAMPLES

The definition of intimate samples is clarified by an amendment to s 65 of **6.50** PACE.[120] The extended definition adds 'a swab taken from any part of a person's genitals (including the pubic hair)', to the previous definition of 'a swab taken from any part of a person's body including the mouth but not any other body orifice'.

Similarly, the definition of non-intimate sample is extended to include 'a **6.51** swab taken from any part of a person's body other than a part from which a swab taken would be an intimate sample'.[121]

K. STAFF CUSTODY OFFICERS

When consulted about the provisions contained in s 120 SOCPA, which seek **6.52** to extend the potential role of civilian police staff to that of custody officers, the Police Federation stated as follows:

---

[116] SOCPA, s 117(2), creating a new s 61(6C) of PACE, to that effect.

[117] Once fingerprints have been taken from a suspect 'in the course of an investigation', s 61(3)(b)(ii) and s 61(3A) PACE impose a bar on the additional taking of such fingerprints unless they are incomplete or of insufficient quality.

[118] SOCPA, s 118(2).

[119] SOCPA, s 118(2), inserting PACE, s 61A(8).

[120] SOCPA, s 119(2).

[121] SOCPA, s 119(3).

This calls for the all the authority and experience that a custody sergeant brings to the role but which a civilian custody officer could not . . . This proposal to civilianise the role of custody officer is one we resist as forcefully as possible. It is essential to maintain the existing structure, including the review of detention functions of inspectors and super-intendents. We urge the Government to abandon this proposal.[122]

6.53   It did not. Instead, s 120 of SOCPA carries through amendments to the PRA and creates a new position of 'staff custody officer'.[123] At Part 4 of Schedule 4 to the PRA (powers exercisable by police civilians), a new paragraph 35A allows those civilian staff designated to the role of 'staff custody officer' to perform almost all the functions of a custody officer. The only ones excluded are those under s 45A(4) and (2)(a) PACE, which relate to the use of video-conferencing facilities for decisions about detention. Section 121 SOCPA makes consequen-tial amendments relating to the custody officer position.

6.54   It is beyond dispute that custody sergeants fulfil a crucial role within the investigative process. Such duties are set out in primary legislation (see, for example, ss 37–40 PACE), and are enhanced by the Codes of Practice to PACE. Custody officers must assess the grounds of arrest and the lawfulness of initial detention when the person is brought to a police station; they are responsible for the welfare of the person in custody at the police station; they must assess whether officers are acting sufficiently expeditiously to justify the continued detention of the suspect; they must ensure the integrity of investigations by monitoring the conduct of the investigative process in so far as it affects contact with the detained person; they must deal with complaints made by detained persons sometimes about the conduct of the investigating officers; and finally assess the suitability of bail and charge. It is unsurprising that the Police Federation, in representing its member officers, sees this role as one that is quintessentially to be reserved for professional police officers.

6.55   Whether it is appropriate for civilian staff to be placed in such a responsible position in the centre of police investigation is largely a political and executive decision, which is beyond the scope of discussion in this work. On one view it is possible that such persons could bring greater independence to such a role. Alternatively, it may be more difficult for persons who are not police officers to question the decision making or conduct of experienced investigating officers. The Association of Chief Police Officers responded to the proposals with qualified approval, provided appropriate training was offered.[124]

---

[122] See p 8 of the *Summary of Response to the Consultation Paper*, January 2005, available at <www.homeoffice.gov.uk/docs4/summary_of_responses.pdf>.

[123] SOCPA, s 120(5).

[124] See p 8 of the *Summary of Response to the Consultation Paper*, January 2005, available at <www.homeoffice.gov.uk/docs4/summary_of_responses.pdf>.

L. ADDITIONAL MATTERS IN PART 3 OF SOCPA

Section 122 amends Part 4 of the PRA in respect of designated and accredited 6.56
persons. Schedule 8 adds to the list of powers which can be assigned to
designated and accredited persons. The new powers for community support
officers include a power to direct traffic and provide assistance at serious road
traffic accidents; a power to deal with begging; a power to search people they are
detaining for items that could cause injury or assist escape; a power to enforce
certain licensing offences; and a power to enter certain licensed premises.

7

PUBLIC ORDER AND CONDUCT
IN PUBLIC PLACES

A. Overview	7.01
B. Harassment	7.06
C. Trespass on Designated Sites	7.18
D. Demonstrations in the Vicinity of Parliament	7.25
E. Anti-social Behaviour	7.31

A. OVERVIEW

1. Introduction

Part 4 of SOCPA (ss 125–144) is entitled 'Public Order and Conduct in Public **7.01** Places etc' and covers a range of activities. It is intended to 'strengthen the protection afforded by the criminal and civil law' against acts of harassment, trespass on sites of national importance, and disruptive behaviour in the vicinity of Parliament. Most of the provisions of this part of the Bill passed without substantial amendment during its passage through Parliament.[1]

The powers relating to harassment (ss 125–127) are designed to allow the **7.02** police to prevent harassment of employees of companies by animal rights protestors.[2] The powers relating to designated site (ss 128–131) and demonstrations in the vicinity of Parliament (ss 132–138) essentially arise out of the one-off actions of two individuals.[3] The Government explained its reasons for introducing these measures in the following terms:

---

[1] Substantial amendments were, however, made to the provisions in ss 132–138 (demonstrations in the vicinity of Parliament). In addition, clause 124 and Sch 10 (which related to offences of 'Racial and Religious Hatred') were removed to ensure the passage of the Bill prior to the 2005 General Election. These topics are now dealt with in the Racial and Religious Hatred Bill 2005 (before Parliament at the time of writing).

[2] See *Animal Welfare—Human Rights: Protecting People from Animal Rights Extremists* (Home Office, Attorney-General, and Department for Trade and Industry, July 2004).

[3] Respectively Aaron Barschak and Brian Haw, see paras 7.18 and 7.25 below.

In a democratic society, every one has the right to voice their opinion and to demonstrate, but human rights of freedom of speech and assembly must be balanced by citizens' responsibilities to others. No one has the right to intimidate or harass others going about their lawful business or to disrupt the workings of Parliament. Those working in the bioscience industry deserve the full protection of the criminal law where their human rights are being threatened.[4]

All these measures have been the subject of criticism and expressions of concern from the Joint Committee on Human Rights[5] and from civil liberties organisations.[6]

2. Freedom of Expression and of Assembly

7.03 The new powers in ss 125 to 138 engage the Convention rights to freedom of expression under Article 10 and freedom of assembly under Article 11. They interfere with the rights of protestors to express their views and to assemble for the purposes of protest. Such interferences will only be justified if they are:

- prescribed by law, and
- for a legitimate aim, and
- necessary in a democratic society.[7]

7.04 The third requirement is the most important and imports the notion of 'proportionality'. The court considers three matters:[8]

- whether the interference complained of corresponded to a 'pressing social need';
- whether it was 'proportionate to the legitimate aim pursued'; and
- whether the reasons given to justify the interference are 'relevant and sufficient'.

7.05 The measures in Part IV provide a sufficiently clear and accessible basis in law to satisfy the 'prescribed by law' requirement. These measures pursue the legitimate aims of protecting the rights and freedoms of others and the prevention

---

[4] Serious Organised Crime and Police Bill, Key Benefits, *Office of Leader of House of Commons*, 29 November 2004.

[5] Joint Committee on Human Rights, *Scrutiny: First Progress Report, 4th Report of Session 2004–2005* (HL Paper 26, HC 224).

[6] Liberty described these as 'excessive, unnecessary or inappropriate', *Serious Organised Crime and Police Bill: Liberty's Briefing for the Second Reading in the House of Commons* (December 2005) para 26; see also JUSTICE, *Serious Organised Crime and Police Bill, Parts 3–6 (not including cl. 124), Briefing for Houses of Lords Second Reading* (March 2005), paras 29–71.

[7] See generally H Tomlinson and R Clayton, *The Law of Human Rights* (Oxford UP, 2000), para 6.125ff.

[8] See generally, *Sunday Times v United Kingdom (No 1)* (1979) 2 EHRR 245, §62, and *R (Daly) v Secretary of State for the Home Department* [2001] 2 AC 532, 546–548.

of disorder (under Articles 10(2) and 11(2)). However, the measure will only be compatible with Convention rights if, in each case in which it is exercised, that exercise is 'proportionate'.

B. HARASSMENT

1. Introduction

Sections 125 to 127 make a number of amendments to the Protection from Harassment Act 1997 (the 1997 Act) and the Criminal Justice and Police Act 2001 (the 2001 Act). According to the Explanatory Notes, the purpose of these amendments is   **7.06**

> to prohibit intimidating conduct designed to stop persons going about their lawful business, introduce a new offence of harassment of a person in his home and confer additional powers on the police to issue directions for the purpose of stopping harassment of a person in his home.[9]

It has been said that the need for these powers has arisen 'largely due to the extremist activities of animal rights protestors'.[10] They are designed to protect people connected with a person or business from harassment arising out of that connection.

2. Amendments to Protection from Harassment Act 1997

Section 125 amends the 1997 Act in a number of important respects. The first concerns the ambit of the criminal offence of harassment. Section 2 of the 1997 Act makes it a criminal offence to pursue a course of conduct which amounts to the harassment of another. 'Harassment' must be of a person and cannot extend to a corporate entity.[11] By s 7(3) of the 1997 Act a course of conduct had to involve conduct on at least two occasions.   **7.07**

Section 125(1) inserts s 1(1A) into the 1997 Act. This extends the definition of 'harassment' to conduct which involves two or more persons by which it is intended to persuade any person (whether or not this person is one of the 'harassed' persons) not to do something he is entitled or required to do or to do something that he is not under an obligation to do. The definition of 'course of conduct' is extended to cover, in the case of conduct in relation to two or more persons, 'conduct on at least one occasion in relation to each of those persons'.[12] This provision means that a campaign against a particular   **7.08**

---

[9] *Serious Organised Crime and Police Bill*, Explanatory Notes, para 19.
[10] ibid, para 467.
[11] See *Daiichi Pharmaceuticals v SHAC* [2004] 1 WLR 1503 (Owen J).
[12] Protection from Harassment Act 1997, s 7(3)(b) (inserted by SOCPA, s 125(7)).

business (or other body) which involves actions relating to different employees on different occasions can constitute harassment.

7.09 Section 125(5) inserts a new s 3A in the 1997 Act which permits a person who is, or may be, a victim of conduct within s 1(1A) to apply to the High Court or the county court for an injunction. In other words, the activities of a campaign against a particular business could be restrained by injunction if it was threatened to approach different employees on different occasions, even if no approaches had actually been made.

7.10 The new 'harassment' offence (and the associated power to grant an injunction) is very broad indeed, applying well beyond the context of 'animal rights' protests. All forms of political protest are, potentially, caught by the provisions provided that the protest takes place more than once. The new powers could, therefore, be exercised in a way which breaches the Article 10 and 11 rights of protestors.[13]

7.11 It is, however, important to note that the 'statutory defences' in s 1(3) of the 1997 Act are extended to cover conduct which involves harassment of two or more persons.[14] A course of conduct will not be harassment if the person who pursued it shows:

- that it was pursued for the purpose of preventing or detecting crime;
- that it was pursued under any enactment or rule of law or to comply with any condition or requirement imposed by any person under any enactment; or
- that in the particular circumstances the pursuit of the course of conduct was reasonable.

This means that a protestor will have a potential 'reasonableness' defence in the course of which the court must take into account the Convention rights of freedom of expression and freedom of assembly.[15]

3. Harassment of a Person at Home

7.12 By s 42 of the 2001 Act a constable can give directions to a person outside a dwelling who is there for the purposes of 'making representations' and whose presence is causing or is likely to cause harassment, alarm, or distress.[16] A

---

[13] See the concerns expressed in the Joint Committee on Human Rights after having taken into account the Government's responses to questions which it raised about the Bill: *Scrutiny: Fourth Progress Report, 8th Report of Session 2004–2005* (HL Paper 60, HC 388), 23 February 2005, paras 2.53–2.54.

[14] This is the effect of SOCPA, s 125(2)(c) which amends s 1(3).

[15] For the approach of the courts in relation to 'reasonableness' under s 5 Public Order Act 1986 see the unsatisfactory decisions in *Norwood v DPP* [2003] Crim LR 888 and *Hammond v DPP* (2004) 168 JP 601.

[16] Section 42(1).

direction is one requiring the person to whom it is given to do all such things as the constable giving it may specify as the things he considers necessary to prevent harassment, alarm, or distress being caused.[17] An offence is committed if a person knowingly contravenes such a direction.[18]

Section 126 amends the 2001 Act by inserting a new s 42A which creates a new **7.13** offence of harassment of a person in his home. This offence can be committed without the need for the police to have given any prior directions. The new offence is committed if:

- a person is outside or in the vicinity of the 'dwelling'[19] of any individual;
- the person is there for the purpose of representing to anyone that he should not do something he is entitled or required to do or that he should do something that he is not under any obligation to do;
- the person intends his presence to amount to harassment or to cause alarm or distress or knows or ought to know that his presence is likely to have these consequences;
- the person's presence does amount to harassment or causes alarm or distress or is likely to have these consequences.

The test as to whether a person ought to know that his presence is likely to **7.14** result in harassment or to cause alarm or distress is an objective one: it will be satisfied if a reasonable person in possession of the same information would think that his presence was likely to have this effect.[20]

The protection of people from harassment in their homes is plainly a legiti- **7.15** mate ground for the restriction of rights of protest. However, the range of conduct covered by the new offence is extremely wide. It could cover, for example, journalists involved in 'doorstepping' a person suspected of misconduct, or people protesting against a former foreign dictator who had taken up residence in England. Unlike the offences under the Protection from Harassment Act 1997 and the Public Order Act 1986, there is no defence of 'reasonableness'. In these circumstances, there is a serious risk that s 42A could breach the Article 10 and/or 11 rights of defendants.[21]

---

[17] Section 42(2).

[18] Section 42(7).

[19] This means the same as in Part 1 of the Public Order Act 1986 (s 42A(7)): that is, 'any structure or part of a structure occupied as a person's home or as other living accommodation (whether the occupation is separate or shared with others)' but does not include any part not so occupied. For this purpose 'structure' includes a tent, caravan, vehicle, vessel, or other temporary or movable structure.

[20] Criminal Justice and Police Act 2001, s 42A(4).

[21] JUSTICE has expressed concerns as to the 'chilling effect' of this provision and has pointed out the range of other powers available to deal with conduct of this type; see *Serious Organised Crime and Police Bill, Parts 3–6 (not including cl. 124), Briefing for Houses of Lords Second Reading* (March 2005), paras 39–40.

7.16   A person who is guilty of an offence under s 42A is liable on summary conviction to a term of imprisonment not exceeding 51 weeks or to a fine not exceeding level 4 or both.[22]

7.17   Section 127 inserts into the 2001 Act new powers to give directions. These directions can now include a requirement to leave the vicinity of the premises in question[23] and not to return within a period of up to three months.[24] The 'direction' given by the police officer is not subject to any appeal.

C. TRESPASS ON DESIGNATED SITES

7.18   The provisions in ss 128 to 131 are designed to deal with a number of well-known cases where royal security has been breached by demonstrators and, in one case, by a comedian.[25] They arise out of the recommendations of an investigation that followed the last of these intrusions into royal security. The Home Secretary accepted that this was using a 'sledgehammer to crack a nut'[26] and the Joint Committee on Human Rights expressed the view that, so far as they interfere with Convention rights, they would be regarded as disproportionate.[27]

7.19   Entering or remaining on the land of another without permission or lawful authority is a civil wrong[28] but is not a criminal offence.[29] By s 128(1), a person commits an offence if he enters, or is on, any 'designated site' as a trespasser. A 'designated site' means a site designated by the Secretary of State. A site can only be designated if:

- it is comprised in Crown land, or

- it is comprised in land belonging to Her Majesty in her private capacity or to the immediate heir to the throne in his private capacity, or

- it appears to the Secretary of State that it is appropriate to designate the site in the interests of national security.

7.20   The power to 'designate' sites in the interests of national security on the basis of what 'appears' to the Secretary of State is a wide one which, potentially,

---

[22] Section 42A(5).

[23] Section 42(4)(a) (inserted by s 127(2) of SOCPA).

[24] Section 42(4)(b) (inserted by s 127(2) of SOCPA).

[25] The so-called 'comedy terrorist' Aaron Barschak who gatecrashed Prince William's 21st birthday party at Windsor Castle on 21 June 2003.

[26] HC Deb, 7 December 2004, col 1059 (Home Secretary)(Second Reading Debate).

[27] Joint Committee on Human Rights, *Scrutiny: First Progress Report, 4th Report of Session 2004–2005* (HL Paper 26, HC 224), para 1.138.

[28] For a discussion of the tort of trespass see H Tomlinson and R Clayton, *Civil Actions against the Police* (Sweet & Maxwell, 3rd edn, 2005), chapter 7.

[29] Unless it is 'aggravated'—that is, where the trespasser's behaviour may disrupt other people's lawful behaviour, see s 68 Criminal Justice and Public Order Act 1994.

allows the Government to criminalise trespass and could severely restrict freedom of assembly.[30] There is no definition of national security. The Secretary of State could designate, for example, embassies, arms fairs, military bases, or government buildings.[31]

It is a defence under this section for the person charged to prove that he did **7.21** not know and had no reasonable cause to suspect that the site was designated (s 128(4)). The Secretary of State may take 'such steps as he considers appropriate' to inform the public of the effect of a designation order (s 130(2)). But this can only be done with the consent of the 'appropriate person'[32] (s 131(3)) and cannot be done in relation to land in relation to which there are rights of public access[33] (s 131(1)). The operation of this defence raises issues under Article 6(2)[34] because it imposes a reverse legal burden on the defence.

Proceedings under this section can only be instituted with the consent of the **7.22** Attorney-General. A person convicted of an offence under this section is liable on summary conviction to imprisonment for a term not exceeding 51 weeks and to a fine not exceeding level 5 or both.

This offence also applies in Northern Ireland. Section 129 creates a corres- **7.23** ponding Scottish offence in relation to 'designated Scottish sites' which can only be sites designated in the interests of national security.

A constable in uniform may arrest a person without warrant on the reason- **7.24** able suspicion of an offence under s 128 (s 130(1)). This power ceases to have effect on the commencement of s 110 (s 130(1)).[35]

D. DEMONSTRATIONS IN THE VICINITY OF PARLIAMENT

The provisions of ss 132 to 138 arise out of the activities of one man. Brian **7.25** Haw protested against Government policy towards Iraq by occupying a place in Parliament Square, opposite the main gates of the Houses of Parliament, for four years from 2 June 2001. An application by Westminster City Council for an injunction to remove him was refused, partly on Article 10 grounds.[36] Demonstrations outside Parliament are subject to Sessional Orders which instruct the Metropolitan Police Commissioner to keep the access to Parliament

---

[30] See the points raised by Liberty, *Serious Organised Crime and Police Bill: Liberty's Briefing for the Second Reading in the House of Commons* (December 2004), paras 34 and 35.

[31] The Joint Committee on Human Rights expressed concern about this provision and was not satisfied with the Government's response, see *Scrutiny: Fourth Progress Report, 8th Report of Session 2004–2005* (HL Paper 60, HC 388), 23 February 2005, para 2.69.

[32] As defined by s 131(4)—curiously this is not the person with actual authority to give consent but the person 'appearing to the Secretary of State' to have such authority.

[33] That is, under s 2(1) Countryside and Rights of Way Act 2000.

[34] Which states that everyone charged with a criminal offence shall be presumed innocent until proved guilty according to law.

[35] For s 110, see para 6.04 above.

[36] *Westminster City Council v Haw* [2002] EWHC 2073 (QB) (Gray J).

free of obstruction. The Procedure Committee conducted an inquiry which reported in November 2003.[37] The Government's response was published in May 2004.[38] Legislation to prohibit long-term demonstrations and ensure access to Parliament was recommended. In the August 2004 Police Powers Green Paper the Government made it clear that it intended to legislate on this point.

7.26   Section 132(1) makes it an offence to organise, take part in,[39] or carry on a demonstration[40] in a public place[41] in the 'designated area' if, when the demonstration starts, appropriate statutory authorisation has not been given. On conviction a person is liable on summary conviction to imprisonment for a term not exceeding 51 weeks, to a fine not exceeding level 5, or both (s 136(1)). A 'designated area' is one specified by the Secretary of State by reference to a map or in any other way but no point in the area so specified may be more than one kilometre from Parliament Square (s 138).

7.26A   Although the purpose of the provisions of this part of the Act was to bring Brian Haw's demonstration to an end, the statutory wording does not have this effect because his demonstration was ongoing at the time the provision came into force.[41A] Although Article 4(2) of the Serious Organised Crime and Police Act 2005 (Commencement No 1, Transitional and Transitory Provisions) Order purported to extend s 132(1) to continuing demonstrations, this was *ultra vires* because it rendered criminal conduct which, but for the alteration, would not have been criminal. This was not a transitional provision but an amendment to the Act. The relevant parts of the orders were quashed by the Divisional Court[41B] which granted a declaration that Mr Haw did not need authorisation for his continuing protest under ss 132–138 SOCPA.

7.27   A person who seeks authorisation for a demonstration in the designated area must give written notice to the Metropolitan Police Commissioner stating the date and time when the demonstration is to be carried out, how it is to be carried out, and whether it is to be carried out by him/herself or not (s 133). The notice must, if reasonably practicable, be given not less than six clear days before

---

[37] Procedure Committee, *Sessional Orders and Resolutions* (HC 855, 2002–2003), 19 November 2003.

[38] Procedure Committee, *Sessional Orders and Resolutions: the Government's Response to the Committee's Third Report of Session 2002–03* (HC 613, 2003–2004), 20 May 2004; the report was debated, HC Deb, 3 November 2004, cols 370ff.

[39] This includes a person carrying on a demonstration by himself (s 132(7)(e)—presumably to ensure that Mr Haw is caught by the provision).

[40] This word is not defined and it is unclear what a person would have to be doing or planning to do to make it necessary for him or her to give notice under this provision.

[41] Defined as 'any highway or any place to which at the material time the public or any section of the public has access, on payment or otherwise, as of right or by virtue of express or implied permission', s 132(7). In other words, the provisions do not affect persons demonstrating on private land.

[41A] See *R (Haw) v Secretary of State for the Home Department*, The Times, 4 August 2005, where this point was conceded by the Secretary of State.

[41B] ibid., *per* Smith LJ and McCombe J, Simon J dissenting. The case is under appeal at the time of writing.

the day on which the demonstration is to start or, if not reasonably practicable, as soon as it is, and in any event not less than 24 hours before the time the demonstration is to start (s 133(2)).

The Commissioner must give authorisation of the demonstration if a notice is given (s 134(2))[42] but may impose such conditions as are, in his reasonable opinion, necessary to prevent: **7.28**

- hindrance to any person wishing to enter or leave Parliament;
- hindrance to the proper operation of Parliament;
- serious public disorder;
- serious damage to property;
- disruption to the life of the community;[43]
- a security risk in any part of the designated area;
- risk to the safety of members of the public (s 134(3)).

The conditions may impose requirements as to time, place, period, numbers of persons, numbers and size of banners and placards, and maximum permissible noise levels (s 134(4)).

By s 137 the use of loudspeakers in designated areas is banned.[44] Loud- **7.29** speakers are often used in large demonstrations and a total ban seems disproportionate.[45]

It is an offence to take part in or organise a demonstration where there is a **7.30** knowing failure to comply with a condition (s 134(7)). On conviction a person is liable on summary conviction to imprisonment for a term not exceeding 51 weeks, to a fine not exceeding level 5, or both (s 136(3)).

E. ANTI-SOCIAL BEHAVIOUR

1. Anti-social Behaviour Orders: General

Anti-social behaviour orders (or ASBOs) were introduced by the Crime and **7.31** Disorder Act 1998 (the 1998 Act). The police, local authorities, or social landlords can apply for an ASBO in relation to any person aged 10 or over. The orders are civil in nature[46] but breach of the order is a criminal offence. ASBOs can be made in free-standing proceedings or on conviction for criminal offences.

---

[42] No time limit is imposed on the Commissioner which may make it difficult to organise a demonstration in accordance with the imposed conditions.

[43] Note that this is not a 'legitimate aim' mentioned in Articles 10(2) or 11(2).

[44] Subject to a list of exceptions for the police, local authorities etc (s 137(2)).

[45] JUSTICE, *Serious Organised Crime and Police Bill, Parts 3–6 (not including cl. 124), Briefing for Houses of Lords Second Reading* (March 2005), paras 56–57.

[46] *R (McCann) v Crown Court at Manchester* [2001] 1 WLR 358.

7.32   Section 139 makes a number of amendments to the procedure relating to ASBOs. These relate to proof that the order has been made,[47] the adjournment of proceedings relating to the making of ASBOs on conviction,[48] and the making of interim orders in such proceedings.[49]

7.33   Section 140 makes amendments to the procedure for the variation and discharge of ASBOs made on conviction.[50] Under the 1998 Act only the offender can apply for variation or discharge of such an order. As a result of these amendments both the DPP and the relevant authorities can apply for variation and discharge.

2. Reporting Restrictions

7.34   The issue of identifying juveniles who are the subject of an ASBO has been of concern to the media in recent years. It has been held that the publication of the photographs of four teenage gang members from Brent was lawful.[51] By s 49 Children and Young Persons Act 1933 there are automatic reporting restrictions when there are proceedings in a Youth Court.[52] Section 141 inserts a new provision into the 1998 Act[53] which has the effect that in relation to proceedings for the making or enforcement of an ASBO in a Youth Court, these automatic reporting restrictions no longer apply and, instead, the court has a discretionary power to restrict reporting under s 45. If the court exercises its discretionary power to give a direction under this provision it must give reasons for doing so.[54]

7.35   The Home Secretary explained that the purpose behind this provision was to

allow local communities to be involved in the justice system by ensuring that breaches of anti-social behaviour orders can be publicised so that people can see who is doing what and where it is being done.[55]

The Joint Committee on Human Rights has expressed doubts about this justification for interfering with the Article 8 rights of the children who are subject to ASBOs and has drawn attention to the primacy of the best interests of the child under the UN Convention on the Rights of the Child.[56]

---

[47] Crime and Disorder Act 1998, s 1(10C) (inserted by s 139(1)).

[48] ibid, s 1C(4A)–(4C) (inserted by s 139(4)).

[49] ibid, s 1D (inserted by s 139(5)).

[50] ibid, s 1CA (inserted by s 140(4)).

[51] *R (Stanley) v Commissioner of Police* [2005] EMLR 5.

[52] There are also discretionary powers to apply reporting restrictions to prevent the disclosure identity of persons aged under 18 (s 39 Children and Young Persons Act 1993 and s 45 Youth Justice and Criminal Evidence Act 1999).

[53] Section 1(10D).

[54] Crime and Disorder Act 1998, s 1(10E).

[55] HC Deb, 7 December 2004, col 1059; see also Explanatory Notes, para 476.

[56] Joint Committee on Human Rights, *Scrutiny: First Progress Report, 4th Report of Session 2004–2005* (HL Paper 26, HC 224), para 1.141ff; see also *Serious Organised Crime and Police Bill: Liberty's Briefing for the Second Reading in the House of Commons* (December 2004), para 41.

3. Contracting Out

Section 142 inserts a new provision into the 1998 Act to allow the contracting out of local authority ASBO functions. The Secretary of State can make an order specifying a person to whom local authorities may contract out all or part of their ASBO functions. The Government has suggested that this provision is 'managerial' in intent but there are obvious concerns about private individuals or companies controlling the sensitive private information which is likely to be obtained in the performance of ASBO functions.[57] It has been made clear that legislative measures will be taken to ensure that local authorities retain responsibility for breaches of Convention rights by contractors who must, in turn, follow guidance from the Secretary of State.[58]

4. Protection of Witnesses

Section 143 makes provision for special measures directions[59] in relation to vulnerable and intimidated witnesses in proceedings for ASBOs. At present such directions can only be made in criminal proceedings.

5. Parental Compensation

Section 144 and Schedule 10 insert ss 13A to 13E into the Crime and Disorder Act 1998 (the 1998 Act), providing power for magistrates' courts to make 'parental compensation orders' on application by a local authority.

A magistrates' court will be able to make a parental compensation order where it is satisfied to the civil standard of proof that a child under the age of 10[60] has taken or caused loss or damage to property in the course of behaving anti-socially or committing an act that would have constituted a criminal offence if he were 10 or over.[61] The magistrates' court must be satisfied that making the order would be desirable in the interests of preventing a repetition of the behaviour in question.[62] The order will require the child's parent(s) or guardian(s) to pay compensation[63] to any person or persons affected by the taking of the property or by its loss or damage.

---

[57] ibid, para 1.143; *Serious Organised Crime and Police Bill: Liberty's Briefing for the Second Reading in the House of Commons* (December 2004), para 39.

[58] This would be the result of new s 1F(7)(a) and 1F(9) Crime and Disorder Act 1998. See the Government's response to the Joint Committee on Human Rights, discussed at *Scrutiny: Fourth Progress Report, 8th Report of Session 2004–2005* (HL Paper 60, HC 388), 23 February 2005, paras 2.81–2.82.

[59] Under Chapter 1 of Part 2 of the Youth Justice and Criminal Evidence Act 1999.

[60] Crime and Disorder Act 1998, s 13A(1).

[61] ibid, s 13A(2).

[62] ibid, s 13(A)(1).

[63] The maximum compensation is currently set at £5,000 but can be varied by order (s 13(A)(5) and (6)).

7.40   A number of concerns have been raised about such orders.[64] A child under 10 is not, as a matter of law, capable of committing a criminal act. The fact that the court must consider whether the order would be desirable to prevent a repetition of the behaviour indicates that it is intended as a sanction on the parents. An appeal against such an order is to the Crown Court.[65] All this suggests that the order is 'criminal' in character for the purposes of Article 6 but, nevertheless, the 'civil standard' of proof is applied and parents can be found liable to pay compensation irrespective of fault.[66]

---

[64] See JUSTICE, *Serious Organised Crime and Police Bill, Parts 3–6 (not including cl. 124), Briefing for Houses of Lords Second Reading* (March 2005), para 67ff.

[65] Crime and Disorder Act 1998, s 36ZD.

[66] JUSTICE, *Serious Organised Crime and Police Bill, Parts 3–6 (not including cl. 124), Briefing for Houses of Lords Second Reading* (March 2005), paras 70–71.

8

MISCELLANEOUS

A. Overview	8.01
B. Protection of Activities of Certain Organisations	8.02
C. Vehicle Registration, Insurance, and Road Traffic Offences	8.10
D. The Publication of Local Policing Information	8.29
E. Other Miscellaneous Police Matters	8.32
F. Abolition of the Royal Parks Constabulary	8.38
G. Criminal Record Checks	8.41
H. Witness Summonses	8.47
I. Private Security Industry Act 2001: Scotland	8.51

A. OVERVIEW

Part 5 of the Serious Organised Crime and Police Act (SOCPA) contains a **8.01** miscellaneous assortment of provisions. Some of the sections were tacked on to the Bill in its final stages because of a failure to secure parliamentary time for other Bills. Part 5 covers:

- new criminal offences to protect the activities of specified organisations;

- new vehicle registration, insurance, and road traffic provisions;

- local policing information;

- miscellaneous police matters, including new provisions for accelerated procedures in police disciplinary matters;

- the abolition of the Royal Parks Constabulary;

- new procedures on criminal record checks;

- new procedures for the issue of witness summonses in the magistrates' and Crown Courts;

- the extension of the Private Security Industry Act 2001 to Scotland.

B. PROTECTION OF ACTIVITIES OF CERTAIN ORGANISATIONS

8.02 Sections 145 to 149 create two new criminal offences and a power to extend their application to other persons or organisations, without parliamentary oversight. These clauses have their origins in the 2004 Government paper 'Animal Welfare, Human Rights—Protecting People from Animal Rights Extremists' which followed reports of apparently escalating animal rights activity.

8.03 The offences, under ss 145 and 146 of SOCPA, seek to protect animal research organisations from any 'economic damage' caused by campaigns of intimidation. Similar legislation was passed in the United States in 1992 with the Animal Enterprise Protection Act, but the need for such laws in the UK has been questioned. There are already numerous existing criminal offences which can be used to protect individuals and legitimate business activities[1] and JUSTICE has claimed that 'to create victim-specific offences in this manner is overtly to politicise the criminal justice system'.[2]

8.04 Section 145 creates the offence of interfering with the contractual relationships of an animal research organisation so as cause it harm. It is essentially aimed at protecting the economic interests of such companies. The offence has two essential components.

(i) Firstly, a person must do, or threaten to do, a 'relevant act' causing loss or damage. Under s 145(3), a 'relevant act' is either a criminal offence or a tortious act. This means that an act, which is already a criminal offence, is further criminalised by this legislation. Further, the inclusion of the term a 'tortious act' is a significant departure because this means that a civil law wrong can be criminalised when committed in compliance with s 145. The phrase 'tortious act' is not defined, which is of concern as some torts are notoriously uncertain in their scope.

The act must be carried out with the intention of harming an 'animal research organisation'. An 'animal research organisation' is defined under s 148 to include the owners, lessees, or licensees of premises where procedures regulated under the Animals (Scientific Procedures) Act 1986 may take place or where animals to be used in these procedures are bred or supplied from; employers of individuals who are licensed to carry out regulated procedures; and persons named in certificates designating places where breeding or supply may take place, and those who engage such people

---

[1] For example, the Criminal Damage Act 1971, s 68 Criminal Justice and Public Order Act 1994, s 16 Offences Against the Person Act 1861, common assault, s 59 Anti-social Behaviour Act 2003, the Public Order Act 1986, and the Protection from Harassment Act 1997.

[2] See JUSTICE, *Briefing on new clauses and amendments relating to the protection of organisations from economic damage or other interference with their activities* (February 2005) available from <www.justice.org.uk>.

under contracts for their services. Under s 145(5), to 'harm' means to cause such an organisation loss or damage of any kind, or to prevent or hinder it from carrying on any of its activities. There is no definition or monetary threshold applied to the term 'loss or damage'.

(ii) Secondly, the act or the threat must be intended to cause or be likely to cause the person to fail to perform a contractual obligation, to withdraw from a contract, or to decide not to enter into a contract.[3] For this purpose 'contract' and 'contractual', defined under s 145(4), is drafted to cover any arrangement whatsoever.

The second new offence, under s 146, is that of the 'intimidation of persons **8.05** connected with an animal research organisation'. The offence has a tortuous construction and is committed where a person (A), with the intention of persuading another person (B) not to do something he is entitled to do, or to do something he is not obliged to do, threatens B that A himself or someone else will commit a crime or do a tortious act causing loss or damage to B or someone else. A must commit the act or threat wholly or mainly because B has a connection with an animal research organisation.[4]

Section 146(2) is extremely broad in its listing of potential 'victims'. For **8.06** example, the protection of this section is not just limited to persons who are connected, directly or indirectly, with an animal research organisation, but it is extended to secondary and tertiary targets, which effectively means anyone with a connection with such an organisation. To this end, the list includes the employees and officers of animal research organisations, students at educational establishments, and people with a financial interest in such organisations (eg shareholders), as well as suppliers and customers. But, it also includes anyone who is contemplating becoming a supplier or customer or lessee of premises, anyone who is known personally to an employee or officer of an animal research organisation, or even a person who is known personally to an employee of a customer. Such wide drafting can be criticised for vagueness and uncertainty because it may lead to inconsistency both in the application of the law and in the sentencing of offenders. It is of further concern that this list can be amended simply by executive order of the Secretary of State.[5]

These 'economic damage' offences have been the subject of criticism both for **8.07** criminalising civil wrongs and for possibly threatening democratic protest as this often seeks to exert economic pressure.[6] Neither s 145 nor 146 applies if the tortious act is done in contemplation or furtherance of a 'trade dispute' as

---

[3] SOCPA, s 145(2).
[4] See Explanatory Note <www.publications.parliament.uk/pa/ld200405/ldbills/024/en/05024x-a.htm>.
[5] SOCPA, s 146(6).
[6] See JUSTICE, n 2 above.

defined in the Trade Union and Labour Relations (Consolidation) Act 1992, but the measures could impose restrictions on other legitimate protests, although those involving consumer boycotts appear to have been exempted.[7]

8.08   Under s 147, a person guilty of an offence under either s 145 or 146 is liable on summary conviction to imprisonment for a term not exceeding 12 months and/or to a fine not exceeding the statutory maximum and on indictment to imprisonment for a term not exceeding 5 years and/or to a fine. The consent of the DPP to any prosecution is required.

8.09   Under s 149, the scope of ss 145 to 147 may be extended by order of the Secretary of State to criminal acts and tortious acts causing loss or damage in relation to other persons or organisations. To make such an order, the Secretary of State must be satisfied that a series of events has taken place which would have been offences under clauses 142 and 143 had they been directed at animal research organisations or people connected with them. There will be no parliamentary oversight of any proposed extension. JUSTICE has criticised this section for allowing the criminalisation of conduct to become a function of the executive rather than the legislature.[8]

C. VEHICLE REGISTRATION, INSURANCE, AND ROAD TRAFFIC OFFENCES

8.10   These offences largely aim to tackle 'driving without entitlement'. This term covers driving without a valid licence, insurance, or vehicle registration. Recent Government consultation papers have concluded that this is a serious issue for road safety because it is alleged that unlicensed and uninsured drivers are significantly more likely to be involved in road crashes than other road users.[9] Notable changes are also made to the law relating to breath tests and to how the revenue raised from driving offences may be applied.

1. Provisions Relating to Vehicle Registration

8.11   Section 150(1) of SOCPA creates the offence of using an incorrectly registered vehicle by inserting s 43C into the Vehicle Excise and Registration Act 1994. It is important to note that this offence is committed by 'using' a vehicle on a public road or in a public place rather than simply 'keeping' it. Case law has

---

[7] See s 145(3) which states: 'paragraph (b) does not include an act which is actionable on the ground only that it induces another person to break a contract with B'. This followed objections from a variety of sources including the Joint Committee on Human Rights in its Fifteenth Report (March 2005) <www.publications.parliament.uk/pa/jt200405/jtselect/jtrights/97/9705.htm>.

[8] See JUSTICE, n 2 above.

[9] See Home Office Consultation Paper *Policing: Modernising Police Powers to Meet Community Needs*, p 17.

demonstrated that the 'use' of a vehicle covers a wide range of scenarios and is not limited to driving the car itself.[10]

Under s 43C(1), the offence of using an 'incorrectly registered' vehicle is committed if either the name or address of the keeper of the vehicle is not recorded in the register, or if any of the particulars recorded in the register are incorrect. The 'keeper' of the vehicle means the person by whom it is kept at the material time.[11] The offence must also relate to a vehicle for which vehicle excise duty is chargeable, or, in the case of an exempt vehicle, to which the regulations under the Vehicle Excise and Registration Act 1994 require a nil licence to be in force.[12]

8.12

The defendant may avail himself of a statutory defence to this charge if he can show either that he had no reasonable opportunity to furnish the name and address of the keeper of the vehicle, or that there was no reasonable opportunity to furnish particulars correcting the incorrect particulars before the material time.[13] It is also a defence for a person to show that either he had reasonable grounds for believing, or that it was reasonable for him to expect, that the name and address of the keeper or the other particulars of registration (as the case may be) were correctly recorded in the register, or that any exception prescribed in regulations under this section is met.[14]

8.13

Using an incorrectly registered vehicle is a summary offence punishable by a fine not exceeding level 3 on the standard scale.[15] It is also an offence in respect of which a fixed penalty may be issued.[16]

8.14

Section 151 also inserts s 28A in the Vehicle Excise and Registration Act 1994, establishing a new obligation to produce registration documents on request. Powers already exist for the production of driving licences, insurance, and test certificates.[17] Under s 28A(1), this power applies to a person using a vehicle in respect of which a registration document has been issued. The request for production may be made by a constable, or 'a person authorised by the Secretary of State for the purposes of this section' who must produce on request evidence of his authority to exercise the power.[18] If the request is made by an authorised person, a person may be asked to produce documents to a police station or an

8.15

---

[10] See the case law in relation to s 143 Road Traffic Act (RTA) 1988 (using a motor vehicle without insurance) which defines 'use' as a degree of control over, managing, or operating the particular vehicle—*Cobb v Williams* [1073] RTR 113, DC; *Bennett v Richardson* [1980] RTT 385, DC; *Jones v DPP* RTR 1, DC.

[11] Vehicle Excise and Registration Act 1994, s 43C(7).

[12] ibid, s 43C(2)(a) and (b).

[13] ibid, s 43C(3).

[14] ibid, s 43C(4).

[15] ibid, s 43 C (5). This allows a maximum fine of £1,000.

[16] SOCPA, s 150(2) amends Sch 3 to the Road Traffic Offenders Act (RTOA) 1988 (fixed penalty offences) to allow for this.

[17] See ss 164 and 165 RTA 1988.

[18] Vehicle Excise and Registration Act 1994, s 28A(2).

authorised testing station provided under s 52(2) Road Traffic Act (RTA) 1988.[19]

8.16   An offence is committed by failing to comply with the request for production.[20] A person guilty of an offence under this section is liable on summary conviction to a fine not exceeding level 2 on the standard scale.[21] However, an offence is not committed if the defendant is able to demonstrate that his situation falls within any of the three conditions set out under s 28A(4). They are as follows

(i)   The defendant produces the registration document, in person, at a police station specified by him at the time of the request, and he does so within seven days after the date on which the request was made or as soon as is reasonably practicable.[22]

(ii)   The vehicle is subject to a lease or hire agreement, and the vehicle is not registered in the name of the lessee or hirer under that agreement and is not required to be so registered.[23] Appropriate evidence[24] of the agreement must be produced at the time of the request or in person, at a police station as requested within seven days after the date of the request, or as soon as is reasonably practicable. It is also necessary for the person to have reasonable grounds for believing, or it is reasonable for him to expect, that the person from whom the vehicle has been leased or hired is able to produce, or require the production of, the registration document.

(iii) A person will not commit an offence if he meets any exception prescribed in regulations under s 28A.[25]

2. Provisions Relating to Unlicensed and Uninsured Drivers

8.17   A Department of Transport report (the Greenaway Report) into uninsured driving was published in August 2004.[26] The report indicated that the incidence of uninsured driving in the UK was high in relation to some EU countries (although not all) and that action needed to be taken to tackle these drivers who

---

[19] Vehicle Excise and Registration Act 1994, s 28A(9).

[20] ibid, s 28A(3).

[21] ibid, s 28A(11). This means a maximum fine of £500. Cf offences under ss 164 and 165 RTA 1988 which are punishable by fines not exceeding level 3 on the standard scale (ie £1,000 maximum).

[22] ibid, s 28A(5).

[23] ibid, s 28A(6).

[24] ibid, s 28A(7). 'Appropriate evidence' means a copy of the agreement, or such other documentary evidence of the agreement as is prescribed in regulations under this section.

[25] ibid, s 28A(8). A person must adduce evidence sufficient to raise an issue with respect to that exception. It is then for the prosecution to disprove the application of the exception beyond reasonable doubt. See s 28A(10).

[26] *Uninsured Driving in the United Kingdom; a report to the Secretary of State for Transport* by Professor David Greenaway. <www.dft.gov.uk/stellent/groups/dft_rdsafety/documents/page/dft_rdsafety_030393.hcsp>.

are apparently more likely to be involved in accidents than insured drivers.[27] Some of its recommendations have been enacted by ss 152 and 153 of SOCPA which enable vehicles driven without insurance or a licence to be seized and removed and then released or disposed of. On a practical level, the development of these new offences is accompanied by plans for better detection and the use of databases. Indeed, s 153 SOCPA allows the Secretary of State to make regulations requiring the Motor Insurers' Information Centre to make available relevant vehicle insurance information to the Police Information Technology Organisation (PITO). This will then be processed and made available to police constables.

Driving without insurance against third party risks is an offence contrary to s 143 RTA 1988.[28] However, the current law enables a convicted uninsured driver to retain his vehicle. This, it has been argued, allows him to continue driving illegally while uninsured. Section 152 aims to change this position by allowing for the seizure of a vehicle driven without insurance or a licence. A new s 165A(1) of the RTA is created, providing police with a power to seize and remove vehicles if one of three conditions is met. **8.18**

(i) A constable in uniform requires a person to produce his licence and its counterpart for examination (under s 164 RTA[29]), and the person fails to produce them. The constable must have reasonable grounds for believing that a motor vehicle is or was being driven by the person in contravention of s 87(1) RTA, ie that he was driving otherwise than in accordance with a licence.

(ii) A constable in uniform requires, under s 165 RTA,[30] a person to produce evidence that a motor vehicle is not or was not being driven in contravention of s 143 and the person fails to produce such evidence. The constable must have reasonable grounds for believing that the vehicle is or was being driven without insurance.

(iii) A constable in uniform requires, under s 163 RTA,[31] a person driving a motor vehicle to stop the vehicle, and the person fails to stop the vehicle, or to stop the vehicle long enough for the constable to make appropriate and lawful enquiries. Again, the constable must also have reasonable grounds for believing that the vehicle is or was being driven in contravention of s 87(1) or 143 RTA (ie otherwise than in accordance with a licence or without insurance).[32]

---

[27] ibid, p 12. There has been no independent research into this in the UK.

[28] Punishable by a maximum fine of £5,000, the automatic endorsement of an offender's licence with 6–8 penalty points, and possible disqualification.

[29] The power to require the production of driving licences and in certain cases details relating to dates of birth.

[30] The power to obtain the names and addresses of drivers and others, and to require production of evidence of insurance or security and test certificates.

[31] This relates to police powers to stop vehicles.

[32] Section 165A(4) RTA 1988.

8.19   Under s 165A(6) RTA, a warning must be given before the vehicle is seized. It must be given to the person who appears to have driven the vehicle. The person must be warned that unless they either produce their licence or insurance documentation immediately, the vehicle will be seized. A warning need not be given if it is considered impracticable. The power to seize allows an officer to enter any premises (other than a private dwelling house[33]) to effect the seizure of the vehicle if he reasonably believes the vehicle to be there. He may use 'reasonable force' to do so.[34] If the vehicle cannot be seized immediately because the person driving the vehicle has failed to stop as requested or has driven off, it can be seized at any time within 24 hours. This 24-hour period begins with the time at which the condition in question is first satisfied.[35]

8.20   The powers provided by s 165A RTA are only available when regulations under s 165B RTA are in force.[36] Section 165B RTA is introduced by s 152 SOCPA. This section allows the Secretary of State to make subsequent regulations for the removal, retention, release, or disposal of seized vehicles. These regulations include relevant charges, periods of retention, and provisions relating to disposal of the vehicle. It would be reasonable to anticipate that these regulations will allow the police to retain a vehicle suspected of being used by an uninsured or unlicensed driver and release it on payment of specified charges and the production of valid documentation. Any vehicle not claimed within a prescribed time will be open to disposal by the police. However, a specific exemption from payment is provided by s 165B(3) if a person can demonstrate that they were not driving the vehicle and that it was used without their knowledge or consent and that they could not reasonably have prevented it from being driven.

8.21   It has been suggested that such powers of seizure may be contrary to the right to the peaceful enjoyment of possessions which is protected by Article 1 of the First Protocol to the European Convention on Human Rights. The second limb of Article 1 specifies that 'No one shall be deprived of his possessions except in the public interest and subject to the conditions provided for by law and by the general principles of international law'. These sections raise issues concerning the executive expropriation of property, the proportionality of the state response, and they engage the fair hearing provisions of the Convention under Article 6, because they may constitute a criminal sanction without a prior judicial determination.[37] For example, they are not imposed by a court as part of a criminal penalty after conviction. The European Court of Human Rights has

---

[33] RTA 1988, s 165A(9)(d). This does not include 'any garage or other structure occupied with the dwelling house, or any land appurtenant to the dwelling house'.

[34] ibid, ss 165A(5)(c).

[35] ibid, s 165A(7).

[36] ibid, s 165A(8).

[37] JUSTICE, *Serious Organised Crime and Police Bill, Parts 3–6, Briefing for House of Lords Second Reading* (March 2005). This argument would also apply to Article 17 of the EU Charter of Fundamental Rights.

considered similar issues in relation to the seizure of property and demand for payment by customs authorities. It has concluded this may not involve a deprivation of property because no transfer of ownership of the property is taking place.[38] The doctrine of the margin of appreciation means that states are deemed to be in the best position to assess what amounts to the 'public interest' in their own jurisdiction.[39] However, the requirement of proportionality means that there must be a reasonable relationship between the means employed and the aim sought to be realised. If the aim is a valid one, the question then is whether the provisions constitute an excessively draconian means of achieving it.

3. Provisions Relating to Drink-driving Offences

Section 154 was originally part of the 2004 Road Safety Bill. However, the **8.22** Serious Organised Crime and Police Bill was amended at report stage to include this provision after the Bill fell due to lack of parliamentary time. Section 154 provides new police powers to take drink-drive evidence at the roadside. This means that officers will no longer have to take a second reading at a police station. It also contains other supplemental provisions.

Section 154(4) to (6) creates new subsections 7(2A) to (2D) in the RTA. The **8.23** old s 7(2) restricted the requirement to provide specimens of breath for analysis (an evidential breath test) to the police station. The amended s 7(2) essentially permits a police constable in uniform to carry out an evidential breath test at a police station, at a hospital, or at or near a place (such as the roadside) where a preliminary breath test has been administered to the person concerned or would have been so administered but for his failure to cooperate with it.[40] After making a request for a relevant breath test at any of these places, the constable is entitled to remain there in order to impose it. The results of this evidential breath test will be admissible as evidence in court. However, this will not prevent a fresh request for a sample to be given at a police station if a reliable device was not available, if it was impractical to use one, or the constable has reasonable cause to believe the device used was not able to provide a reliable result.[41] In the event of a positive result, a refusal, or if the police officer believes the equipment not to be working properly, the person may be arrested and taken to a police station.

Section 154(1) to (3) also inserts new ss 6D(1A) and 6D(2A) in the RTA. **8.24** Section 6D(1) provides that a constable may arrest a person without warrant if, as a result of a preliminary breath test, the constable reasonably suspects that the

---

[38] *Air Canada v the United Kingdom* (1995) 20 EHRR 15.
[39] *James and others v the United Kingdom*, 21 February 1986, Series A no 98.
[40] RTA, s 7(2)(c). Under the new s 7(2B), this is only permissible if the constable is in uniform, or has imposed a requirement on the person concerned to cooperate with a relevant breath test under s 6(5) RTA.
[41] RTA, s 7(2D).

proportion of alcohol in the person's breath or blood exceeds the prescribed limit. The new s 6D(1A) allows this to happen even if specimens have already been given, provided that the constable has reasonable cause to believe that the device used to analyse the specimens was not reliable. In addition, a new s 6D(2A) is also inserted allowing a person arrested in this way to be detained with a view to imposing on him there a requirement under s 7 RTA.[42] This enables a constable, who reasonably believes that the device used to analyse the specimen has not produced a reliable indication, to arrest a person and take them to the police station so that they can be required to provide a specimen of blood or urine.

8.25   If a person is unable to provide breath he may be required to provide a specimen of blood or urine, which must be taken at a police station. If the breath reading is no more than 50 microgrammes of alcohol per 100 millilitres of breath, the person who provided it may ask for it to be replaced by a specimen of blood or urine, which again must be taken at a police station. Section 154(7) amends s 8 RTA to enable a constable to arrest a suspect for this purpose.

8.26   Section 154(6) amends s 7(3) RTA (which deals with the circumstances in which a requirement to provide a specimen of blood or urine arises) to allow for a request to be made where no reliable device under s 7(1)(a) is available at the police station (or where it is not practicable to use such a device) but only if specimens of breath have not been provided elsewhere (unless the constable has reasonable cause to believe that the device was not reliable).

8.27   Section 154(9) to (12) amends s 10 RTA which deals with detention at a police station. It enables a person who was required to provide a specimen of breath, blood, or urine to be detained at a police station after the test if a constable has reasonable grounds for believing that, if the person were to drive or attempt to drive a motor vehicle on a road, he would commit an offence under s 4 or 5 RTA. However, this will not apply 'if it ought reasonably to appear' to the constable that there is no likelihood of the person driving or attempting to drive a motor vehicle while over the limit. It will also not apply if a person is at a hospital as a patient and taking him from there to a police station would be prejudicial to his proper care and treatment.

4. Payments by Secretary of State to Police Authorities

8.28   Section 155 enables the Secretary of State to make payments to police authorities in respect of the whole or any part of their expenditure on the prevention and detection of the motoring offences specified in a lengthy list in s 155(3) and on enforcement action relating to such offences. This effectively allows money from fixed penalties for offences such as driving without insurance

---

[42] Section 7 concerns the provision of specimens for analysis in the course of an investigation into whether a person has committed an offence under s 4 or 5 RTA.

and failure to wear a seatbelt to be recycled to fund future prevention, detection, and enforcement activities. Section 156 applies a similar clause to Scotland.

D. THE PUBLICATION OF LOCAL POLICING INFORMATION

This proposal arose from a White Paper in November 2004 which was aimed at strengthening community policing.[43] A provision on the publication of local policing information was then incorporated into s 157 of SOCPA. **8.29**

Section 157 places a duty on police authorities to produce an annual summary of local policing information to the public soon after the end of each financial year by inserting a new s 8A into the Police Act 1996. Examples are given of the type of information[44] to be included but the Secretary of State may, under the new s 8A(3) (and by order), specify what is to be included, after consultation with appropriate stakeholders.[45] The police must have regard to this guidance relating to the form and content of the summary. **8.30**

Police authorities are under a duty to try to distribute this 'local policing summary' to all households in their areas.[46] **8.31**

E. OTHER MISCELLANEOUS POLICE MATTERS

This section encompasses three unrelated provisions relating to police matters. **8.32**

1. Responsibilities in Relation to the Health and Safety etc of Police

Section 158 amends s 51A Health and Safety at Work Act 1974 to enable the prosecution of a chief officer of police to be brought against the office itself rather than against the individual incumbent. This action was prompted by the 2003 Health and Safety Executive prosecution of the Commissioner of the Metropolitan Police, Sir John Stevens and his predecessor, Sir Paul Condon who appeared in court in person for five weeks for failing to ensure the safety of their officers following a prosecution by the Health and Safety Executive.[47] It brings the position of a chief officer into line with that of police authorities which are liable as bodies corporate for breaches of health and safety legislation in respect of police staff (who are employees of police authorities). **8.33**

---

[43] Home Office, *Building Communities, Beating Crime: A Better Police Service for the 21st Century*, Cm 6360, November 2004, <www.policereform.gov.uk/docs/prwp2004.html>.

[44] eg crime statistics, local and force-level policing priorities, numbers of officers, contact details, and local projects/initiatives that are under way.

[45] Under s 8A(6) Police Act 1996, they include the Association of Police Authorities and the Association of Chief Police Officers.

[46] Police Act 1996, s 8A(4).

[47] See House of Commons Library Research Paper 04/89, 2 December 2004, p 31.

8.34 However, under new s 51A(2B) and (2C), the chief officer may also be prosecuted in a personal capacity if it can be shown that he personally consented to the commission of an offence or personally connived in its commission, or was personally negligent. This does not apply in respect of anything occurring before the passing of the Bill. The effects of the amendments to the 1974 Act are backdated to 1 July 1998 for the purpose of any legal proceedings commenced on or after the commencement.[48] The provision is extended to Scotland.[49]

2. Investigations: Accelerated Procedure in Special Cases

8.35 Section 159 introduces Schedule 11 which makes provision for an accelerated procedure for certain investigations into the conduct of police officers. This makes amendments to Schedule 3 to the Police Reform Act 2002 to allow disciplinary procedures to be brought more quickly if certain conditions are met. These conditions are set out in a new s 20A(7) of the Police Reform Act 2002. Firstly, there must be sufficient evidence (in the form of written statements or documents) that a person may have committed an imprisonable offence and that their conduct is of a serious nature. Secondly, there must be sufficient evidence to establish, on the balance of probabilities, that conduct justifying a dismissal has taken place.[50] Thirdly, the appropriate authority must consider that it is in the public interest to investigate without delay. If these special conditions are met, a report can be submitted before the investigation has been completed and disciplinary proceedings can be brought earlier than previously. A new paragraph 20A of Schedule 3 is inserted and this sets out the accelerated procedure to be followed.

8.36 Disciplinary proceedings may also be brought before any related criminal proceedings are concluded (although the appropriate authority must consult the Director of Public Prosecutions (DPP) before proceeding in this way). The DPP may ask the appropriate authority not to bring disciplinary proceedings if they might prejudice the criminal proceedings.[51]

3. Investigations: Deaths and Serious Injuries During or After Contact with the Police

8.37 Section 160 gives effect to Schedule 12 which amends Part 2 of the Police Reform Act 2002 to bring a new category of case under the jurisdiction of the Independent Police Complaints Commission (IPCC). The IPCC was established by the Police Reform Act 2002. Section 10(2) (the general functions of the

---

[48] Section 158(5).

[49] ibid, s 158(6).

[50] Paragraph 20A(8), Sch 3 to the Police Reform Act 2002 defines this as 'conduct so serious that disciplinary proceedings brought in respect of it would be likely to result in dismissal'.

[51] Paragraph 20G, Sch 3 to the Police Reform Act 2002.

Commission) will be amended by the addition of a new category, 'deaths and serious injury matters' (DSI). To be included, a case must be one where a person has died or been seriously injured following arrest or detention or direct or indirect contact with the police and there is reason to believe that the contact may have caused or contributed to the death or serious injury.[52] This section will concern cases that do not involve a complaint or a conduct matter when first identified and categorised.

F. ABOLITION OF THE ROYAL PARKS CONSTABULARY

The Royal Parks Constabulary (RPC) was responsible for the policing of 17 Royal Parks, gardens, and open spaces in and around London. A report by Anthony Speed found it was underfunded and that the tasks it faced were beyond its resources.[53] Section 161 abolishes the RPC and provides for a merger with the Metropolitan Police Service. Schedule 13 provides for transfer of constables, property, rights, and liabilities to the Metropolitan Police Authority. **8.38**

Paragraph 13 of Part 2 of Schedule 13 amends the Police Reform Act 2002 to add breaches of park regulations to the list of 'relevant offences' in relation to which community support officers have limited powers of detention and to provide them with a power to take temporary possession of items which they suspect have been used in the commission of a park trading offence. **8.39**

Section 162 disapplies the Parks Regulation Act 1872 to the Royal Parks. It preserves the power of the Secretary of State to make regulations in respect of the specified parks. Under s 162(3) the Secretary of State is responsible for ensuring that copies of any regulations in force, made under s 2 Parks Regulation (Amendment) Act 1926, are displayed in a suitable position in that park. **8.40**

G. CRIMINAL RECORD CHECKS

The Criminal Records Bureau (CRB) was established by Part V of the Police Act 1997 and came into existence in March 2002. It provides access not only to criminal records but also to lists held by the Department for Education and Skills and the Department of Health of people considered unsuitable to work with children and with vulnerable adults. The Police Act allows the Secretary of State to issue three types of document containing information on a person's criminal record. These certificates are provided in response to applications from persons seeking posts and positions within the scope of the Rehabilitation of **8.41**

---

[52] Police Reform Act 2002, ss 10(2A) to (2D).
[53] Anthony Speed, *A Formal Inspection of the Royal Parks Constabulary*, September 2000, <www.dcms.gov.uk/PDF/royal_parks_insp.PDF>.

Offenders Act 1974 (Exceptions) Order 1975 or, in relation to Scotland, the Rehabilitation of Offenders Act 1974 (Exclusions and Exceptions) (Scotland) Order 2003.

8.42 Sections 163 to 168 make changes to the existing system. Sections 113 and 115 of the 1997 Act (which deal respectively with criminal record certificates and 'enhanced' criminal record certificates) have already been subject to a variety of amendments and are now replaced altogether by s 163 of SOCPA which inserts new ss 113A to F into the Police Act 1997.[54] Section 163 also introduces Schedule 14 which makes the necessary consequential amendments to Part 5 of the Police Act 1997.

8.43 The new sections contain the following provisions.

(i) Section 113A deals with criminal records certificates.

(ii) Section 113B sets out the provisions for enhanced criminal record certificates. The range of police forces and other organisations from which the CRB can seek non-conviction information for the purposes of enhanced criminal records certificates is extended.

(iii) Section 113C deals with additional protection in relation to an individual's suitability to work with children. The CRB is given access to comparable protection lists held in Scotland and Northern Ireland and vice versa. The scope of the section is extended to individuals specified in the new s 113C(5).

(iv) Section 113D establishes provisions relating to an individual's suitability to work with vulnerable adults. Again, the CRB is given access to comparable protection lists held in Scotland and Northern Ireland and vice versa.

(v) Section 113E creates an additional service for urgent cases which allows a person to start work in advance of the CRB's certificate being issued.

(vi) Section 113F contains various supplementary provisions.

8.44 Section 164 inserts a new s 118(2A) into the Police Act 1997. This enables the CRB to access information held by the UK Passport Agency, the Driver and Vehicle Licensing Agency, and Department of Work and Pension's database of national insurance numbers and 'such other persons or for such other purposes as prescribed' in order to verify an individual's identity. This gives effect to one of the recommendations made by Sir Michael Bichard following the Soham murders inquiry.[55]

8.45 Section 165 also makes several amendments to the Police Act 1997. Firstly, s 165(1)(a) amends subsection 119(3) to allow the Secretary of State to determine the fees for requests for information made to police authorities

---

[54] Explanatory Notes to the Bill, prepared by the Home Office, Bill 005-EN: para 378, <www.publications.parliament.uk/pa/cm200405/cmbills/005/en/05005x--.htm>.

[55] See Bichard Inquiry, Recommendation 23.

(they are currently set by statutory instrument). Section 165(1)(b) inserts new subsections 119(6) and (7) to include bodies such as the Northern Ireland Policing Board in the definition of 'police authority'. Subsections 165(2) and (3) make similar amendments to ss 120A and 124A of the Police Act 1997 in the same way.

Section 166 makes minor amendments to the Police Act 1997 as it applies **8.46** to Scotland. Section 167 extends Part V of the Police Act 1997 to Northern Ireland. As a consequence, a new Criminal Records Disclosure body will be established with the same powers and flexibility as the CRB in England and Wales.[56] Similarly, s 168 extends Part V of the Police Act 1997 to the Channel Islands and the Isle of Man.

H. WITNESS SUMMONSES

The Criminal Procedure and Investigations Act 1996 removed the requirement **8.47** for examining justices to make witness orders in respect of attendance at the Crown Court at committal. The procedure for issue of witness summonses in the Crown Court was also amended. In order to issue a summons, the Crown Court had to be satisfied that a person was likely to be able to produce material evidence and that they would not voluntarily attend as a witness or would not voluntarily produce the document or thing requested without being summonsed.[57]

In 2003, the Home Office published a consultation paper 'Securing the **8.48** Attendance of Witnesses in Court' which invited views on whether to 're-introduce witness orders'.[58] It asserted that the threshold for obtaining such orders had been set too high so that often a summons was only issued following a witness's failure to attend trial, leading to inevitable delay and prejudice to the trial process. The consultation paper proposed the reintroduction of a new form of witness order. However, '[t]he general view of respondents was that the re-introduction of witness orders might undermine existing initiatives to encourage witnesses to come forward and remain engaged in the criminal justice process'.[59] It was finally concluded that witness summonses should be used more effectively as a pre-emptive measure in specific cases. Consequently, a provision was inserted into the Serious Organised Crime and Police Bill, amending the

---

[56] See Explanatory Notes to the Bill, prepared by the Home Office, Bill 005-EN: para 433, <www.publications.parliament.uk/pa/cm200405/cmbills/005/en/05005x--.htm>.

[57] Criminal Procedure (Attendance of Witnesses) Act 1965, s 2 as amended. The Magistrates' Courts Act 1980 makes similar provision.

[58] <www.homeoffice.gov.uk/justice/legalprocess/witnesses/index.html#Consultation%20Papers>.

[59] Explanatory Notes to the Bill, prepared by the Home Office, Bill 005-EN: para 62, <www.publications.parliament.uk/pa/cm200405/cmbills/005/en/05005x--.htm>.

evidential test for obtaining a summons and making it easier to obtain one before the commencement of a trial.

8.49   Under s 169 SOCPA, the issue of a summons in the Crown Court is now governed by an 'interests of justice' test. The Court must be satisfied that it is in the interests of justice to issue a summons to secure a person's attendance to give evidence or to produce a 'document or thing'. Similarly, a new s 97(1) of the Magistrates' Courts Act 1980 is created, allowing a summons to be issued by a justice of the peace if they are satisfied that a person 'is likely to be able to give material evidence, or produce any document or thing likely to be material evidence, at the summary trial of an information or hearing of a complaint by a magistrates' court' and that 'it is in the interests of justice to issue a summons under this subsection to secure the attendance of that person to give evidence or produce the document or thing'.

8.50   Powers relating to summonses for committal proceedings, the taking of depositions, and the issue of summonses in Northern Ireland are similarly amended to include the 'interests of justice test'.[60] Finally, s 170 SOCPA applies the interest of justice test to the powers of courts-martial etc to issue warrants of arrest for witnesses.

I. PRIVATE SECURITY INDUSTRY ACT 2001: SCOTLAND

8.51   Section 171 and Schedule 15 extend the Private Security Industry Act 2001 to Scotland.[61] This Act established a mandatory national licensing scheme for individuals working in the following industry sectors: door supervisors; vehicle immobilisers (wheel clampers); security guards; key holders; security consultants; and private investigators. It set up the Security Industry Authority to issue licences and regulate the industry. The 2001 Act also provided for a voluntary approved contractor scheme with powers to make it mandatory.

---

[60] Section 169(3) SOCPA amends s 97A(1)(b) Magistrates' Courts Act 1980 in respect of committal proceedings and s 169(4) amends para 4(1)(b) of Sch 3 to the Crime and Disorder Act 1998 for dispositions. Section 169(5) amends s 51A(1)(b) Judicature (Northern Ireland) Act 1978.

[61] Following a Scottish Executive consultation paper ('Regulating the Private Security Industry in Scotland') in September 2001, it was concluded that the most effective way of regulating the private security industry in Scotland would be to extend the remit of the Act.

APPENDIX

Serious Organised Crime and Police Act 2005

2005 CHAPTER 15

CONTENTS

PART 1

THE SERIOUS ORGANISED CRIME AGENCY

CHAPTER 1

SOCA: ESTABLISHMENT AND ACTIVITIES

Establishment of SOCA   129

Section
1 Establishment of Serious Organised Crime Agency

Functions   129

2 Functions of SOCA as to serious organised crime
3 Functions of SOCA as to information relating to crime
4 Exercise of functions: general considerations

General powers   131

5 SOCA's general powers

Annual plans and reports   131

6 Annual plans
7 Annual reports

Central supervision and direction   132

8 General duty of Secretary of State and Scottish Ministers
9 Strategic priorities
10 Codes of practice
11 Reports to Secretary of State

12 Power to direct submission of action plan
13 Revision of inadequate action plan
14 Procedure for giving directions under section 12
15 Reports relating to directions under section 12
16 Inspections

Financial provisions 137

17 Grants by Secretary of State
18 Determinations relating to grants under section 17
19 Charges by SOCA and other receipts
20 Accounts

Operational matters 138

21 Operational responsibility of Director General
22 Activities in Scotland in relation to crime
23 Mutual assistance between SOCA and law enforcement agencies: voluntary arrangements
24 Mutual assistance between SOCA and law enforcement agencies: directed arrangements
25 Directed arrangements: Scotland
26 Use by SOCA of police premises etc.
27 Regulations as to equipment

Liability for unlawful conduct 143

28 Liability of SOCA for acts of seconded staff etc.
29 Payment by SOCA of amounts in connection with unlawful conduct of employees etc.
30 Application of sections 28 and 29 to members of joint investigation teams
31 Liability of special police forces and law enforcement agencies for unlawful conduct of SOCA staff

Use and disclosure of information 146

32 Use of information by SOCA
33 Disclosure of information by SOCA
34 Disclosure of information to SOCA
35 Restrictions on further disclosure

General duties of police etc. 147

36 General duty of police to pass information to SOCA
37 General duty of police etc. to assist SOCA

Prosecutions 147

38 Prosecution of offences investigated by SOCA
39 Directions as to reference of cases and proceedings to appropriate prosecutor
40 Functions of Director of Revenue and Customs Prosecutions as to persons arrested for designated offence

Miscellaneous and supplementary 150

41 Directions
42 Interpretation of Chapter 1

CHAPTER 2
SOCA: SPECIAL POWERS OF DESIGNATED STAFF

Designations 151

43 Designation of SOCA staff as persons having powers of constable etc.
44 Delegation of power to designate
45 Modification or withdrawal of designations

Powers exercisable 152

46 Person having powers of a constable
47 Person having powers of constable: Scotland and Northern Ireland
48 Person having customs powers
49 Person having powers of an immigration officer

Exercise of powers 155

50 Designations: supplementary
51 Assaults, obstruction or deception in connection with designations

Supplementary 156

52 Modification of enactments
53 Employment provisions
54 Interpretation of Chapter 2

CHAPTER 3
SOCA: MISCELLANEOUS AND SUPPLEMENTARY

Complaints and misconduct 157

55 Complaints and misconduct

Application of discrimination legislation   158

56   Application of discrimination legislation to SOCA seconded staff

Joint investigation teams   158

57   Assaults or obstruction in connection with joint investigation teams

Transfers   159

58   Transfers to SOCA

Amendments   159

59   Minor and consequential amendments relating to SOCA

PART 2
INVESTIGATIONS, PROSECUTIONS, PROCEEDINGS
AND PROCEEDS OF CRIME

CHAPTER 1
INVESTIGATORY POWERS OF DPP, ETC.

Introductory   159

60   Investigatory powers of DPP etc.
61   Offences to which this Chapter applies

Disclosure notices   161

62   Disclosure notices
63   Production of documents
64   Restrictions on requiring information etc.
65   Restrictions on use of statements

Enforcement   163

66   Power to enter and seize documents
67   Offences in connection with disclosure notices or search warrants

Supplementary   165

68   Procedure applicable to search warrants
69   Manner in which disclosure notice may be given
70   Interpretation of Chapter 1

CHAPTER 2
OFFENDERS ASSISTING INVESTIGATIONS AND PROSECUTIONS

71 Assistance by offender: immunity from prosecution
72 Assistance by offender: undertakings as to use of evidence
73 Assistance by defendant: reduction in sentence
74 Assistance by defendant: review of sentence
75 Proceedings under section 74: exclusion of public

CHAPTER 3
FINANCIAL REPORTING ORDERS

76 Financial reporting orders: making
77 Financial reporting orders: making in Scotland
78 Financial reporting orders: making in Northern Ireland
79 Financial reporting orders: effect
80 Financial reporting orders: variation and revocation
81 Financial reporting orders: verification and disclosure

CHAPTER 4
PROTECTION OF WITNESSES AND OTHER PERSONS

82 Protection of persons involved in investigations or proceedings
83 Joint arrangements
84 Transfer of responsibility to other protection provider
85 Duty to assist protection providers
86 Offence of disclosing information about protection arrangements
87 Defences to liability under section 86
88 Offences of disclosing information relating to persons assuming new identity
89 Defences to liability under section 88
90 Protection from liability
91 Transitional provision
92 Transitional provision: supplemental
93 Provision of information
94 Interpretation of Chapter 4

CHAPTER 5
INTERNATIONAL OBLIGATIONS

95 Enforcement of overseas forfeiture orders
96 Mutual assistance in freezing property or evidence

CHAPTER 6
PROCEEDS OF CRIME

97   Confiscation orders by magistrates' courts
98   Civil recovery: freezing orders
99   Civil recovery: interim receivers' expenses etc.
100 Detention of seized cash: meaning of '48 hours'
101 Appeal in proceedings for forfeiture of cash
102 Money laundering: defence where overseas conduct is legal under local law
103 Money laundering: threshold amounts
104 Money laundering: disclosures to identify persons and property
105 Money laundering: form and manner of disclosures
106 Money laundering: miscellaneous amendments
107 Money laundering offences
108 International cooperation
109 Minor and consequential amendments relating to Chapter 6

PART 3
POLICE POWERS ETC.

Powers of arrest   195

110 Powers of arrest
111 Powers of arrest: supplementary

Exclusion zones   197

112 Power to direct a person to leave a place

Search warrants   197

113 Search warrants: premises
114 Search warrants: other amendments

Fireworks   200

115 Power to stop and search for prohibited fireworks

Photographing of suspects etc.   201

116 Photographing of suspects etc.

Fingerprints and footwear impressions   201

117 Fingerprints
118 Impressions of footwear

Intimate samples   204

119 Intimate samples

Custody officers   204

120 Staff custody officers: designation
121 Custody officers: amendments to PACE

Designated and accredited persons   206

122 Powers of designated and accredited persons

Provision of information for use by police staff   207

123 Provision of information for use by police staff

Interpretation of Part 3   208

124 Interpretation of Part 3

PART 4
PUBLIC ORDER AND CONDUCT IN PUBLIC PLACES ETC.

Harassment   208

125 Harassment intended to deter lawful activities
126 Harassment etc. of a person in his home
127 Harassment etc: police direction to stay away from person's home

Trespass on designated site   210

128 Offence of trespassing on designated site
129 Corresponding Scottish offence
130 Designated sites: powers of arrest
131 Designated sites: access

Demonstrations in vicinity of Parliament   213

132 Demonstrating without authorisation in designated area
133 Notice of demonstrations in designated area
134 Authorisation of demonstrations in designated area
135 Supplementary directions
136 Offences under sections 132 to 135: penalties
137 Loudspeakers in designated area
138 The designated area

Anti-social behaviour 217

139 Orders about anti-social behaviour etc.
140 Variation and discharge of anti-social behaviour orders made on conviction
141 Anti-social behaviour orders etc: reporting restrictions
142 Contracting out of local authority functions relating to anti-social behaviour orders
143 Special measures for witnesses in proceedings for anti-social behaviour orders etc.

Parental compensation orders 222

144 Parental compensation orders

PART 5
MISCELLANEOUS

Protection of activities of certain organisations 222

145 Interference with contractual relationships so as to harm animal research organisation
146 Intimidation of persons connected with animal research organisation
147 Penalty for offences under sections 145 and 146
148 Animal research organisations
149 Extension of sections 145 to 147

Vehicle registration and insurance and road traffic offences 225

150 Offence in respect of incorrectly registered vehicles
151 Power of constables etc. to require production of registration documents in respect of a vehicle
152 Power to seize etc. vehicles driven without licence or insurance
153 Disclosure of information about insurance status of vehicles
154 Power to require specimens of breath at roadside or at hospital etc.
155 Payments by Secretary of State to police authorities in relation to the prevention, detection and enforcement of certain traffic offences
156 Payments by Scottish Ministers to police authorities etc. in relation to the prevention, detection and enforcement of certain traffic offences

Local policing information 233

157 Publication of local policing information

Other miscellaneous police matters 234

158 Responsibilities in relation to the health and safety etc. of police
159 Investigations: accelerated procedure in special cases
160 Investigations: deaths and serious injuries during or after contact with the police

Royal Parks etc.   235

161   Abolition of Royal Parks Constabulary
162   Regulation of specified parks

Criminal record checks   236

163   Criminal record certificates
164   Criminal records checks: verification of identity
165   Certain references to police forces
166   Further amendments to Police Act 1997 as it applies to Scotland[1]
167   Part 5 of the Police Act 1997: Northern Ireland
168   Part 5 of the Police Act 1997: Channel Islands and Isle of Man

Witness summonses   243

169   Powers of Crown Court and Magistrates' Court to issue witness summons
170   Powers of courts-martial etc. to issue warrants of arrest in respect of witnesses

Private Security Industry Act 2001: Scotland   244

171   Private Security Industry Act 2001: Scottish extent

PART 6
FINAL PROVISIONS

172   Orders and regulations
173   Supplementary, incidental, consequential etc. provision
174   Minor and consequential amendments, repeals and revocations
175   Penalties for offences: transitional modification for England and Wales
176   Expenses
177   Interpretation
178   Commencement
179   Short title and extent

Schedule 1   The Serious Organised Crime Agency   250
                   Part 1: The Board of SOCA
                   Part 2: Director General and other staff
                   Part 3: Committees, procedure etc.
                   Part 4: General
Schedule 2   Functions of Independent Police Complaints Commission in
                   relation to SOCA   256
Schedule 3   Transfers to SOCA   259

---

[1] Amended by correction slip

Schedule 4   Minor and consequential amendments relating to SOCA   262

Schedule 5   Persons specified for the purposes of section 82   284

Schedule 6   Minor and consequential amendments relating to Chapter 6 of
Part 2   286

Schedule 7   Powers of Arrest: supplementary   290
Part 1: Specific repeals
Part 2: General repeal
Part 3: Amendments relating to references to arrestable offences
and serious arrestable offences
Part 4: Other amendments

Schedule 8   Powers of designated and accredited persons   301
Part 1: Designated persons
Part 2: Accredited persons

Schedule 9   Additional powers and duties of designated persons   309

Schedule 10   Parental compensation orders   311
Part 1: England and Wales
Part 2: Northern Ireland

Schedule 11   Investigations into conduct of police officers: accelerated
procedure in special cases   317

Schedule 12   Investigations of deaths and serious injuries during or after
contact with the police   323

Schedule 13   Abolition of Royal Parks Constabulary: supplementary   330
Part 1: Transfers to Metropolitan Police Authority
Part 2: Amendments

Schedule 14   Amendments of Part 5 of Police Act 1997   333

Schedule 15   Private Security Industry Act 2001: Scottish extent   334

Schedule 16   Remaining minor and consequential amendments (search warrants) 338

Schedule 17   Repeals and revocations   339
Part 1: Repeals coming into force on Royal Assent
Part 2: Other repeals and revocations

An Act to provide for the establishment and functions of the Serious Organised Crime Agency; to make provision about investigations, prosecutions, offenders and witnesses in criminal proceedings and the protection of persons involved in investigations or proceedings; to provide for the implementation of certain international obligations relating to criminal matters; to amend the Proceeds of Crime Act 2002; to make further provision for combatting crime and disorder, including new provision about powers of arrest and search warrants and about parental compensation orders; to make further provision about the police and policing and persons supporting the police; to make provision for protecting certain organisations from interference with their activities; to make provision about criminal records; to provide for the Private Security Industry Act 2001 to extend to Scotland; and for connected purposes.

[7th April 2005]

BE IT ENACTED by the Queen's most Excellent Majesty, by and with the advice and consent of the Lords Spiritual and Temporal, and Commons, in this present Parliament assembled, and by the authority of the same, as follows:—

PART 1
THE SERIOUS ORGANISED CRIME AGENCY

CHAPTER 1
SOCA: ESTABLISHMENT AND ACTIVITIES

Establishment of SOCA

1 Establishment of Serious Organised Crime Agency

(1) There shall be a body corporate to be known as the Serious Organised Crime Agency ('SOCA').

(2) Schedule 1 makes provision about the constitution, members and staff of SOCA and other matters relating to it.

(3) Each of the following bodies shall cease to exist on such date as the Secretary of State appoints by order—

(a) the National Criminal Intelligence Service and its Service Authority, and

(b) the National Crime Squad and its Service Authority.

Functions

2 Functions of SOCA as to serious organised crime

(1) SOCA has the functions of—

(a) preventing and detecting serious organised crime, and

(b) contributing to the reduction of such crime in other ways and to the mitigation of its consequences.

(2) SOCA's functions under subsection (1) are exercisable subject to subsections (3) to (5) (but subsection (3) does not apply to Scotland).

(3) If, in exercising its function under subsection (1)(a), SOCA becomes aware of conduct appearing to SOCA to involve serious or complex fraud, SOCA may thereafter exercise that function in relation to the fraud in question only—

(a) with the agreement of the Director, or an authorised officer, of the Serious Fraud Office, or

(b) if the Serious Fraud Office declines to act in relation to it.

(4) If, in exercising its function under subsection (1)(a), SOCA becomes aware of conduct appearing to SOCA to involve revenue fraud, SOCA may thereafter exercise that function in relation to the fraud in question only with the agreement of the Commissioners.

(5) Before exercising its function under subsection (1)(b) in any way in relation to revenue fraud, SOCA must consult the Commissioners.

(6) The issue of whether SOCA's function under subsection (1)(a) continued to be exercisable in any circumstances within subsection (3) or (4) may not be raised in any criminal proceedings.

(7) In this section 'revenue fraud' includes fraud relating to taxes, duties and national insurance contributions.

(8) In this Chapter 'the Commissioners' means the Commissioners for Her Majesty's Revenue and Customs.

3 Functions of SOCA as to information relating to crime

(1) SOCA has the function of gathering, storing, analysing and disseminating information relevant to—

(a) the prevention, detection, investigation or prosecution of offences, or

(b) the reduction of crime in other ways or the mitigation of its consequences.

(2) SOCA may disseminate such information to—

(a) police forces within subsection (3),

(b) special police forces,

(c) law enforcement agencies, or

(d) such other persons as it considers appropriate in connection with any of the matters mentioned in subsection (1)(a) or (b).

(3) The police forces within this subsection are—

(a) police forces in the United Kingdom, and

(b) the States of Jersey Police Force, the salaried police force of the Island of Guernsey and the Isle of Man Constabulary.

(4) In this section 'law enforcement agency' means—

(a) the Commissioners or any other government department,

(b) the Scottish Administration,

(c) any other person who is charged with the duty of investigating offences or charging offenders, or

(d) any other person who is engaged outside the United Kingdom in the carrying on of activities similar to any carried on by SOCA or a police force.

(5) In this Chapter 'special police force' means—

(a) the Ministry of Defence Police,

(b) the British Transport Police Force,

(c) the Civil Nuclear Constabulary, or

(d) the Scottish Drug Enforcement Agency.

4 Exercise of functions: general considerations

(1) In exercising its functions SOCA must have regard to the matters mentioned in subsection (2).

(2) The matters are—

(a) SOCA's current annual plan under section 6 together with any priorities determined by SOCA under that section that are specified in the plan,

(b) any current strategic priorities determined by the Secretary of State under section 9, and

(c) any current performance targets established by SOCA.

(3) In exercising any function to which a code of practice under section 10 relates, SOCA must have regard to the code.

General powers

5 SOCA's general powers

(1) SOCA has the general powers conferred by this section.

(2) SOCA may—

   (a) institute criminal proceedings in England and Wales or Northern Ireland;

   (b) at the request of the chief officer of a police force within section 3(3) or of a special police force, act in support of any activities of that force;

   (c) at the request of any law enforcement agency, act in support of any activities of that agency;

   (d) enter into other arrangements for cooperating with bodies or persons (in the United Kingdom or elsewhere) which it considers appropriate in connection with the exercise of any of SOCA's functions under section 2 or 3 or any activities within subsection (3).

(3) Despite the references to serious organised crime in section 2(1), SOCA may carry on activities in relation to other crime if they are carried on for the purposes of any of the functions conferred on SOCA by section 2 or 3.

(4) Subsection (3) does not affect the generality of section 3(1).

(5) SOCA may furnish such assistance as it considers appropriate in response to requests made by any government or other body exercising functions of a public nature in any country or territory outside the United Kingdom.

(6) Subsection (5) does not apply to any request for assistance which—

   (a) could be made under section 13 of the Crime (International Cooperation) Act 2003 (c. 32) (requests by overseas authorities to obtain evidence), and

   (b) is not a request in relation to which SOCA has functions under that section by virtue of an order under section 27(2) of that Act.

(7) In this section 'law enforcement agency' has the meaning given by section 3(4).

Annual plans and reports

6 Annual plans

(1) Before the beginning of each financial year SOCA must issue a plan setting out how SOCA intends to exercise its functions during that year ('the annual plan').

(2) The annual plan must (in particular) set out how SOCA intends to exercise its functions in Scotland and in Northern Ireland.

(3) The annual plan must also include a statement of—

   (a) any priorities which SOCA has determined for that year,

   (b) any current strategic priorities determined by the Secretary of State under section 9,

   (c) any current performance targets established by SOCA, and

   (d) the financial resources that are expected to be available to SOCA for that year.

(4) Any priorities within subsection (3)(a) may relate—

   (a) to matters to which strategic priorities determined under section 9 also relate, or

   (b) to other matters,

   but in any event must be so framed as to be consistent with strategic priorities determined under that section.

(5) The annual plan must state, in relation to each priority within subsection (3)(a) or (b), how SOCA intends to give effect to that priority.

(6) SOCA must arrange for the annual plan to be published in such manner as it considers appropriate.

(7) SOCA must send a copy of the annual plan to—

(a) the Secretary of State,

(b) the Scottish Ministers,

(c) the Commissioners,

(d) each police authority for an area in Great Britain, each joint police board and the Northern Ireland Policing Board,

(e) the chief officer of each police force in the United Kingdom, and

(f) such other persons as SOCA considers appropriate.

(8) In subsection (7)(d) the reference to a police authority for an area in Great Britain does not include a constituent authority in an amalgamation scheme approved under section 19(1) of the Police (Scotland) Act 1967 (c. 77).

(9) Before issuing its annual plan for any financial year, SOCA must—

(a) consult the Scottish Ministers and agree with them what provision the plan is to make for Scotland by virtue of subsection (2); and

(b) consult such other persons as it considers appropriate.

7 Annual reports

(1) As soon as possible after the end of each financial year SOCA must issue a report on the exercise of its functions during that year (an 'annual report').

(2) The annual report must include an assessment of the extent to which the annual plan for that year under section 6 has been carried out.

(3) SOCA must arrange for the annual report to be published in such manner as it considers appropriate.

(4) SOCA must send a copy of the annual report to—

(a) the Secretary of State,

(b) the Scottish Ministers,

(c) the Commissioners,

(d) each police authority for an area in Great Britain, each joint police board and the Northern Ireland Policing Board,

(e) the chief officer of each police force in the United Kingdom, and

(f) such other persons as SOCA considers appropriate.

(5) In subsection (4)(d) the reference to a police authority for an area in Great Britain does not include a constituent authority in an amalgamation scheme approved under section 19(1) of the Police (Scotland) Act 1967.

(6) The Secretary of State must lay a copy of the annual report before Parliament.

(7) The Scottish Ministers must lay a copy of the annual report before the Scottish Parliament.

Central supervision and direction

8 General duty of Secretary of State and Scottish Ministers

The Secretary of State and the Scottish Ministers must exercise the powers respectively conferred on him and them under this Chapter in such manner and to such extent as appear to him and them to be best calculated to promote the efficiency and effectiveness of SOCA.

9 Strategic priorities

(1) The Secretary of State may determine strategic priorities for SOCA.

(2) Before determining any such priorities the Secretary of State must consult—

(a) SOCA,

(b) the Scottish Ministers, and

(c) such other persons as he considers appropriate.

(3) The Secretary of State must arrange for any priorities determined under this section to be published in such manner as he considers appropriate.

10 Codes of practice

(1) The Secretary of State may issue codes of practice relating to the exercise by SOCA of any of its functions.

(2) The Secretary of State may from time to time revise the whole or any part of a code of practice issued under this section.

(3) Before issuing or revising a code of practice issued under this section the Secretary of State must consult—

(a) SOCA,

(b) the Scottish Ministers, and

(c) such other persons as he considers appropriate.

(4) The Secretary of State must lay before Parliament—

(a) any code of practice issued under this section, and

(b) any revisions of such a code.

(5) The Secretary of State—

(a) is not required by subsection (4) to lay before Parliament, or

(b) may exclude from what he does lay before Parliament,

anything to which subsection (6) applies.

(6) This subsection applies to anything the publication of which, in the opinion of the Secretary of State—

(a) would be against the interests of national security, or

(b) could prejudice the prevention or detection of crime or the apprehension or prosecution of offenders, or

(c) could jeopardise the safety of any person.

(7) The Secretary of State must provide the Scottish Ministers with a copy of—

(a) any code of practice issued under this section, or

(b) any revisions of such a code.

11 Reports to Secretary of State

(1) The Secretary of State may require SOCA to submit a report to him on such matters—

(a) connected with the exercise of SOCA's functions, or

(b) otherwise connected with any of SOCA's activities,

as may be specified in the requirement.

(2) A report submitted under subsection (1) must be in such form as may be so specified.

(3) The Secretary of State must consult the Scottish Ministers before imposing any requirement under that subsection relating to any functions or activities of SOCA—

(a) exercised or carried out in Scotland, or

(b) exercised or carried out outside, but in relation to, Scotland.

(4) The Secretary of State may—

(a) arrange, or

(b) require SOCA to arrange,

for a report under this section to be published in such manner as he considers appropriate.

(5) But the Secretary of State may exclude any part of a report from publication under subsection (4) if, in his opinion, publication of that part—

(a) would be against the interests of national security, or

(b) could prejudice the prevention or detection of crime or the apprehension or prosecution of offenders, or

(c) could jeopardise the safety of any person.

12 Power to direct submission of action plan

(1) This section applies where an inspection report made to the Secretary of State states—

(a) that, in the opinion of the person making the report, the whole or any part of SOCA is (whether generally or in particular respects) not efficient or not effective; or

(b) that, in that person's opinion, the whole or part of SOCA will cease to be efficient or effective (whether generally or in particular respects) unless remedial measures are taken.

(2) If the Secretary of State considers that remedial measures are required in relation to any matters identified by the report, he may direct SOCA—

(a) to submit an action plan to him, and

(b) to do so within such period as is specified in the direction (which must be a period ending not less than 4, and not more than 12, weeks after the direction is given).

(3) An 'action plan' is a plan setting out the remedial measures which SOCA proposes to take in relation to the matters in respect of which the direction is given.

(4) The provision that a direction under this section may require to be included in an action plan includes—

(a) provision setting out the steps that SOCA proposes should be taken in respect of the matters in respect of which the direction is given, and the performance targets that SOCA proposes should be met;

(b) provision setting out SOCA's proposals as to the times within which those steps are to be taken and those targets met, and the means by which the success of the plan's implementation is to be measured;

(c) provision for the making of progress reports to the Secretary of State about the plan's implementation;

(d) provision as to the times at which, and the manner in which, any progress report is to be made; and

(e) provision for the duration of the plan and for it to cease to apply in circumstances determined by the Secretary of State.

(5) But nothing in this section authorises the Secretary of State to direct the inclusion in an action plan of any requirement to do or not to do anything—

(a) in a particular case identified for the purposes of the requirement, or

(b) in relation to a particular person so identified.

(6) The Secretary of State must consult the Scottish Ministers before giving any direction under this section in connection with any functions or activities of SOCA—

(a) exercised or carried out in Scotland, or

(b) exercised or carried out outside, but in relation to, Scotland.

(7) In this section 'an inspection report' means a report under section 16.

(8) If this section applies at a time when there is already an action plan in force—

(a) references in this section to the submission of an action plan to the Secretary of State include references to the submission of revisions of the existing plan, and

(b) the other provisions of this section have effect accordingly.

13 Revision of inadequate action plan

(1) This section applies where the Secretary of State is of the opinion that any remedial measures contained in an action plan submitted to him under section 12 are inadequate.

(2) The Secretary of State may notify SOCA of that opinion and of his reasons for it.

(3) The Secretary of State must consult the Scottish Ministers before forming an opinion for the purposes of subsection (1) as to any remedial measures proposed in connection with any functions or activities of SOCA—

(a) exercised or carried out in Scotland, or

(b) exercised or carried out outside, but in relation to, Scotland.

(4) If SOCA receives a notification under subsection (2)—

(a) it must consider whether to revise the plan in the light of the matters notified to it, and

(b) if it does revise the plan, it must send a copy of the revised plan to the Secretary of State.

(5) References in this section to an action plan submitted to the Secretary of State under section 12 include references to revisions submitted to him by virtue of subsection (8) of that section.

14 Procedure for giving directions under section 12

(1) The Secretary of State may not give a direction under section 12 unless the conditions in subsection (2) are satisfied.

(2) The conditions are—

(a) SOCA must have been given such information about the Secretary of State's grounds for proposing to give the direction as he considers appropriate for enabling it to make representations or proposals under paragraphs (b) and (c) below;

135

    (b) SOCA must have been given an opportunity of making representations about those grounds;

    (c) SOCA must have had an opportunity of making proposals for the taking of remedial measures that would make it unnecessary to give the direction; and

    (d) the Secretary of State must have considered any such representations and any such proposals.

15 Reports relating to directions under section 12

(1) This section applies where the Secretary of State exercises his power to give a direction under section 12.

(2) The Secretary of State must prepare a report on his exercise of that power.

(3) A report under subsection (2)—

    (a) is to be prepared at such time as the Secretary of State considers appropriate, and

    (b) may relate to more than one exercise of the power.

(4) The Secretary of State must—

    (a) lay before each House of Parliament a copy of any report prepared under subsection (2), and

    (b) send a copy of any such report to the Scottish Ministers.

(5) The Scottish Ministers must lay before the Scottish Parliament any copy of a report sent to them under subsection (4).

16 Inspections

(1) Her Majesty's Inspectors of Constabulary ('HMIC') must inspect SOCA from time to time.

(2) HMIC must also inspect SOCA if requested to do so by the Secretary of State either—

    (a) generally, or

    (b) in respect of a particular matter.

(3) Before requesting an inspection that would fall to be carried out wholly or partly in Scotland, the Secretary of State must consult the Scottish Ministers.

(4) Any inspection under this section must be carried out jointly by HMIC and the Scottish inspectors—

    (a) if it is carried out wholly in Scotland, or

    (b) in a case where it is carried out partly in Scotland, to the extent that it is carried out there.

(5) Following an inspection under this section, HMIC must report to the Secretary of State on the efficiency and effectiveness of SOCA either—

    (a) generally, or

    (b) in the case of an inspection under subsection (2)(b), in respect of the matter to which the inspection related.

(6) A report under subsection (5) must be in such form as the Secretary of State may direct.

(7) The Secretary of State must arrange for every report which he receives under subsection (5) to be published in such manner as he considers appropriate.

(8) The Secretary of State may exclude from publication under subsection (7) any part of a report if, in his opinion, the publication of that part—

(a) would be against the interests of national security, or

(b) could prejudice the prevention or detection of crime or the apprehension or prosecution of offenders, or

(c) might jeopardise the safety of any person.

(9) The Secretary of State must send a copy of the published report—

(a) to SOCA, and

(b) if subsection (4) applied to the inspection, to the Scottish Ministers.

(10) SOCA must—

(a) prepare comments on the published report, and

(b) arrange for its comments to be published in such manner as it considers appropriate.

(11) SOCA must send a copy of any document published under subsection (10)(b)—

(a) to the Secretary of State, and

(b) if subsection (4) applied to the inspection, to the Scottish Ministers.

(12) The inspectors shall carry out such other duties for the purpose of furthering the efficiency and effectiveness of SOCA as the Secretary of State may from time to time direct.

(13) In this section 'the Scottish inspectors' means the inspectors of constabulary appointed under section 33(1) of the Police (Scotland) Act 1967 (c. 77).

Financial provisions

17 Grants by Secretary of State

(1) The Secretary of State must make a grant to SOCA in respect of each of its financial years.

(2) The grant in respect of a financial year is to be paid—

(a) at such time, or

(b) in instalments of such amounts and at such time,

as the Secretary of State may determine (and any such time may fall within or after that year).

18 Determinations relating to grants under section 17

(1) The Secretary of State must determine the amount of the grant to be made under section 17 in respect of each of SOCA's financial years.

(2) But a determination under subsection (1) may, if the Secretary of State thinks fit, specify a single amount in respect of two or more financial years.

(3) A determination under that subsection may be varied by a subsequent determination.

(4) Where the Secretary of State makes any determination under subsection (1), he must prepare a report—

(a) setting out the determination, and

(b) stating the considerations which he took into account in making it.

(5) The Secretary of State must—

(a) send SOCA a copy of each report under subsection (4), and

(b) lay a copy of each such report before the House of Commons.

(6) In connection with the exercise of his functions under this section, the Secretary of State may require SOCA—

(a) to provide him with such information as he may specify, and

(b) to do so within such period as he may specify.

19 Charges by SOCA and other receipts

(1) SOCA may make charges in respect of—

(a) the provision by SOCA of any goods or services to any person, or

(b) an agreement for the provision by SOCA of any such goods or services.

(2) Any charges made under subsection (1) may include amounts calculated by reference to expenditure incurred, or expected to be incurred, by SOCA otherwise than directly in connection with the provision of the goods or services concerned.

(3) Apart from—

(a) grants under section 17,

(b) sums received under section 30(6), and

(c) sums borrowed by SOCA under paragraph 21 of Schedule 1,

all sums received by SOCA in the course of, or in connection with, the exercise of its functions must be paid to the Secretary of State.

(4) Subsection (3) does not apply where the Secretary of State so directs.

(5) Any sums received by the Secretary of State under subsection (3) must be paid into the Consolidated Fund.

20 Accounts

(1) SOCA must—

(a) keep proper accounts and proper records in relation to the accounts; and

(b) prepare a statement of accounts in respect of each financial year.

(2) A statement of accounts under subsection (1) must be in such form, and contain such information, as the Secretary of State may direct.

(3) SOCA must send copies of the statement of accounts for a financial year—

(a) to the Secretary of State, and

(b) to the Comptroller and Auditor General,

within such period following the end of the financial year as the Secretary of State may specify.

(4) The Comptroller and Auditor General must—

(a) examine, certify and report on the statement of accounts, and

(b) lay copies of the statement and of his report before each House of Parliament.

Operational matters

21 Operational responsibility of Director General

(1) The Director General of SOCA has the function of exercising general operational control in relation to the activities carried out in the exercise of SOCA's functions.

(2) This function includes deciding—

(a) which particular operations are to be mounted in the exercise of any of those functions, and

(b) how such operations are to be conducted.

22 Activities in Scotland in relation to crime

(1) SOCA may only carry out activities in Scotland in relation to an offence which it suspects has been committed (or is being committed) if it does so with the agreement of the Lord Advocate.

(2) In carrying out any such activities in Scotland SOCA must comply with such directions (whether general or special) as it may receive from the Lord Advocate or from the procurator fiscal.

(3) If it suspects that an offence has been committed (or is being committed) in Scotland, SOCA must report the matter to the procurator fiscal as soon as is practicable.

23 Mutual assistance between SOCA and law enforcement agencies: voluntary arrangements

(1) Subsection (2) applies if—
  (a) the chief officer of a police force in the British Islands or of a special police force, or
  (b) a law enforcement agency operating in the British Islands,
  notifies the Director General of SOCA that that force or agency has a special need for assistance from SOCA and requests the Director General of SOCA to provide it with such assistance.

(2) In such a case the Director General of SOCA may provide that force or agency with—
  (a) such members of the staff of SOCA, or
  (b) such other assistance,
  as the Director General of SOCA considers appropriate in the circumstances.

(3) Subsection (4) applies if the Director General of SOCA notifies—
  (a) the chief officer of a police force in the United Kingdom or of a special police force, or
  (b) a law enforcement agency operating in the United Kingdom,
  that SOCA has a special need for assistance from that force or agency and requests it to provide SOCA with such assistance.

(4) In such a case the chief officer of that force or the agency in question may provide SOCA with—
  (a) such constables or members of the staff of the agency, or
  (b) such other assistance,
  as the chief officer or the agency considers appropriate in the circumstances.

(5) But before the Scottish Drug Enforcement Agency provides any constable under subsection (4), its Director must obtain the agreement of the chief constable of the police force from which the constable is seconded to the Agency.

(6) Where a member of the staff of SOCA is provided under this section for the assistance of a police force, a special police force or a law enforcement agency, he shall be under the direction and control of the chief officer of the force or the head of the agency (as the case may be).

(7) Where—
  (a) a constable,
  (b) a member of the staff of the Scottish Drug Enforcement Agency, or
  (c) a member of the staff of a law enforcement agency,

is provided under this section for the assistance of SOCA, he shall be under the direction and control of the Director General of SOCA (despite anything in, or in any agreement made under, any other enactment).

(8) Where SOCA provides assistance under this section for—

(a) a police force in the United Kingdom or a special police force, or

(b) a law enforcement agency operating in the United Kingdom,

the relevant police authority or (as the case may be) that agency must pay to SOCA such contribution, if any, as may be agreed between them or, in the absence of agreement, as may be determined by the Secretary of State.

(9) Where SOCA is provided with assistance under this section by—

(a) a police force in the United Kingdom or a special police force, or

(b) a law enforcement agency operating in the United Kingdom,

SOCA must pay to the relevant police authority or (as the case may be) that agency such contribution, if any, as may be agreed between them or, in the absence of agreement, as may be determined by the Secretary of State.

(10) If the assistance mentioned in subsection (8) or (9) is provided for or (as the case may be) by—

(a) a police force in Scotland,

(b) the Scottish Drug Enforcement Agency, or

(c) the Scottish Administration,

the Secretary of State must, before making a determination under the subsection in question, consult the Scottish Ministers.

(11) In this section—

'law enforcement agency' has the meaning given by section 3(4) (subject to any territorial restrictions contained in this section);

'police force', in relation to the British Islands, includes the States of Jersey Police Force, the salaried police force of the Island of Guernsey and the Isle of Man Constabulary;

'relevant police authority' means—

(a) in relation to a police force in Great Britain, the police authority maintaining that force (or, in the case of a police force for a combined area, the joint police board for that area),

(b) in relation to the Police Service of Northern Ireland or the Police Service of Northern Ireland Reserve, the Northern Ireland Policing Board,

(c) in relation to the Ministry of Defence Police, the Secretary of State,

(d) in relation to the British Transport Police Force, the British Transport Police Authority,

(e) in relation to the Civil Nuclear Constabulary, the Civil Nuclear Police Authority, and

(f) in relation to the Scottish Drug Enforcement Agency, the Agency itself.

24 Mutual assistance between SOCA and law enforcement agencies: directed arrangements

(1) This section applies where it appears to the Secretary of State—

(a) that a body within subsection (2) has a special need for assistance from SOCA or SOCA has a special need for assistance from a body within that subsection,

(b) that it is expedient for such assistance to be provided by SOCA or (as the case may be) the body, and

(c) that satisfactory arrangements cannot be made, or cannot be made in time, under section 23.

(2) The bodies within this subsection are—

(a) any police force in England and Wales or Northern Ireland,

(b) any special police force other than the Scottish Drug Enforcement Agency, and

(c) any law enforcement agency operating in the United Kingdom other than the Scottish Administration.

(3) In a case where this section applies the Secretary of State may (as appropriate)—

(a) direct the chief officer of the police force to provide such constables or other assistance for the purpose of meeting the need in question as may be specified in the direction;

(b) direct the chief officer of the special police force to provide such constables or other persons, or such other assistance, for the purpose of meeting the need in question as may be so specified;

(c) direct the head of the law enforcement agency to provide such members of the staff of that agency or other assistance for the purpose of meeting the need in question as may be so specified;

(d) direct the Director General of SOCA to provide such members of the staff of SOCA or other assistance for the purpose of meeting the need in question as may be so specified.

(4) A direction under subsection (3) requires the consent of the Treasury if it is to be given to the Commissioners.

(5) Subsections (6) to (9) of section 23 apply in relation to assistance provided under this section—

(a) by SOCA to a police force, a special police force or a law enforcement agency, or

(b) to SOCA by a police force, a special police force or a law enforcement agency, as they apply in relation to assistance so provided under that section.

(6) In this section 'law enforcement agency' has the meaning given by section 3(4) (subject to the territorial restriction contained in subsection (2) above).

25 Directed arrangements: Scotland

(1) This section applies where it appears to the Scottish Ministers—

(a) that a body within subsection (2) has a special need for assistance from SOCA or SOCA has a special need for assistance from a body within that subsection,

(b) that it is expedient for such assistance to be provided by SOCA or (as the case may be) the body, and

(c) that satisfactory arrangements cannot be made, or cannot be made in time, under section 23.

(2) The bodies within this subsection are—

(a) any police force in Scotland, and

(b) the Scottish Drug Enforcement Agency.

(3) In a case where this section applies the Scottish Ministers may (as appropriate)—

    (a) direct the chief officer of the police force to provide such constables or other assistance for the purpose of meeting the need in question as may be specified in the direction;

    (b) direct the Director of the Scottish Drug Enforcement Agency to provide such constables or other persons, or other assistance, for the purpose of meeting the need in question as may be so specified;

    (c) with the agreement of the Secretary of State, direct the Director General of SOCA to provide such members of the staff of SOCA or other assistance for the purpose of meeting the need in question as may be so specified.

(4) Subsections (6) to (10) of section 23 apply in relation to assistance provided under this section—

    (a) by SOCA to a police force in Scotland or to the Scottish Drug Enforcement Agency, or

    (b) to SOCA by a police force in Scotland or by the Scottish Drug Enforcement Agency,

as they apply in relation to assistance so provided under that section.

26 Use by SOCA of police premises etc.

(1) Arrangements may be made between—

    (a) SOCA, and

    (b) the relevant police authority,

under which SOCA may use such premises, equipment or other material, facilities or services made available by a police force in England and Wales or Northern Ireland as are specified or described in the arrangements.

(2) If it appears to the Secretary of State—

    (a) that it is expedient for arrangements within subsection (1) to be made between SOCA and the relevant police authority, and

    (b) that satisfactory arrangements cannot be made, or cannot be made in time, under that subsection,

he may direct SOCA and that authority to enter into such arrangements within that subsection as are specified in the direction.

(3) Before giving such a direction to SOCA or the relevant police authority the Secretary of State must—

    (a) notify that body that he is proposing to give the directions, and

    (b) consider any representations made to him by that body.

(4) Any arrangements under this section may be varied or terminated by agreement between the parties.

(5) But arrangements entered into in pursuance of a direction under subsection (2) may not be so terminated without the consent of the Secretary of State.

(6) Where any expenditure is incurred by the relevant police authority by virtue of any arrangements under this section, SOCA must pay to the authority such contribution, if any, in respect of that expenditure—

    (a) as may be agreed between them, or

    (b) in the absence of agreement, as may be determined by the Secretary of State.

(7) In this section 'relevant police authority' means—

    (a) in relation to a police force in England and Wales, the police authority maintaining that force, and

    (b) in relation to the Police Service of Northern Ireland or the Police Service of Northern Ireland Reserve, the Northern Ireland Policing Board.

27 Regulations as to equipment

(1) The Secretary of State may make regulations requiring equipment used by SOCA to satisfy such requirements as to design and performance as may be prescribed by the regulations.

(2) The Secretary of State may be regulations make any of the following kinds of provision—

    (a) provision requiring SOCA, when using equipment for the purposes specified in the regulations, to use only—

        (i) the equipment which is specified in the regulations,

        (ii) equipment which is of a description so specified, or

        (iii) equipment which is of a type approved by the Secretary of State in accordance with the regulations;

    (b) provision prohibiting SOCA from using equipment of a type approved as mentioned in paragraph (a)(iii) except—

        (i) where the conditions subject to which the approval was given are satisfied, and

        (ii) in accordance with the other terms of that approval;

    (c) provision requiring equipment used by SOCA to comply with such conditions as may be specified in the regulations, or as may be approved by the Secretary of State in accordance with the regulations;

    (d) provision prohibiting SOCA from using equipment specified in the regulations, or any equipment of a description so specified.

(3) Before making regulations under this section Secretary of State must consult—

    (a) SOCA, and

    (b) such other persons as he considers appropriate.

(4) In this section 'equipment' includes—

    (a) vehicles, and

    (b) headgear and protective and other clothing.

Liability for unlawful conduct

28 Liability of SOCA for acts of seconded staff etc.

(1) SOCA is liable in respect of unlawful conduct of persons to whom this section applies in the carrying out, or the purported carrying out, of their functions as such persons in the same manner as an employer is liable in respect of any unlawful conduct of his employees in the course of their employment.

(2) In the case of any such unlawful conduct of persons to whom this section applies which is a tort, SOCA is accordingly to be treated as a joint tortfeasor.

This subsection does not apply to Scotland.

(3) This section applies to—

    (a) any constable or other person who has been seconded to SOCA to serve as a member of its staff, and

    (b) any constable or other person who has been provided for the assistance of SOCA under section 23, 24 or 25.

29 Payment by SOCA of amounts in connection with unlawful conduct of employees etc.

(1) SOCA may, in such cases and to such extent as appear to it to be appropriate, pay—

    (a) any damages or costs awarded against a person to whom this section applies in proceedings for any unlawful conduct of that person;

    (b) any costs (or, in Scotland, expenses) incurred and not recovered by such a person in such proceedings, and

    (c) any sum required in connection with the settlement of a claim that has, or might have, given rise to such proceedings.

(2) This section applies to—

    (a) any person who is employed by SOCA,

    (b) any constable or other person who has been seconded to SOCA to serve as a member of its staff, and

    (c) any constable or other person who has been provided for the assistance of SOCA under section 23, 24 or 25.

30 Application of sections 28 and 29 to members of joint investigation teams

(1) Subsection (2) applies where an international joint investigation team has been formed under the leadership of a member of SOCA's staff.

(2) In such a case—

    (a) section 28 has effect in relation to any member of that team who is not a member of SOCA's staff as if any unlawful conduct in the carrying out, or purported carrying out, of his functions as a member of the team were unlawful conduct of a person to whom that section applies; and

    (b) section 29(1) has effect as if it applied to every member of the team to whom it would not apply apart from this subsection.

(3) Subsection (4) applies where a person ('the relevant person') is carrying out surveillance under section 76A of the Regulation of Investigatory Powers Act 2000 (c. 23) (foreign surveillance operations).

(4) In such a case—

    (a) section 28 has effect as if any unlawful conduct of the relevant person in the course of carrying out the surveillance were unlawful conduct of a person to whom that section applies; and

    (b) section 29(1) has effect as if it applied to the relevant person.

(5) In this section 'international joint investigation team' means any investigation team formed in accordance with—

    (a) any framework decision on joint investigation teams adopted under Article 34 of the Treaty on European Union;

    (b) the Convention on Mutual Assistance in Criminal Matters between the Member States of the European Union and the Protocol to that Convention established in accordance with that Article of the Treaty; or

    (c) any international agreement to which the United Kingdom is a party and which is specified in an order made by the Secretary of State.

(6) Where—

    (a) a sum is paid by SOCA by virtue of this section, and

    (b) the Secretary of State receives under any international agreement a sum by way of reimbursement (in whole or in part) of the sum paid by SOCA,

he must pay to SOCA the sum received by him by way of reimbursement.

31 Liability of special police forces and law enforcement agencies for unlawful conduct of SOCA staff

(1) The relevant authority is liable in respect of unlawful conduct of persons to whom this section applies in the carrying out, or the purported carrying out, of their functions as such persons in the same manner as an employer is liable in respect of any unlawful conduct of his employees in the course of their employment.

(2) In the case of any such unlawful conduct of persons to whom this section applies which is a tort, the relevant authority is accordingly to be treated as a joint tortfeasor.

This subsection does not apply to Scotland.

(3) In so far as a relevant authority does not already have power to do so it may, in such cases and to such extent as appear to it to be appropriate, pay—

(a) any damages or costs awarded against a person to whom this section applies in proceedings for any unlawful conduct of that person,

(b) any costs (or, in Scotland, expenses) incurred and not recovered by such a person in such proceedings, and

(c) any sum required in connection with the settlement of a claim that has, or might have, given rise to such proceedings.

(4) This section applies to a member of the staff of SOCA who under section 23, 24 or 25 is provided for the assistance of—

(a) a special police force, or

(b) a law enforcement agency operating in the United Kingdom.

(5) In this section—

'law enforcement agency' has the meaning given by section 3(4) (subject to the territorial restriction contained in subsection (4)(b) above), and

'relevant authority'—

(a) in relation to a member of the staff of SOCA provided for the assistance of the Ministry of Defence Police, means the Secretary of State,

(b) in relation to a member of the staff of SOCA provided for the assistance of the British Transport Police Force, means the British Transport Police Authority,

(c) in relation to a member of the staff of SOCA provided for the assistance of the Civil Nuclear Constabulary, means the Civil Nuclear Police Authority,

(d) in relation to a member of the staff of SOCA provided for the assistance of the Scottish Drug Enforcement Agency, means that Agency,

(e) in relation to a member of the staff of SOCA provided for the assistance of the Commissioners, means the Commissioners,

(f) in relation to a member of the staff of SOCA provided for the assistance of the Scottish Administration, means the Scottish Ministers, and

(g) in relation to a member of the staff of SOCA provided for the assistance of any other law enforcement agency, means such person as is prescribed in relation to that agency by regulations made by the Secretary of State.

Use and disclosure of information

32 Use of information by SOCA

Information obtained by SOCA in connection with the exercise of any of its functions may be used by SOCA in connection with the exercise of any of its other functions.

33 Disclosure of information by SOCA

(1) Information obtained by SOCA in connection with the exercise of any of its functions may be disclosed by SOCA if the disclosure is for any permitted purposes.

(2) 'Permitted purposes' means the purposes of any of the following—

   (a) the prevention, detection, investigation or prosecution of criminal offences, whether in the United Kingdom or elsewhere;

   (b) the prevention, detection or investigation of conduct for which penalties other than criminal penalties are provided under the law of any part of the United Kingdom or of any country or territory outside the United Kingdom;

   (c) the exercise of any function conferred on SOCA by section 2, 3 or 5 (so far as not falling within paragraph (a) or (b));

   (d) the exercise of any functions of any intelligence service within the meaning of the Regulation of Investigatory Powers Act 2000 (c. 23);

   (e) the exercise of any functions under Part 2 of the Football Spectators Act 1989 (c. 37);

   (f) the exercise of any function which appears to the Secretary of State to be a function of a public nature and which he designates by order.

(3) A disclosure under this section does not breach—

   (a) any obligation of confidence owed by the person making the disclosure, or

   (b) any other restriction on the disclosure of information (however imposed).

(4) But nothing in this section authorises—

   (a) a disclosure, in contravention of any provisions of the Data Protection Act 1998 (c. 29), of personal data which are not exempt from those provisions,

   (b) a disclosure which is prohibited by Part 1 of the Regulation of Investigatory Powers Act 2000, or

   (c) a disclosure in contravention of section 35(2).

34 Disclosure of information to SOCA

(1) Any person may disclose information to SOCA if the disclosure is made for the purposes of the exercise by SOCA of any of its functions.

(2) A disclosure under this section does not breach—

   (a) any obligation of confidence owed by the person making the disclosure, or

   (b) any other restriction on the disclosure of information (however imposed).

(3) But nothing in this section authorises—

   (a) a disclosure, in contravention of any provisions of the Data Protection Act 1998, of personal data which are not exempt from those provisions, or

   (b) a disclosure which is prohibited by Part 1 of the Regulation of Investigatory Powers Act 2000.

(4) Information may not be disclosed under subsection (1) on behalf of the

Commissioners unless the disclosure is authorised by the Commissioners or by an authorised officer of theirs.

35 Restrictions on further disclosure

(1) Information disclosed by SOCA under section 33 to any person or body must not be further disclosed except—
  (a) for a purpose connected with any function of that person or body for the purposes of which the information was disclosed by SOCA, or otherwise for any permitted purposes, and
  (b) with the consent of SOCA.

(2) Information disclosed to SOCA under any enactment by the Commissioners or a person acting on their behalf must not be further disclosed except—
  (a) for any permitted purposes, and
  (b) with the consent of the Commissioners or an authorised officer of Revenue and Customs.

(3) Consent under subsection (1) or (2) may be given—
  (a) in relation to a particular disclosure, or
  (b) in relation to disclosures made in circumstances specified or described in the consent.

(4) In this section 'permitted purposes' has the meaning given by section 33(2).

General duties of police etc.

36 General duty of police to pass information to SOCA

(1) The chief officer of a police force in Great Britain must keep SOCA informed of any information relating to crime in his police area that appears to him to be likely to be relevant to the exercise by SOCA of any of its functions.

(2) The Chief Constable of the Police Service of Northern Ireland has a corresponding duty in relation to crime in Northern Ireland.

(3) The chief officer of a special police force must keep SOCA informed of any information relating to crime that he has become aware of in his capacity as chief officer and appears to him to be likely to be relevant to the exercise by SOCA of any of its functions.

37 General duty of police etc. to assist SOCA

(1) It is the duty of every person to whom this section applies to assist SOCA in the exercise of its functions in relation to serious organised crime.

(2) This section applies to—
  (a) any constable,
  (b) any officer of Revenue and Customs, and
  (c) any member of Her Majesty's armed forces or Her Majesty's coastguard.

Prosecutions

38 Prosecution of offences investigated by SOCA

(1) The Director of Revenue and Customs Prosecutions—
  (a) may institute and conduct criminal proceedings in England and Wales that

arise out of a criminal investigation by SOCA relating to a designated offence, and

    (b) must take over the conduct of criminal proceedings instituted by SOCA in England and Wales in respect of a designated offence.

(2) The Director of Revenue and Customs Prosecutions must provide such advice as he thinks appropriate, to such persons as he thinks appropriate, in relation to—

    (a) a criminal investigation by SOCA relating to a designated offence, or

    (b) criminal proceedings instituted in England and Wales that arise out of such an investigation.

(3) The Director of Public Prosecutions—

    (a) may institute and conduct criminal proceedings in England and Wales that arise out of a criminal investigation by SOCA relating to a non-designated offence, and

    (b) must take over the conduct of criminal proceedings instituted by SOCA in England and Wales in respect of such an offence.

But paragraph (b) does not apply where the Director of the Serious Fraud Office has the conduct of the proceedings.

(4) The Director of Public Prosecutions must provide such advice as he thinks appropriate, to such persons as he thinks appropriate, in relation to—

    (a) a criminal investigation by SOCA relating to a non-designated offence, or

    (b) criminal proceedings instituted in England and Wales that arise out of such an investigation.

(5) Sections 23 and 23A of the Prosecution of Offences Act 1985 (c. 23) (power to discontinue proceedings) apply (with any necessary modifications) to proceedings conducted by the Director of Revenue and Customs Prosecutions in accordance with this section as they apply to proceedings conducted by the Director of Public Prosecutions.

(6) In the Commissioners for Revenue and Customs Act 2005 (c. 11)—

    (a) section 37(1) (prosecutors), and

    (b) section 38(1) (conduct of prosecutions by appointed persons),

have effect as if the reference to section 35 of that Act included a reference to this section.

(7) For the purposes of this section and section 39—

    (a) 'criminal investigation' means any process—

        (i)   for considering whether an offence has been committed,

        (ii) for discovering by whom an offence has been committed, or

        (iii) as a result of which an offence is alleged to have been committed;

    (b) an offence is a 'designated offence' if criminal proceedings instituted by SOCA in respect of the offence fall (or, as the case may be, would fall) to be referred to the Director of Revenue and Customs Prosecutions by virtue of directions under section 39(1);

    (c) 'non-designated offence' means an offence which is not a designated offence;

    (d) a reference to the institution of criminal proceedings is to be construed in accordance with section 15(2) of the Prosecution of Offences Act 1985 (c. 23); and

    (e) a reference to the institution of proceedings by SOCA includes a reference to their institution by the Director General of SOCA or a person authorised by him.

39 Directions as to reference of cases and proceedings to appropriate prosecutor

(1) The Directors may give directions to SOCA—

    (a) for enabling SOCA to determine whether cases arising out of criminal investigations by SOCA are to be referred to the Director of Revenue and Customs Prosecutions, or to the Director of Public Prosecutions, in order for him to consider whether to institute proceedings in accordance with section 38(1)(a) or (3)(a);

    (b) for enabling SOCA to determine whether criminal proceedings instituted by SOCA are to be referred to the Director of Revenue and Customs Prosecutions, or to the Director of Public Prosecutions, in order for him to take over their conduct in accordance with section 38(1)(b) or (3)(b);

    (c) specifying, in relation to any cases or proceedings that are to be so referred to the Director of Revenue and Customs Prosecutions or the Director of Public Prosecutions, the steps to be taken by SOCA in connection with referring them to him.

(2) Directions under subsection (1) may provide for cases or proceedings to be referred to one or other of the Directors by reference to—

    (a) whether the cases or proceedings relate to an offence falling within a category of offences specified in the directions; or

    (b) whether any criteria so specified are satisfied with respect to the cases or proceedings; or

    (c) such other matters as the Directors think fit.

(3) The Directors may from time to time revise any directions given under this section.

(4) The Directors must publish in such manner as they think fit—

    (a) any directions given under this section, and

    (b) any revisions made to such directions;

and they must give a copy of any such directions or revisions to SOCA.

(5) A report to which this subsection applies must set out—

    (a) any directions given under this section, and

    (b) any revisions made to such directions,

in the year to which the report relates.

(6) Subsection (5) applies to—

    (a) a report under section 9 of the Prosecution of Offences Act 1985 (c. 23) (report to Attorney General by Director of Public Prosecutions), and

    (b) a report under paragraph 6 of Schedule 3 to the Commissioners for Revenue and Customs Act 2005 (c. 11) (report to Attorney General by Director of Revenue and Customs Prosecutions).

(7) Directions under this section may make different provision for different cases, circumstances or areas.

(8) If there is a failure to comply with directions under this section in relation to the reference of any matter to one of the Directors, neither—

    (a) the reference, nor

    (b) anything subsequently done in connection with the matter,

is invalid by reason of anything in the directions or in section 38.

(9) In this section 'the Directors' means the Director of Public Prosecutions and the Director of Revenue and Customs Prosecutions, acting jointly.

40 Functions of Director of Revenue and Customs Prosecutions as to persons arrested for designated offence

(1) Sections 37 to 37B of the Police and Criminal Evidence Act 1984 (c. 60) (duties of custody officers; guidance etc.) have effect, in relation to a person arrested following a criminal investigation by SOCA relating to a designated offence, as if references to the Director of Public Prosecutions were references to the Director of Revenue and Customs Prosecutions.

(2) In subsection (1) the reference to a designated offence is to be read in accordance with section 38(7)(b) of this Act.

Miscellaneous and supplementary

41 Directions

Any person to whom a direction is given by the Secretary of State or the Scottish Ministers under this Chapter must comply with the direction.

42 Interpretation of Chapter 1

(1) In this Chapter—

'chief officer' means—
(a) in relation to a police force in England and Wales, the chief officer of police,
(b) in relation to a police force in Scotland, the chief constable,
(c) in relation to the Police Service of Northern Ireland or the Police Service of Northern Ireland Reserve, the Chief Constable of the Police Service of Northern Ireland;
(d) in relation to the States of Jersey Police Force or the salaried police force of the Island of Guernsey, the chief officer of that force;
(e) in relation to the Isle of Man Constabulary, the chief constable;
(f) in relation to a special police force mentioned in section 3(5)(a), (b) or (c), the Chief Constable;
(g) in relation to the Scottish Drug Enforcement Agency, the Director of that Agency;

'the Commissioners' has the meaning given by section 2(8);

'constable', in relation to Northern Ireland, means a member of the Police Service of Northern Ireland or the Police Service of Northern Ireland Reserve;

'financial year', in relation to SOCA, means—
(a) the period beginning with the date on which SOCA is established and ending with the following 31st March, and
(b) each successive period of 12 months ending with 31st March;

'functions' includes powers and duties;

'government department' includes a Northern Ireland department;

'joint police board' has the same meaning as in the Police (Scotland) Act 1967 (c. 77);

'police force' means (unless the context otherwise requires)—
(a) a police force in England, Wales or Scotland, or

(b) the Police Service of Northern Ireland or the Police Service of Northern Ireland Reserve;

'special police force' has the meaning given by section 3(5).

(2) In this Chapter—
  (a) 'the Scottish Drug Enforcement Agency' means the organisation known by that name and established under section 36(1)(a)(ii) of the Police (Scotland) Act 1967; and
  (b) 'the Director' of that Agency means the person engaged on central service (as defined by section 38(5) of that Act) and for the time being appointed by the Scottish Ministers to exercise control in relation to the activities carried out in the exercise of the Agency's functions.

(3) Section 81(5) of the Regulation of Investigatory Powers Act 2000 (c. 23) (meaning of 'prevention' and 'detection') applies for the purposes of this Chapter as it applies for the purposes of the provisions of that Act not contained in Chapter 1 of Part 1.

CHAPTER 2
SOCA: SPECIAL POWERS OF DESIGNATED STAFF

Designations

43 Designation of SOCA staff as persons having powers of constable etc.

(1) The Director General of SOCA may designate a member of the staff of SOCA as one or more of the following—
  (a) a person having the powers of a constable;
  (b) a person having the customs powers of an officer of Revenue and Customs;
  (c) a person having the powers of an immigration officer.

(2) A designation under this section—
  (a) may be made subject to any limitations specified in the designation (whether as to the powers exercisable by virtue of it, the purposes for which they are exercisable or otherwise); and
  (b) has effect either for a period so specified or without limit of time.

(3) Subsection (2) applies subject to any modification or withdrawal of the designation under section 45.

(4) A member of SOCA's staff may be designated as a person having the powers mentioned in any of paragraphs (a) to (c) of subsection (1) whether or not—
  (a) he already has (for any reason) any powers falling within any of those paragraphs, or
  (b) he had any such powers before becoming a member of SOCA's staff.

(5) But a person may not be designated as a person having the powers mentioned in any of paragraphs (a) to (c) of subsection (1) unless the Director General is satisfied that that person—
  (a) is capable of effectively exercising the powers that would be exercisable by virtue of the designation,
  (b) has received adequate training in respect of the exercise of those powers, and
  (c) is otherwise a suitable person to exercise those powers.

(6) Where an employee of SOCA—

    (a) before becoming such an employee, held an office by virtue of which he had any powers falling within subsection (1)(a), (b) or (c), and

    (b) has not resigned that office,

that office is to be treated as suspended so long as he remains in SOCA's employment, and revives if (and only if) on ceasing to be so employed he returns to service as the holder of that office.

(7) References in this section to the powers of a constable, the customs powers of an officer of Revenue and Customs or the powers of an immigration officer are to be read in accordance with sections 46 to 49.

44 Delegation of power to designate

(1) The Director General of SOCA may, to such extent as he may specify, delegate his functions under section 43 to an employee of SOCA at the prescribed level.

(2) 'At the prescribed level' means employed in a grade or on a pay scale not lower than that specified in an order made by the Secretary of State.

45 Modification or withdrawal of designations

(1) The Director General of SOCA may at any time modify or withdraw a designation made under section 43 by giving a notice to that effect to the designated person.

(2) An employee of SOCA by whom the power to make designations under section 43 is exercisable by virtue of section 44 may at any time modify or withdraw a relevant designation by giving a notice to that effect to the designated person.

(3) For the purposes of this section 'a relevant designation', in relation to such an employee, means a designation of a kind that the employee is authorised to make by virtue of section 44.

Powers exercisable

46 Person having powers of a constable

(1) This section applies to a member of SOCA's staff who is for the time being designated under section 43 as a person having the powers of a constable.

(2) The designated person has all the powers and privileges of a constable.

(3) Those powers and privileges are exercisable by the designated person—

    (a) throughout England and Wales and the adjacent United Kingdom waters, and

    (b) in accordance with section 47, in Scotland or Northern Ireland and the adjacent United Kingdom waters.

(4) If any of those powers and privileges, when exercisable by a constable, are subject to any territorial restrictions on their exercise, they are similarly subject to those restrictions when exercised by the designated person.

(5) If any of those powers and privileges, when exercisable by a constable, are exercisable elsewhere than in the United Kingdom or the adjacent United Kingdom waters, they are similarly exercisable by the designated person.

(6) The designated person also has any powers exercisable by virtue of subsection (7).

(7) Any enactment under which a constable may be authorised by warrant to exercise any power in relation to any matter has effect, for the purpose of enabling the designated person to be authorised to exercise the power in relation to any such matter, as if he were a constable.

(8) Subsections (2) to (7) have effect subject to any limitation specified in the designation under section 43(2).

(9) In this section references to the powers and privileges of a constable are references to the powers and privileges of a constable whether under any enactment or otherwise.

47 Person having powers of constable: Scotland and Northern Ireland

(1) This section provides for persons designated as mentioned in section 46(1) ('relevant persons') to exercise the powers and privileges mentioned in section 46(2) in Scotland or Northern Ireland and the adjacent United Kingdom waters.

(2) If so agreed by—
  (a) the Scottish Ministers, and
  (b) SOCA,
  the powers and privileges are exercisable by relevant persons in Scotland and the adjacent United Kingdom waters to such extent and in such circumstances as may be specified in the agreement.

(3) If so agreed by—
  (a) the Director of the Scottish Drug Enforcement Agency or a person nominated by him for the purposes of this subsection, and
  (b) SOCA,
  a relevant person may exercise the powers and privileges in Scotland in connection with a particular operation.

(4) A person nominated for the purposes of subsection (3) must be either—
  (a) a person for the time being appointed as Deputy Director of that Agency, or
  (b) an appropriate officer of a police force for an area in Scotland.

(5) If so agreed by—
  (a) the Secretary of State, and
  (b) SOCA,
  the powers and privileges are exercisable by relevant persons in Northern Ireland and the adjacent United Kingdom waters to such extent and in such circumstances as may be specified in the agreement.

(6) If—
  (a) an agreement under subsection (5) ('the general authorisation') is in force, and
  (b) an appropriate officer of the Police Service of Northern Ireland and SOCA so agree in conformity with the general authorisation,
  a relevant person may exercise the powers and privileges in Northern Ireland in connection with a particular operation in accordance with the agreement mentioned in paragraph (b).

(7) In this section—

'appropriate officer' means an officer of or above the rank of assistant chief constable;

'the Scottish Drug Enforcement Agency' and 'the Director' of that Agency have the meanings given by section 42(2).

48 Person having customs powers

(1) This section applies to a member of SOCA's staff who is for the time being designated under section 43 as a person having the customs powers of an officer of Revenue and Customs.

(2) The designated person has, in relation to any customs matter, the same powers as an officer of Revenue and Customs would have.

(3) The designated person also has any powers exercisable by virtue of subsection (4).

(4) Any enactment under which an officer of Revenue and Customs may be authorised by warrant to exercise any power in relation to any customs matter has effect, for the purpose of enabling the designated person to be authorised to exercise the power in relation to any such matter, as if he were an officer of Revenue and Customs.

(5) Where any power is exercisable by an officer of Revenue and Customs both—
  (a) in relation to a customs matter, and
  (b) in relation to any other matter,
  it is exercisable by the designated person only in relation to the customs matter.

(6) Subsections (2) to (5) have effect subject to any limitation specified in the designation under section 43(2).

(7) In this section 'customs matter' means any matter other than—
  (a) a matter to which section 7 of the Commissioners for Revenue and Customs Act 2005 (c. 11) applies (former Inland Revenue matters), or
  (b) any tax or duty not mentioned in Schedule 1 to that Act (which lists such matters).

49 Person having powers of an immigration officer

(1) This section applies to a member of SOCA's staff who is for the time being designated under section 43 as a person having the powers of an immigration officer.

(2) The designated person has, in relation to any matter in relation to which powers are exercisable by an immigration officer, the same powers as such an officer would have.

(3) The designated person also has any powers exercisable by virtue of subsection (4).

(4) Any enactment under which an immigration officer may be authorised by warrant to exercise any power in relation to any matter has effect, for the purpose of enabling the designated person to be authorised to exercise the power in relation to any such matter, as if he were an immigration officer.

(5) Subsections (2) to (4) have effect subject to any limitation specified in the designation under section 43(2).

(6) In this section 'immigration officer' means a person who is an immigration officer within the meaning of the Immigration Act 1971 (c. 77).

Exercise of powers

50 Designations: supplementary

(1) If a designated person—
   (a) exercises any power in relation to another person in reliance on his designation under section 43, or
   (b) purports to do so,
   he must produce evidence of his designation to the other person if requested to do so.

(2) A failure to comply with subsection (1) does not make the exercise of the power invalid.

(3) For the purpose of determining liability for the unlawful conduct of members of SOCA's staff, any conduct by a designated person in reliance, or purported reliance, on his designation is to be taken to be—
   (a) if he is employed by SOCA, conduct in the course of his employment, or
   (b) if he is a person to whom section 28 applies by virtue of subsection (3)(a) of that section, conduct falling within subsection (1) of that section.

(4) In this case of any unlawful conduct within subsection (3) which is a tort, SOCA is accordingly to be treated as a joint tortfeasor.
   This subsection does not apply to Scotland.

51 Assaults, obstruction or deception in connection with designations

(1) A person commits an offence if he assaults—
   (a) a designated person acting in the exercise of a relevant power, or
   (b) a person who is assisting a designated person in the exercise of such a power.

(2) A person commits an offence if he resists or wilfully obstructs—
   (a) a designated person acting in the exercise of a relevant power, or
   (b) a person who is assisting a designated person in the exercise of such a power.

(3) A person commits an offence if, with intent to deceive—
   (a) he impersonates a designated person,
   (b) he makes any statement or does any act calculated falsely to suggest that he is a designated person, or
   (c) he makes any statement or does any act calculated falsely to suggest that he has powers as a designated person that exceed the powers he actually has.

(4) A person guilty of an offence under subsection (1) or (3) is liable on summary conviction—
   (a) to imprisonment for a term not exceeding 51 weeks, or
   (b) to a fine not exceeding level 5 on the standard scale, or to both.

(5) A person guilty of an offence under subsection (2) is liable on summary conviction—
   (a) to imprisonment for a term not exceeding 51 weeks, or
   (b) to a fine not exceeding level 3 on the standard scale,
   or to both.

(6) In this section 'relevant power', in relation to a designated person, means a power or privilege exercisable by that person by virtue of the designation under section 43.

(7) In the application of this section to Scotland the references to 51 weeks in subsections (4)(a) and (5)(a) are to be read as references to 12 months in each case.

(8) In the application of this section to Northern Ireland the references to 51 weeks are to be read as follows—

(a) in subsection (4)(a) the reference is to be read as a reference to 6 months, and

(b) in subsection (5)(a) the reference is to be read as a reference to 1 month.

Supplementary

52 Modification of enactments

(1) The Secretary of State may by order provide for any enactment (or description of enactments) to apply in relation to—

(a) designated persons, or

(b) the exercise of powers by such persons under this Chapter,

with such modifications as he considers necessary or expedient.

(2) An order under this section may include provision for or in connection with—

(a) extending to such persons any exemption or protection afforded by an enactment to any other description of persons;

(b) providing for the disclosure of information to, or the doing of other things in relation to, such persons under any enactment;

(c) conferring on the Director General of SOCA functions exercisable in relation to such persons.

(3) Subsection (2) does not affect the generality of subsection (1).

(4) In this section any reference to designated persons includes a reference to any description of such persons.

(5) Before exercising the power conferred by subsection (1) in relation to an enactment which (expressly or otherwise) confers any function on—

(a) the Commissioners for Her Majesty's Revenue and Customs, or

(b) an officer of Revenue and Customs,

the Secretary of State must consult the Commissioners.

(6) Before exercising the power conferred by subsection (1) in relation to an enactment which extends to Scotland, the Secretary of State must consult the Scottish Ministers.

(7) The power conferred by subsection (1) is exercisable by the Scottish Ministers (rather than by the Secretary of State) where the provision to be made is within the legislative competence of the Scottish Parliament.

53 Employment provisions

(1) A member of SOCA's staff who is for the time being designated under section 43 as a person having the powers of a constable is not, by virtue of section 46(2), to be treated as being in police service for the purposes of the enactments mentioned in subsection (2).

(2) The enactments are—

(a) section 280 of the Trade Union and Labour Relations (Consolidation) Act 1992 (c. 52) (person in police service excluded from definitions of 'worker' and 'employee');

(b) section 200 of the Employment Rights Act 1996 (c. 18) (certain provisions of the Act not to apply to persons in police service);

(c) Article 145 of the Trade Union and Labour Relations (Northern Ireland) Order 1995 (S.I. 1995/1980 (N.I. 12)); and

(d) Article 243 of the Employment Rights (Northern Ireland) Order 1996 (S.I. 1996/1919 (N.I. 16)).

54 Interpretation of Chapter 2

(1) In this Chapter—

'designated person' means a person for the time being designated under section 43;

'United Kingdom waters' means the sea and other waters within the seaward limits of the United Kingdom's territorial sea.

(2) Any reference in this Chapter to the exercise of powers by virtue of a designation under section 43 is, in a case where any limitations were imposed under subsection (2) of that section, a reference to their exercise in conformity with those limitations.

CHAPTER 3
SOCA: MISCELLANEOUS AND SUPPLEMENTARY

Complaints and misconduct

55 Complaints and misconduct

(1) Schedule 2 makes provision for, and in connection with, the operation in relation to SOCA of Part 2 of the Police Reform Act 2002 (c. 30) (which relates to complaints and misconduct).

(2) In the Police (Northern Ireland) Act 1998 (c. 32)—

(a) after section 60 insert—

'60ZA Serious Organised Crime Agency

(1) An agreement for the establishment in relation to members of the staff of the Serious Organised Crime Agency of procedures corresponding or similar to any of those established by virtue of this Part may, with the approval of the Secretary of State, be made between the Ombudsman and the Agency.

(2) Where no such procedures are in force in relation to the Agency, the Secretary of State may by order establish such procedures.

(3) An agreement under this section may at any time be varied or terminated with the approval of the Secretary of State.

(4) Before making an order under this section the Secretary of State shall consult—

(a) the Ombudsman; and

(b) the Agency.

(5) Nothing in any other statutory provision shall prevent the Agency from carrying into effect procedures established by virtue of this section.

(6) No such procedures shall have effect in relation to anything done by a member of the staff of the Agency outside Northern Ireland.'; and

(b) in section 61(5) (reports), at the end of paragraph (b) insert'; and

(c) if the report concerns the Serious Organised Crime Agency, to the Agency.'

Application of discrimination legislation

56 Application of discrimination legislation to SOCA seconded staff

(1) For the purposes of the provisions to which this subsection applies any constable or other person who has been seconded to SOCA to serve as a member of its staff shall be treated as being employed by SOCA as respects any act done by it in relation to that person.

(2) Subsection (1) applies to—

    (a) Part 2 of the Sex Discrimination Act 1975 (c. 65);

    (b) Part 2 of the Race Relations Act 1976 (c. 74);

    (c) Part II of the Sex Discrimination (Northern Ireland) Order 1976 (S.I. 1976/1042 (N.I. 15));

    (d) Part 2 of the Disability Discrimination Act 1995 (c. 50);

    (e) Part II of the Race Relations (Northern Ireland) Order 1997 (S.I. 1997/869 (N.I. 6)); and

    (f) the Fair Employment and Treatment (Northern Ireland) Order 1998 (S.I. 1998/3162 (N.I. 21)), except Part VII.

(3) For the purposes of the provisions to which this subsection applies—

    (a) any constable or other person who has been seconded to SOCA to serve as a member of its staff shall be treated as being employed by SOCA (and as not being employed by any other person); and

    (b) anything done by such a person in the performance, or purported performance, of his functions as such a person shall be treated as done in the course of that employment.

(4) Subsection (3) applies to—

    (a) section 41 of the Sex Discrimination Act 1975;

    (b) section 32 of the Race Relations Act 1976;

    (c) Article 42 of the Sex Discrimination (Northern Ireland) Order 1976;

    (d) section 58 of the Disability Discrimination Act 1995;

    (e) Article 32 of the Race Relations (Northern Ireland) Order 1997; and

    (f) Article 36 of the Fair Employment and Treatment (Northern Ireland) Order 1998.

Joint investigation teams

57 Assaults or obstruction in connection with joint investigation teams

(1) This section applies where an international joint investigation team has been formed under the leadership of a member of SOCA's staff.

(2) A person commits an offence if he assaults a member of the team who is carrying out his functions as a member of the team.

(3) A person commits an offence if he resists or wilfully obstructs a member of the team who is carrying out his functions as a member of that team.

(4) A person guilty of an offence under subsection (2) is liable on summary conviction—

    (a) to imprisonment for a term not exceeding 51 weeks, or

    (b) to a fine not exceeding level 5 on the standard scale,

    or to both.

(5) A person guilty of an offence under subsection (3) is liable on summary conviction—

(a) to imprisonment for a term not exceeding 51 weeks, or

(b) to a fine not exceeding level 3 on the standard scale,

or to both.

(6) In this section 'international joint investigation team' means any investigation team formed in accordance with—

(a) any framework decision on joint investigation teams adopted under Article 34 of the Treaty on European Union,

(b) the Convention on Mutual Assistance in Criminal Matters between the Member States of the European Union and the Protocol to that Convention established in accordance with that Article of the Treaty, or

(c) any international agreement to which the United Kingdom is a party and which is specified in an order made by the Secretary of State.

(7) In the application of this section to Scotland the references to 51 weeks in subsections (4)(a) and (5)(a) are to be read as references to 12 months in each case.

(8) In the application of this section to Northern Ireland the references to 51 weeks are to be read as follows—

(a) in subsection (4)(a) the reference is to be read as a reference to 6 months, and

(b) in subsection (5)(a) the reference is to be read as a reference to 1 month.

Transfers

58 Transfers to SOCA

Schedule 3 makes provision about the transfer of staff, property, rights and liabilities to SOCA.

Amendments

59 Minor and consequential amendments relating to SOCA

Schedule 4 contains minor and consequential amendments relating to SOCA.

PART 2

INVESTIGATIONS, PROSECUTIONS, PROCEEDINGS AND PROCEEDS OF CRIME

CHAPTER 1

INVESTIGATORY POWERS OF DPP, ETC.

Introductory

60 Investigatory powers of DPP etc.

(1) This Chapter confers powers on—

(a) the Director of Public Prosecutions,

(b) the Director of Revenue and Customs Prosecutions, and

(c) the Lord Advocate,

in relation to the giving of disclosure notices in connection with the investigation of offences to which this Chapter applies.

(2) T... ...ublic Prosecutions may, to such extent as he may determine,
d... ...se of his powers under this Chapter to a Crown prosecutor.

(3) ... ...evenue and Customs Prosecutions may, to such extent as he
... ...legate the exercise of his powers under this Chapter to a Rev-
e... ...s Prosecutor.

(4) Th... ...ite may, to such extent as he may determine, delegate the exercise... ...under this Chapter to a procurator fiscal.

(5) In thi... ...he Investigating Authority' means—
  (a) the... ...of Public Prosecutions,
  (b) the... ...of Revenue and Customs Prosecutions, or
  (c) the L... ...ocate.

(6) But, in ci... ...ances where the powers of any of those persons are exercisable
by any o... ...rson by virtue of subsection (2), (3) or (4), references to 'the
Investigat... ...thority' accordingly include any such other person.

61 Offences to which this Chapter applies

(1) This Chapter applies to the following offences—
  (a) any offence listed in Schedule 2 to the Proceeds of Crime Act 2002 (c. 29) (lifestyle offences: England and Wales);
  (b) any offence listed in Schedule 4 to that Act (lifestyle offences: Scotland);
  (c) any offence under sections 15 to 18 of the Terrorism Act 2000 (c. 11) (offences relating to fund-raising, money laundering etc.);
  (d) any offence under section 170 of the Customs and Excise Management Act 1979 (c. 2) (fraudulent evasion of duty) or section 72 of the Value Added Tax Act 1994 (c. 23) (offences relating to VAT) which is a qualifying offence;
  (e) any offence under section 17 of the Theft Act 1968 (c. 60) (false accounting), or any offence at common law of cheating in relation to the public revenue, which is a qualifying offence;
  (f) any offence under section 1 of the Criminal Attempts Act 1981 (c. 47), or in Scotland at common law, of attempting to commit any offence in paragraph (c) or any offence in paragraph (d) or (e) which is a qualifying offence;
  (g) any offence under section 1 of the Criminal Law Act 1977 (c. 45), or in Scotland at common law, of conspiracy to commit any offence in paragraph (c) or any offence in paragraph (d) or (e) which is a qualifying offence.

(2) For the purposes of subsection (1) an offence in paragraph (d) or (e) of that subsection is a qualifying offence if the Investigating Authority certifies that in his opinion—
  (a) in the case of an offence in paragraph (d) or an offence of cheating the public revenue, the offence involved or would have involved a loss, or potential loss, to the public revenue of an amount not less than £5,000;
  (b) in the case of an offence under section 17 of the Theft Act 1968 (c. 60), the offence involved or would have involved a loss or gain, or potential loss or gain, of an amount not less than £5,000.

(3) A document purporting to be a certificate under subsection (2) is to be received in evidence and treated as such a certificate unless the contrary is proved.

(4) The Secretary of State may by order—
  (a) amend subsection (1), in its application to England and Wales, so as to remove an offence from it or add an offence to it;

    (b) amend subsection (2), in its application to England and Wales, so as to—
        (i) take account of any amendment made by virtue of paragraph (a) above, or
        (ii) vary the sums for the time being specified in subsection (2)(a) and (b).
(5) The Scottish Ministers may be order—
    (a) amend subsection (1), in its application to Scotland, so as to remove an offence from it or add an offence to it;
    (b) amend subsection (2), in its application to Scotland, so as to—
        (i) take account of any amendment made by virtue of paragraph (a) above, or
        (ii) vary the sums for the time being specified in subsection (2)(a) and (b).

Disclosure notices

62 Disclosure notices

(1) If it appears to the Investigating Authority—
    (a) that there are reasonable grounds for suspecting that an offence to which this Chapter applies has been committed,
    (b) that any person has information (whether or not contained in a document) which relates to a matter relevant to the investigation of that offence, and
    (c) that there are reasonable grounds for believing that information which may be provided by that person in compliance with a disclosure notice is likely to be of substantial value (whether or not by itself) to that investigation,
he may give, or authorise an appropriate person to give, a disclosure notice to that person.
(2) In this Chapter 'appropriate person' means—
    (a) a constable,
    (b) a member of the staff of SOCA who is for the time being designated under section 43, or
    (c) an officer of Revenue and Customs.
(3) In this Chapter 'disclosure notice' means a notice in writing requiring the person to whom it is given to do all or any of the following things in accordance with the specified requirements, namely—
    (a) answer questions with respect to any matter relevant to the investigation;
    (b) provide information with respect to any such matter as is specified in the notice;
    (c) produce such documents, or documents of such descriptions, relevant to the investigation as are specified in the notice.
(4) In subsection (3) 'the specified requirements' means such requirements specified in the disclosure notice as relate to—
    (a) the time at or by which,
    (b) the place at which, or
    (c) the manner in which,
the person to whom the notice is given is to do any of the things mentioned in paragraphs (a) to (c) of that subsection; and those requirements may include a requirement to do any of those things at once.
(5) A disclosure notice must be signed or counter-signed by the Investigating Authority.

(6) This section has effect subject to section 64 (restrictions on requiring information etc.).

63 Production of documents

(1) This section applies where a disclosure notice has been given under section 62.
(2) An authorised person may—
  (a) take copies of or extracts from any documents produced in compliance with the notice, and
  (b) require the person producing them to provide an explanation of any of them.
(3) Documents so produced may be retained for so long as the Investigating Authority considers that it is necessary to retain them (rather than copies of them) in connection with the investigation for the purposes of which the disclosure notice was given.
(4) If the Investigating Authority has reasonable grounds for believing—
  (a) that any such documents may have to be produced for the purposes of any legal proceedings, and
  (b) that they might otherwise be unavailable for those purposes,
  they may be retained until the proceedings are concluded.
(5) If a person who is required by a disclosure notice to produce any documents does not produce the documents in compliance with the notice, an authorised person may require that person to state, to the best of his knowledge and belief, where they are.
(6) In this section 'authorised person' means any appropriate person who either—
  (a) is the person by whom the notice was given, or
  (b) is authorised by the Investigating Authority for the purposes of this section.
(7) This section has effect subject to section 64 (restrictions on requiring information etc.).

64 Restrictions on requiring information etc.

(1) A person may not be required under section 62 or 63—
  (a) to answer any privileged question,
  (b) to provide any privileged information, or
  (c) to produce any privileged document,
  except that a lawyer may be required to provide the name and address of a client of his.
(2) A 'privileged question' is a question which the person would be entitled to refuse to answer on grounds of legal professional privilege in proceedings in the High Court.
(3) 'Privileged information' is information which the person would be entitled to refuse to provide on grounds of legal professional privilege in such proceedings.
(4) A 'privileged document' is a document which the person would be entitled to refuse to produce on grounds of legal professional privilege in such proceedings.
(5) A person may not be required under section 62 to produce any excluded material (as defined by section 11 of the Police and Criminal Evidence Act 1984 (c. 60)).
(6) In the application of this section to Scotland—
  (a) subsections (1) to (5) do not have effect, but

(b) a person may not be required under section 62 or 63 to answer any question, provide any information or produce any document which he would be entitled, on grounds of legal privilege, to refuse to answer or (as the case may be) provide or produce.

(7) In subsection (6)(b), 'legal privilege' has the meaning given by section 412 of the Proceeds of Crime Act 2002 (c. 29).

(8) A person may not be required under section 62 or 63 to disclose any information or produce any document in respect of which he owes an obligation of confidence by virtue of carrying on any banking business, unless—

    (a) the person to whom the obligation of confidence is owed consents to the disclosure or production, or

    (b) the requirement is made by, or in accordance with a specific authorisation given by, the Investigating Authority.

(9) Subject to the preceding provisions, any requirement under section 62 or 63 has effect despite any restriction on disclosure (however imposed).

65 Restrictions on use of statements

(1) A statement made by a person in response to a requirement imposed under section 62 or 63 ('the relevant statement') may not be used in evidence against him in any criminal proceedings unless subsection (2) or (3) applies.

(2) This subsection applies where the person is being prosecuted—

    (a) for an offence under section 67 of this Act, or

    (b) for an offence under section 5 of the Perjury Act 1911 (c. 6) (false statements made on oath otherwise than in judicial proceedings or made otherwise than on oath), or

    (c) for an offence under section 2 of the False Oaths (Scotland) Act 1933 (c. 20) (false statutory declarations and other false statements without oath) or at common law for an offence of attempting to pervert the course, or defeat the ends, of justice.

(3) This subsection applies where the person is being prosecuted for some other offence and—

    (a) the person, when giving evidence in the proceedings, makes a statement inconsistent with the relevant statement, and

    (b) in the proceedings evidence relating to the relevant statement is adduced, or a question about it is asked, by or on behalf of the person.

Enforcement

66 Power to enter and seize documents

(1) A justice of the peace may issue a warrant under this section if, on an information on oath laid by the Investigating Authority, he is satisfied—

    (a) that any of the conditions mentioned in subsection (2) is met in relation to any documents of a description specified in the information, and

    (b) that the documents are on premises so specified.

(2) The conditions are—

    (a) that a person has been required by a disclosure notice to produce the documents but has not done so;

    (b) that it is not practicable to give a disclosure notice requiring their production;

    (c) that giving such a notice might seriously prejudice the investigation of an offence to which this Chapter applies.

(3) A warrant under this section is a warrant authorising an appropriate person named in it—

    (a) to enter and search the premises, using such force as is reasonably necessary;

    (b) to take possession of any documents appearing to be documents of a description specified in the information, or to take any other steps which appear to be necessary for preserving, or preventing interference with, any such documents;

    (c) in the case of any such documents consisting of information recorded otherwise than in legible form, to take possession of any computer disk or other electronic storage device which appears to contain the information in question, or to take any other steps which appear to be necessary for preserving, or preventing interference with, that information;

    (d) to take copies of or extracts from any documents or information falling within paragraph (b) or (c);

    (e) to require any person on the premises to provide an explanation of any such documents or information or to state where any such documents or information may be found;

    (f) to require any such person to give the appropriate person such assistance as he may reasonably require for the taking of copies or extracts as mentioned in paragraph (d).

(4) A person executing a warrant under this section may take other persons with him, if it appears to him to be necessary to do so.

(5) A warrant under this section must, if so required, be produced for inspection by the owner or occupier of the premises or anyone acting on his behalf.

(6) If the premises are unoccupied or the occupier is temporarily absent, a person entering the premises under the authority of a warrant under this section must leave the premises as effectively secured against trespassers as he found them.

(7) Where possession of any document or device is taken under this section—

    (a) the document may be retained for so long as the Investigating Authority considers that it is necessary to retain it (rather than a copy of it) in connection with the investigation for the purposes of which the warrant was sought, or

    (b) the device may be retained for so long as he considers that it is necessary to retain it in connection with that investigation,

as the case may be.

(8) If the Investigating Authority has reasonable grounds for believing—

    (a) that any such document or device may have to be produced for the purposes of any legal proceedings, and

    (b) that it might otherwise be unavailable for those purposes,

it may be retained until the proceedings are concluded.

(9) Nothing in this section authorises a person to take possession of, or make copies of or take extracts from, any document or information which, by virtue of section 64, could not be required to be produced or disclosed under section 62 or 63.

(10) In the application of this section to Scotland—

(a) subsection (1) has effect as if, for the words from the beginning to 'satisfied-', there were substituted 'A sheriff may issue a warrant under this section, on the application of a procurator fiscal, if he is satisfied—';

(b) subsections (1)(a) and (3)(b) have effect as if, for 'in the information', there were substituted 'in the application'; and

(c) subsections (4) to (6) do not have effect.

67 Offences in connection with disclosure notices or search warrants

(1) A person commits an offence if, without reasonable excuse, he fails to comply with any requirement imposed on him under section 62 or 63.

(2) A person commits an offence if, in purported compliance with any requirement imposed on him under section 62 or 63—

(a) he makes a statement which is false or misleading, and

(b) he either knows that it is false or misleading or is reckless as to whether it is false or misleading.

'False or misleading' means false or misleading in a material particular.

(3) A person commits an offence if he wilfully obstructs any person in the exercise of any rights conferred by a warrant under section 66.

(4) A person guilty of an offence under subsection (1) or (3) is liable on summary conviction—

(a) to imprisonment for a term not exceeding 51 weeks, or

(b) to a fine not exceeding level 5 on the standard scale,

or to both.

(5) A person guilty of an offence under subsection (2) is liable—

(a) on conviction on indictment, to imprisonment for a term not exceeding two years or to a fine, or to both;

(b) on summary conviction, to imprisonment for a term not exceeding 12 months or to a fine not exceeding the statutory maximum, or to both.

(6) In the application of this section to Scotland, the reference to 51 weeks in subsection (4)(a) is to be read as a reference to 12 months.

Supplementary

68 Procedure applicable to search warrants

In Part 1 of Schedule 1 to the Criminal Justice and Police Act 2001 (c. 16) (powers of seizure to which section 50 applies) after paragraph 73E (inserted by the Human Tissue Act 2004 (c. 30)) insert—

'73F *Serious Organised Crime and Police Act 2005*

The power of seizure conferred by section 66 of the Serious Organised Crime and Police Act 2005 (seizure of documents for purposes of investigation by DPP or other Investigating Authority).'

69 Manner in which disclosure notice may be given

(1) This section provides for the manner in which a disclosure notice may be given under section 62.

(2) The notice may be given to a person by—

(a) delivering it to him,

     (b) leaving it at his proper address,

     (c) sending it by post to him at that address.

(3) The notice may be given—

     (a) in the case of a body corporate, to the secretary or clerk of that body;

     (b) in the case of a partnership, to a partner or a person having the control or management of the partnership business;

     (c) in the case of an unincorporated association (other than a partnership), to an officer of the association.

(4) For the purposes of this section and section 7 of the Interpretation Act 1978 (c. 30) (service of documents by post) in its application to this section, the proper address of a person is his usual or last-known address (whether residential or otherwise), except that—

     (a) in the case of a body corporate or its secretary or clerk, it is the address of the registered office of that body or its principal office in the United Kingdom,

     (b) in the case of a partnership, a partner or a person having the control or management of the partnership business, it is that of the principal office of the partnership in the United Kingdom, and

     (c) in the case of an unincorporated association (other than a partnership) or an officer of the association, it is that of the principal office of the association in the United Kingdom.

(5) This section does not apply to Scotland.

70 Interpretation of Chapter 1

(1) In this Chapter—

'appropriate person' has the meaning given by section 62(2);

'the Investigating Authority' is to be construed in accordance with section 60(5) and (6);

'disclosure notice' has the meaning given by section 62(3);

'document' includes information recorded otherwise than in legible form.

(2) In relation to information recorded otherwise than in legible form, any reference in this Chapter to the production of documents is a reference to the production of a copy of the information in legible form.

CHAPTER 2
OFFENDERS ASSISTING INVESTIGATIONS AND PROSECUTIONS

71 Assistance by offender: immunity from prosecution

(1) If a specified prosecutor thinks that for the purposes of the investigation or prosecution of any offence it is appropriate to offer any person immunity from prosecution he may give the person a written notice under this subsection (an 'immunity notice').

(2) If a person is given an immunity notice, no proceedings for an offence of a description specified in the notice may be brought against that person in England and Wales or Northern Ireland except in circumstances specified in the notice.

(3) An immunity notice ceases to have effect in relation to the person to whom it is given if the person fails to comply with any conditions specified in the notice.

(4) Each of the following is a specified prosecutor—
  (a) the Director of Public Prosecutions;
  (b) the Director of Revenue and Customs Prosecutions;
  (c) the Director of the Serious Fraud Office;
  (d) the Director of Public Prosecutions for Northern Ireland;
  (e) a prosecutor designated for the purposes of this section by a prosecutor mentioned in paragraphs (a) to (d).

(5) The Director of Public Prosecutions or a person designated by him under subsection (4)(e) may not give an immunity notice in relation to proceedings in Northern Ireland.

(6) The Director of Public Prosecutions for Northern Ireland or a person designated by him under subsection (4)(e) may not give an immunity notice in relation to proceedings in England and Wales.

(7) An immunity notice must not be given in relation to an offence under section 188 of the Enterprise Act 2002 (c. 40) (cartel offences).

72 Assistance by offender: undertakings as to use of evidence

(1) If a specified prosecutor thinks that for the purposes of the investigation or prosecution of any offence it is appropriate to offer any person an undertaking that information of any description will not be used against the person in any proceedings to which this section applies he may give the person a written notice under this subsection (a 'restricted use undertaking').

(2) This section applies to—
  (a) criminal proceedings;
  (b) proceedings under Part 5 of the Proceeds of Crime Act 2002 (c. 29).

(3) If a person is given a restricted use undertaking the information described in the undertaking must not be used against that person in any proceedings to which this section applies brought in England and Wales or Northern Ireland except in the circumstances specified in the undertaking.

(4) A restricted use undertaking ceases to have effect in relation to the person to whom it is given if the person fails to comply with any conditions specified in the undertaking.

(5) The Director of Public Prosecutions for Northern Ireland or a person designated by him under section 71(4)(e) may not give a restricted use undertaking in relation to proceedings in England and Wales.

(6) The Director of Public Prosecutions or a person designated by him under section 71(4)(e) may not give a restricted use undertaking in relation to proceedings in Northern Ireland.

(7) Specified prosecutor must be construed in accordance with section 71(4).

73 Assistance by defendant: reduction in sentence

(1) This section applies if a defendant—
  (a) following a plea of guilty is either convicted of an offence in proceedings in the Crown Court or is committed to the Crown Court for sentence, and
  (b) has, pursuant to a written agreement made with a specified prosecutor, assisted or offered to assist the investigator or prosecutor in relation to that or any other offence.

(2) In determining what sentence to pass on the defendant the court may take into account the extent and nature of the assistance given or offered.

(3) If the court passes a sentence which is less than it would have passed but for the assistance given or offered, it must state in open court—

(a) that it has passed a lesser sentence than it would otherwise have passed, and

(b) what the greater sentence would have been.

(4) Subsection (3) does not apply if the court thinks that it would not be in the public interest to disclose that the sentence has been discounted; but in such a case the court must give written notice of the matters specified in paragraphs (a) and (b) of subsection (3) to both the prosecutor and the defendant.

(5) Nothing in any enactment which—

(a) requires that a minimum sentence is passed in respect of any offence or an offence of any description or by reference to the circumstances of any offender (whether or not the enactment also permits the court to pass a lesser sentence in particular circumstances), or

(b) in the case of a sentence which is fixed by law, requires the court to take into account certain matters for the purposes of making an order which determines or has the effect of determining the minimum period of imprisonment which the offender must serve (whether or not the enactment also permits the court to fix a lesser period in particular circumstances),

affects the power of a court to act under subsection (2).

(6) If, in determining what sentence to pass on the defendant, the court takes into account the extent and nature of the assistance given or offered as mentioned in subsection (2), that does not prevent the court from also taking account of any other matter which it is entitled by virtue of any other enactment to take account of for the purposes of determining—

(a) the sentence, or

(b) in the case of a sentence which is fixed by law, any minimum period of imprisonment which an offender must serve.

(7) If subsection (3) above does not apply by virtue of subsection (4) above, sections 174(1)(a) and 270 of the Criminal Justice Act 2003 (c. 44) (requirement to explain reasons for sentence or other order) do not apply to the extent that the explanation will disclose that a sentence has been discounted in pursuance of this section.

(8) In this section—

(a) a reference to a sentence includes, in the case of a sentence which is fixed by law, a reference to the minimum period an offender is required to serve, and a reference to a lesser sentence must be construed accordingly;

(b) a reference to imprisonment includes a reference to any other custodial sentence within the meaning of section 76 of the Powers of Criminal Courts (Sentencing) Act 2000 (c. 6) or Article 2 of the Criminal Justice (Northern Ireland) Order 1996 (S.I. 1996/3160).

(9) An agreement with a specified prosecutor may provide for assistance to be given to that prosecutor or to any other prosecutor.

(10) References to a specified prosecutor must be construed in accordance with section 71.

74 Assistance by defendant: review of sentence

(1) This section applies if—
   (a) the Crown Court has passed a sentence on a person in respect of an offence, and
   (b) the person falls within subsection (2).

(2) A person falls within this subsection if—
   (a) he receives a discounted sentence in consequence of his having offered in pursuance of a written agreement to give assistance to the prosecutor or investigator of an offence but he knowingly fails to any extent to give assistance in accordance with the agreement;
   (b) he receives a discounted sentence in consequence of his having offered in pursuance of a written agreement to give assistance to the prosecutor or investigator of an offence and, having given the assistance in accordance with the agreement, in pursuance of another written agreement gives or offers to give further assistance;
   (c) he receives a sentence which is not discounted but in pursuance of a written agreement he subsequently gives or offers to give assistance to the prosecutor or investigator of an offence.

(3) A specified prosecutor may at any time refer the case back to the court by which the sentence was passed if—
   (a) the person is still serving his sentence, and
   (b) the specified prosecutor thinks it is in the interests of justice to do so.

(4) A case so referred must, if possible, be heard by the judge who passed the sentence to which the referral relates.

(5) If the court is satisfied that a person who falls within subsection (2)(a) knowingly failed to give the assistance it may substitute for the sentence to which the referral relates such greater sentence (not exceeding that which it would have passed but for the agreement to give assistance) as it thinks appropriate.

(6) In a case of a person who falls within subsection (2)(b) or (c) the court may—
   (a) take into account the extent and nature of the assistance given or offered;
   (b) substitute for the sentence to which the referral relates such lesser sentence as it thinks appropriate.

(7) Any part of the sentence to which the referral relates which the person has already served must be taken into account in determining when a greater or lesser sentence imposed by subsection (5) or (6) has been served.

(8) A person in respect of whom a reference is made under this section and the specified prosecutor may with the leave of the Court of Appeal appeal to the Court of Appeal against the decision of the Crown Court.

(9) Section 33(3) of the Criminal Appeal Act 1968 (c. 19) (limitation on appeal from the criminal division of the Court of Appeal) does not prevent an appeal to the Supreme Court under this section.

(10) A discounted sentence is a sentence passed in pursuance of section 73 or subsection (6) above.

(11) References—
   (a) to a written agreement are to an agreement made in writing with a specified prosecutor;
   (b) to a specified prosecutor must be construed in accordance with section 71.

(12) In relation to any proceedings under this section, the Secretary of State may make an order containing provision corresponding to any provision in—
  (a) the Criminal Appeal Act 1968 (subject to any specified modifications), or
  (b) the Criminal Appeal (Northern Ireland) Act 1980 (c. 47) (subject to any specified modifications).

(13) A person does not fall within subsection (2) if—
  (a) he was convicted of an offence for which the sentence is fixed by law, and
  (b) he did not plead guilty to the offence for which he was sentenced.

(14) Section 174(1)(a) or 270 of the Criminal Justice Act 2003 (c. 44) (as the case may be) applies to a sentence substituted under subsection (5) above unless the court thinks that it is not in the public interest to disclose that the person falls within subsection (2)(a) above.

(15) Subsections (3) to (9) of section 73 apply for the purposes of this section as they apply for the purposes of that section and any reference in those subsections to subsection (2) of that section must be construed as a reference to subsection (6) of this section.

75 Proceedings under section 74: exclusion of public

(1) This section applies to—
  (a) any proceedings relating to a reference made under section 74(3), and
  (b) any other proceedings arising in consequence of such proceedings.

(2) The court in which the proceedings will be or are being heard may make such order as it thinks appropriate—
  (a) to exclude from the proceedings any person who does not fall within subsection (4);
  (b) to give such directions as it thinks appropriate prohibiting the publication of any matter relating to the proceedings (including the fact that the reference has been made).

(3) An order under subsection (2) may be made only to the extent that the court thinks—
  (a) that it is necessary to do so to protect the safety of any person, and
  (b) that it is in the interests of justice.

(4) The following persons fall within this subsection—
  (a) a member or officer of the court;
  (b) a party to the proceedings;
  (c) counsel or a solicitor for a party to the proceedings;
  (d) a person otherwise directly concerned with the proceedings.

(5) This section does not affect any other power which the court has by virtue of any rule of law or other enactment—
  (a) to exclude any person from proceedings, or
  (b) to restrict the publication of any matter relating to proceedings.

CHAPTER 3
FINANCIAL REPORTING ORDERS

76 Financial reporting orders: making

(1) A court sentencing or otherwise dealing with a person convicted of an offence

mentioned in subsection (3) may also make a financial reporting order in respect of him.

(2) But it may do so only if it is satisfied that the risk of the person's committing another offence mentioned in subsection (3) is sufficiently high to justify the making of a financial reporting order.

(3) The offences are—

    (a) an offence under any of the following provisions of the Theft Act 1968 (c. 60)—

        section 15 (obtaining property by deception),

        section 15A (obtaining a money transfer by deception),

        section 16 (obtaining a pecuniary advantage by deception),

        section 20(2) (procuring execution of valuable security, etc.),

    (b) an offence under either of the following provisions of the Theft Act 1978 (c. 31)—

    section 1 (obtaining services by deception),

    section 2 (evasion of liability by deception),

    (c) any offence specified in Schedule 2 to the Proceeds of Crime Act 2002 (c. 29) ('lifestyle offences').

(4) The Secretary of State may by order amend subsection (3) so as to remove an offence from it or add an offence to it.

(5) A financial reporting order—

    (a) comes into force when it is made, and

    (b) has effect for the period specified in the order, beginning with the date on which it is made.

(6) If the order is made by a magistrates' court, the period referred to in subsection (5)(b) must not exceed 5 years.

(7) Otherwise, that period must not exceed—

    (a) if the person is sentenced to imprisonment for life, 20 years,

    (b) otherwise, 15 years.

77 Financial reporting orders: making in Scotland

(1) A court sentencing or otherwise dealing with a person convicted of an offence mentioned in subsection (3) may also make a financial reporting order in respect of him.

(2) But he or it may do so only if satisfied that the risk of the person's committing another offence mentioned in subsection (3) is sufficiently high to justify the making of a financial reporting order.

(3) The offences are—

    (a) at common law, the offence of fraud,

    (b) any offence specified in Schedule 4 to the Proceeds of Crime Act 2002 (c. 29) ('lifestyle offences': Scotland).

(4) The Scottish Ministers may by order amend subsection (3) so as to remove an offence from it or add an offence to it.

(5) A financial reporting order—

    (a) comes into force when it is made, and

    (b) has effect for the period specified in the order, beginning with the date on which it is made.

(6) If the order is made by the sheriff, the period referred to in subsection (5)(b) must not exceed 5 years.

(7) If the order is made by the High Court of Justiciary, that period must not exceed—

(a) if the person is sentenced to imprisonment for life, 20 years,

(b) otherwise, 15 years.

78 Financial reporting orders: making in Northern Ireland

(1) A court sentencing or otherwise dealing with a person convicted of an offence mentioned in subsection (3) may also make a financial reporting order in respect of him.

(2) But the court may do so only if it is satisfied that the risk of the person's committing another offence mentioned in subsection (3) is sufficiently high to justify the making of a financial reporting order.

(3) The offences are—

(a) an offence under any of the following provisions of the Theft Act (Northern Ireland) 1969 (c. 16 (N.I.))—

section 15 (obtaining property by deception),
section 15A (obtaining a money transfer by deception),
section 16 (obtaining a pecuniary advantage by deception),
section 19(2) (procuring execution of valuable security, etc.),

(b) an offence under either of the following provisions of the Theft (Northern Ireland) Order 1978 (S.I. 1978/1407 (N.I. 23))—

Article 3 (obtaining services by deception),

Article 4 (evasion of liability by deception)

(c) any offence specified in Schedule 5 to the Proceeds of Crime Act 2002 ('life-style offences': Northern Ireland).

(4) A financial reporting order—

(a) comes into force when it is made, and

(b) has effect for the period specified in the order, beginning with the date on which it is made.

(5) If the order is made by a magistrates' court, or by the county court on appeal, the period referred to in subsection (4)(b) must not exceed 5 years.

(6) Otherwise, that period must not exceed—

(a) if the person is sentenced to imprisonment for life, 20 years,

(b) otherwise, 15 years.

79 Financial reporting orders: effect

(1) A person in relation to whom a financial reporting order has effect must do the following.

(2) He must make a report, in respect of—

(a) the period of a specified length beginning with the date on which the order comes into force, and

(b) subsequent periods of specified lengths, each period beginning immediately after the end of the previous one.

(3) He must set out in each report, in the specified manner, such particulars of his financial affairs relating to the period in question as may be specified.

(4) He must include any specified documents with each report.

(5) He must make each report within the specified number of days after the end of the period in question.

(6) He must make each report to the specified person.

(7) Rules of court may provide for the maximum length of the periods which may be specified under subsection (2).

(8) In this section, 'specified' means specified by the court in the order.

(9) In Scotland the specified person must be selected by the court from a list set out in an order made for the purposes of this section by the Scottish Ministers.

(10) A person who without reasonable excuse includes false or misleading information in a report, or otherwise fails to comply with any requirement of this section, is guilty of an offence and is liable on summary conviction to—

    (a) imprisonment for a term not exceeding—

        (i) in England and Wales, 51 weeks,

        (ii) in Scotland, 12 months,

        (iii) in Northern Ireland, 6 months, or

    (b) a fine not exceeding level 5 on the standard scale,

    or to both.

80 Financial reporting orders: variation and revocation

(1) An application for variation or revocation of a financial reporting order may be made by—

    (a) the person in respect of whom it has been made,

    (b) the person to whom reports are to be made under it (see section 79(6)).

(2) The application must be made to the court which made the order.

(3) But if the order was made on appeal, the application must be made to the court which originally sentenced the person in respect of whom the order was made.

(4) If (in either case) that court was a magistrates' court, the application may be made to any magistrates' court acting in the same local justice area (or in Northern Ireland for the same county court division) as that court.

(5) Subsections (3) and (4) do not apply to Scotland.

81 Financial reporting orders: verification and disclosure

(1) In this section, 'the specified person' means the person to whom reports under a financial reporting order are to be made.

(2) The specified person may, for the purpose of doing either of the things mentioned in subsection (4), disclose a report to any person who he reasonably believes may be able to contribute to doing either of those things.

(3) Any other person may disclose information to—

    (a) the specified person, or

    (b) a person to whom the specified person has disclosed a report,

    for the purpose of contributing to doing either of the things mentioned in subsection (4).

(4) The things mentioned in subsections (2) and (3) are—

    (a) checking the accuracy of the report or of any other report made pursuant to the same order,

    (b) discovering the true position.

(5) The specified person may also disclose a report for the purposes of—
    (a) the prevention, detection, investigation or prosecution of criminal offences, whether in the United Kingdom or elsewhere,
    (b) the prevention, detection or investigation of conduct for which penalties other than criminal penalties are provided under the law of any part of the United Kingdom or of any country or territory outside the United Kingdom.

(6) A disclosure under this section does not breach—
    (a) any obligation of confidence owed by the person making the disclosure, or
    (b) any other restriction on the disclosure of information (however imposed).

(7) But nothing in this section authorises a disclosure, in contravention of any provisions of the Data Protection Act 1998 (c. 29), of personal data which are not exempt from those provisions.

(8) In this section, references to a report include any of its contents, any document included with the report, or any of the contents of such a document.

CHAPTER 4
PROTECTION OF WITNESSES AND OTHER PERSONS

82 Protection of persons involved in investigations or proceedings

(1) A protection provider may make such arrangements as he considers appropriate for the purpose of protecting a person of a description specified in Schedule 5 if—
    (a) the protection provider considers that the person's safety is at risk by virtue of his being a person of a description so specified, and
    (b) the person is ordinarily resident in the United Kingdom.

(2) A protection provider may vary or cancel any arrangements made by him under subsection (1) if he considers it appropriate to do so.

(3) If a protection provider makes arrangements under subsection (1) or cancels arrangements made under that subsection, he must record that he has done so.

(4) In determining whether to make arrangements under subsection (1), or to vary or cancel arrangements made under that subsection, a protection provider must, in particular, have regard to—
    (a) the nature and extent of the risk to the person's safety,
    (b) the cost of the arrangements,
    (c) the likelihood that the person, and any person associated with him, will be able to adjust to any change in their circumstances which may arise from the making of the arrangements or from their variation or cancellation (as the case may be), and
    (d) if the person is or might be a witness in legal proceedings (whether or not in the United Kingdom), the nature of the proceedings and the importance of his being a witness in those proceedings.

(5) A protection provider is—
    (a) a chief officer of a police force in England and Wales;
    (b) a chief constable of a police force in Scotland;
    (c) the Chief Constable of the Police Service of Northern Ireland;
    (d) the Director General of SOCA;

    (e) any of the Commissioners for Her Majesty's Revenue and Customs;

    (f) the Director of the Scottish Drug Enforcement Agency;

    (g) a person designated by a person mentioned in any of the preceding paragraphs to exercise his functions under this section.

(6) The Secretary of State may, after consulting the Scottish Ministers, by order amend Schedule 5 so as to add, modify or omit any entry.

(7) Nothing in this section affects any power which a person has (otherwise than by virtue of this section) to make arrangements for the protection of another person.

83 Joint arrangements

(1) Arrangements may be made under section 82(1) by two or more protection providers acting jointly.

(2) If arrangements are made jointly by virtue of subsection (1), any powers conferred on a protection provider by this Chapter are exercisable in relation to the arrangements by—

    (a) all of the protection providers acting together, or

    (b) one of the protection providers, or some of the protection providers acting together, with the agreement of the others.

(3) Nothing in this section or in section 84 affects any power which a protection provider has to request or obtain assistance from another protection provider.

84 Transfer of responsibility to other protection provider

(1) A protection provider who makes arrangements under section 82(1) may agree with another protection provider that, as from a date specified in the agreement—

    (a) the protection provider will cease to discharge any responsibilities which he has in relation to the arrangements, and

    (b) the other protection provider will discharge those responsibilities instead.

(2) Any such agreement may include provision for the making of payments in respect of any costs incurred or likely to be incurred in consequence of the agreement.

(3) If an agreement is made under subsection (1), any powers conferred on a protection provider by this Chapter (including the power conferred by subsection (1)) are, as from the date specified in the agreement, exercisable by the other protection provider as if he had made the arrangements under section 82(1).

(4) Each protection provider who makes an agreement under subsection (1) must record that he has done so.

85 Duty to assist protection providers

(1) This section applies if a protection provider requests assistance from a public authority in connection with the making of arrangements under section 82(1) or the implementation, variation or cancellation of such arrangements.

(2) The public authority must take reasonable steps to provide the assistance requested.

(3) 'Public authority' includes any person certain of whose functions are of a public nature but does not include—

    (a) a court or tribunal,

    (b) either House of Parliament or a person exercising functions in connection with proceedings in Parliament, or

    (c) the Scottish Parliament or a person exercising functions in connection with proceedings in the Scottish Parliament.

86 Offence of disclosing information about protection arrangements

(1) A person commits an offence if—

    (a) he discloses information which relates to the making of arrangements under section 82(1) or to the implementation, variation or cancellation of such arrangements, and

    (b) he knows or suspects that the information relates to the making of such arrangements or to their implementation, variation or cancellation.

(2) A person who commits an offence under this section is liable—

    (a) on conviction on indictment, to imprisonment for a term not exceeding two years, to a fine or to both;

    (b) on summary conviction, to imprisonment for a term not exceeding 12 months, to a fine not exceeding the statutory maximum or to both.

(3) In the application of this section to Scotland or Northern Ireland, the reference in subsection (2)(b) to 12 months is to be read as a reference to 6 months.

87 Defences to liability under section 86

(1) A person (P) is not guilty of an offence under section 86 if—

    (a) at the time when P disclosed the information, he was or had been a protected person,

    (b) the information related only to arrangements made for the protection of P or for the protection of P and a person associated with him, and

    (c) at the time when P disclosed the information, it was not likely that its disclosure would endanger the safety of any person.

(2) A person (D) is not guilty of an offence under section 86 if—

    (a) D disclosed the information with the agreement of a person (P) who, at the time the information was disclosed, was or had been a protected person,

    (b) the information related only to arrangements made for the protection of P or for the protection of P and a person associated with him, and

    (c) at the time when D disclosed the information, it was not likely that its disclosure would endanger the safety of any person.

(3) A person is not guilty of an offence under section 86 if he disclosed the information for the purposes of safeguarding national security or for the purposes of the prevention, detection or investigation of crime.

(4) A person is not guilty of an offence under section 86 if—

    (a) at the time when he disclosed the information, he was a protection provider or involved in the making of arrangements under section 82(1) or in the implementation, variation or cancellation of such arrangements, and

    (b) he disclosed the information for the purposes of the making, implementation, variation or cancellation of such arrangements.

(5) The Secretary of State may by order make provision prescribing circumstances in which a person who discloses information as mentioned in section 86(1) is not

guilty in England and Wales or in Northern Ireland of an offence under that section.

(6) The Scottish Ministers may by order make provision prescribing circumstances in which a person who discloses information as mentioned in section 86(1) is not guilty in Scotland of an offence under that section.

(7) If sufficient evidence is adduced to raise an issue with respect to a defence under or by virtue of this section, the court or jury must assume that the defence is satisfied unless the prosecution proves beyond reasonable doubt that it is not.

88 Offences of disclosing information relating to persons assuming new identity

(1) A person (P) commits an offence if—
   (a) P is or has been a protected person,
   (b) P assumed a new identity in pursuance of arrangements made under section 82(1),
   (c) P discloses information which indicates that he assumed, or might have assumed, a new identity, and
   (d) P knows or suspects that the information disclosed by him indicates that he assumed, or might have assumed, a new identity.

(2) A person (D) commits an offence if—
   (a) D discloses information which relates to a person (P) who is or has been a protected person,
   (b) P assumed a new identity in pursuance of arrangements made under section 82(1),
   (c) the information disclosed by D indicates that P assumed, or might have assumed, a new identity, and
   (d) D knows or suspects—
      (i) that P is or has been a protected person, and
      (ii) that the information disclosed by D indicates that P assumed, or might have assumed, a new identity.

(3) A person who commits an offence under this section is liable—
   (a) on conviction on indictment, to imprisonment for a term not exceeding two years, to a fine or to both;
   (b) on summary conviction, to imprisonment for a term not exceeding 12 months, to a fine not exceeding the statutory maximum or to both.

(4) In the application of this section to Scotland or Northern Ireland, the reference in subsection (3)(b) to 12 months is to be read as a reference to 6 months.

89 Defences to liability under section 88

(1) P is not guilty of an offence under section 88(1) if, at the time when he disclosed the information, it was not likely that its disclosure would endanger the safety of any person.

(2) D is not guilty of an offence under section 88(2) if—
   (a) D disclosed the information with the agreement of P, and
   (b) at the time when D disclosed the information, it was not likely that its disclosure would endanger the safety of any person.

(3) D is not guilty of an offence under section 88(2) if he disclosed the information for the purposes of safeguarding national security or for the purposes of the prevention, detection or investigation of crime.

(4) D is not guilty of an offence under section 88(2) if—

    (a) at the time when he disclosed the information, he was a protection provider or involved in the making of arrangements under section 82(1) or in the implementation, variation or cancellation of such arrangements, and

    (b) he disclosed the information for the purposes of the making, implementation, variation or cancellation of such arrangements.

(5) The Secretary of State may by order make provision prescribing circumstances in which a person who discloses information as mentioned in subsection (1) or (2) of section 88 is not guilty in England and Wales or in Northern Ireland of an offence under that subsection.

(6) The Scottish Ministers may by order make provision prescribing circumstances in which a person who discloses information as mentioned in subsection (1) or (2) of section 88 is not guilty in Scotland of an offence under that subsection.

(7) If sufficient evidence is adduced to raise an issue with respect to a defence under or by virtue of this section, the court or jury must assume that the defence is satisfied unless the prosecution proves beyond reasonable doubt that it is not.

90 Protection from liability

(1) This section applies if—

    (a) arrangements are made for the protection of a person under section 82(1), and

    (b) the protected person assumes a new identity in pursuance of the arrangements.

(2) No proceedings (whether civil or criminal) may be brought against a person to whom this section applies in respect of the making by him of a false or misleading representation if the representation—

    (a) relates to the protected person, and

    (b) is made solely for the purpose of ensuring that the arrangements made for him to assume a new identity are, or continue to be, effective.

(3) The persons to whom this section applies are—

    (a) the protected person;

    (b) a person who is associated with the protected person;

    (c) a protection provider;

    (d) a person involved in the making of arrangements under section 82(1) or in the implementation, variation or cancellation of such arrangements.

91 Transitional provision

(1) This section applies to arrangements which were, at any time before the commencement of section 82, made by a protection provider, or any person acting with his authority, for the purpose of protecting a person of a description specified in Schedule 5.

(2) If the following three conditions are satisfied, the arrangements are to be treated as having been made by the protection provider under section 82(1).

(3) The first condition is that the protection provider could have made the arrangements under section 82(1) had it been in force at the time when the arrangements were made.

(4) The second condition is that the arrangements were in operation immediately before the commencement of section 82.

(5) The third condition is that the protection provider determines that it is appropriate to treat the arrangements as having been made under section 82(1).

(6) A determination under subsection (5) may be made at any time before the end of the period of six months beginning with the day on which section 82 comes into force.

(7) A protection provider must make a record of a determination under subsection (5).

(8) Subsection (9) applies if—

    (a) at any time before the commencement of section 82, arrangements were made by a person specified in subsection (11), or any person acting with the authority of such a person, for the purpose of protecting a person of a description specified in Schedule 5, and

    (b) functions in relation to the arrangements are, at any time before the end of the period of six months mentioned in subsection (6), exercisable by a protection provider.

(9) The provision made by subsections (1) to (7) applies in relation to the arrangements as if they had been made by the protection provider.

(10) Accordingly, if the three conditions mentioned in subsections (3) to (5) are satisfied in relation to the arrangements, they are to be treated, by virtue of subsection (2), as having been made by the protection provider under section 82(1).

(11) The persons specified in this subsection are—

    (a) the Director General of the National Criminal Intelligence Service;

    (b) the Director General of the National Crime Squad;

    (c) any of the Commissioners of Her Majesty's Customs and Excise.

92 Transitional provision: supplemental

(1) In this section—

    (a) 'the arrangements' are arrangements which are treated as having been made by a protection provider by virtue of section 91(2), and

    (b) 'the relevant date' is the date of the record made by the protection provider, in relation to the arrangements, in pursuance of section 91(7).

(2) A person does not commit an offence under section 86(1) by disclosing information relating to the arrangements unless the information is disclosed on or after the relevant date.

(3) But it is immaterial whether the information relates to something done in connection with the arrangements before or on or after the relevant date.

(4) A person does not commit an offence under section 88(1) or (2) by disclosing information relating to a person who assumed a new identity in pursuance of the arrangements unless the information is disclosed on or after the relevant date.

(5) But it is immaterial whether the person assumed a new identity before or on or after the relevant date.

(6) Section 90 applies in relation to a false or misleading representation relating to a person who assumed a new identity in pursuance of the arrangements only if the false or misleading representation is made on or after the relevant date.

(7) But it is immaterial whether the person assumed a new identity before or on or after the relevant date.

93 Provision of information

(1) This section applies if—

    (a) a protection provider makes arrangements under section 82(1), or

    (b) a protection provider determines under section 91(5) that it is appropriate to treat arrangements to which that section applies as having been made under section 82(1).

(2) The protection provider must inform the person to whom the arrangements relate of the provisions of this Chapter as they apply in relation to the arrangements.

(3) If the protection provider considers that the person would be unable to understand the information, by reason of his age or of any incapacity, the information must instead be given to a person who appears to the protection provider—

    (a) to be interested in the welfare of the person to whom the arrangements relate, and

    (b) to be the appropriate person to whom to give the information.

(4) If arrangements are made jointly under section 82(1) (by virtue of section 83), the protection providers involved in the arrangements must nominate one of those protection providers to perform the duties imposed by this section.

94 Interpretation of Chapter 4

(1) This section applies for the purposes of this Chapter.

(2) 'Protection provider' is to be construed in accordance with section 82.

(3) A person is a protected person if—

    (a) arrangements have been made for his protection under subsection (1) of section 82, and

    (b) the arrangements have not been cancelled under subsection (2) of that section.

(4) A person is associated with another person if any of the following apply—

    (a) they are members of the same family;

    (b) they live in the same household;

    (c) they have lived in the same household.

(5) A person assumes a new identity if either or both of the following apply—

    (a) he becomes known by a different name;

    (b) he makes representations about his personal history or circumstances which are false or misleading.

(6) A reference to a person who is a witness in legal proceedings includes a reference to a person who provides any information or any document or other thing which might be used in evidence in those proceedings or which (whether or not admissible as evidence in those proceedings)—

    (a) might tend to confirm evidence which will or might be admitted in those proceedings,

    (b) might be referred to in evidence given in those proceedings by another witness, or

    (c) might be used as the basis for any cross examination in the course of those proceedings,

and a reference to a person who might be, or to a person who has been, a witness in legal proceedings is to be construed accordingly.

(7) A reference to a person who is a witness in legal proceedings does not include a reference to a person who is an accused person in criminal proceedings unless he is a witness for the prosecution and a reference to a person who might be, or to a person who has been, a witness in legal proceedings is to be construed accordingly.

(8) A reference to a person who is or has been a member of staff of an organisation includes a reference to a person who is or has been seconded to the organisation to serve as a member of its staff.

(9) 'The Scottish Drug Enforcement Agency' and 'the Director' of that Agency have the meanings given by section 42(2).

CHAPTER 5
INTERNATIONAL OBLIGATIONS

95 Enforcement of overseas forfeiture orders

In section 9 of the Criminal Justice (International Cooperation) Act 1990 (c. 5) (enforcement of overseas forfeiture orders), for subsection (6) (offences to which section applies) substitute—

'(6) This section applies to any offence that corresponds to or is similar to—
    (a) an offence under the law of England and Wales;
    (b) an offence under the law of Scotland; or
    (c) an offence under the law of Northern Ireland.'

96 Mutual assistance in freezing property or evidence

(1) The Secretary of State or the Scottish Ministers may by order make provision—
    (a) for the purpose of implementing any obligation of the United Kingdom created or arising by or under the Decision or enabling any such obligation to be implemented,
    (b) for the purpose of enabling any rights enjoyed or to be enjoyed by the United Kingdom under or by virtue of the Decision to be exercised, or
    (c) for the purpose of dealing with matters arising out of or related to any such obligation or rights.

(2) In subsection (1) 'the Decision' means Council Framework Decision 2003/577/JHA of 22 July 2003 on the execution in the European Union of orders freezing property or evidence.

(3) The provision that may be made under subsection (1) by the Secretary of State includes, subject to subsections (5) and (7), any provision (of any extent) that might be made by Act of Parliament.

(4) The provision that may be made under subsection (1) by the Scottish Ministers includes, subject to subsections (6) and (7), any provision that might be made by Act of the Scottish Parliament.

(5) The power conferred by subsection (1) on the Secretary of State does not include power to make provision that would be within the legislative competence of the Scottish Parliament if it were included in an Act of that Parliament.

(6) The power conferred by subsection (1) on the Scottish Ministers is limited to the making of provision that would be within the legislative competence of the Scottish Parliament if it were included in an Act of that Parliament.

(7) The powers conferred by subsection (1) do not include power—

    (a) to make any provision imposing or increasing taxation,

    (b) to make any provision taking effect from a date earlier than that of the making of the instrument containing the provision,

    (c) to confer any power to legislate by means of orders, rules, regulations or other subordinate instrument, other than rules of procedure for a court or tribunal, or

    (d) to create criminal offences.

(8) Subsection (7)(c) does not preclude—

    (a) the modification of a power to legislate conferred otherwise than under subsection (1), or

    (b) the extension of any such power to purposes of the like nature as those for which it was conferred,

and a power to give directions as to matters of administration is not to be regarded as a power to legislate within the meaning of subsection (7)(c).

CHAPTER 6
PROCEEDS OF CRIME

97 Confiscation orders by magistrates' courts

(1) The Secretary of State may by order make such provision as he considers appropriate for or in connection with enabling confiscation orders under—

    (a) Part 2 of the Proceeds of Crime Act 2002 (c. 29) (confiscation: England and Wales), or

    (b) Part 4 of that Act (confiscation: Northern Ireland),

to be made by magistrates' courts in England and Wales or Northern Ireland (as the case may be).

(2) But an order under subsection (1) may not enable such a confiscation order to be made by any magistrates' court in respect of an amount exceeding £10,000.

(3) An order under subsection (1) may amend, repeal, revoke or otherwise modify any provision of Part 2 or 4 of the 2002 Act or any other enactment relating to, or to things done under or for the purposes of, either (or any provision) of those Parts.

98 Civil recovery: freezing orders

(1) In the Proceeds of Crime Act 2002 (c. 29), after section 245 insert—

'Property freezing orders (England and Wales and Northern Ireland)

245A Application for property freezing order

(1) Where the enforcement authority may take proceedings for a recovery order in the High Court, the authority may apply to the court for a property freezing order (whether before or after starting the proceedings).

(2) A property freezing order is an order that—

    (a) specifies or describes the property to which it applies, and

    (b) subject to any exclusions (see section 245C(1)(b) and (2)), prohibits any person to whose property the order applies from in any way dealing with the property.

(3) An application for a property freezing order may be made without notice if the circumstances are such that notice of the application would prejudice any right of the enforcement authority to obtain a recovery order in respect of any property.

(4) The court may make a property freezing order on an application if it is satisfied that the condition in subsection (5) is met and, where applicable, that the condition in subsection (6) is met.

(5) The first condition is that there is a good arguable case—
   (a) that the property to which the application for the order relates is or includes recoverable property, and
   (b) that, if any of it is not recoverable property, it is associated property.

(6) The second condition is that, if—
   (a) the property to which the application for the order relates includes property alleged to be associated property, and
   (b) the enforcement authority has not established the identity of the person who holds it,
   the authority has taken all reasonable steps to do so.

245B Variation and setting aside of order

(1) The court may at any time vary or set aside a property freezing order.

(2) If the court makes an interim receiving order that applies to all of the property to which a property freezing order applies, it must set aside the property freezing order.

(3) If the court makes an interim receiving order that applies to some but not all of the property to which a property freezing order applies, it must vary the property freezing order so as to exclude any property to which the interim receiving order applies.

(4) If the court decides that any property to which a property freezing order applies is neither recoverable property nor associated property, it must vary the order so as to exclude the property.

(5) Before exercising power under this Chapter to vary or set aside a property freezing order, the court must (as well as giving the parties to the proceedings an opportunity to be heard) give such an opportunity to any person who may be affected by its decision.

(6) Subsection (5) does not apply where the court is acting as required by subsection (2) or (3).

245C Exclusions

(1) The power to vary a property freezing order includes (in particular) power to make exclusions as follows—
   (a) power to exclude property from the order, and
   (b) power, otherwise than by excluding property from the order, to make exclusions from the prohibition on dealing with the property to which the order applies.

(2) Exclusions from the prohibition on dealing with the property to which the order applies (other than exclusions of property from the order) may also be made when the order is made.

(3) An exclusion may, in particular, make provision for the purpose of enabling any person—
   (a) to meet his reasonable living expenses, or
   (b) to carry on any trade, business, profession or occupation.

(4) An exclusion may be made subject to conditions.

(5) Where the court exercises the power to make an exclusion for the purpose of enabling a person to meet legal expenses that he has incurred, or may incur, in respect of proceedings under this Part, it must ensure that the exclusion—

    (a) is limited to reasonable legal expenses that the person has reasonably incurred or that he reasonably incurs,

    (b) specifies the total amount that may be released for legal expenses in pursuance of the exclusion, and

    (c) is made subject to the required conditions (see section 286A) in addition to any conditions imposed under subsection (4).

(6) The court, in deciding whether to make an exclusion for the purpose of enabling a person to meet legal expenses of his in respect of proceedings under this Part—

    (a) must have regard (in particular) to the desirability of the person being represented in any proceedings under this Part in which he is a participant, and

    (b) must, where the person is the respondent, disregard the possibility that legal representation of the person in any such proceedings might, were an exclusion not made, be funded by the Legal Services Commission or the Northern Ireland Legal Services Commission.

(7) If excluded property is not specified in the order it must be described in the order in general terms.

(8) The power to make exclusions must, subject to subsection (6), be exercised with a view to ensuring, so far as practicable, that the satisfaction of any right of the enforcement authority to recover the property obtained through unlawful conduct is not unduly prejudiced.

(9) Subsection (8) does not apply where the court is acting as required by section 245B(3) or (4).

245D Restriction on proceedings and remedies

(1) While a property freezing order has effect—

    (a) the court may stay any action, execution or other legal process in respect of the property to which the order applies, and

    (b) no distress may be levied against the property to which the order applies except with the leave of the court and subject to any terms the court may impose.

(2) If a court (whether the High Court or any other court) in which proceedings are pending in respect of any property is satisfied that a property freezing order has been applied for or made in respect of the property, it may either stay the proceedings or allow them to continue on any terms it thinks fit.

(3) If a property freezing order applies to a tenancy of any premises, no landlord or other person to whom rent is payable may exercise the right of forfeiture by peaceable re-entry in relation to the premises in respect of any failure by the tenant to comply with any term or condition of the tenancy, except with the leave of the court and subject to any terms the court may impose.

(4) Before exercising any power conferred by this section, the court must (as well as giving the parties to any of the proceedings concerned an opportunity to be heard) give such an opportunity to any person who may be affected by the court's decision.'

(2) In the Proceeds of Crime Act 2002 (c. 29), after section 255 insert—

'Prohibitory property orders (Scotland)

255A Application for prohibitory property order

(1) Where the enforcement authority may take proceedings for a recovery order in the Court of Session, the authority may apply to the court for a prohibitory property order (whether before or after starting the proceedings).

(2) A prohibitory property order is an order that—

    (a) specifies or describes the property to which it applies, and

(b) subject to any exclusions (see section 255C(1)(b) and (2)), prohibits any person to whose property the order applies from in any way dealing with the property.

(3) An application for a prohibitory property order may be made without notice if the circumstances are such that notice of the application would prejudice any right of the enforcement authority to obtain a recovery order in respect of any property.

(4) The court may make a prohibitory property order on an application if it is satisfied that the condition in subsection (5) is met and, where applicable, that the condition in subsection (6) is met.

(5) The first condition is that there is a good arguable case—
  (a) that the property to which the application for the order relates is or includes recoverable property, and
  (b) that, if any of it is not recoverable property, it is associated property.

(6) The second condition is that, if—
  (a) the property to which the application for the order relates includes property alleged to be associated property, and
  (b) the enforcement authority has not established the identity of the person who holds it,
  the authority has taken all reasonable steps to do so.

255B Variation and recall of prohibitory property order

(1) The court may at any time vary or recall a prohibitory property order.

(2) If the court makes an interim administration order that applies to all of the property to which a prohibitory property order applies, it must recall the prohibitory property order.

(3) If the court makes an interim administration order that applies to some but not all of the property to which a prohibitory property order applies, it must vary the prohibitory property order so as to exclude any property to which the interim administration order applies.

(4) If the court decides that any property to which a prohibitory property order applies is neither recoverable property nor associated property, it must vary the order so as to exclude the property.

(5) Before exercising power under this Chapter to vary or recall a prohibitory property order, the court must (as well as giving the parties to the proceedings an opportunity to be heard) give such an opportunity to any person who may be affected by its decision.

(6) Subsection (5) does not apply where the court is acting as required by subsection (2) or (3).

255C Exclusions

(1) The power to vary a prohibitory property order includes (in particular) power to make exclusions as follows—
  (a) power to exclude property from the order, and
  (b) power, otherwise than by excluding property from the order, to make exclusions from the prohibition on dealing with the property to which the order applies.

(2) Exclusions from the prohibition on dealing with the property to which the order applies (other than exclusions of property from the order) may also be made when the order is made.

(3) An exclusion may, in particular, make provision for the purpose of enabling any person—
  (a) to meet his reasonable living expenses, or
  (b) to carry on any trade, business, profession or occupation.

(4) An exclusion may be made subject to conditions.

(5) An exclusion may not be made for the purpose of enabling any person to meet any legal expenses in respect of proceedings under this Part.

(6) If excluded property is not specified in the order it must be described in the order in general terms.

(7) The power to make exclusions must be exercised with a view to ensuring, so far as practicable, that the satisfaction of any right of the enforcement authority to recover the property obtained through unlawful conduct is not unduly prejudiced.

(8) Subsection (7) does not apply where the court is acting as required by section 255B(3) or (4).

255D Restriction on proceedings and remedies

(1) While a prohibitory property order has effect the court may sist any action, execution or other legal process in respect of the property to which the order applies.

(2) If a court (whether the Court of Session or any other court) in which proceedings are pending in respect of any property is satisfied that a prohibitory property order has been applied for or made in respect of the property, it may either sist the proceedings or allow them to continue on any terms it thinks fit.

(3) Before exercising any power conferred by this section, the court must (as well as giving the parties to any of the proceedings concerned an opportunity to be heard) give such an opportunity to any person who may be affected by the court's decision.

255E Arrestment of property affected by prohibitory property order

(1) On the application of the enforcement authority the Court of Session may, in relation to moveable recoverable property to which a prohibitory property order applies (whether generally or to such of it as is specified in the application), grant warrant for arrestment.

(2) An application under subsection (1) may be made at the same time as the application for the prohibitory property order or at any time thereafter.

(3) Such a warrant for arrestment may be granted only if the property would be arrestable if the person entitled to it were a debtor.

(4) A warrant under subsection (1) has effect as if granted on the dependence of an action for debt at the instance of the enforcement authority against the person and may be executed, recalled, loosed or restricted accordingly.

(5) An arrestment executed under this section ceases to have effect when, or in so far as, the prohibitory property order ceases to apply in respect of the property in relation to which the warrant for arrestment was granted.

(6) If an arrestment ceases to have effect to any extent by virtue of subsection (5) the enforcement authority must apply to the Court of Session for an order recalling or, as the case may be, restricting the arrestment.

255F Inhibition of property affected by prohibitory property order

(1) On the application of the enforcement authority, the Court of Session may, in relation to the property mentioned in subsection (2), grant warrant for inhibition against any person specified in a prohibitory property order.

(2) That property is heritable property situated in Scotland to which the prohibitory property order applies (whether generally or to such of it as is specified in the application).

(3) The warrant for inhibition—

    (a) has effect as if granted on the dependence of an action for debt by the enforcement authority against the person and may be executed, recalled, loosed or restricted accordingly, and

    (b) has the effect of letters of inhibition and must forthwith be registered by the enforcement authority in the register of inhibitions and adjudications.

(4) Section 155 of the Titles to Land Consolidation (Scotland) Act 1868 (c. 101) (effective date of inhibition) applies in relation to an inhibition for which warrant is granted under subsection (1) as it applies to an inhibition by separate letters or contained in a summons.

(5) An inhibition executed under this section ceases to have effect when, or in so far as, the prohibitory property order ceases to apply in respect of the property in relation to which the warrant for inhibition was granted.

(6) If an inhibition ceases to have effect to any extent by virtue of subsection (5) the enforcement authority must—

    (a) apply for the recall or, as the case may be, the restriction of the inhibition, and

    (b) ensure that the recall or restriction is reflected in the register of inhibitions and adjudications.'

99 Civil recovery: interim receivers' expenses etc.

(1) The Proceeds of Crime Act 2002 (c. 29) is amended as follows.

(2) In section 280 (civil recovery orders: applying realised proceeds), after subsection (2) insert—

'(3) The Director may apply a sum received by him under subsection (2) in making payment of the remuneration and expenses of—

    (a) the trustee, or

    (b) any interim receiver appointed in, or in anticipation of, the proceedings for the recovery order.

(4) Subsection (3)(a) does not apply in relation to the remuneration of the trustee if the trustee is a member of the staff of the Agency.'

(3) In section 284 (payment of interim administrator or trustee (Scotland)—

    (a) the existing words become subsection (1), and

    (b) after that subsection insert—

'(2) The Scottish Ministers may apply a sum received by them under section 280(2) in making payment of such fees or expenses.

(3) Subsection (2) does not apply in relation to the fees of a trustee for civil recovery if the trustee is a member of their staff.'

(4) In paragraph 5 of Schedule 1 (finances of the Assets Recovery Agency), after sub-paragraph (1) (paragraph (b) of which provides for the expenses of the Director and staff of the Agency to be paid out of money provided by Parliament) insert—

'(1A) Sub-paragraph (1)(b) has effect subject to anything in this Act.'

100 Detention of seized cash: meaning of '48 hours'

(1) In the Proceeds of Crime Act 2002 (c. 29), Chapter 3 of Part 5 (civil recovery of cash in summary proceedings) is amended as follows.

(2) In section 295 (detention of seized cash, initially for 48 hours), after subsection (1) insert—

'(1A) The period of 48 hours mentioned in subsection (1) is to be calculated in accordance with subsection (1B).

(1B) In calculating a period of 48 hours in accordance with this subsection, no account shall be taken of—

    (a)   any Saturday or Sunday,

    (b)   Christmas Day,

    (c)   Good Friday,

    (d)   any day that is a bank holiday under the Banking and Financial Dealings Act 1971 in the part of the United Kingdom within which the cash is seized, or

    (e)   any day prescribed under section 8(2) of the Criminal Procedure (Scotland) Act 1995 as a court holiday in a sheriff court in the sheriff court district within which the cash is seized.'

(3)   In sections 290(6), 296(1) and 302(2), after '48 hours' insert '(calculated in accordance with section 295(1B))'.

101 Appeal in proceedings for forfeiture of cash

(1)   For section 299 of the Proceeds of Crime Act 2002 (appeal against forfeiture of cash) substitute—

'299 Appeal against decision under section 298

(1)   Any party to proceedings for an order for the forfeiture of cash under section 298 who is aggrieved by an order under that section or by the decision of the court not to make such an order may appeal—

    (a) in relation to England and Wales, to the Crown Court;

    (b) in relation to Scotland, to the Sheriff Principal;

    (c) in relation to Northern Ireland, to a county court.

(2)   An appeal under subsection (1) must be made before the end of the period of 30 days starting with the day on which the court makes the order or decision.

(3)   The court hearing the appeal may make any order it thinks appropriate.

(4)   If the court upholds an appeal against an order forfeiting the cash, it may order the release of the cash.'

(2)   This section does not apply to a decision of a court not to order the forfeiture of cash under section 298 of that Act taken before this section comes into force.

102 Money laundering: defence where overseas conduct is legal under local law

(1)   In the Proceeds of Crime Act 2002 (c. 29), Part 7 (money laundering) is amended as follows.

(2)   In section 327 (concealing etc.), after subsection (2) insert—

'(2A) Nor does a person commit an offence under subsection (1) if—

    (a) he knows, or believes on reasonable grounds, that the relevant criminal conduct occurred in a particular country or territory outside the United Kingdom, and

    (b) the relevant criminal conduct—

       (i) was not, at the time it occurred, unlawful under the criminal law then applying in that country or territory, and

      (ii) is not of a description prescribed by an order made by the Secretary of State.

(2B) In subsection (2A) 'the relevant criminal conduct' is the criminal conduct by reference to which the property concerned is criminal property.'

(3)   In section 328 (arrangements), after subsection (2) insert—

'(3) Nor does a person commit an offence under subsection (1) if—

    (a) he knows, or believes on reasonable grounds, that the relevant criminal conduct occurred in a particular country or territory outside the United Kingdom, and

   (b)   the relevant criminal conduct—
         (i)   was not, at the time it occurred, unlawful under the criminal law then
               applying in that country or territory, and
         (ii) is not of a description prescribed by an order made by the Secretary of State.
   (4) In subsection (3) 'the relevant criminal conduct' is the criminal conduct by reference to
        which the property concerned is criminal property.'

(4) In section 329 (acquisition, use and possession), after subsection (2) insert—

   '(2A) Nor does a person commit an offence under subsection (1) if—
      (a) he knows, or believes on reasonable grounds, that the relevant criminal conduct
           occurred in a particular country or territory outside the United Kingdom, and
      (b) the relevant criminal conduct—
           (i)   was not, at the time it occurred, unlawful under the criminal law then apply-
                 ing in that country or territory, and
           (ii) is not of a description prescribed by an order made by the Secretary of State.

   (2B) In subsection (2A) 'the relevant criminal conduct' is the criminal conduct by reference
         to which the property concerned is criminal property.'

(5) In section 330 (failure to disclose: regulated sector), after subsection (7) insert—

   '(7A) Nor does a person commit an offence under this section if—
      (a) he knows, or believes on reasonable grounds, that the money laundering is
           occurring in a particular country or territory outside the United Kingdom, and
      (b) the money laundering—
           (i)   is not unlawful under the criminal law applying in that country or territory,
                 and
           (ii) is not of a description prescribed in an order made by the Secretary of State.'

(6) In section 331 (failure to disclose: nominated officers in the regulated sector),
     after subsection (6) insert—

   '(6A) Nor does a person commit an offence under this section if—
      (a) he knows, or believes on reasonable grounds, that the money laundering is occur-
           ring in a particular country or territory outside the United Kingdom, and
      (b) the money laundering—
           (i)   is not unlawful under the criminal law applying in that country or territory,
                 and
           (ii) is not of a description prescribed in an order made by the Secretary of State.'

(7) In section 332 (failure to disclose: other nominated officers), after subsection (6)
     insert—

   '(7) Nor does a person commit an offence under this section if—
      (a) he knows, or believes on reasonable grounds, that the money laundering is occur-
           ring in a particular country or territory outside the United Kingdom, and
      (b) the money laundering—
           (i)   is not unlawful under the criminal law applying in that country or territory,
                 and
           (ii) is not of a description prescribed in an order made by the Secretary of State.'

103 Money laundering: threshold amounts

   (1) The Proceeds of Crime Act 2002 (c. 29) is amended as follows.
   (2) In section 327 (concealing etc.), after subsection (2B) (which is inserted by
        section 102 of this Act) insert—

'(2C) A deposit-taking body that does an act mentioned in paragraph (c) or (d) of subsection (1) does not commit an offence under that subsection if—
- (a) it does the act in operating an account maintained with it, and
- (b) the value of the criminal property concerned is less than the threshold amount determined under section 339A for the act.'

(3) In section 328 (arrangements), after subsection (4) (which is inserted by section 102 of this Act) insert—

'(5) A deposit-taking body that does an act mentioned in subsection (1) does not commit an offence under that subsection if—
- (a) it does the act in operating an account maintained with it, and
- (b) the arrangement facilitates the acquisition, retention, use or control of criminal property of a value that is less than the threshold amount determined under section 339A for the act.'

(4) In section 329 (acquisition, use and possession), after subsection (2B) (which is inserted by section 102 of this Act) insert—

'(2C) A deposit-taking body that does an act mentioned in subsection (1) does not commit an offence under that subsection if—
- (a) it does the act in operating an account maintained with it, and
- (b) the value of the criminal property concerned is less than the threshold amount determined under section 339A for the act.'

(5) In Part 7 (money laundering), after section 339 insert—

'Threshold amounts

339A Threshold amounts

(1) This section applies for the purposes of sections 327(2C), 328(5) and 329(2C).

(2) The threshold amount for acts done by a deposit-taking body in operating an account is £250 unless a higher amount is specified under the following provisions of this section (in which event it is that higher amount).

(3) An officer of Revenue and Customs, or a constable, may specify the threshold amount for acts done by a deposit-taking body in operating an account—
- (a) when he gives consent, or gives notice refusing consent, to the deposit-taking body's doing of an act mentioned in section 327(1), 328 (1) or 329(1) in opening, or operating, the account or a related account, or
- (b) on a request from the deposit-taking body.

(4) Where the threshold amount for acts done in operating an account is specified under subsection (3) or this subsection, an officer of Revenue and Customs, or a constable, may vary the amount (whether on a request from the deposit-taking body or otherwise) by specifying a different amount.

(5) Different threshold amounts may be specified under subsections (3) and (4) for different acts done in operating the same account.

(6) The amount specified under subsection (3) or (4) as the threshold amount for acts done in operating an account must, when specified, not be less than the amount specified in subsection (2).

(7) The Secretary of State may by order vary the amount for the time being specified in subsection (2).

(8) For the purposes of this section, an account is related to another if each is maintained with the same deposit-taking body and there is a person who, in relation to each account, is the person or one of the persons entitled to instruct the body as respects the operation of the account.'

(6) In section 340 (interpretation of Part 7), after subsection (13) insert—

'(14) "Deposit-taking body" means—
  (a) a business which engages in the activity of accepting deposits, or
  (b) the National Savings Bank.'

(7) In section 459(4)(a) and (6)(a) (provision for certain orders to be subject to affirmative procedure), after '309,' insert '339A(7),'.

104 Money laundering: disclosures to identify persons and property

(1) In the Proceeds of Crime Act 2002 (c. 29), Part 7 (money laundering) is amended as follows.

(2) In section 330(1) (regulated sector: failure to disclose: offence committed if three conditions satisfied), for 'each of the following three conditions is satisfied' substitute 'the conditions in subsections (2) to (4) are satisfied'.

(3) For section 330(4) to (6) (the required disclosure) substitute—

'(3A) The third condition is—
  (a) that he can identify the other person mentioned in subsection (2) or the whereabouts of any of the laundered property, or
  (b) that he believes, or it is reasonable to expect him to believe, that the information or other matter mentioned in subsection (3) will or may assist in identifying that other person or the whereabouts of any of the laundered property.

(4) The fourth condition is that he does not make the required disclosure to—
  (a) a nominated officer, or
  (b) a person authorised for the purposes of this Part by the Director General of the Serious Organised Crime Agency,
as soon as is practicable after the information or other matter mentioned in subsection (3) comes to him.

(5) The required disclosure is a disclosure of—
  (a) the identity of the other person mentioned in subsection (2), if he knows it,
  (b) the whereabouts of the laundered property, so far as he knows it, and
  (c) the information or other matter mentioned in subsection (3).

(5A) The laundered property is the property forming the subject-matter of the money laundering that he knows or suspects, or has reasonable grounds for knowing or suspecting, that other person to be engaged in.

(6) But he does not commit an offence under this section if—
  (a) he has a reasonable excuse for not making the required disclosure,
  (b) he is a professional legal adviser and—
    (i) if he knows either of the things mentioned in subsection (5)(a) and (b), he knows the thing because of information or other matter that came to him in privileged circumstances, or
    (ii) the information or other matter mentioned in subsection (3) came to him in privileged circumstances, or
  (c) subsection (7) applies to him.'

(4) For section 331(4) to (6) (failure to disclose: nominated officers in the regulated sector: the required disclosure) substitute—

'(3A) The third condition is—
  (a) that he knows the identity of the other person mentioned in subsection (2), or the whereabouts of any of the laundered property, in consequence of a disclosure made under section 330,

191

    (b) that that other person, or the whereabouts of any of the laundered property, can be identified from the information or other matter mentioned in subsection (3), or

    (c) that he believes, or it is reasonable to expect him to believe, that the information or other matter will or may assist in identifying that other person or the whereabouts of any of the laundered property.

(4) The fourth condition is that he does not make the required disclosure to a person authorised for the purposes of this Part by the Director General of the Serious Organised Crime Agency as soon as is practicable after the information or other matter mentioned in subsection (3) comes to him.

(5) The required disclosure is a disclosure of—

    (a) the identity of the other person mentioned in subsection (2), if disclosed to him under section 330,

    (b) the whereabouts of the laundered property, so far as disclosed to him under section 330, and

    (c) the information or other matter mentioned in subsection (3).

(5A) The laundered property is the property forming the subject-matter of the money laundering that he knows or suspects, or has reasonable grounds for knowing or suspecting, that other person to be engaged in.

(6) But he does not commit an offence under this section if he has a reasonable excuse for not making the required disclosure.'

(5) In section 332(3) (failure to disclose: other nominated officers: the second condition), for 'section 337 or 338' substitute 'the applicable section'.

(6) For section 332(4) to (6) (the required disclosure) substitute—

'(3A) The third condition is—

    (a) that he knows the identity of the other person mentioned in subsection (2), or the whereabouts of any of the laundered property, in consequence of a disclosure made under the applicable section,

    (b) that that other person, or the whereabouts of any of the laundered property, can be identified from the information or other matter mentioned in subsection (3), or

    (c) that he believes, or it is reasonable to expect him to believe, that the information or other matter will or may assist in identifying that other person or the whereabouts of any of the laundered property.

(4) The fourth condition is that he does not make the required disclosure to a person authorised for the purposes of this Part by the Director General of the Serious Organised Crime Agency as soon as is practicable after the information or other matter mentioned in subsection (3) comes to him.

(5) The required disclosure is a disclosure of—

    (a) the identity of the other person mentioned in subsection (2), if disclosed to him under the applicable section,

    (b) the whereabouts of the laundered property, so far as disclosed to him under the applicable section, and

    (c) the information or other matter mentioned in subsection (3).

(5A) The laundered property is the property forming the subject-matter of the money laundering that he knows or suspects that other person to be engaged in.

(5B) The applicable section is section 337 or, as the case may be, section 338.

(6) But he does not commit an offence under this section if he has a reasonable excuse for not making the required disclosure.'

(7) In section 337 (protected disclosures), after subsection (4) insert—

'(4A) Where a disclosure consists of a disclosure protected under subsection (1) and a disclosure of either or both of—

(a) the identity of the other person mentioned in subsection (3), and

(b) the whereabouts of property forming the subject-matter of the money laundering that the discloser knows or suspects, or has reasonable grounds for knowing or suspecting, that other person to be engaged in,

the disclosure of the thing mentioned in paragraph (a) or (b) (as well as the disclosure protected under subsection (1)) is not to be taken to breach any restriction on the disclosure of information (however imposed).'

105 Money laundering: form and manner of disclosures

(1) In the Proceeds of Crime Act 2002 (c. 29), Part 7 (money laundering) is amended as follows.

(2) In each of sections 330(9)(b), 337(5)(b) and 338(5)(b) (disclosure to nominated officer is ineffective if employer's procedures not followed), omit 'and in accordance with the procedure established by the employer for the purpose'.

(3) In section 334 (penalties), after subsection (2) insert—

'(3) A person guilty of an offence under section 339(1A) is liable on summary conviction to a fine not exceeding level 5 on the standard scale.'

(4) In section 338(1) (authorised disclosures), omit paragraph (b) (disclosure must be made in prescribed form and manner) but not the 'and' at the end.

(5) In section 339 (form and manner of disclosures), for subsections (2) and (3) substitute—

'(1A) A person commits an offence if he makes a disclosure under section 330, 331, 332 or 338 otherwise than in the form prescribed under subsection (1) or otherwise than in the manner so prescribed.

(1B) But a person does not commit an offence under subsection (1A) if he has a reasonable excuse for making the disclosure otherwise than in the form prescribed under subsection (1) or (as the case may be) otherwise than in the manner so prescribed.

(2) The power under subsection (1) to prescribe the form in which a disclosure must be made includes power to provide for the form to include a request to a person making a disclosure that the person provide information specified or described in the form if he has not provided it in making the disclosure.

(3) Where under subsection (2) a request is included in a form prescribed under subsection (1), the form must—

(a) state that there is no obligation to comply with the request, and

(b) explain the protection conferred by subsection (4) on a person who complies with the request.'

106 Money laundering: miscellaneous amendments

(1) In the Proceeds of Crime Act 2002, Part 7 (money laundering) is amended as follows.

(2) In section 330 (regulated sector: failure to disclose), after subsection (9) insert—

'(9A) But a disclosure which satisfies paragraphs (a) and (b) of subsection (9) is not to be taken as a disclosure to a nominated officer if the person making the disclosure—

(a) is a professional legal adviser,

(b) makes it for the purpose of obtaining advice about making a disclosure under this section, and

(c) does not intend it to be a disclosure under this section.'

(3) In section 337(5)(a) (disclosure to person nominated to receive disclosures under section 337), after 'disclosures under' insert 'section 330 or'.

(4) In section 338(1)(c) (first or second condition must be satisfied for disclosure to be authorised), for 'or second' substitute', second or third'.

(5) In section 338 (authorised disclosures), after subsection (2) insert—

'(2A) The second condition is that—
(a) the disclosure is made while the alleged offender is doing the prohibited act,
(b) he began to do the act at a time when, because he did not then know or suspect that the property constituted or represented a person's benefit from criminal conduct, the act was not a prohibited act, and
(c) the disclosure is made on his own initiative and as soon as is practicable after he first knows or suspects that the property constitutes or represents a person's benefit from criminal conduct.'

(6) In section 338(3) (the second condition), for 'second' substitute 'third'.

107 Money laundering offences

(1) The Proceeds of Crime Act 2002 (c. 29) is amended as follows.

(2) In section 364 (meaning of customer information) in subsection (5)—
(a) after paragraph (a) insert—

'(aa) constitutes an offence specified in section 415(1A) of this Act,';

(b) in paragraph (b) after 'paragraph (a)' insert 'or (aa)'.

(3) In section 398 (meaning of customer information: Scotland) in subsection (5)—
(a) after paragraph (a) insert—

'(aa) constitutes an offence specified in section 415(1A) of this Act,';

(b) in paragraph (b) after 'paragraph (a)' insert 'or (aa)'.

(4) In section 415 (money laundering offences) after subsection (1) insert—

'(1A) Each of the following is a money laundering offence—
(a) an offence under section 93A, 93B or 93C of the Criminal Justice Act 1988;
(b) an offence under section 49, 50 or 51 of the Drug Trafficking Act 1994;
(c) an offence under section 37 or 38 of the Criminal Law (Consolidation) (Scotland) Act 1995;
(d) an offence under article 45, 46 or 47 of the Proceeds of Crime (Northern Ireland) Order 1996.'

108 International cooperation

(1) Part 11 of the Proceeds of Crime Act 2002 (c. 29) (cooperation) is amended as follows.

(2) In section 444 (external requests and orders), for subsection (3)(a) (Order under the section may include provision about the functions of the Secretary of State, the Lord Advocate, the Scottish Ministers and the Director of the Assets Recovery Agency) substitute—

'(a) provision about the functions of any of the listed persons in relation to external requests and orders;'.

(3) In that section, after subsection (3) insert—

'(4) For the purposes of subsection (3)(a) "the listed persons" are—

    (a) the Secretary of State;
    (b) the Lord Advocate;
    (c) the Scottish Ministers;
    (d) the Director;
    (e) the Director of Public Prosecutions;
    (f) the Director of Public Prosecutions for Northern Ireland;
    (g) the Director of the Serious Fraud Office; and
    (h) the Director of Revenue and Customs Prosecutions.'

(4) In section 447(3) (meaning of 'external investigation'), after paragraph (a) insert—

    '(aa) the extent or whereabouts of property obtained as a result of or in connection with criminal conduct, or'.

109 Minor and consequential amendments relating to Chapter 6

Schedule 6, which contains minor and consequential amendments relating to provisions of this Chapter, has effect.

PART 3
POLICE POWERS ETC.

Powers of arrest

110 Powers of arrest

(1) For section 24 of PACE (arrest without warrant for arrestable offences) substitute—

'24 Arrest without warrant: constables

(1) A constable may arrest without a warrant—
    (a) anyone who is about to commit an offence;
    (b) anyone who is in the act of committing an offence;
    (c) anyone whom he has reasonable grounds for suspecting to be about to commit an offence;
    (d) anyone whom he has reasonable grounds for suspecting to be committing an offence.
(2) If a constable has reasonable grounds for suspecting that an offence has been committed, he may arrest without a warrant anyone whom he has reasonable grounds to suspect of being guilty of it.
(3) If an offence has been committed, a constable may arrest without a warrant—
    (a) anyone who is guilty of the offence;
    (b) anyone whom he has reasonable grounds for suspecting to be guilty of it.
(4) But the power of summary arrest conferred by subsection (1), (2) or (3) is exercisable only if the constable has reasonable grounds for believing that for any of the reasons mentioned in subsection (5) it is necessary to arrest the person in question.
(5) The reasons are—
    (a) to enable the name of the person in question to be ascertained (in the case where the constable does not know, and cannot readily ascertain, 'the person's name, or has reasonable grounds for doubting whether a name given by the person as his name is his real name);

    (b) correspondingly as regards the person's address;

    (c) to prevent the person in question—

        (i) causing physical injury to himself or any other person;

        (ii) suffering physical injury;

        (iii) causing loss of or damage to property;

        (iv) committing an offence against public decency (subject to subsection (6)); or

        (v) causing an unlawful obstruction of the highway;

    (d) to protect a child or other vulnerable person from the person in question;

    (e) to allow the prompt and effective investigation of the offence or of the conduct of the person in question;

    (f) to prevent any prosecution for the offence from being hindered by the disappearance of the person in question.

(6) Subsection (5)(c)(iv) applies only where members of the public going about their normal business cannot reasonably be expected to avoid the person in question.

24A Arrest without warrant: other persons

(1) A person other than a constable may arrest without a warrant—

    (a) anyone who is in the act of committing an indictable offence;

    (b) anyone whom he has reasonable grounds for suspecting to be committing an indictable offence.

(2) Where an indictable offence has been committed, a person other than a constable may arrest without a warrant—

    (a) anyone who is guilty of the offence;

    (b) anyone whom he has reasonable grounds for suspecting to be guilty of it.

(3) But the power of summary arrest conferred by subsection (1) or (2) is exercisable only if—

    (a) the person making the arrest has reasonable grounds for believing that for any of the reasons mentioned in subsection (4) it is necessary to arrest the person in question; and

    (b) it appears to the person making the arrest that it is not reasonably practicable for a constable to make it instead.

(4) The reasons are to prevent the person in question—

    (a) causing physical injury to himself or any other person;

    (b) suffering physical injury;

    (c) causing loss of or damage to property; or

    (d) making off before a constable can assume responsibility for him.'

(2) Section 25 of PACE (general arrest conditions) shall cease to have effect.

(3) In section 66 of PACE (codes of practice), in subsection (1)(a)—

    (a) omit 'or' at the end of sub-paragraph (i),

    (b) at the end of sub-paragraph (ii) insert 'or (iii) to arrest a person;'

(4) The sections 24 and 24A of PACE substituted by subsection (1) are to have effect in relation to any offence whenever committed.

111 Powers of arrest: supplementary

Schedule 7, which supplements section 110 by providing for the repeal of certain enactments (including some which are spent) and by making further supplementary provision, has effect.

Exclusion zones

112 Power to direct a person to leave a place

(1) A constable may direct a person to leave a place if he believes, on reasonable grounds, that the person is in the place at a time when he would be prohibited from entering it by virtue of—

    (a) an order to which subsection (2) applies, or

    (b) a condition to which subsection (3) applies.

(2) This subsection applies to an order which—

    (a) was made, by virtue of any enactment, following the person's conviction of an offence, and

    (b) prohibits the person from entering the place or from doing so during a period specified in the order.

(3) This subsection applies to a condition which—

    (a) was imposed, by virtue of any enactment, as a condition of the person's release from a prison in which he was serving a sentence of imprisonment following his conviction of an offence, and

    (b) prohibits the person from entering the place or from doing so during a period specified in the condition.

(4) A direction under this section may be given orally.

(5) Any person who knowingly contravenes a direction given to him under this section is guilty of an offence and liable on summary conviction to imprisonment for a term not exceeding 51 weeks or to a fine not exceeding level 4 on the standard scale, or to both.

(6) A constable in uniform may arrest without warrant any person he reasonably suspects is committing or has committed an offence under subsection (5).

(7) Subsection (6) ceases to have effect on the commencement of section 110.

(8) In subsection (3)(a)—

    (a) 'sentence of imprisonment' and 'prison' are to be construed in accordance with section 62(5) of the Criminal Justice and Court Service Act 2000 (c. 43);

    (b) the reference to a release from prison includes a reference to a temporary release.

(9) In this section, 'place' includes an area.

(10) This section applies whether or not the order or condition mentioned in subsection (1) was made or imposed before or after the commencement of this section.

Search warrants

113 Search warrants: premises

(1) PACE is amended as follows.

(2) Section 8 (power to authorise entry and search of premises) is amended as provided in subsections (3) and (4).

(3) In subsection (1)—

    (a) in paragraph (b), for 'specified in the application' substitute 'mentioned in subsection (1A) below',

    (b) in paragraph (e), at the end add 'in relation to each set of premises specified in the application'.

(4) After subsection (1) insert—

'(1A) The premises referred to in subsection (1)(b) above are—

  (a) one or more sets of premises specified in the application (in which case the application is for a 'specific premises warrant'); or

  (b) any premises occupied or controlled by a person specified in the application, including such sets of premises as are so specified (in which case the application is for an 'all premises warrant').

(1B) If the application is for an all premises warrant, the justice of the peace must also be satisfied—

  (a) that because of the particulars of the offence referred to in paragraph (a) of subsection (1) above, there are reasonable grounds for believing that it is necessary to search premises occupied or controlled by the person in question which are not specified in the application in order to find the material referred to in paragraph (b) of that subsection; and

  (b) that it is not reasonably practicable to specify in the application all the premises which he occupies or controls and which might need to be searched.'

(5) Section 15 (search warrants—safeguards) is amended as provided in subsections (6) to (8).

(6) For subsection (2)(b) substitute—

'(b) to specify the matters set out in subsection (2A) below; and'.

(7) After subsection (2) insert—

'(2A) The matters which must be specified pursuant to subsection (2)(b) above are—

  (a) if the application is for a specific premises warrant made by virtue of section 8(1A)(a) above or paragraph 12 of Schedule 1 below, each set of premises which it is desired to enter and search;

  (b) if the application is for an all premises warrant made by virtue of section 8(1A)(b) above or paragraph 12 of Schedule 1 below—

    (i) as many sets of premises which it is desired to enter and search as it is reasonably practicable to specify;

    (ii) the person who is in occupation or control of those premises and any others which it is desired to enter and search;

    (iii) why it is necessary to search more premises than those specified under sub-paragraph (i); and

    (iv) why it is not reasonably practicable to specify all the premises which it is desired to enter and search.'

(8) For subsection (6)(a)(iv) substitute—

'(iv) each set of premises to be searched, or (in the case of an all premises warrant) the person who is in occupation or control of premises to be searched, together with any premises under his occupation or control which can be specified and which are to be searched; and'.

(9) In section 16 (execution of warrants)—

  (a) after subsection (3) insert—

'(3A) If the warrant is an all premises warrant, no premises which are not specified in it may be entered or searched unless a police officer of at least the rank of inspector has in writing authorised them to be entered.',

  (b) in subsection (9), after paragraph (b) add—

'and, unless the warrant is a specific premises warrant specifying one set of premises only, he shall do so separately in respect of each set of premises entered and searched, which he shall in each case state in the endorsement.',

    (c) in subsection (12), for 'the premises' substitute 'premises'.

(10) Schedule 1 (special procedure) is amended as follows.

(11) In each of paragraphs 2(a)(ii) and 3(a), at the end add', or on premises occupied or controlled by a person specified in the application (including all such premises on which there are reasonable grounds for believing that there is such material as it is reasonably practicable so to specify);'

(12) In paragraph 3(b), for 'the premises' substitute 'such premises'.

(13) In paragraph 12—

    (a) in sub-paragraph (a)(ii), after 'fulfilled' insert 'in relation to each set of premises specified in the application',

    (b) at the end add 'or (as the case may be) all premises occupied or controlled by the person referred to in paragraph 2(a)(ii) or 3(a), including such sets of premises as are specified in the application (an "all premises warrant")'.

(14) After paragraph 12 insert—

    '12A The judge may not issue an all premises warrant unless he is satisfied—

        (a) that there are reasonable grounds for believing that it is necessary to search premises occupied or controlled by the person in question which are not specified in the application, as well as those which are, in order to find the material in question; and

        (b) that it is not reasonably practicable to specify all the premises which he occupies or controls which might need to be searched.'

(15) In paragraph 14(a), omit 'to which the application relates'.

114 Search warrants: other amendments

    (1) PACE is amended as follows.

    (2) In section 8 (power to authorise entry and search of premises), after the subsection (1B) inserted by section 113(4) of this Act insert—

        '(1C) The warrant may authorise entry to and search of premises on more than one occasion if, on the application, the justice of the peace is satisfied that it is necessary to authorise multiple entries in order to achieve the purpose for which he issues the warrant.

        (1D) If it authorises multiple entries, the number of entries authorised may be unlimited, or limited to a maximum.'

    (3) Section 15 (search warrants—safeguards) is amended as provided in subsections (4) to (7).

    (4) In subsection (2)(a)—

        (a) omit 'and' at the end of sub-paragraph (i),

        (b) at the end of sub-paragraph (ii) insert 'and',

        (c) after that sub-paragraph insert—

            '(iii) if the application is for a warrant authorising entry and search on more than one occasion, the ground on which he applies for such a warrant, and whether he seeks a warrant authorising an unlimited number of entries, or (if not) the maximum number of entries desired;'.

    (5) In subsection (5), at the end add 'unless it specifies that it authorises multiple entries'.

    (6) After subsection (5) insert—

        '(5A) If it specifies that it authorises multiple entries, it must also specify whether the number of entries authorised is unlimited, or limited to a specified maximum.'

(7) For subsection (7) substitute—

'(7) Two copies shall be made of a specific premises warrant (see section 8(1A) (a) above) which specifies only one set of premises and does not authorise multiple entries; and as many copies as are reasonably required may be made of any other kind of warrant.'

(8) In section 16 (execution of warrants)—
(a) in subsection (3), for 'one month' substitute 'three months',
(b) after the subsection (3A) inserted by section 113(9)(a) of this Act, insert—

'(3B) No premises may be entered or searched for the second or any subsequent time under a warrant which authorises multiple entries unless a police officer of at least the rank of inspector has in writing authorised that entry to those premises.',

(c) for subsection (10) substitute—

'(10) A warrant shall be returned to the appropriate person mentioned in subsection (10A) below—
(a) when it has been executed; or
(b) in the case of a specific premises warrant which has not been executed, or an all premises warrant, or any warrant authorising multiple entries, upon the expiry of the period of three months referred to in subsection (3) above or sooner.
(10A) The appropriate person is—
(a) if the warrant was issued by a justice of the peace, the designated officer for the local justice area in which the justice was acting when he issued the warrant;
(b) if it was issued by a judge, the appropriate officer of the court from which he issued it.'

(9) In Schedule 1 (special procedure), in paragraph 17, for 'a Circuit judge' substitute 'a judge of the High Court, a Circuit judge, a Recorder'.

Fireworks

115 Power to stop and search for prohibited fireworks

(1) Section 1 of PACE (powers of constables to stop and search) is amended as follows.
(2) In subsection (2), for 'or any article to which subsection (8A) below applies' substitute', any article to which subsection (8A) below applies or any firework to which subsection (8B) below applies'.
(3) In subsection (3), for 'or any article to which subsection (8A) below applies' substitute', any article to which subsection (8A) below applies or any firework to which subsection (8B) below applies'.
(4) In subsection (6), for 'or an article to which subsection (8A) below applies' substitute', an article to which subsection (8A) below applies or a firework to which subsection (8B) below applies'.
(5) After subsection (8A) insert—

'(8B) This subsection applies to any firework which a person possesses in contravention of a prohibition imposed by fireworks regulations.
(8C) In this section—
(a) "firework" shall be construed in accordance with the definition of "fireworks" in section 1(1) of the Fireworks Act 2003; and
(b) "fireworks regulations" has the same meaning as in that Act.'

Photographing of suspects etc.

116 Photographing of suspects etc.

(1) Section 64A of PACE (photographing of suspects etc.) is amended as follows.

(2) After subsection (1) insert—

'(1A) A person falling within subsection (1B) below may, on the occasion of the relevant event referred to in subsection (1B), be photographed elsewhere than at a police station—

(a) with the appropriate consent; or

(b) if the appropriate consent is withheld or it is not practicable to obtain it, without it.

(1B) A person falls within this subsection if he has been—

(a) arrested by a constable for an offence;

(b) taken into custody by a constable after being arrested for an offence by a person other than a constable;

(c) made subject to a requirement to wait with a community support officer under paragraph 2(3) or (3B) of Schedule 4 to the Police Reform Act 2002 ('the 2002 Act');

(d) given a penalty notice by a constable in uniform under Chapter 1 of Part 1 of the Criminal Justice and Police Act 2001, a penalty notice by a constable under section 444A of the Education Act 1996, or a fixed penalty notice by a constable in uniform under section 54 of the Road Traffic Offenders Act 1988;

(e) given a notice in relation to a relevant fixed penalty offence (within the meaning of paragraph 1 of Schedule 4 to the 2002 Act) by a community support officer by virtue of a designation applying that paragraph to him; or

(f) given a notice in relation to a relevant fixed penalty offence (within the meaning of paragraph 1 of Schedule 5 to the 2002 Act) by an accredited person by virtue of accreditation specifying that that paragraph applies to him.'

(3) In subsection (4)(a), after 'prosecution' insert 'or to the enforcement of a sentence'.

(4) In subsection (5), after paragraph (b) insert '; and

(c) "sentence" includes any order made by a court in England and Wales when dealing with an offender in respect of his offence.'

(5) After subsection (6) insert—

'(6A) In this section, a "photograph" includes a moving image, and corresponding expressions shall be construed accordingly.'

Fingerprints and footwear impressions

117 Fingerprints

(1) Section 61 of PACE (fingerprinting) is amended as provided in subsections (2) to (4).

(2) After subsection (6) insert—

'(6A) A constable may take a person's fingerprints without the appropriate consent if—

(a) the constable reasonably suspects that the person is committing or attempting to commit an offence, or has committed or attempted to commit an offence; and

(b) either of the two conditions mentioned in subsection (6B) is met.

(6B) The conditions are that—

    (a) the name of the person is unknown to, and cannot be readily ascertained by, the constable;

    (b) the constable has reasonable grounds for doubting whether a name furnished by the person as his name is his real name.

  (6C) The taking of fingerprints by virtue of subsection (6A) does not count for any of the purposes of this Act as taking them in the course of the investigation of an offence by the police.'

  (3) In subsection (7), for 'or (6)' substitute', (6) or (6A)'.

  (4) In subsection (7A)—

    (a) after 'police station,' insert 'or by virtue of subsection (6A) at a place other than a police station,',

    (b) in paragraph (a), after 'an officer' insert '(or, in a subsection (6A) case, the constable)'.

  (5) In section 63A of PACE (fingerprints and samples: supplementary provisions)—

    (a) after subsection (1) insert—

'(1ZA) Fingerprints taken by virtue of section 61(6A) above may be checked against other fingerprints to which the person seeking to check has access and which are held by or on behalf of any one or more relevant law-enforcement authorities or which are held in connection with or as a result of an investigation of an offence.',

    (b) in subsection (1A), after 'subsection (1)' insert 'and (1ZA)'.

  (6) Section 64 of PACE (destruction of fingerprints and samples) is amended as follows.

  (7) In subsection (1A), for 'or the conduct of a prosecution' substitute', the conduct of a prosecution or the identification of a deceased person or of the person from whom a body part came'.

  (8) After subsection (1B) insert—

'(1BA) Fingerprints taken from a person by virtue of section 61(6A) above must be destroyed as soon as they have fulfilled the purpose for which they were taken.'

  (9) In subsection (3AB), for 'subsection (3)' substitute 'subsection (1BA) or (3)'.

  (10) In subsection (3AC)—

    (a) in paragraph (a), after 'that' insert 'fingerprint or',

    (b) at the end add the following new sentence—

'This subsection does not apply to fingerprints taken from a person by virtue of section 61(6A) above.'

118 Impressions of footwear

  (1) PACE is amended as provided in subsections (2) to (4).

  (2) After section 61 insert—

'61A Impressions of footwear

  (1) Except as provided by this section, no impression of a person's footwear may be taken without the appropriate consent.

  (2) Consent to the taking of an impression of a person's footwear must be in writing if it is given at a time when he is at a police station.

(3) Where a person is detained at a police station, an impression of his footwear may be taken without the appropriate consent if—

    (a) he is detained in consequence of his arrest for a recordable offence, or has been charged with a recordable offence, or informed that he will be reported for a recordable offence; and

    (b) he has not had an impression taken of his footwear in the course of the investigation of the offence by the police.

(4) Where a person mentioned in paragraph (a) of subsection (3) above has already had an impression taken of his footwear in the course of the investigation of the offence by the police, that fact shall be disregarded for the purposes of that subsection if the impression of his footwear taken previously is—

    (a) incomplete; or

    (b) is not of sufficient quality to allow satisfactory analysis, comparison or matching (whether in the case in question or generally).

(5) If an impression of a person's footwear is taken at a police station, whether with or without the appropriate consent—

    (a) before it is taken, an officer shall inform him that it may be the subject of a speculative search; and

    (b) the fact that the person has been informed of this possibility shall be recorded as soon as is practicable after the impression has been taken, and if he is detained at a police station, the record shall be made on his custody record.

(6) In a case where, by virtue of subsection (3) above, an impression of a person's footwear is taken without the appropriate consent—

    (a) he shall be told the reason before it is taken; and

    (b) the reason shall be recorded on his custody record as soon as is practicable after the impression is taken.

(7) The power to take an impression of the footwear of a person detained at a police station without the appropriate consent shall be exercisable by any constable.

(8) Nothing in this section applies to any person—

    (a) arrested or detained under the terrorism provisions;

    (b) arrested under an extradition arrest power.'

(3) Section 63A (fingerprints and samples: supplementary provisions) is amended as follows—

    (a) in subsection (1), after 'fingerprints', in both places, insert', impressions of footwear',

    (b) in subsection (1C)—

        (i) in paragraph (a), after 'fingerprints' insert', impressions of footwear',

        (ii) in paragraph (b), after 'fingerprints' insert', of the impressions of footwear',

        (iii) after the third 'fingerprints' insert 'or impressions of footwear',

        (iv) after the fourth 'fingerprints' insert', impressions of footwear'.

(4) Section 64 (destruction of fingerprints and samples) is amended as follows—

    (a) in subsection (1A), after 'fingerprints' in both places where it occurs insert', impressions of footwear',

    (b) in subsection (1B)(a), after 'fingerprint' insert 'or an impression of footwear',

    (c) in subsection (3), after 'fingerprints' insert', impressions of footwear',

    (d) in subsection (3AA)—

        (i) for 'and fingerprints' substitute', fingerprints and impressions of footwear',

(ii) in paragraph (b), for 'or, as the case may be, fingerprint' substitute', fingerprint, (or as the case may be) an impression of footwear',

(e) in subsection (3AB)—

    (i) after each of the first and third places 'fingerprint' occurs insert', impression of footwear',

    (ii) after the second place 'fingerprint' occurs, insert', nor the impression of footwear,',

(f) in subsection (3AC), after 'fingerprint' in each place where it occurs (including the 'fingerprint' in paragraph (a) inserted by section 117(10)(a) of this Act), insert', impression of footwear',

(g) in subsection (3AD), after 'fingerprint' insert', impression of footwear',

(h) in subsection (5), after 'fingerprints' in each place where it occurs insert 'or impressions of footwear',

(i) in subsection (6), after 'fingerprints' insert 'or impressions of footwear',

(j) in subsection (6A), after 'fingerprints' insert 'or impressions of footwear'.

Intimate samples

119 Intimate samples

(1) Section 65 of PACE (which defines certain terms for the purposes of Part 5 of that Act) is amended as follows.

(2) In the definition of 'intimate sample', for paragraph (c) substitute—

'(c) a swab taken from any part of a person's genitals (including pubic hair) or from a person's body orifice other than the mouth;'.

(3) In the definition of 'non-intimate sample', for paragraph (c) substitute—

'(c) a swab taken from any part of a person's body other than a part from which a swab taken would be an intimate sample;'.

Custody officers

120 Staff custody officers: designation

(1) Section 38 of the Police Reform Act 2002 (c. 30) (police powers for police authority employees) is amended as provided in subsections (2) to (4).

(2) In subsection (2), after paragraph (d) add—

'(e) staff custody officer.'

(3) In subsection (6), after paragraph (d) add—

'(e) in the case of a person designated as a staff custody officer, Part 4A.'

(4) After subsection (9) add—

'(10) References in this section, section 42 or section 46(4) to powers and duties conferred or imposed on a designated person, or to a designated person's being authorised or required to do anything by virtue of a designation under this section, or to a power or duty exercisable by a designated person in reliance on or by virtue of a designation under this section are, in the case of a staff custody officer at a police station designated under section 35(1) of the 1984 Act, references to those things in relation to him after his appointment as a custody officer for that police station under section 36(2) of that Act.'

(5) After Part 4 of Schedule 4 to the Police Reform Act 2002 (powers exercisable by police civilians) insert—

'PART 4A
STAFF CUSTODY OFFICERS

35A *Exercise of functions of custody officers*

    (1) Where a designation applies this paragraph to any person, he may (subject to sub-paragraph (2)) perform all the functions of a custody officer under the 1984 Act (except those under section 45A(4) of that Act) and under any other enactment which confers functions on such a custody officer.

    (2) But in relation to a police station designated under section 35(1) of the 1984 Act, the person must first also be appointed a custody officer for that police station under section 36(2) of that Act.

    (3) A person performing the functions of a custody officer by virtue of a designation under this paragraph (together with, if appropriate, an appointment as such) shall have all the powers and duties of a custody officer.

    (4) Except in sections 36 and 45A(4) of the 1984 Act, references in any enactment to a custody officer within the meaning of that Act include references to a person performing the functions of a custody officer by virtue of a designation under this paragraph.'

121 Custody officers: amendments to PACE

    (1) Section 36 of PACE (custody officers at police stations) is amended as provided in subsections (2) to (6).

    (2) For subsection (3) substitute—

        '(3) No person may be appointed a custody officer unless—
            (a) he is a police officer of at least the rank of sergeant; or
            (b) he is a staff custody officer.'

    (3) In subsection (5), for 'an officer' substitute 'an individual'.

    (4) In subsection (7)—
        (a) in paragraph (a)—
            (i) after 'by an officer' insert 'or a staff custody officer',
            (ii) for 'such an officer' substitute 'such a person',
        (b) in paragraph (b), for 'such officer' substitute 'such person'.

    (5) In subsection (8)—
        (a) after 'in' insert 'section 34 above or in',
        (b) for 'an officer' substitute 'a person'.

    (6) After subsection (10) add—

        '(11) In this section, "staff custody officer" means a person who has been designated as such under section 38 of the Police Reform Act 2002.'

    (7) In section 39 of PACE (responsibilities in relation to persons detained)—
        (a) in subsection (6)(a), after 'custody officer' insert '(or, if the custody officer is a staff custody officer, any police officer or any police employee)',
        (b) after subsection (6) add—

'(7) In subsection (6) above—
"police employee" means a person employed under section 15 of the Police Act 1996;
"staff custody officer" has the same meaning as in the Police Reform Act 2002.'

Designated and accredited persons

122 Powers of designated and accredited persons

(1) The Police Reform Act 2002 (c. 30) is amended as follows.

(2) In section 42 (supplementary provisions relating to designations)—
    (a) in subsection (2), after 'section 41 shall' insert', subject to subsection (2A),',
    (b) after subsection (2) insert—

'(2A) A police officer of or above the rank of inspector may direct a particular investigating officer not to wear a uniform for the purposes of a particular operation; and if he so directs, subsection (2) shall not apply in relation to that investigating officer for the purposes of that operation.

(2B) In subsection (2A), "investigating officer" means a person designated as an investigating officer under section 38 by the chief officer of police of the same force as the officer giving the direction.'

(3) Schedule 4 (powers exercisable by police civilians) is amended as follows—
    (a) in paragraph 1, after sub-paragraph (2) insert—

'(2A) The reference to the powers mentioned in sub-paragraph (2)(a) does not include those powers so far as they relate to an offence under the provisions in the following list—
    section 1 of the Theft Act 1968,
    section 87 of the Environmental Protection Act 1990.',

    (b) in paragraph 15A (power to modify paragraph 1(2)(a)), for sub-paragraph (1) substitute—

'(1) The Secretary of State may by order amend paragraph 1(2A) so as to remove a provision from the list or add a provision to the list; but the list must contain only provisions mentioned in the first column of the Table in section 1(1) of the Criminal Justice and Police Act 2001.',

and in the heading to paragraph 15A, for '1(2)(a)' substitute '1(2A)'.

(4) Schedule 5 (powers exercisable by accredited persons) is amended as provided in subsections (5) and (6).

(5) In paragraph 1 (power to issue fixed penalty notices)—
    (a) in sub-paragraph (2)(aa), omit 'except in respect of an offence under section 12 of the Licensing Act 1872 or section 91 of the Criminal Justice Act 1967',
    (b) after sub-paragraph (2) insert—

'(2A) The reference to the powers mentioned in sub-paragraph (2)(aa) does not include those powers so far as they relate to an offence under the provisions in the following list—
    section 12 of the Licensing Act 1872,
    section 91 of the Criminal Justice Act 1967,
    section 1 of the Theft Act 1968,
    section 1(1) of the Criminal Damage Act 1971,
    section 87 of the Environmental Protection Act 1990.'

(6) In paragraph 9A (power to modify paragraph 1(2)(aa)), for sub-paragraph (1) substitute—

'(1) The Secretary of State may by order amend paragraph 1(2A) so as to remove a provision from the list or add a provision to the list; but the list must contain only provisions mentioned in the first column of the Table in section 1(1) of the Criminal Justice and Police Act 2001.',

and in the heading to paragraph 9A, for '1(2)(aa)' substitute '1(2A)'.

(7) Schedules 8 and 9 to this Act, which provide for additional powers and duties for designated and accredited persons under the Police Reform Act 2002 (c. 30), have effect.

Provision of information for use by police staff

123 Provision of information for use by police staff

(1) In section 71 of the Criminal Justice and Court Services Act 2000 (c. 43) (access to driver licensing records), in subsection (4), after 'In this section' insert'—

'constables' includes—
- (a) persons employed by a police authority under section 15(1) of the Police Act 1996 who are under the direction and control of the chief officer of police of the police force maintained by that authority,
- (b) persons employed by a police authority under section 9(1) of the Police (Scotland) Act 1967 who are under the direction and control of the chief constable of the police force maintained for the authority's area,
- (c) police support staff (within the meaning of the Police (Northern Ireland) Act 2000), and
- (d) persons employed by the British Transport Police Authority under section 27(1) of the Railways and Transport Safety Act 2003 who are under the direction and control of the Chief Constable of the British Transport Police Force'.

(2) In section 18 of the Vehicles (Crime) Act 2001 (c. 3) (register of registration plate suppliers), after subsection (8) insert—

'(9) In this section, "constables" includes—
- (a) persons employed by a police authority under section 15(1) of the Police Act 1996 who are under the direction and control of the chief officer of police of the police force maintained by that authority,
- (b) persons employed by a police authority under section 9(1) of the Police (Scotland) Act 1967 who are under the direction and control of the chief constable of the police force maintained for the authority's area, and
- (c) persons employed by the British Transport Police Authority under section 27(1) of the Railways and Transport Safety Act 2003 who are under the direction and control of the Chief Constable of the British Transport Police Force.'

(3) In section 36 of the Vehicles (Crime) Act 2001 (c. 3) (access to certain motor insurance information), in subsection (3), after 'In this section—' insert

' "constables" includes—
- (a) persons employed by a police authority under section 15(1) of the Police Act 1996 who are under the direction and control of the chief officer of police of the police force maintained by that authority,
- (b) persons employed by a police authority under section 9(1) of the Police (Scotland) Act 1967 who are under the direction and control of the chief constable of the police force maintained for the authority's area, and

(c) persons employed by the British Transport Police Authority under section 27(1) of the Railways and Transport Safety Act 2003 who are under the direction and control of the Chief Constable of the British Transport Police Force;'.

Interpretation of Part 3

124 Interpretation of Part 3

In this Part, 'PACE' means the Police and Criminal Evidence Act 1984 (c. 60).

PART 4
PUBLIC ORDER AND CONDUCT IN PUBLIC PLACES ETC.

Harassment

125 Harassment intended to deter lawful activities

(1) The Protection from Harassment Act 1997 (c. 40) is amended as follows.

(2) In section 1 (prohibition of harassment)—
   (a) after subsection (1) insert—

'(1A) A person must not pursue a course of conduct—
   (a) which involves harassment of two or more persons, and
   (b) which he knows or ought to know involves harassment of those persons, and
   (c) by which he intends to persuade any person (whether or not one of those mentioned above)—
      (i) not to do something that he is entitled or required to do, or
      (ii) to do something that he is not under any obligation to do.';

   (b) in subsection (2), after 'amounts to' insert 'or involves' and after 'amounted to' insert 'or involved';
   (c) in subsection (3), after 'Subsection (1)' insert 'or (1A)'.

(3) In section 2(1) (offence of harassment) for 'section 1' substitute 'section 1(1) or (1A)'.

(4) In section 3(1) (civil remedy) for 'section 1' substitute 'section 1(1)'.

(5) After section 3 insert—

'3A Injunctions to protect persons from harassment within section 1(1A)

(1) This section applies where there is an actual or apprehended breach of section 1(1A) by any person ("the relevant person").

(2) In such a case—
   (a) any person who is or may be a victim of the course of conduct in question, or
   (b) any person who is or may be a person falling within section 1(1A)(c),
   may apply to the High Court or a county court for an injunction restraining the relevant person from pursuing any conduct which amounts to harassment in relation to any person or persons mentioned or described in the injunction.

(3) Section 3(3) to (9) apply in relation to an injunction granted under subsection (2) above as they apply in relation to an injunction granted as mentioned in section 3(3)(a).'

(6) In section 5(2) (restraining orders) after 'victim' insert 'or victims'.

(7) In section 7 (interpretation of sections 1 to 5)—

(a) for subsection (3) substitute—

'(3) A "course of conduct" must involve—
  (a) in the case of conduct in relation to a single person (see section 1(1)), conduct on at least two occasions in relation to that person, or
  (b) in the case of conduct in relation to two or more persons (see section 1 (1A)), conduct on at least one occasion in relation to each of those persons.';

and

(b) after subsection (4) add—

'(5) References to a person, in the context of the harassment of a person, are references to a person who is an individual.'

126 Harassment etc. of a person in his home

(1) After section 42 of the Criminal Justice and Police Act 2001 (c. 16) insert—

'42A Offence of harassment etc. of a person in his home

(1) A person commits an offence if—
  (a) that person is present outside or in the vicinity of any premises that are used by any individual ("the resident") as his dwelling;
  (b) that person is present there for the purpose (by his presence or otherwise) of representing to the resident or another individual (whether or not one who uses the premises as his dwelling), or of persuading the resident or such another individual—
    (i) that he should not do something that he is entitled or required to do; or
    (ii) that he should do something that he is not under any obligation to do;
  (c) that person—
    (i) intends his presence to amount to the harassment of, or to cause alarm or distress to, the resident; or
    (ii) knows or ought to know that his presence is likely to result in the harassment of, or to cause alarm or distress to, the resident; and
  (d) the presence of that person—
    (i) amounts to the harassment of, or causes alarm or distress to, any person falling within subsection (2); or
    (ii) is likely to result in the harassment of, or to cause alarm or distress to, any such person.
(2) A person falls within this subsection if he is—
  (a) the resident,
  (b) a person in the resident's dwelling, or
  (c) a person in another dwelling in the vicinity of the resident's dwelling.
(3) The references in subsection (1)(c) and (d) to a person's presence are references to his presence either alone or together with that of any other persons who are also present.
(4) For the purposes of this section a person (A) ought to know that his presence is likely to result in the harassment of, or to cause alarm or distress to, a resident if a reasonable person in possession of the same information would think that A's presence was likely to have that effect.
(5) A person guilty of an offence under this section shall be liable, on summary conviction, to imprisonment for a term not exceeding 51 weeks or to a fine not exceeding level 4 on the standard scale, or to both.

(6) In relation to an offence committed before the commencement of section 281(5) of the Criminal Justice Act 2003 (alteration of penalties for summary offences), the reference in subsection (5) to 51 weeks is to be read as a reference to 6 months.

(7) In this section "dwelling" has the same meaning as in Part 1 of the Public Order Act 1986.'

(2) A constable in uniform may arrest without warrant any person he reasonably suspects is committing or has committed an offence under section 42A (as inserted by subsection (1)).

(3) Subsection (2) ceases to have effect on the commencement of section 110 of this Act.

127 Harassment etc: police direction to stay away from person's home

(1) Section 42 of the Criminal Justice and Police Act 2001 (c. 16) (police directions stopping harassment of a person in his home) is amended as follows.

(2) For subsection (4) substitute—

'(4) The requirements that may be imposed by a direction under this section include—
(a) a requirement to leave the vicinity of the premises in question, and
(b) a requirement to leave that vicinity and not to return to it within such period as the constable may specify, not being longer than 3 months;
and (in either case) the requirement to leave the vicinity may be to do so immediately or after a specified period of time.'

(3) In subsection (7), for 'contravenes a direction given to him under this section' substitute 'fails to comply with a requirement in a direction given to him under this section (other than a requirement under subsection (4)(b))'.

(4) After subsection (7) insert—

'(7A) Any person to whom a constable has given a direction including a requirement under subsection (4)(b) commits an offence if he—
(a) returns to the vicinity of the premises in question within the period specified in the direction beginning with the date on which the direction is given; and
(b) does so for the purpose described in subsection (1)(b).

(7B) A person guilty of an offence under subsection (7A) shall be liable, on summary conviction, to imprisonment for a term not exceeding 51 weeks or to a fine not exceeding level 4 on the standard scale, or to both.

(7C) In relation to an offence committed before the commencement of section 281(5) of the Criminal Justice Act 2003 (alteration of penalties for summary offences), the reference in subsection (7B) to 51 weeks is to be read as a reference to 6 months.'

Trespass on designated site

128 Offence of trespassing on designated site

(1) A person commits an offence if he enters, or is on, any designated site in England and Wales or Northern Ireland as a trespasser.

(2) A 'designated site' means a site—
(a) specified or described (in any way) in an order made by the Secretary of State, and
(b) designated for the purposes of this section by the order.

(3) The Secretary of State may only designate a site for the purposes of this section if—

    (a) it is comprised in Crown land; or

    (b) it is comprised in land belonging to Her Majesty in Her private capacity or to the immediate heir to the Throne in his private capacity; or

    (c) it appears to the Secretary of State that it is appropriate to designate the site in the interests of national security.

(4) It is a defence for a person charged with an offence under this section to prove that he did not know, and had no reasonable cause to suspect, that the site in relation to which the offence is alleged to have been committed was a designated site.

(5) A person guilty of an offence under this section is liable on summary conviction—

    (a) to imprisonment for a term not exceeding 51 weeks, or

    (b) to a fine not exceeding level 5 on the standard scale,

    or to both.

(6) No proceedings for an offence under this section may be instituted against any person—

    (a) in England and Wales, except by or with the consent of the Attorney General, or

    (b) in Northern Ireland, except by or with the consent of the Attorney General for Northern Ireland.

(7) For the purposes of this section a person who is on any designated site as a trespasser does not cease to be a trespasser by virtue of being allowed time to leave the site.

(8) In this section—

    (a) 'site' means the whole or part of any building or buildings, or any land, or both;

    (b) 'Crown land' means land in which there is a Crown interest or a Duchy interest.

(9) For this purpose—

'Crown interest' means an interest belonging to Her Majesty in right of the Crown, and

'Duchy interest' means an interest belonging to Her Majesty in right of the Duchy of Lancaster or belonging to the Duchy of Cornwall.

(10) In the application of this section to Northern Ireland, the reference to 51 weeks in subsection (5)(a) is to be read as a reference to 6 months.

129 Corresponding Scottish offence

(1) A person commits an offence if he enters, or is on, any designated Scottish site without lawful authority.

(2) A 'designated Scottish site' means a site in Scotland—

    (a) specified or described (in any way) in an order made by the Secretary of State, and

    (b) designated for the purposes of this section by the order.

(3) The Secretary of State may only designate a site for the purposes of this section if it appears to him that it is appropriate to designate the site in the interests of national security.

(4) It is a defence for a person charged with an offence under this section to prove that he did not know, and had no reasonable cause to suspect, that the site in relation to which the offence is alleged to have been committed was a designated Scottish site.

(5) A person guilty of an offence under this section is liable on summary conviction—
(a) to imprisonment for a term not exceeding 12 months, or
(b) to a fine not exceeding level 5 on the standard scale,
or to both.

(6) For the purposes of subsection (1), a person who is on any designated Scottish site without lawful authority does not acquire lawful authority by virtue of being allowed time to leave the site.

(7) In this section 'site' means the whole or part of any building or buildings, or any land, or both.

130 Designated sites: powers of arrest

(1) A constable in uniform may, in England or Wales, arrest without warrant any person he reasonably suspects is committing or has committed an offence under section 128.
This subsection ceases to have effect on the commencement of section 110.

(2) An offence under section 128 is to be treated as an arrestable offence for the purposes of the Police and Criminal Evidence (Northern Ireland) Order 1989 (S.I. 1989/1341 (N.I. 12)).

(3) A constable in uniform may, in Scotland, arrest without warrant any person he reasonably suspects is committing or has committed an offence under section 129.

131 Designated sites: access

(1) The following provisions do not apply to land in respect of which a designation order is in force—
(a) section 2(1) of the Countryside and Rights of Way Act 2000 (c. 37) (rights of public in relation to access land),
(b) Part III of the Countryside (Northern Ireland) Order 1983 (S.I. 1983/1895 (N.I. 18)) (access to open country), and
(c) section 1 of the Land Reform (Scotland) Act 2003 (asp 2) (access rights).

(2) The Secretary of State may take such steps as he considers appropriate to inform the public of the effect of any designation order, including, in particular, displaying notices on or near the site to which the order relates.

(3) But the Secretary of State may only—
(a) display any such notice, or
(b) take any other steps under subsection (2),
in or on any building or land, if the appropriate person consents.

(4) The 'appropriate person' is—
(a) a person appearing to the Secretary of State to have a sufficient interest in the building or land to consent to the notice being displayed or the steps being taken, or
(b) a person acting on behalf of such a person.

(5) In this section a 'designation order' means—
   (a) in relation to England and Wales or Northern Ireland, an order under section 128, or
   (b) in relation to Scotland, an order under section 129.

Demonstrations in vicinity of Parliament

132 Demonstrating without authorisation in designated area

(1) Any person who—
   (a) organises a demonstration in a public place in the designated area, or
   (b) takes part in a demonstration in a public place in the designated area, or
   (c) carries on a demonstration by himself in a public place in the designated area,
   is guilty of an offence if, when the demonstration starts, authorisation for the demonstration has not been given under section 134(2).
(2) It is a defence for a person accused of an offence under subsection (1) to show that he reasonably believed that authorisation had been given.
(3) Subsection (1) does not apply if the demonstration is—
   (a) a public procession of which notice is required to be given under subsection (1) of section 11 of the Public Order Act 1986 (c. 64), or of which (by virtue of subsection (2) of that section) notice is not required to be given, or
   (b) a public procession for the purposes of section 12 or 13 of that Act.
(4) Subsection (1) also does not apply in relation to any conduct which is lawful under section 220 of the Trade Union and Labour Relations (Consolidation) Act 1992 (c. 52).
(5) If subsection (1) does not apply by virtue of subsection (3) or (4), nothing in sections 133 to 136 applies either.
(6) Section 14 of the Public Order Act 1986 (imposition of conditions on public assemblies) does not apply in relation to a public assembly which is also a demonstration in a public place in the designated area.
(7) In this section and in sections 133 to 136—
   (a) 'the designated area' means the area specified in an order under section 138,
   (b) 'public place' means any highway or any place to which at the material time the public or any section of the public has access, on payment or otherwise, as of right or by virtue of express or implied permission,
   (c) references to any person organising a demonstration include a person participating in its organisation,
   (d) references to any person organising a demonstration do not include a person carrying on a demonstration by himself,
   (e) references to any person or persons taking part in a demonstration (except in subsection (1) of this section) include a person carrying on a demonstration by himself.

133 Notice of demonstrations in designated area

(1) A person seeking authorisation for a demonstration in the designated area must give written notice to that effect to the Commissioner of Police of the Metropolis (referred to in this section and section 134 as 'the Commissioner').

213

(2) The notice must be given—
  (a) if reasonably practicable, not less than 6 clear days before the day on which the demonstration is to start, or
  (b) if that is not reasonably practicable, then as soon as it is, and in any event not less than 24 hours before the time the demonstration is to start.

(3) The notice must be given—
  (a) if the demonstration is to be carried on by more than one person, by any of the persons organising it,
  (b) if it is to be carried on by a person by himself, by that person.

(4) The notice must state—
  (a) the date and time when the demonstration is to start,
  (b) the place where it is to be carried on,
  (c) how long it is to last,
  (d) whether it is to be carried on by a person by himself or not,
  (e) the name and address of the person giving the notice.

(5) A notice under this section must be given by—
  (a) delivering it to a police station in the metropolitan police district, or
  (b) sending it by post by recorded delivery to such a police station.

(6) Section 7 of the Interpretation Act 1978 (c. 30) (under which service of a document is deemed to have been effected at the time it would be delivered in the ordinary course of post) does not apply to a notice under this section.

134 Authorisation of demonstrations in designated area

(1) This section applies if a notice complying with the requirements of section 133 is received at a police station in the metropolitan police district by the time specified in section 133(2).

(2) The Commissioner must give authorisation for the demonstration to which the notice relates.

(3) In giving authorisation, the Commissioner may impose on the persons organising or taking part in the demonstration such conditions specified in the authorisation and relating to the demonstration as in the Commissioner's reasonable opinion are necessary for the purpose of preventing any of the following—
  (a) hindrance to any person wishing to enter or leave the Palace of Westminster,
  (b) hindrance to the proper operation of Parliament,
  (c) serious public disorder,
  (d) serious damage to property,
  (e) disruption to the life of the community,
  (f) a security risk in any part of the designated area,
  (g) risk to the safety of members of the public (including any taking part in the demonstration).

(4) The conditions may, in particular, impose requirements as to—
  (a) the place where the demonstration may, or may not, be carried on,
  (b) the times at which it may be carried on,
  (c) the period during which it may be carried on,
  (d) the number of persons who may take part in it,
  (e) the number and size of banners or placards used,
  (f) maximum permissible noise levels.

(5) The authorisation must specify the particulars of the demonstration given in the notice under section 133 pursuant to subsection (4) of that section, with any modifications made necessary by any condition imposed under subsection (3) of this section.

(6) The Commissioner must give notice in writing of—
   (a) the authorisation,
   (b) any conditions imposed under subsection (3), and
   (c) the particulars mentioned in subsection (5),
   to the person who gave the notice under section 133.

(7) Each person who takes part in or organises a demonstration in the designated area is guilty of an offence if—
   (a) he knowingly fails to comply with a condition imposed under subsection (3) which is applicable to him (except where it is varied under section 135), or
   (b) he knows or should have known that the demonstration is carried on otherwise than in accordance with the particulars set out in the authorisation by virtue of subsection (5).

(8) It is a defence for a person accused of an offence under subsection (7) to show—
   (a) (in a paragraph (a) case) that the failure to comply, or
   (b) (in a paragraph (b) case) that the divergence from the particulars,
   arose from circumstances beyond his control, or from something done with the agreement, or by the direction, of a police officer.

(9) The notice required by subsection (6) may be sent by post to the person who gave the notice under section 133 at the address stated in that notice pursuant to subsection (4) (e) of that section.

(10) If the person to whom the notice required by subsection (6) is to be given has agreed, it may be sent to him by email or by facsimile transmission at the address or number notified by him for the purpose to the Commissioner (and a notice so sent is 'in writing' for the purposes of that subsection).

135 Supplementary directions

(1) This section applies if the senior police officer reasonably believes that it is necessary, in order to prevent any of the things mentioned in paragraphs (a) to (g) of subsection (3) of section 134—
   (a) to impose additional conditions on those taking part in or organising a demonstration authorised under that section, or
   (b) to vary any condition imposed under that subsection or under paragraph (a) (including such a condition as varied under subsection (2)).

(2) The senior police office may give directions to those taking part in or organising the demonstration imposing such additional conditions or varying any such condition already imposed.

(3) A person taking part in or organising the demonstration who knowingly fails to comply with a condition which is applicable to him and which is imposed or varied by a direction under this section is guilty of an offence.

(4) It is a defence for him to show that the failure to comply arose from circumstances beyond his control.

(5) In this section, 'the senior police officer' means the most senior in rank of the police officers present at the scene (or any one of them if there are more than one of the same rank).

136 Offences under sections 132 to 135: penalties

(1) A person guilty of an offence under section 132(1)(a) is liable on summary conviction to imprisonment for a term not exceeding 51 weeks, to a fine not exceeding level 4 on the standard scale, or to both.

(2) A person guilty of an offence under section 132(1)(b) or (c) is liable on summary conviction to a fine not exceeding level 3 on the standard scale.

(3) A person guilty of an offence under section 134(7) or 135(3) is liable on summary conviction—

    (a) if the offence was in relation to his capacity as organiser of the demonstration, to imprisonment for a term not exceeding 51 weeks, to a fine not exceeding level 4 on the standard scale, or to both,

    (b) otherwise, to a fine not exceeding level 3 on the standard scale.

(4) A person who is guilty of the offence of inciting another to—

    (a) do anything which would constitute an offence mentioned in subsection (1), (2) or (3), or

    (b) fail to do anything where the failure would constitute such an offence,

is liable on summary conviction to imprisonment for a term not exceeding 51 weeks, to a fine not exceeding level 4 on the standard scale, or to both, notwithstanding section 45(3) of the Magistrates' Courts Act 1980 (c. 43).

(5) A constable in uniform may arrest without warrant anyone he reasonably believes is committing an offence mentioned in subsections (1) to (4).

This subsection ceases to have effect on the coming into force of section 110.

137 Loudspeakers in designated area

(1) Subject to subsection (2), a loudspeaker shall not be operated, at any time or for any purpose, in a street in the designated area.

(2) Subsection (1) does not apply to the operation of a loudspeaker—

    (a) in case of emergency,

    (b) for police, fire and rescue authority or ambulance purposes,

    (c) by the Environment Agency, a water undertaker or a sewerage undertaker in the exercise of any of its functions,

    (d) by a local authority within its area,

    (e) for communicating with persons on a vessel for the purpose of directing the movement of that or any other vessel,

    (f) if the loudspeaker forms part of a public telephone system,

    (g) if the loudspeaker is in or fixed to a vehicle and subsection (3) applies,

    (h) otherwise than on a highway, by persons employed in connection with a transport undertaking used by the public, but only if the loudspeaker is operated solely for making announcements to passengers or prospective passengers or to other persons so employed,

    (i) in accordance with a consent granted by a local authority under Schedule 2 to the Noise and Statutory Nuisance Act 1993 (c. 40).

(3) This subsection applies if the loudspeaker referred to in subsection (2)(g)—

    (a) is operated solely for the entertainment of or for communicating with the driver or a passenger of the vehicle (or, if the loudspeaker is or forms part of the horn or similar warning instrument of the vehicle, solely for giving warning to other traffic), and

(b) is so operated as not to give reasonable cause for annoyance to persons in the vicinity.

(4) A person who operates or permits the operation of a loudspeaker in contravention of subsection (1) is guilty of an offence and is liable on summary conviction to—

(a) a fine not exceeding level 5 on the standard scale, together with

(b) a further fine not exceeding £50 for each day on which the offence continues after the conviction.

(5) In this section—

'local authority' means a London borough council (and, in subsection (2)(d), the Greater London Authority),

'street' means a street within the meaning of section 48(1) of the New Roads and Street Works Act 1991 (c. 22) which is for the time being open to the public,

'the designated area' means the area specified in an order under section 138,

'vessel' includes a hovercraft within the meaning of the Hovercraft Act 1968 (c. 59).

(6) In Schedule 2 to the Noise and Statutory Nuisance Act 1993 (consent to the operation of loudspeakers in streets or roads), in paragraph 1(1), at the end add 'or of section 137(1) of the Serious Organised Crime and Police Act 2005'.

138 The designated area

(1) The Secretary of State may by order specify an area as the designated area for the purposes of sections 132 to 137.

(2) The area may be specified by description, by reference to a map or in any other way.

(3) No point in the area so specified may be more than one kilometre in a straight line from the point nearest to it in Parliament Square.

Anti-social behaviour

139 Orders about anti-social behaviour etc.

(1) The Crime and Disorder Act 1998 (c. 37) is amended as provided in subsections (2) to (9).

(2) In section 1 (anti-social behaviour orders), after subsection (10B) insert—

'(10C) In proceedings for an offence under subsection (10), a copy of the original anti-social behaviour order, certified as such by the proper officer of the court which made it, is admissible as evidence of its having been made and of its contents to the same extent that oral evidence of those things is admissible in those proceedings.'

(3) The existing text of section 1A (power of Secretary of State to add to relevant authorities) is to be subsection (1) of that section, and after that subsection add—

'(2) The Secretary of State may by order—

(a) provide that a person or body of any other description specified in the order is, in such cases and circumstances as may be prescribed by the order, to be a relevant authority for the purposes of such of sections 1 above and 1B, 1CA and 1E below as are specified in the order; and

217

(b) prescribe the description of persons who are to be "relevant persons" in relation to that person or body.'

(4) In section 1C (orders about anti-social behaviour on conviction in criminal proceedings)—

(a) after subsection (4) insert—

'(4A) The court may adjourn any proceedings in relation to an order under this section even after sentencing the offender.

(4B) If the offender does not appear for any adjourned proceedings, the court may further adjourn the proceedings or may issue a warrant for his arrest.

(4C) But the court may not issue a warrant for the offender's arrest unless it is satisfied that he has had adequate notice of the time and place of the adjourned proceedings.',

(b) in subsection (9), after '(10)' insert ', (10C)'.

(5) Section 1D (interim orders) is amended as provided in subsections (6) to (9).

(6) For subsections (1) and (2) substitute—

'(1) This section applies where—

(a) an application is made for an anti-social behaviour order;

(b) an application is made for an order under section 1B;

(c) a request is made by the prosecution for an order under section 1C; or

(d) the court is minded to make an order under section 1C of its own motion.

(2) If, before determining the application or request, or before deciding whether to make an order under section 1C of its own motion, the court considers that it is just to make an order under this section pending the determination of that application or request or before making that decision, it may make such an order.'

(7) In subsection (4)(c), for 'main application' substitute 'application or request mentioned in subsection (1), or on the court's making a decision as to whether or not to make an order under section 1C of its own motion.'

(8) In subsection (5), at the beginning insert 'In relation to cases to which this section applies by virtue of paragraph (a) or (b) of subsection (1),'

(9) After subsection (5) add—

'(6) In relation to cases to which this section applies by virtue of paragraph (c) or (d) of subsection (1)—

(a) subsections (6) and (10) to (12) of section 1 apply for the purposes of the making and effect of orders under this section as they apply for the purposes of the making and effect of anti-social behaviour orders; and

(b) section 1CA applies for the purposes of the variation or discharge of an order under this section as it applies for the purposes of the variation or discharge of an order under section 1C.'

(10) In section 14A of the Football Spectators Act 1989 (c. 37) (banning orders on conviction of an offence), after subsection (4) insert—

'(4A) The court may adjourn any proceedings in relation to an order under this section even after sentencing the offender.

(4B) If the offender does not appear for any adjourned proceedings, the court may further adjourn the proceedings or may issue a warrant for his arrest.

(4C) But the court may not issue a warrant for the offender's arrest unless it is satisfied that he has had adequate notice of the time and place of the adjourned proceedings.'

140 Variation and discharge of anti-social behaviour orders made on conviction

(1) The Crime and Disorder Act 1998 (c. 37) is amended as follows.

(2) In section 1 (anti-social behaviour orders), in subsection (1A), after '1B' insert', 1CA'.

(3) In section 1C (orders on conviction), omit subsections (6) to (8).

(4) After section 1C insert—

'1CA Variation and discharge of orders under section 1C

(1) An offender subject to an order under section 1C may apply to the court which made it for it to be varied or discharged.

(2) If he does so, he must also send written notice of his application to the Director of Public Prosecutions.

(3) The Director of Public Prosecutions may apply to the court which made an order under section 1C for it to be varied or discharged.

(4) A relevant authority may also apply to the court which made an order under section 1C for it to be varied or discharged if it appears to it that—

    (a) in the case of variation, the protection of relevant persons from anti-social acts by the person subject to the order would be more appropriately effected by a variation of the order;

    (b) in the case of discharge, that it is no longer necessary to protect relevant persons from anti-social acts by him by means of such an order.

(5) If the Director of Public Prosecutions or a relevant authority applies for the variation or discharge of an order under section 1C, he or it must also send written notice of the application to the person subject to the order.

(6) In the case of an order under section 1C made by a magistrates' court, the references in subsections (1), (3) and (4) to the court by which the order was made include a reference to any magistrates' court acting in the same local justice area as that court.

(7) No order under section 1C shall be discharged on an application under this section before the end of the period of two years beginning with the day on which the order takes effect, unless—

    (a) in the case of an application under subsection (1), the Director of Public Prosecutions consents, or

    (b) in the case of an application under subsection (3) or (4), the offender consents.'

(5) In section 3 of the Prosecution of Offences Act 1985 (c. 23) (functions of the Director of Public Prosecutions), in subsection (2), after paragraph (fa) insert—

'(fb) where it appears to him appropriate to do so, to have the conduct of applications under section 1CA(3) of the Crime and Disorder Act 1998 for the variation or discharge of orders made under section 1C of that Act;

(fc) where it appears to him appropriate to do so, to appear on any application under section 1CA of that Act made by a person subject to an order under section 1C of that Act for the variation or discharge of the order.'

141 Anti-social behaviour orders etc: reporting restrictions

(1) The Crime and Disorder Act 1998 (c. 37) is amended as follows.

(2) In section 1 (anti-social behaviour orders)—

    (a) after subsection (10C) (inserted by section 139(2) of this Act), insert—

'(10D) In relation to proceedings brought against a child or a young person for an offence under subsection (10)—

(a) section 49 of the Children and Young Persons Act 1933 (restrictions on reports of proceedings in which children and young persons are concerned) does not apply in respect of the child or young person against whom the proceedings are brought;

(b) section 45 of the Youth Justice and Criminal Evidence Act 1999 (power to restrict reporting of criminal proceedings involving persons under 18) does so apply.

(10E) If, in relation to any such proceedings, the court does exercise its power to give a direction under section 45 of the Youth Justice and Criminal Evidence Act 1999, it shall give its reasons for doing so.',

(b) in subsection (12), before the definition of 'the commencement date' insert—

' "child" and "young person" shall have the same meaning as in the Children and Young Persons Act 1933;'.

(3) In section 1C (orders about anti-social behaviour on conviction in criminal proceedings), in subsection (9), after '(10C)' (inserted by section 139(4)(b) of this Act) insert', (10D), (10E)'.

(4) Subject to paragraph 2(2) of Schedule 2 to the Youth Justice and Criminal Evidence Act 1999 (c. 23), until section 45 of that Act comes into force, the references to it in section 1 (10D)(b) and (10E) of the Crime and Disorder Act 1998 (c. 37) (inserted by subsection (2) of this section) shall be read as references to section 39 of the Children and Young Persons Act 1933 (c. 12).

142 Contracting out of local authority functions relating to anti-social behaviour orders

(1) In the Crime and Disorder Act 1998 after section 1E (consultation requirements relating to individual support orders) insert—

'1F Contracting out of local authority functions

(1) The Secretary of State may by order provide that a relevant authority which is a local authority may make arrangements with a person specified (or of a description specified) in the order for the exercise of any function it has under sections 1 to 1E above—
(a) by such a person, or
(b) by an employee of his.

(2) The order may provide—
(a) that the power of the relevant authority to make the arrangements is subject to such conditions as are specified in the order;
(b) that the arrangements must be subject to such conditions as are so specified;
(c) that the arrangements may be made subject to such other conditions as the relevant authority thinks appropriate.

(3) The order may provide that the arrangements may authorise the exercise of the function—
(a) either wholly or to such extent as may be specified in the order or arrangements;
(b) either generally or in such cases or areas as may be so specified.

(4) An order may provide that the person with whom arrangements are made in pursuance of the order is to be treated as if he were a public body for the purposes of section 1 of the Local Authorities (Goods and Services) Act 1970.

(5) The Secretary of State must not make an order under this section unless he first consults—

    (a) the National Assembly for Wales, if the order relates to a relevant authority in Wales;

    (b) such representatives of local government as he thinks appropriate;

    (c) such other persons as he thinks appropriate.

(6) Any arrangements made by a relevant authority in pursuance of an order under this section do not prevent the relevant authority from exercising the function to which the arrangements relate.

(7) The following provisions of the Deregulation and Contracting Out Act 1994 apply for the purposes of arrangements made in pursuance of an order under this section as they apply for the purposes of an authorisation to exercise functions by virtue of an order under section 70(2) of that Act—

    (a) section 72 (effect of contracting out);

    (b) section 73 (termination of contracting out);

    (c) section 75 and Schedule 15 (provision relating to disclosure of information);

    (d) paragraph 3 of Schedule 16 (authorised persons to be treated as officers of local authority).

(8) For the purposes of subsection (7), any reference in the provisions specified in paragraphs (a) to (d) to a person authorised to exercise a function must be construed as a reference to a person with whom an arrangement is made for the exercise of the function in pursuance of an order under this section.

(9) Relevant authorities and any person with whom arrangements are made in pursuance of an order under this section must have regard to any guidance issued by the Secretary of State for the purposes of this section.

(10) An order under this section may make different provision for different purposes.

(11) An order under this section may contain—

    (a) such consequential, supplemental or incidental provisions (including provision modifying any enactment), or

    (b) such transitional provisions or savings,

as the person making the order thinks appropriate.

(12) Each of the following is a local authority—

    (a) a local authority within the meaning of section 270 of the Local Government Act 1972;

    (b) the Common Council of the City of London;

    (c) the Council of the Isles of Scilly.'

(2) In subsection (1) of section 1A of that Act (definition of relevant authority) (as renumbered by section 139(3) of this Act) for 'and 1E' substitute', 1E and 1F'.

(3) In section 114(3) of that Act (orders and regulations) after 'section' insert '1F,'.

143 Special measures for witnesses in proceedings for anti-social behaviour orders etc.

After section 1H of the Crime and Disorder Act 1998 (c. 37) (as amended by the Drugs Act 2005 (c. 17)) insert—

'1I Special measures for witnesses

(1) This section applies to the following proceedings—

    (a) any proceedings in a magistrates' court on an application for an anti-social behaviour order,

    (b) any proceedings in a magistrates' court or the Crown Court so far as relating to the issue whether to make an order under section 1C, and

    (c) any proceedings in a magistrates' court so far as relating to the issue whether to make an order under section 1D.

(2) Chapter 1 of Part 2 of the Youth Justice and Criminal Evidence Act 1999 (special measures directions in the case of vulnerable and intimidated witnesses) shall apply in relation to any such proceedings as it applies in relation to criminal proceedings, but with—

    (a) the omission of the provisions of that Act mentioned in subsection (3) (which make provision appropriate only in the context of criminal proceedings), and

    (b) any other necessary modifications.

(3) The provisions are—

    (a) section 17(4),

    (b) section 21(1)(b) and (5) to (7),

    (c) section 22(1)(b) and (2)(b) and (c),

    (d) section 27(10), and

    (e) section 32.

(4) Any rules of court made under or for the purposes of Chapter 1 of Part 2 of that Act shall apply in relation to proceedings to which this section applies—

    (a) to such extent as may be provided by rules of court, and

    (b) subject to such modifications as may be so provided.

(5) Section 47 of that Act (restrictions on reporting special measures directions etc.) applies, with any necessary modifications, in relation to—

    (a) a direction under section 19 of the Act as applied by this section, or

    (b) a direction discharging or varying such a direction,

and sections 49 and 51 of that Act (offences) apply accordingly.'

Parental compensation orders

144 Parental compensation orders

Schedule 10 is to have effect.

PART 5
MISCELLANEOUS

Protection of activities of certain organisations

145 Interference with contractual relationships so as to harm animal research organisation

(1) A person (A) commits an offence if, with the intention of harming an animal research organisation, he—

    (a) does a relevant act, or

    (b) threatens that he or somebody else will do a relevant act,

in circumstances in which that act or threat is intended or likely to cause a second person (B) to take any of the steps in subsection (2).

(2) The steps are—

    (a) not to perform any contractual obligation owed by B to a third person (C) (whether or not such non-performance amounts to a breach of contract);

    (b) to terminate any contract B has with C;

    (c) not to enter into a contract with C.

(3) For the purposes of this section, a 'relevant act' is—

    (a) an act amounting to a criminal offence, or

    (b) a tortious act causing B to suffer loss or damage of any description;

but paragraph (b) does not include an act which is actionable on the ground only that it induces another person to break a contract with B.

(4) For the purposes of this section, 'contract' includes any other arrangement (and 'contractual' is to be read accordingly).

(5) For the purposes of this section, to 'harm' an animal research organisation means—

    (a) to cause the organisation to suffer loss or damage of any description, or

    (b) to prevent or hinder the carrying out by the organisation of any of its activities.

(6) This section does not apply to any act done wholly or mainly in contemplation or furtherance of a trade dispute.

(7) In subsection (6) 'trade dispute' has the same meaning as in Part 4 of the Trade Union and Labour Relations (Consolidation) Act 1992 (c. 52), except that section 218 of that Act shall be read as if—

    (a) it made provision corresponding to section 244(4) of that Act, and

    (b) in subsection (5), the definition of 'worker' included any person falling within paragraph (b) of the definition of 'worker' in section 244(5).

146 Intimidation of persons connected with animal research organisation

(1) A person (A) commits an offence if, with the intention of causing a second person (B) to abstain from doing something which B is entitled to do (or to do something which B is entitled to abstain from doing)—

    (a) A threatens B that A or somebody else will do a relevant act, and

    (b) A does so wholly or mainly because B is a person falling within subsection (2).

(2) A person falls within this subsection if he is—

    (a) an employee or officer of an animal research organisation;

    (b) a student at an educational establishment that is an animal research organisation;

    (c) a lessor or licensor of any premises occupied by an animal research organisation;

    (d) a person with a financial interest in, or who provides financial assistance to, an animal research organisation;

    (e) a customer or supplier of an animal research organisation;

    (f) a person who is contemplating becoming someone within paragraph (c), (d) or (e);

    (g) a person who is, or is contemplating becoming, a customer or supplier of someone within paragraph (c), (d), (e) or (f);

    (h) an employee or officer of someone within paragraph (c), (d), (e), (f) or (g);

    (i) a person with a financial interest in, or who provides financial assistance to, someone within paragraph (c), (d), (e), (f) or (g);

    (j) a spouse, civil partner, friend or relative of, or a person who is known personally to, someone within any of paragraphs (a) to (i);

    (k) a person who is, or is contemplating becoming, a customer or supplier of someone within paragraph (a), (b), (h), (i) or (j); or

    (l) an employer of someone within paragraph (j).

(3) For the purposes of this section, an 'officer' of an animal research organisation or a person includes—

    (a) where the organisation or person is a body corporate, a director, manager or secretary;

    (b) where the organisation or person is a charity, a charity trustee (within the meaning of the Charities Act 1993 (c. 10));

    (c) where the organisation or person is a partnership, a partner.

(4) For the purposes of this section—

    (a) a person is a customer or supplier of another person if he purchases goods, services or facilities from, or (as the case may be) supplies goods, services or facilities to, that other; and

    (b) 'supplier' includes a person who supplies services in pursuance of any enactment that requires or authorises such services to be provided.

(5) For the purposes of this section, a 'relevant act' is—

    (a) an act amounting to a criminal offence, or

    (b) a tortious act causing B or another person to suffer loss or damage of any description.

(6) The Secretary of State may by order amend this section so as to include within subsection (2) any description of persons framed by reference to their connection with—

    (a) an animal research organisation, or

    (b) any description of persons for the time being mentioned in that subsection.

(7) This section does not apply to any act done wholly or mainly in contemplation or furtherance of a trade dispute.

(8) In subsection (7) 'trade dispute' has the meaning given by section 145(7).

147 Penalty for offences under sections 145 and 146

(1) A person guilty of an offence under section 145 or 146 is liable—

    (a) on summary conviction, to imprisonment for a term not exceeding 12 months or to a fine not exceeding the statutory maximum, or to both;

    (b) on conviction on indictment, to imprisonment for a term not exceeding five years or to a fine, or to both.

(2) No proceedings for an offence under either of those sections may be instituted except by or with the consent of the Director of Public Prosecutions.

148 Animal research organisations

(1) For the purposes of sections 145 and 146 'animal research organisation' means any person or organisation falling within subsection (2) or (3).

(2) A person or organisation falls within this subsection if he or it is the owner, lessee or licensee of premises constituting or including—

    (a) a place specified in a licence granted under section 4 or 5 of the 1986 Act,

    (b) a scientific procedure establishment designated under section 6 of that Act, or

    (c) a breeding or supplying establishment designated under section 7 of that Act.

(3) A person or organisation falls within this subsection if he or it employs, or engages under a contract for services, any of the following in his capacity as such—

    (a) the holder of a personal licence granted under section 4 of the 1986 Act,

    (b) the holder of a project licence granted under section 5 of that Act,

    (c) a person specified under section 6(5) of that Act, or

    (d) a person specified under section 7(5) of that Act.

(4) The Secretary of State may by order amend this section so as to include a reference to any description of persons whom he considers to be involved in, or to have a direct connection with persons who are involved in, the application of regulated procedures.

(5) In this section—

'the 1986 Act' means the Animals (Scientific Procedures) Act 1986 (c. 14);

'organisation' includes any institution, trust, undertaking or association of persons;

'premises' includes any place within the meaning of the 1986 Act.

'regulated procedures' has the meaning given by section 2 of the 1986 Act.

149 Extension of sections 145 to 147

(1) The Secretary of State may by order provide for sections 145, 146 and 147 to apply in relation to persons or organisations of a description specified in the order as they apply in relation to animal research organisations.

(2) The Secretary of State may, however, only make an order under this section if satisfied that a series of acts has taken place and—

    (a) that those acts were directed at persons or organisations of the description specified in the order or at persons having a connection with them, and

    (b) that, if those persons or organisations had been animal research organisa- tions, those acts would have constituted offences under section 145 or 146.

(3) In this section 'organisation' and 'animal research organisation' have the mean- ings given by section 148.

Vehicle registration and insurance and road traffic offences

150 Offence in respect of incorrectly registered vehicles

(1) After section 43B of the Vehicle Excise and Registration Act 1994 (c. 22) insert—

'Offence in respect of incorrectly registered vehicles

43C Offence of using an incorrectly registered vehicles

(1) A person is guilty of an offence if, on a public road or in a public place, he uses a vehicle to which subsection (2) applies and in respect of which—

    (a) the name and address of the keeper are not recorded in the register, or

    (b) any of the particulars recorded in the register are incorrect.

(2) This sebsection applies to a vehicle if—

    (a) vehicle excise duty is chargeable in respect of it, or

    (b) it is an exempt vehicle in respect of which regulations under this Act require a nil licence to be in force.

(3) It is a defence for a person charged with an offence under subsection (1) to show (as the case may be)—

    (a) that there was no reasonable opportunity, before the material time, to furnish the name and address of the keeper of the vehicle, or

    (b) that there was no reasonable opportunity, before the material time, to furnish particulars correcting the incorrect particulars.

(4) It is also a defence for a person charged with an offence under subsection (1) to show—

      (a) that he had reasonable grounds for believing, or that it was reasonable for him to expect, that the name and address of the keeper or the other particulars of registration (as the case may be) were correctly recorded in the register, or

      (b) that any exception prescribed in regulations under this section is met.

(5) A person guilty of an offence under this section is liable on summary conviction to a fine not exceeding level 3 on the standard scale.

(6) The Secretary of State may make regulations prescribing, varying or revoking exceptions for the purposes of subsection (4)(b).

(7) In this section—

"keeper", in relation to a vehicle, means the person by whom it is kept at the material time; "the register" means the register kept by the Secretary of State under Part 2.'

(2) In Schedule 3 to the Road Traffic Offenders Act 1988 (c. 53) (fixed penalty offences) after the entry relating to section 43 of the Vehicle Excise and Registration Act 1994 insert—

'Section 43C of that Act   Using an incorrectly registered vehicle.'

151 Power of constables etc. to require production of registration documents in respect of a vehicle

After section 28 of the Vehicle Excise and Registration Act 1994 (c. 22) insert—

'Power of constables etc. to require production of documents

28A Power of constables etc. to require production of registration documents

(1) A person using a vehicle in respect of which a registration document has been issued must produce the document for inspection on being so required by—
      (a) a constable, or
      (b) a person authorised by the Secretary of State for the purposes of this section (an "authorised person").

(2) An authorised person exercising the power conferred by subsection (1) must, if so requested, produce evidence of his authority to exercise the power.

(3) A person is guilty of an offence if he fails to comply with subsection (1).

(4) Subsection (3) does not apply if any of the following conditions is satisfied.

(5) The first condition is that—
      (a) the person produces the registration document, in person, at a police station specified by him at the time of the request, and
      (b) he does so within 7 days after the date on which the request was made or as soon as is reasonably practicable.

(6) The second condition is that—
      (a) the vehicle is subject to a lease or hire agreement,
      (b) the vehicle is not registered in the name of the lessee or hirer under that agreement and is not required to be so registered,
      (c) the person produces appropriate evidence of the agreement to the constable or authorised person at the time of the request or he produces such evidence in person, at a police station specified by him at the time of the request—
         (i) within 7 days after the date of the request, or
         (ii) as soon as is reasonably practicable, and
      (d) the person has reasonable grounds for believing, or it is reasonable for him to expect, that the person from whom the vehicle has been leased or hired is able to produce, or require the production of, the registration document.

(7) In subsection (6)(c) "appropriate evidence" means—

(a) a copy of the agreement, or

(b) such other documentary evidence of the agreement as is prescribed in regulations under this section.

(8) The third condition is that any exception prescribed in regulations under this section is met.

(9) Where a requirement is imposed under subsection (1) by an authorised person, a testing station provided under section 52(2) of the Road Traffic Act 1988 may be specified under subsection (5)(a) or (6)(c) instead of a police station.

(10) A person accused of an offence under this section is not entitled to the benefit of an exception conferred by or under this section unless evidence is adduced that is sufficient to raise an issue with respect to that exception, but where evidence is so adduced it is for the prosecution to prove beyond reasonable doubt that the exception does not apply.

(11) A person guilty of an offence under this section is liable on summary conviction to a fine not exceeding level 2 on the standard scale.

(12) The Secretary of State may make regulations—

(a) prescribing descriptions of evidence for the purposes of subsection (7);

(b) prescribing, varying or revoking exceptions for the purposes of subsection (8).

(13) In this section "registration document" means a registration document issued in accordance with regulations under section 22(1)(e).'

152 Power to seize etc. vehicles driven without licence or insurance

After section 165 of the Road Traffic Act 1988 (c. 52) insert—

'165A Power to seize vehicles driven without licence or insurance

(1) Subsection (5) applies if any of the following conditions is satisfied.

(2) The first condition is that—

(a) a constable in uniform requires, under section 164, a person to produce his licence and its counterpart for examination,

(b) the person fails to produce them, and

(c) the constable has reasonable grounds for believing that a motor vehicle is or was being driven by the person in contravention of section 87(1).

(3) The second condition is that—

(a) a constable in uniform requires, under section 165, a person to produce evidence that a motor vehicle is not or was not being driven in contravention of section 143,

(b) the person fails to produce such evidence, and

(c) the constable has reasonable grounds for believing that the vehicle is or was being so driven.

(4) The third condition is that—

(a) a constable in uniform requires, under section 163, a person driving a motor vehicle to stop the vehicle,

(b) the person fails to stop the vehicle, or to stop the vehicle long enough, for the constable to make such lawful enquiries as he considers appropriate, and

(c) the constable has reasonable grounds for believing that the vehicle is or was being driven in contravention of section 87(1) or 143.

(5) Where this subsection applies, the constable may—

(a) seize the vehicle in accordance with subsections (6) and (7) and remove it;

(b) enter, for the purpose of exercising a power falling within paragraph

(a) , any premises (other than a private dwelling house) on which he has reasonable grounds for believing the vehicle to be;

    (c) use reasonable force, if necessary, in the exercise of any power conferred by paragraph (a) or (b).

(6) Before seizing the motor vehicle, the constable must warn the person by whom it appears that the vehicle is or was being driven in contravention of section 87(1) or 143 that he will seize it—

    (a) in a section 87(1) case, if the person does not produce his licence and its counterpart immediately;

    (b) in a section 143 case, if the person does not provide him immediately with evidence that the vehicle is not or was not being driven in contravention of that section.

But the constable is not required to give such a warning if the circumstances make it impracticable for him to do so.

(7) If the constable is unable to seize the vehicle immediately because the person driving the vehicle has failed to stop as requested or has driven off, he may seize it at any time within the period of 24 hours beginning with the time at which the condition in question is first satisfied.

(8) The powers conferred on a constable by this section are exercisable only at a time when regulations under section 165B are in force.

(9) In this section—

    (a) a reference to a motor vehicle does not include an invalid carriage;

    (b) a reference to evidence that a motor vehicle is not or was not being driven in contravention of section 143 is a reference to a document or other evidence within section 165(2)(a);

    (c) "counterpart" and "licence" have the same meanings as in section 164;

    (d) "private dwelling house" does not include any garage or other structure occupied with the dwelling house, or any land appurtenant to the dwelling house.

165B Retention etc. of vehicles seized under section 165A

(1) The Secretary of State may by regulations make provision as to—

    (a) the removal and retention of motor vehicles seized under section 165A; and

    (b) the release or disposal of such motor vehicles.

(2) Regulations under subsection (1) may, in particular, make provision—

    (a) for the giving of notice of the seizure of a motor vehicle under section 165A to a person who is the registered keeper, the owner or the driver of that vehicle;

    (b) for the procedure by which a person who claims to be the registered keeper or the owner of a motor vehicle seized under section 165A may seek to have it released;

    (c) for requiring the payment, by the registered keeper, owner or driver of the vehicle, of fees, charges or costs in relation to the removal and retention of such a motor vehicle and to any application for its release;

    (d) as to the circumstances in which a motor vehicle seized under section 165A may be disposed of;

    (e) as to the destination—

        (i) of any fees or charges payable in accordance with the regulations;

        (ii) of the proceeds (if any) arising from the disposal of a motor vehicle seized under section 165A;

    (f) for the delivery to a local authority, in circumstances prescribed by or determined in accordance with the regulations, of any motor vehicle seized under section 165A.

(3) Regulations under subsection (1) must provide that a person who would otherwise be liable to pay any fee or charge under the regulations is not liable to pay it if—

    (a) he was not driving the motor vehicle at the time in question, and

    (b) he did not know that the vehicle was being driven at that time, had not consented to its being driven and could not, by the taking of reasonable steps, have prevented it from being driven.

(4) Regulations under subsection (1) may make different provision for different cases.

(5) In this section—

"local authority"—

    (a) in relation to England, means—

        (i)   a county council,

        (ii) the council of a district comprised in an area for which there is no county council,

        (iii) a London borough council,

        (iv) the Common Council of the City of London, or

        (v) transport for London;

    (b) in relation to Wales, means the council of a county or county borough; and

    (c) in relation to Scotland, means a council constituted under section 2 of the Local Government etc. (Scotland) Act 1994;

"registered keeper", in relation to a motor vehicle, means the person in whose name the vehicle is registered under the Vehicle Excise and Registration Act 1994.'

153 Disclosure of information about insurance status of vehicles

(1) The Secretary of State may by regulations make provision for and in connection with requiring MIIC to make available relevant vehicle insurance information to PITO for it to process with a view to making the processed information available for use by constables.

(2) 'Relevant vehicle insurance information' means information relating to vehicles the use of which has been (but no longer is) insured under a policy of insurance, or security in respect of third party risks, complying with the requirements of Part 6 of the Road Traffic Act 1988 (c. 52).

(3) The regulations may in particular—

    (a) require all relevant vehicle insurance information or any particular description of such information to be made available to PITO,

    (b) determine the purposes for which information processed from such information by PITO may be made available for use by constables, and

    (c) determine the circumstances in which any of the processed information which has been made available for use by constables may be further disclosed by them.

(4) In this section—

'information' means information held in any form,

'MIIC' means the Motor Insurers' Information Centre (a company limited by guarantee and incorporated under the Companies Act 1985 (c. 6) on 8th December 1998), and

'PITO' means the Police Information Technology Organisation.

154 Power to require specimens of breath at roadside or at hospital etc.

(1) Section 6D of the Road Traffic Act 1988 (preliminary tests for drink and drugs: arrest) is amended as follows.

(2) After subsection (1) insert—

'(1A) The fact that specimens of breath have been provided under section 7 of this Act by the person concerned does not prevent subsection (1) above having effect if the constable who imposed on him the requirement to provide the specimens has reasonable cause to believe that the device used to analyse the specimens has not produced a reliable indication of the proportion of alcohol in the breath of the person.'

(3) After subsection (2) insert—

'(2A) A person arrested under this section may, instead of being taken to a police station, be detained at or near the place where the preliminary test was, or would have been, administered, with a view to imposing on him there a requirement under section 7 of this Act.'

(4) Section 7 of that Act (provision of specimens for analysis) is amended as follows.

(5) For subsection (2) substitute—

'(2) A requirement under this section to provide specimens of breath can only be made—
   (a) at a police station,
   (b) at a hospital, or
   (c) at or near a place where a relevant breath test has been administered to the person concerned or would have been so administered but for his failure to cooperate with it.

(2A) For the purposes of this section "a relevant breath test" is a procedure involving the provision by the person concerned of a specimen of breath to be used for the purpose of obtaining an indication whether the proportion of alcohol in his breath or blood is likely to exceed the prescribed limit.

(2B) A requirement under this section to provide specimens of breath may not be made at or near a place mentioned in subsection (2)(c) above unless the constable making it—
   (a) is in uniform, or
   (b) has imposed a requirement on the person concerned to cooperate with a relevant breath test in circumstances in which section 6(5) of this Act applies.

(2C) Where a constable has imposed a requirement on the person concerned to cooperate with a relevant breath test at any place, he is entitled to remain at or near that place in order to impose on him there a requirement under this section.

(2D) If a requirement under subsection (1)(a) above has been made at a place other than at a police station, such a requirement may subsequently be made at a police station if (but only if)—
   (a) a device or a reliable device of the type mentioned in subsection (1)(a) above was not available at that place or it was for any other reason not practicable to use such a device there, or
   (b) the constable who made the previous requirement has reasonable cause to believe that the device used there has not produced a reliable indication of the proportion of alcohol in the breath of the person concerned.'

(6) In subsection (3) (circumstances in which requirement to provide a specimen of blood or urine may be made)—
   (a) in paragraph (b) (breath-testing device not available etc.) insert at the beginning 'specimens of breath have not been provided elsewhere and', and
   (b) in paragraph (bb) (police station breath-testing device has not provided a reliable indication of alcohol level) for 'at the police station' substitute '(at the police station or elsewhere)'.

(7) In section 8 of that Act (choice of specimens of breath) after subsection (2) insert—

'(2A) If the person who makes a claim under subsection (2) above was required to provide specimens of breath under section 7 of this Act at or near a place mentioned in subsection (2)(c) of that section, a constable may arrest him without warrant.'

(8) In section 9(1) of that Act (protection for hospital patients) for 'for a laboratory test' substitute 'under section 7 of this Act'.

(9) Section 10 of that Act (detention of persons affected by alcohol or a drug) is amended as follows.

(10) In subsection (1) (detention at a police station)—
    (a) for 'until it appears to the constable' substitute '(or, if the specimen was provided otherwise than at a police station, arrested and taken to and detained at a police station) if a constable has reasonable grounds for believing', and
    (b) for 'not be committing' substitute 'commit'.

(11) In subsection (2) (grounds for detention) for 'A person shall not be detained in pursuance of this section if it appears to a' 'substitute 'Subsection (1) above does not apply to the person if it ought reasonably to appear to the'.

(12) After that subsection insert—

'(2A) A person who is at a hospital as a patient shall not be arrested and taken from there to a police station in pursuance of this section if it would be prejudicial to his proper care and treatment as a patient.'

155 Payments by Secretary of State to police authorities in relation to the prevention, detection and enforcement of certain traffic offences

(1) The Secretary of State may make payments in respect of the whole or any part of the expenditure of a police authority in relation to—
    (a) the prevention and detection of offences to which subsection (3) applies, or
    (b) any enforcement action or proceedings in respect of such offences or any alleged such offences.

(2) Payments under this section shall be made at such times, in such manner and subject to such conditions as the Secretary of State may determine.

(3) This subsection applies to offences committed in England and Wales under the following provisions—

Road Traffic Act 1988 (c. 52)

section 14 (requirements regarding seat belts: adults);

section 15(2) and (4) (restriction on carrying children not wearing seat belts in motor vehicles);

section 42 (motor vehicles and trailers: other construction and use requirements) in relation to the construction and use requirements imposed by the following regulations—
    (a) regulations 54, 57, 104 and 110 of the Road Vehicles (Construction and Use) Regulations 1986 (S.I. 1986/1078);
    (b) regulations 11(1) and 25 of the Road Vehicles Lighting Regulations 1989 (S.I. 1989/1796);

section 47 (obligatory test certificates for motor vehicles);

section 87(1) (drivers of motor vehicles to have driving licences);

section 143 (users of motor vehicles to be insured or secured against third-party risks);

section 163 (power of police to stop vehicles); section 172 (duty to give information as to the identity of driver etc. in certain circumstances);

Vehicle Excise and Registration Act 1994 (c. 22)

section 33 (not exhibiting vehicle licence);

section 42 (not fixing registration mark);

section 43 (obscured registration mark);

section 43C (using an incorrectly registered vehicle);

section 59 (regulations: offences) in relation to the requirements imposed by regulation 11 of the Road Vehicles (Display of Registration Marks) Regulations 2001 (S.I. 2001/561).

(4) The Secretary of State may by order amend the list of offences in subsection (3) so as to add, modify or omit any entry.

(5) In subsection (3) 'construction and use requirements' has the meaning given by section 41(7) of the Road Traffic Act 1988 (c. 52).

156 Payments by Scottish Ministers to police authorities etc. in relation to the prevention, detection and enforcement of certain traffic offences

(1) The Scottish Ministers may make payments in respect of the whole or any part of the expenditure of a police authority or joint police board (within the meaning of the Police (Scotland) Act 1967 (c. 77)) in relation to—

(a) the prevention and detection of offences to which subsection (3) applies, or

(b) any enforcement action or proceedings in respect of such offences or any alleged such offences.

(2) Payments under this section shall be made at such times, in such manner and subject to such conditions as the Scottish Ministers may determine.

(3) This subsection applies to offences committed in Scotland under the following provisions—

Road Traffic Act 1988 (c. 52)

section 14 (requirements regarding seat belts: adults);

section 15(2) and (4) (restriction on carrying children not wearing seat belts in motor vehicles);

section 42 (motor vehicles and trailers: other construction and use requirements) in relation to the construction and use requirements imposed by the following regulations—

(a) regulations 54, 57, 104 and 110 of the Road Vehicles (Construction and Use) Regulations 1986 (S.I. 1986/1078);

(b) regulations 11(1) and 25 of the Road Vehicles Lighting Regulations 1989 (S.I. 1989/1796);

section 47 (obligatory test certificates for motor vehicles);

section 87(1) (drivers of motor vehicles to have driving licences);

section 143 (users of motor vehicles to be insured or secured against third-party risks);

section 163 (power of police to stop vehicles);
section 172 (duty to give information as to the identity of driver etc. in certain circumstances);

Vehicle Excise and Registration Act 1994 (c. 22)

section 33 (not exhibiting vehicle licence);
section 42 (not fixing registration mark);
section 43 (obscured registration mark);
section 43C (using an incorrectly registered vehicle);
section 59 (regulations: offences) in relation to the requirements imposed by regulation 11 of the Road Vehicles (Display of Registration Marks) Regulations 2001 (S.I. 2001/561).

(4) The Scottish Ministers may by order amend the list of offences in subsection (3) so as to add, modify or omit any entry.
(5) In subsection (3) 'construction and use requirements' has the meaning given by section 41(7) of the Road Traffic Act 1988 (c. 52).
(6) In section 95 of the Road Traffic Offenders Act 1988 (c. 53) (destination of fines imposed in respect of road traffic offences etc.) insert—

'(3) There shall be paid into the Scottish Consolidated Fund all fixed penalties imposed in respect of offences, committed in Scotland, to which section 156(3) of the Serious Organised Crime and Police Act 2005 applies.'

Local policing information

157 Publication of local policing information

After section 8 of the Police Act 1996 (c. 16) insert—

'8A Local policing summaries

(1) As soon as possible after the end of each financial year, every police authority established under section 3 shall issue a report for members of the public in the authority's area on matters relating to the policing of that area for the year.
(2) Such a report is referred to in this section as a "local policing summary".
(3) The Secretary of State may by order specify matters which are to be included in a local policing summary.
(4) A police authority shall arrange—
    (a) for every local policing summary issued by it under this section to be published in such manner as appears to it to be appropriate, and
    (b) for a copy of every such summary to be sent, by whatever means appear to the authority to be appropriate, to each person liable to pay any tax, precept or levy to or in respect of the authority.
(5) It shall be the duty of a police authority, in preparing and publishing a local policing summary, to have regard to any guidance given by the Secretary of State about the form and content of local policing summaries and the manner of their publication.
(6) Before making an order under subsection (3), and before giving any such guidance as is referred to in subsection (5), the Secretary of State must consult—
    (a) persons whom he considers to represent the interests of police authorities,
    (b) persons whom he considers to represent the interests of chief officers of police, and
    (c) such other persons as he thinks fit.

(7) This section shall apply in relation to the Metropolitan Police Authority as it applies to a police authority established under section 3.

(8) A statutory instrument containing an order under subsection (3) shall be subject to annulment in pursuance of a resolution of either House of Parliament.'

Other miscellaneous police matters

158 Responsibilities in relation to the health and safety etc. of police

(1) In section 51A of the Health and Safety at Work etc. Act 1974 (c. 37) (application of Part 1 of that Act to police) after subsection (2) insert—

'(2A) For the purposes of this Part the relevant officer, as defined by subsection (2)(a) or (c) above, shall be treated as a corporation sole.

(2B) Where, in a case in which the relevant officer, as so defined, is guilty of an offence by virtue of this section, it is proved—

(a) that the officer-holder personally consented to the commission of the offence,

(b) that he personally connived in its commission, or

(c) that the commission of the offence was attributable to personal neglect on his part,

the office-holder (as well as the corporation sole) shall be guilty of the offence and shall be liable to be proceeded against and punished accordingly.

(2C) In subsection (2B) above "the office-holder", in relation to the relevant officer, means an individual who, at the time of the consent, connivance or neglect—

(a) held the office or other position mentioned in subsection (2) above as the office or position of that officer; or

(b) was for the time being responsible for exercising and performing the powers and duties of that office or position.

(2D) The provisions mentioned in subsection (2E) below (which impose the same liability for unlawful conduct of constables on persons having their direction or control as would arise if the constables were employees of those persons) do not apply to any liability by virtue of this Part.

(2E) Those provisions are—

(a) section 39 of the Police (Scotland) Act 1967;

(b) section 88(1) of the Police Act 1996;

(c) section 97(9) of that Act;

(d) paragraph 7(1) of Schedule 8 to the Police Act 1997;

(e) paragraph 14(1) of Schedule 3 to the Criminal Justice and Police Act 2001;

(f) section 28 of the Serious Organised Crime and Police Act 2005.

(2F) In the application of this section to Scotland—

(a) subsection (2A) shall have effect as if for the words "corporation sole" there were substituted "distinct juristic person (that is to say, as a juristic person distinct from the individual who for the time being is the office-holder)";

(b) subsection (2B) shall have effect as if for the words "corporation sole" there were substituted "juristic person"; and

(c) subsection (2C) shall have effect as if for the words "subsection (2B)" there were substituted "subsections (2A) and (2B)".'

(2) For subsection (2) of each of the following sections of the Employment Rights Act 1996 (c. 18)—

(a) section 49A (right of police officers not to suffer detriment in relation to health and safety issues), and

(b) section 134A (right of police officers not to be unfairly dismissed in relation to health and safety issues),

substitute the subsection set out in subsection (3) of this section.

(3) The subsection to be substituted is—

'(2) In this section "the relevant officer", in relation to—

(a) a person holding the office of constable, or

(b) a person holding an appointment as a police cadet,

means the person who under section 51A of the Health and Safety at Work etc. Act 1974 is to be treated as his employer for the purposes of Part 1 of that Act.'

(4) The following provisions of the Police Reform Act 2002 (c. 30) (which relate to duties and rights in relation to the health and safety of police) cease to have effect—

(a) section 95, and

(b) in Schedule 8, the reference to section 5 of the Police (Health and Safety) Act 1997 (c. 42).

(5) The amendments made by subsections (1) to (3) have effect for the purposes of any proceedings in or before a court or tribunal that are commenced on or after the day on which this Act is passed as if the amendments had come into force on 1st July 1998.

(6) For the purposes of proceedings commenced against a person in his capacity by virtue of this section as a corporation sole (or, in Scotland, as a distinct juristic person) anything done by or in relation to that person before the passing of this Act shall be deemed to have been done by or in relation to that person in that capacity.

(7) No person shall be liable by virtue of section 51A(2B) of the Health and Safety at Work etc. Act 1974 (c. 37) in respect of anything occurring before the passing of this Act.

159 Investigations: accelerated procedure in special cases

Schedule 11 (which makes provision for an accelerated procedure for certain investigations into the conduct of police officers) has effect.

160 Investigations: deaths and serious injuries during or after contact with the police

Schedule 12 (which makes provision for the investigation of deaths and serious injuries which occur during or after contact with persons serving with the police) has effect.

Royal Parks etc.

161 Abolition of Royal Parks Constabulary

(1) The Royal Parks Constabulary is abolished.

(2) Every relevant person shall cease to be a park constable on the appointed day.

(3) Subsection (2) is not to be taken as terminating the Crown employment of any relevant person.

(4) In this section, section 162 and Schedule 13—

'appointed day' means such day as the Secretary of State may by order appoint for the purposes of this section,

'Crown employment' has the same meaning as in the Employment Rights Act 1996 (c. 18), and

'relevant person' means a person who immediately before the appointed day is serving as a park constable with the Royal Parks Constabulary.

(5) Schedule 13 (which provides for transfers to the Metropolitan Police Authority and makes amendments) has effect.

162 Regulation of specified parks

(1) From the appointed day the Parks Regulation Act 1872 (c. 15) does not apply to the specified parks.

(2) But from the appointed day section 2 of the Parks Regulation (Amendment) Act 1926 (c. 36) applies in relation to the specified parks in the same way as it applies in relation to parks to which the Parks Regulation Act 1872 applies.

(3) The Secretary of State must ensure that copies of any regulations made under section 2 of the Parks Regulation (Amendment) Act 1926 (c. 36) which are in force in relation to a specified park are displayed in a suitable position in that park.

(4) In this section 'specified park' means a park, garden, recreation ground, open space or other land in the metropolitan police district—

(a) which is specified in an order made by the Secretary of State before the appointed day, and

(b) to which the Parks Regulation Act 1872 (c. 15) then applied by virtue of section 1 of the Parks Regulation (Amendment) Act 1926.

Criminal record checks

163 Criminal record certificates

(1) Sections 113 and 115 of the Police Act 1997 (c. 50) (criminal record certificates) are omitted.

(2) Before section 114 of that Act insert—

'113A Criminal record certificates

(1) The Secretary of State must issue a criminal record certificate to any individual who—

(a) makes an application in the prescribed manner and form, and

(b) pays in the prescribed manner any prescribed fee.

(2) The application must—

(a) be countersigned by a registered person, and

(b) be accompanied by a statement by the registered person that the certificate is required for the purposes of an exempted question.

(3) A criminal record certificate is a certificate which—

(a) gives the prescribed details of every relevant matter relating to the applicant which is recorded in central records, or

(b) states that there is no such matter.

(4) The Secretary of State must send a copy of a criminal record certificate to the registered person who countersigned the application.

(5) The Secretary of State may treat an application under this section as an application under section 113B if—

    (a) in his opinion the certificate is required for a purpose prescribed under subsection (2) of that section,

    (b) the registered person provides him with the statement required by that subsection, and

    (c) the applicant consents and pays to the Secretary of State the amount (if any) by which the fee payable in relation to an application under that section exceeds the fee paid in relation to the application under this section.

(6) In this section—

    "central records" means such records of convictions and cautions held for the use of police forces generally as may be prescribed;

    "exempted question" means a question in relation to which section 4(2)(a) or (b) of the Rehabilitation of Offenders Act 1974 (effect of rehabilitation) has been excluded by an order of the Secretary of State under section 4(4) of that Act;

    "relevant matter" means—

        (a) a conviction within the meaning of the Rehabilitation of Offenders Act 1974, including a spent conviction, and

        (b) a caution.

113B Enhanced criminal record certificates

(1) The Secretary of State must issue an enhanced criminal record certificate to any individual who—

    (a) makes an application in the prescribed manner and form, and

    (b) pays in the prescribed manner any prescribed fee.

(2) The application must—

    (a) be countersigned by a registered person, and

    (b) be accompanied by a statement by the registered person that the certificate is required for a prescribed purpose.

(3) An enhanced criminal record certificate is a certificate which—

    (a) gives the prescribed details of every relevant matter relating to the applicant which is recorded in central records and any information provided in accordance with subsection (4), or

    (b) states that there is no such matter or information.

(4) Before issuing an enhanced criminal record certificate the Secretary of State must request the chief officer of every relevant police force to provide any information which, in the chief officer's opinion—

    (a) might be relevant for the purpose described in the statement under subsection (2), and

    (b) ought to be included in the certificate.

(5) The Secretary of State must also request the chief officer of every relevant police force to provide any information which, in the chief officer's opinion—

    (a) might be relevant for the purpose described in the statement under subsection (2),

    (b) ought not to be included in the certificate, in the interests of the prevention or detection of crime, and

    (c) can, without harming those interests, be disclosed to the registered person.

(6) The Secretary of State must send to the registered person who countersigned the application—

    (a) a copy of the enhanced criminal record certificate, and

    (b) any information provided in accordance with subsection (5).

(7) The Secretary of State may treat an application under this section as an application under section 113A if in his opinion the certificate is not required for a purpose prescribed under subsection (2).

(8) If by virtue of subsection (7) the Secretary of State treats an application under this section as an application under section 113A, he must refund to the applicant the amount (if any) by which the fee paid in relation to the application under this section exceeds the fee payable in relation to an application under section 113A.

(9) In this section—

"central records", "exempted question", and "relevant matter" have the same meaning as in section 113A;

"relevant police force", in relation to an application under this section, means a police force which is a relevant police force in relation to that application under regulations made by the Secretary of State.

(10) For the purposes of this section references to a police force include any of the following—

(a) the Royal Navy Regulating Branch;

(b) the Royal Marines Police;

(c) the Royal Military Police;

(d) the Royal Air Force Police;

(e) the Ministry of Defence Police;

(f) the National Criminal Intelligence Service;

(g) the National Crime Squad;

(h) the British Transport Police;

(i) the Civil Nuclear Constabulary;

(j) the States of Jersey Police Force;

(k) the salaried police force of the Island of Guernsey;

(l) the Isle of Man Constabulary;

(m) a body with functions in any country or territory outside the British Islands which correspond to those of a police force in any part of the United Kingdom,

and any reference to the chief officer of a police force includes the person responsible for the direction of a body mentioned in this subsection.

(11) For the purposes of this section each of the following must be treated as if it were a police force—

(a) the Commissioners for Her Majesty's Revenue and Customs (and for this purpose a reference to the chief officer of a police force must be taken to be a reference to any one of the Commissioners);

(b) the Serious Organised Crime Agency (and for this purpose a reference to the chief officer of a police force must be taken to be a reference to the Director General of the Agency);

(c) such other department or body as is prescribed (and regulations may prescribe in relation to the department or body the person to whom a reference to the chief officer is to be taken to be).

113C Criminal record certificates: suitability relating to children

(1) If an application under section 113A or 113B is accompanied by a children's suitability statement the criminal record certificate or enhanced criminal record certificate (as the case may be) must also state—

(a) whether the applicant is included in a specified children's list;

(b) if he is included in such a list, such details of his inclusion as may be prescribed;

(c) whether he is subject to a specified children's direction;

(d) if he is subject to such a direction, the grounds on which it was given and such details as may be prescribed of the circumstances in which it was given.

(2) A children's suitability statement is a statement by the registered person that the certificate is required for the purpose of considering—

(a) the applicant's suitability to be employed, supplied to work, found work or given work in a position (whether paid or unpaid) within subsection (5),

(b) the applicant's suitability to be a foster parent or to adopt a child,

(c) the applicant's suitability to be a child's special guardian for the purposes of sections 14A and 14C of the Children Act 1989,

(d) the applicant's suitability to have a child placed with him by virtue of section 70 of the Children (Scotland) Act 1995 or by virtue of section 5(2), (3) and (4) of the Social Work (Scotland) Act 1968, or

(e) the suitability of a person living in the same household as the applicant to be a person mentioned in paragraph (b) or (c) or to have a child placed with him as mentioned in paragraph (d).

(3) Each of the following is a specified children's list—

(a) the list kept under section 1 of the Protection of Children Act 1999;

(b) the list kept under section 1(1) of the Protection of Children (Scotland) Act 2003;

(c) the list kept under Article 3 of the Protection of Children and Vulnerable Adults (Northern Ireland) Order 2003;

(d) any list kept for the purposes of regulations under Article 70(2)(e) or 88A(2)(b) of the Education and Libraries (Northern Ireland) Order 1986;

(e) any such other list as the Secretary of State specifies by order if he thinks that the list corresponds to a list specified in paragraphs (a) to (c) and is kept in pursuance of a country or territory outside the United Kingdom.

(4) Each of the following is a specified children's direction—

(a) a direction under section 142 of the Education Act 2002;

(b) anything which the Secretary of State specifies by order which he thinks corresponds to such a direction and which is done for the purposes of the law of Scotland or of Northern Ireland or of a country or territory outside the United Kingdom.

(5) A position falls within this subsection if it is any of the following—

(a) a child care position within the meaning of the Protection of Children Act 1999;

(b) a child care position within the meaning of the Protection of Children (Scotland) Act 2003;

(c) a child care position within the meaning of Chapter 1 of Part 2 of the Protection of Children and Vulnerable Adults (Northern Ireland) Order 2003;

(d) a position, employment or further employment in which may be prohibited or restricted by regulations under Article 70(2)(e) or 88A(2)(b) of the Education and Libraries (Northern Ireland) Order 1986;

(e) a position which involves work to which section 142 of the Education Act 2002 applies;

(f) a position of such other description as may be prescribed.

(6) An order under subsection (4)(b) may make such modifications of subsection (1)(d) as the Secretary of State thinks necessary or expedient in consequence of the order.

113D Criminal record certificates: suitability relating to adults

(1) If an application under section 113A or 113B is accompanied by an adults' suitability statement the criminal record certificate or enhanced criminal record certificate (as the case may be) must also state—

(a) whether the applicant is included in a specified adults' list;

(b) if he is included in such a list, such details of his inclusion as may be prescribed.

(2) An adults' suitability statement is a statement by the registered person that the certificate is required for the purpose of considering the applicant's suitability to be employed, supplied to work, found work or given work in a position (whether paid or unpaid) falling within subsection (4).

(3) Each of the following is a specified adults' list—
    (a) the list kept under section 81 of the Care Standards Act 2000;
    (b) the list kept under Article 35 of the Protection of Children and Vulnerable Adults (Northern Ireland) Order 2003;
    (c) any such other list as the Secretary of State specifies by order if he thinks that the list corresponds to a list specified in paragraph (a) or (b) and is kept in pursuance of the law of Scotland or of a country or territory outside the United Kingdom.

(4) A position falls within this subsection if it is any of the following—
    (a) a care position within the meaning of Part 7 of the Care Standards Act 2000;
    (b) a care position within the meaning of Part 3 of the Protection of Children and Vulnerable Adults (Northern Ireland) Order 2003;
    (c) a position concerned with providing a care service (as defined by section 2(1) of the Regulation of Care (Scotland) Act 2001);
    (d) a position of such other description as may be prescribed.

113E Criminal record certificates: specified children's and adults' lists: urgent cases

(1) Subsection (2) applies to an application under section 113A or 113B if—
    (a) it is accompanied by a children's suitability statement,
    (b) the registered person requests an urgent preliminary response, and
    (c) the applicant pays in the prescribed manner such additional fee as is prescribed in respect of the application.

(2) The Secretary of State must notify the registered person—
    (a) if the applicant is not included in a specified children's list, of that fact;
    (b) if the applicant is included in such a list, of the details prescribed for the purposes of section 113C(1)(b) above;
    (c) if the applicant is not subject to a specified children's direction, of that fact;
    (d) if the applicant is subject to such a direction, of the grounds on which the direction was given and the details prescribed for the purposes of section 113C(1)(d) above.

(3) Subsection (4) applies to an application under section 113A or 113B if—
    (a) it is accompanied by an adults' suitability statement,
    (b) the registered person requests an urgent preliminary response, and
    (c) the applicant pays in the prescribed manner such additional fee as is prescribed in respect of the application.

(4) The Secretary of State must notify the registered person either—
    (a) that the applicant is not included in a specified adults' list, or
    (b) that a criminal record certificate or enhanced criminal record certificate will be issued in due course.

(5) In this section—
"criminal record certificate" has the same meaning as in section 113A;
"enhanced criminal record certificate" has the same meaning as in section 113B;
"children's suitability statement", "specified children's direction" and
"specified children's list" have the same meaning as in section 113C;
"adults' suitability statement" and "specified adults' list" have the same meaning as in section 113D.

113F Criminal record certificates: supplementary

(1) References in sections 113C(2) and 113D(2) to considering the applicant's suitability to be employed, supplied to work, found work or given work in a position falling within section 113C(5) or 113D(4) include references to considering—

   (a) for the purposes of Part 10A of the Children Act 1989 (child minding and day care in England and Wales), the applicant's suitability to look after or be in regular contact with children under the age of eight;

   (b) for the purposes of that Part of that Act, in the case of an applicant for or holder of a certificate under section 79W of that Act, or a person prescribed under subsection (4) of that section, his suitability to look after children within the meaning of that section;

   (c) the applicant's suitability to be registered for child minding or providing day care under section 71 of the Children Act 1989 or Article 118 of the Children (Northern Ireland) Order 1995 (child minding and day care);

   (d) for the purposes of section 3 of the Teaching and Higher Education Act 1998 (registration of teachers with the General Teaching Council for England or the General Teaching Council for Wales) or of section 6 of the Teaching Council (Scotland) Act 1965 (registration of teachers with the General Teaching Council for Scotland), the applicant's suitability to be a teacher;

   (e) the applicant's suitability to be registered under Part 2 of the Care Standards Act 2000 (establishments and agencies);

   (f) the applicant's suitability to be registered under Part 4 of that Act (social care workers);

   (g) the applicant's suitability to be registered under Part 1 of the Regulation of Care (Scotland) Act 2001 (applications by persons seeking to provide a care service);

   (h) the applicant's suitability to be registered under Part 3 of that Act (social workers and other social service workers);

   (i) the applicant's application to have a care service, consisting of the provision of child minding or the day care of children, registered under Part 1 of that Act (care services);

   (j) the applicant's suitability to be registered under Part 1 of the Health and Personal Social Services Act (Northern Ireland) 2001 (social care workers);

   (k) the applicant's suitability to be registered under Part 3 of the Health and Personal Social Services (Quality, Improvement and Regulation) (Northern Ireland) Order 2003 (regulation of establishments and agencies).

  (2) The power to make an order under section 113C or 113D is exercisable by statutory instrument, but no such order may be made unless a draft of the order has been laid before and approved by a resolution of each House of Parliament.

  (3) If the power mentioned in subsection (2) is exercised by the Scottish Ministers, the reference in that subsection to each House of Parliament must be construed as a reference to the Scottish Parliament.'

(3) Schedule 14 (which makes consequential amendments to Part 5 of the Police Act 1997 (c. 50)) has effect.

(4) If section 115(1) of the Adoption and Children Act 2002 (c. 38) comes into force before the preceding provisions of this section, the Secretary of State may by order apply Part 5 of the Police Act 1997 subject to such modifications as he thinks necessary or expedient for the purpose of enabling a certificate or statement to be issued under section 113 or 115 of that Act of 1997 in connection with consideration by a court of whether to make a special guardianship order under section 14A of the Children Act 1989 (c. 41).

164 Criminal records checks: verification of identity

(1) Section 118 of the Police Act 1997 (evidence of identity) is amended as follows.

(2) In subsection (1) after '117' insert 'or 120'.

(3) After subsection (2) insert—

'(2A) For the purpose of verifying evidence of identity supplied in pursuance of subsection (1) the Secretary of State may obtain such information as he thinks is appropriate from data held—

(a) by the United Kingdom Passport Agency;

(b) by the Driver and Vehicle Licensing Agency;

(c) by Driver and Vehicle Licensing Northern Ireland;

(d) by the Secretary of State in connection with keeping records of national insurance numbers;

(e) by such other persons or for such purposes as is prescribed.'

165 Certain references to police forces

(1) In section 119 of the Police Act 1997 (c. 50) (sources of information),

(a) in subsection (3) for 'the prescribed fee' substitute 'such fee as he thinks appropriate';

(b) after subsection (5) insert—

'(6) For the purposes of this section references to a police force include any body mentioned in subsections (10)(a) to (i) and (11) of section 113B and references to a chief officer must be construed accordingly.

(7) In the case of such a body the reference in subsection (3) to the appropriate police authority must be construed as a reference to such body as is prescribed.'

(2) In each version of section 120A of that Act (as inserted respectively by section 134 (1) of the Criminal Justice and Police Act 2001 (c. 16) and section 70 of the Criminal Justice (Scotland) Act 2003 (asp 7)), after subsection (5) insert—

'(6) For the purposes of this section references to a police force include any body mentioned in subsections (10)(a) to (i) and (11) of section 113B and references to a chief officer must be construed accordingly.'

(3) In section 124A of that Act (offences relating to disclosure of information) (inserted by section 328 of and paragraphs 1 and 11 of Schedule 35 to the Criminal Justice Act 2003 (c. 44)), after subsection (5) insert—

'(6) For the purposes of this section the reference to a police force includes any body mentioned in subsections (10)(a) to (i) and (11) of section 113B and the reference to a chief officer must be construed accordingly.'

166 Further amendments to Police Act 1997 as it applies to Scotland

(1) In section 120A of the Police Act 1997 (as inserted by section 70 of the Criminal Justice (Scotland) Act 2003 (asp 7)), in subsection (5) for the words from 'the prescribed fee' to the end substitute 'such fee as they consider appropriate'.

(2) In section 126 of that Act of 1997 after subsection (2) insert—

'(3) In the application of this Part to Scotland references to the Secretary of State must be construed as references to the Scottish Ministers.

(4) Subsection (3) does not apply to section 118(2A)(d)[a] or 124A(1) and (2).'

167 Part 5 of the Police Act 1997: Northern Ireland

The amendments made by Schedule 35 to the Criminal Justice Act 2003 (c. 44) to Part 5 of the Police Act 1997 (c. 50) extend to Northern Ireland as well as to England and Wales, and accordingly in section 337(5) of that Act of 2003 (extent)—

(a) after 'section 315' insert—
'section 328;';
(b) after 'Schedule 5' insert—
'Schedule 35.'

168 Part 5 of the Police Act 1997: Channel Islands and Isle of Man

(1) Her Majesty may by Order in Council extend any provision of Part 5 of the Police Act 1997 (certificates of criminal records etc.), with such modifications as appear to Her Majesty in Council to be appropriate, to any of the Channel Islands or the Isle of Man.

(2) An order under this section may make such consequential, incidental, supplementary, transitory or transitional provision or savings as Her Majesty in Council thinks appropriate.

Witness summonses

169 Powers of Crown Court and Magistrates' Court to issue witness summons

(1) In section 2(1) of the Criminal Procedure (Attendance of Witnesses) Act 1965 (c. 69) (issue of witness summons on application to Crown Court) for paragraph (b) substitute—

'(b) it is in the interests of justice to issue a summons under this section to secure the attendance of that person to give evidence or to produce the document or thing.'

(2) In section 97 of the Magistrates' Courts Act 1980 (c. 43) (summons to witness) for subsection (1) substitute—

'(1) Where a justice of the peace is satisfied that—
(a) any person in England or Wales is likely to be able to give material evidence, or produce any document or thing likely to be material evidence, at the summary trial of an information or hearing of a complaint by a magistrates' court, and
(b) it is in the interests of justice to issue a summons under this subsection to secure the attendance of that person to give evidence or produce the document or thing,
the justice shall issue a summons directed to that person requiring him to attend before the court at the time and place appointed in the summons to give evidence or to produce the document or thing.'

(3) In section 97A(1) of that Act (summons as to committal proceedings) for paragraph (b) substitute—

'(b) it is in the interests of justice to issue a summons under this section to secure the attendance of that person to give evidence or to produce the document or other exhibit, and'.

(4) In paragraph 4(1) of Schedule 3 to the Crime and Disorder Act 1998 (c. 37) (power of justice to take depositions etc.) for paragraph (b) substitute—

'(b) it is in the interests of justice to issue a summons under this paragraph to secure the attendance of the witness to have his evidence taken as a deposition or to produce the document or other exhibit.'

(5) In section 51A(1) of the Judicature (Northern Ireland) Act 1978 (c. 23) (issue of witness summons on application to Crown Court) for paragraph (b) substitute—

'(b) it is in the interests of justice to issue a summons under this section to secure the attendance of that person to give evidence or to produce the document or thing.'

170 Powers of courts-martial etc. to issue warrants of arrest in respect of witnesses

(1) Section 25 of the Armed Forces Act 2001 (c. 19) (powers to compel attendance of witnesses) is amended as follows.

(2) In subsection (1) (which inserts a new section 101A in the Army Act 1955 (3 & 4 Eliz. 2 c. 18)), in subsection (1) of the new section 101A, for paragraph (b) substitute—

'(b) that it is in the interests of justice that the person should attend to give evidence or to produce the document or other thing, and'.

(3) In subsection (2) (which inserts a new section 101A in the Air Force Act 1955 (3 & 4 Eliz. 2 c. 19)), in subsection (1) of the new section 101A, for paragraph (b) substitute—

'(b) that it is in the interests of justice that the person should attend to give evidence or to produce the document or other thing, and'.

(4) In subsection (3) (which inserts a new section 65A in the Naval Discipline Act 1957), in subsection (1) of the new section 65A, for paragraph (b) substitute—

'(b) that it is in the interests of justice that the person should attend to give evidence or to produce the document or other thing, and'.

Private Security Industry Act 2001: Scotland

171 Private Security Industry Act 2001: Scottish extent

(1) Schedule 15 amends the Private Security Industry Act 2001 (c. 12) in relation to its extent to Scotland.

(2) In Schedule 2 to the Scottish Public Services Ombudsman Act 2002 (asp 11) (persons liable to investigation) after paragraph 90 add—

'91 The Security Industry Authority.'

PART 6
FINAL PROVISIONS

172 Orders and regulations

(1) Any power of the Secretary of State to make an order or regulations under this Act, and any power of the Scottish Ministers to make an order under this Act, is exercisable by statutory instrument.

(2) Any such power—
(a) may be exercised so as to make different provision for different cases or descriptions of case or different purposes or areas, and
(b) includes power to make such incidental, supplementary, consequential, transitory, transitional or saving provision as the Secretary of State considers appropriate (or, in the case of an order made by the Scottish Ministers, as they consider appropriate).

(3) Subject to subsections (4) and (5), orders or regulations made by the Secretary of State under this Act are to be subject to annulment in pursuance of a resolution of either House of Parliament.

(4) Subsection (3) does not apply to any order under section 1(3), 161(4) or 178.

(5) Subsection (3) also does not apply to—
   (a) any order under section 33(2)(f);
   (b) any order under section 52;
   (c) any order under section 61(4);
   (d) any order under section 76(4);
   (e) any order under section 82(6);
   (f) any order under section 87(5);
   (g) any order under section 89(5);
   (h) any order under section 96(1);
   (i) any order under section 97(1);
   (j) any order under section 146(6), 148(4) or 149;
   (k) any order under section 173 which amends or repeals any provision of an Act;

and no such order may be made by the Secretary of State (whether alone or with other provisions) unless a draft of the statutory instrument containing the order has been laid before, and approved by a resolution of, each House of Parliament.

(6) Subject to subsections (7) and (8), orders made by the Scottish Ministers under this Act are to be subject to annulment in pursuance of a resolution of the Scottish Parliament.

(7) Subsection (6) does not apply to any order under section 178.

(8) Subsection (6) also does not apply to—
   (a) any order under section 52;
   (b) any order under section 61(5);
   (c) any order under section 77(4);
   (d) any order under section 87(6);
   (e) any order under section 89(6);
   (f) any order under section 96(1);
   (g) any order under section 173 which amends or repeals any provision of an Act;

and no such order may be made by the Scottish Ministers (whether alone or with other provisions) unless a draft of the statutory instrument containing the order has been laid before, and approved by a resolution of, the Scottish Parliament.

173 Supplementary, incidental, consequential etc. provision

(1) The Secretary of State may by order make—
   (a) such supplementary, incidental or consequential provision, or
   (b) such transitory, transitional or saving provision,
   as he considers appropriate for the general purposes, or any particular purpose, of this Act, or in consequence of, or for giving full effect to, any provision made by this Act.

(2) An order under subsection (1) may amend, repeal, revoke or otherwise modify any enactment (including this Act).

(3) The power to make an order under subsection (1) includes power to repeal or revoke an enactment which is spent.

(4) Before exercising the power conferred by subsection (1) in relation to an enactment which extends to Scotland, the Secretary of State must consult the Scottish Ministers.

(5) The power conferred by subsection (1) is exercisable by the Scottish Ministers (rather than by the Secretary of State) where the provision to be made is—

(a) for the general purposes of this Act and would be within the legislative competence of the Scottish Parliament if it were included in an Act of that Parliament; or

(b) for the purposes of, in consequence of, or for giving full effect to—

(i) section 77, 156, 171 or Schedule 15,

(ii) so far as extending to Scotland, any provision mentioned in section 178 (4),

(iii) so far as relating as mentioned in section 178(5), section 174(2) and Schedule 17,

(iv) so far as having effect as mentioned in section 178(6)(a), section 96.

(6) But an order under—

(a) paragraph (b)(i) of subsection (5) in relation to section 171 or Schedule 15, or

(b) paragraph (b)(iv) of that subsection,

may be made only after consulting the Secretary of State.

(7) Nothing in this Act affects the generality of the power conferred by this section.

174 Minor and consequential amendments, repeals and revocations

(1) Schedule 16 makes provision for remaining minor and consequential amendments (search warrants).

(2) Schedule 17 makes provision for the repeal and revocation of enactments (including enactments which are spent).

175 Penalties for offences: transitional modification for England and Wales

(1) This section contains transitional modifications in respect of penalties for certain offences committed in England or Wales.

(2) In relation to an offence committed before the commencement of section 154(1) of the Criminal Justice Act 2003 (c. 44) (general limit on magistrates' court's power to impose imprisonment), the references in the following provisions to periods of imprisonment of 12 months are to be read as references to periods of imprisonment of 6 months—

section 67(5)(b);

section 86(2)(b);

section 88(3)(b);

section 147(1)(a).

(3) In relation to an offence committed before the commencement of section 281(5) of the Criminal Justice Act 2003 (alteration of penalties for summary offences), the references in the following provisions of this Act to periods of imprisonment of 51 weeks are to be read as references to the periods of imprisonment specified in respect of those provisions as follows—

Section	Modified period of imprisonment
section 51(4)(a)	6 months
section 51(5)(a)	1 months
section 57(4)(a)	6 months
section 57(5)(a)	6 months
section 67(4)(a)	1 months
section 79(10)(a)(i)	6 months
section 112(5)	6 months
section 128(5)(a)	4 months
section 136(1)	3 months
section 136(3)(a)	3 months
section 136(4)	3 months

176 Expenses

(1) There shall be paid out of money provided by Parliament—
    (a) any expenditure incurred by the Secretary of State by virtue of this Act;
    (b) any increase attributable to this Act in the sums payable out of money so provided under any other enactment.
(2) Subsection (1)(a) does not apply to any expenditure of the Secretary of State under section 155.

177 Interpretation

(1) In this Act 'SOCA' means the Serious Organised Crime Agency.
(2) In this Act 'enactment' includes—
    (a) an enactment contained in or made under an Act of the Scottish Parliament or Northern Ireland legislation, and
    (b) an enactment comprised in subordinate legislation (within the meaning of the Interpretation Act 1978 (c. 30)).
(3) In this Act references to enactments include enactments passed or made after the passing of this Act.
(4) Subsections (2) and (3) apply except where the context otherwise requires.

178 Commencement

(1) The following provisions come into force on the day on which this Act is passed—
    (a) sections 117(7) (and section 117(6) so far as relates to it), 158, 167, 172, 173, 176, 177, this section and section 179, and
    (b) Part 1 of Schedule 17 and (so far as it relates to that Part of that Schedule) section 174(2).
(2) Section 163(4) comes into force at the end of the period of three months beginning with the day on which this Act is passed.
(3) Sections 77 and 156 come into force on such day as the Scottish Ministers may by order appoint.
(4) So far as they extend to Scotland—
    (a) Chapter 1 of Part 2,

    (b) sections 79 to 81,

    (c) Chapter 4 of Part 2 (including Schedule 5),

    (d) sections 163 to 166, and

    (e) Schedule 14,

come into force on such day as the Scottish Ministers may by order appoint.

  (5) So far as they relate—

    (a) to sections 113 and 115 of the Police Act 1997 (c. 50) as those sections apply to Scotland;

    (b) to section 125 of that Act, to the Regulation of Care (Scotland) Act 2001 (asp 8), to the Protection of Children (Scotland) Act 2003 (asp 5) and to the Criminal Justice (Scotland) Act 2003 (asp 7),

section 174(2) and Schedule 17 come into force on such day as the Scottish Ministers may by order appoint.

  (6) The following provisions come into force on such day as the Scottish Ministers may by order appoint after consulting the Secretary of State—

    (a) section 96 so far as it has effect for the purpose of conferring functions on the Scottish Ministers, and

    (b) section 171 and Schedule 15.

  (7) The following provisions come into force on such day as the Secretary of State may by order appoint after consulting the Scottish Ministers—

    (a) sections 95, 98(2), 99(2) and (3), 100, 101 and 107, and

    (b) paragraphs 1 and 6 of Schedule 6, and section 109 so far as relating to those paragraphs.

  (8) Otherwise, this Act comes into force on such day as the Secretary of State may by order appoint.

  (9) Different days may be appointed for different purposes or different areas.

  (10) The Secretary of State may by order make such provision as he considers appropriate for transitory, transitional or saving purposes in connection with the coming into force of any provision of this Act.

  (11) The power conferred by subsection (10) is exercisable by the Scottish Ministers (rather than the Secretary of State) in connection with any provision of this Act which comes into force by order made by the Scottish Ministers.

179   Short title and extent

  (1) This Act may be cited as the Serious Organised Crime and Police Act 2005.

  (2) Subject to the following provisions, this Act extends to England and Wales only.

  (3) The following extend also to Scotland—

    (a) sections 1 to 54, 57 and 58,

    (b) sections 60 to 68, 70, 79 to 96, 98 to 106, 107(1) and (4) and 108,

    (c) section 123,

    (d) section 131,

    (e) sections 150 to 153, 156(6), 158, 163(1) and (2), 164, 165(1) and (2), 166(2), 167 and 171(1),

    (f) sections 172, 173, 176 to 178 and this section,

    (g) Schedules 1, 3, 5 and 15.

  (4) The following extend to Scotland only—

    (a) section 77 and 107(3),

    (b) sections 129 and 130(3),

    (c) sections 156(1) to (5), 166(1) and 171(2).

(5) The following extend also to Northern Ireland—

    (a) sections 1 to 54, 57 and 58,

    (b) sections 68, 71 to 75, 79 to 106, 107(1), (2) and (4) and 108,

    (c) section 123(1),

    (d) sections 128, 131 and 144,

    (e) sections 150(1), 151, 163(1) and (2), 164, 165, 166(2) and 167,

    (f) sections 172, 173, 176 to 178 and this section,

    (g) Schedules 1, 3 and 5.

(6) The following extend to Northern Ireland only—

    (a) section 55(2),

    (b) section 78,

    (c) section 130(2),

    (d) Part 2 of Schedule 10.

(7) The following have the same extent as the enactments to which they relate—

    (a) section 55(1) and Schedule 2,

    (b) section 59 and Schedule 4,

    (c) section 109 and Schedule 6,

    (d) section 154,

    (e) section 159 and Schedule 11,

    (f) section 160 and Schedule 12,

    (g) section 161(5) (so far as it has effect for the purposes of Part 2 of Schedule 13) and that Part of that Schedule,

    (h) section 163(3) and Schedule 14,

    (i) sections 169(5) and 170,

    (j) (subject to subsection (8)) section 174(2) and Schedule 17.

(8) So far as Schedule 17 contains a repeal or revocation of an enactment which corresponds to the repeal or revocation of that enactment by another provision of this Act, that Schedule and section 174(2) have the same extent as that other provision.

(9) So far as they relate to any provision of this Act which extends to any place outside the United Kingdom, sections 172, 173, 177, 178 and this section also extend there.

(10) Subsection (2) does not apply to the following—

    (a) section 168, or

    (b) any provision of Schedule 7 which makes provision as to its extent.

SCHEDULE 1

THE SERIOUS ORGANISED CRIME AGENCY

PART 1
THE BOARD OF SOCA

Membership

1 (1) SOCA shall consist of—
    (a) a chairman,
    (b) such number of ex-officio members as SOCA may from time to time determine, and
    (c) such number of other members ('ordinary members') as the Secretary of State may so determine.

  (2) The following limits apply for the purposes of sub-paragraph (1)—
    (a) the number of ex-officio members determined under sub-paragraph (1)(b) must not at any time exceed such number as may for the time being be specified by the Secretary of State,
    (b) the number of ordinary members determined under sub-paragraph (1)(c) must not at any time be less than the number of ex-officio members for the time being determined under sub-paragraph (1)(b), and
    (c) the total of the numbers determined under sub-paragraph (1)(b) and (c) must not at any time be less than four.

  (3) The chairman and the ordinary members are to be appointed by the Secretary of State.

  (4) Before appointing a person to hold office as chairman the Secretary of State must consult the Scottish Ministers.

  (5) For the purposes of this Schedule the 'ex-officio members' are—
    (a) the Director-General of SOCA (see paragraph 9), and
    (b) such other employees of SOCA as may for the time being be appointed by the Director General after consulting the chairman.

  (6) References in any enactment to members of SOCA are (unless the context otherwise requires) references to any of its members mentioned in sub-paragraph (1).

Tenure of office: chairman and ordinary members

2 The chairman and the ordinary members shall hold and vacate office as such in accordance with the terms of their respective appointments.
    This is subject to paragraphs 3 and 4.

3 (1) An appointment of a person to hold office as chairman or ordinary member shall be for a term not exceeding five years.

(2) A person holding office as chairman or ordinary member may at any time resign that office by giving notice in writing to the Secretary of State.

4 The Secretary of State may by notice in writing remove a person from office as chairman or ordinary member if satisfied that—

(a) he has without reasonable excuse failed, for a continuous period of three months, to carry out his functions as chairman or ordinary member;

(b) he has without reasonable excuse been absent from three consecutive meetings of SOCA;

(c) he has been convicted (whether before or after his appointment) of a criminal offence;

(d) he is an undischarged bankrupt or his estate has been sequestrated and he has not been discharged;

(e) he is the subject of a bankruptcy restrictions order or an interim order under Schedule 4A to the Insolvency Act 1986 (c. 45) or an order to the like effect made under any corresponding enactment in force in Scotland or Northern Ireland;

(f) he has made a composition or arrangement with, or granted a trust deed for, his creditors;

(g) he has failed to comply with the terms of his appointment; or

(h) he is otherwise unable or unfit to carry out his functions as chairman or ordinary member.

5 A person who ceases to be the chairman or an ordinary member is eligible for re-appointment, except where he is removed from office under paragraph 4.

Remuneration, pensions etc. of chairman and ordinary members

6 (1) SOCA shall pay to the chairman and each of the ordinary members such remuneration and allowances as may be determined by the Secretary of State.

(2) SOCA shall, if required to do so by the Secretary of State—

(a) pay such pension, allowances or gratuities as may be determined by the Secretary of State to or in respect of a person who is or has been the chairman or an ordinary member, or

(b) make such payments as may be so determined towards provision for the payment of a pension, allowances or gratuities to or in respect of such a person.

(3) If the Secretary of State determines that there are special circumstances which make it right for a person ceasing to hold office as chairman or ordinary member to receive compensation, SOCA shall pay to him a sum by way of compensation of such amount as may be determined by the Secretary of State.

(4) Service as chairman of SOCA shall be included among the kinds of service to which a scheme under section 1 of the Superannuation Act 1972 (c. 11) can apply, and accordingly in Schedule 1 to that Act (in which those kinds of service are listed) insert at the appropriate place—

'Chairman of the Serious Organised Crime Agency.'

(5) SOCA must pay to the Minister for the Civil Service, at such times as he may direct, such sums as he may determine in respect of any increase attributable to sub-paragraph (4) in the sums payable out of money provided by Parliament under that Act.

Termination of office of ex-officio members

7 (1) The Director General ceases to be an ex-officio member of SOCA on ceasing to be Director General.

(2) Any other ex-officio member of SOCA ceases to be such a member—

(a) on ceasing to be an employee of SOCA, or

(b) if the Director General by notice in writing revokes his appointment as ex-officio member.

(3) Before revoking an appointment under sub-paragraph (2)(b) the Director General must consult the chairman of SOCA.

(4) An ex-officio member other than the Director General may at any time resign his office as ex-officio member by giving notice in writing to the Director General.

PART 2
DIRECTOR GENERAL AND OTHER STAFF

SOCA's staff

8 (1) SOCA shall have—

(a) a Director General (see paragraph 9), and

(b) such other employees as SOCA may appoint.

(2) SOCA may make arrangements for persons to be seconded to SOCA to serve as members of its staff.

(3) A member of a police force on temporary service with SOCA shall be under the direction and control of SOCA.

(4) References in any enactment to members of staff of SOCA are (unless the context otherwise requires) references to persons who either are employees of SOCA or have been seconded to SOCA to serve as members of its staff.

The Director General

9 (1) The Director General shall be—

(a) appointed by the Secretary of State, and

(b) employed by SOCA on such terms and conditions as the Secretary of State may determine.

(2) But a person may not be so appointed for a term exceeding five years.

(3) Before appointing a person as Director General the Secretary of State must consult—

(a) the chairman of SOCA, and

(b) the Scottish Ministers.

(4) SOCA shall pay to its Director General such remuneration and allowances as the Secretary of State may determine.

Termination or suspension of appointment of Director General

10 (1) The Secretary of State may call on the Director General to retire or to resign from his office as Director General—

    (a) in the interests of efficiency or effectiveness, or

    (b) by reason of any misconduct by the Director General.

(2) But before doing so the Secretary of State must have complied with sub-paragraphs (3) to (6).

(3) The Secretary of State must give the Director General—

    (a) an explanation in writing of the grounds on which the Secretary of State proposes to call upon the Director General to retire or resign as mentioned in sub-paragraph (1)(a) or (b), and

    (b) an opportunity to make representations to the Secretary of State (including an opportunity to make them in person).

(4) The Secretary of State must consider any representations made by or on behalf of the Director General.

(5) The Secretary of State must send a copy of the explanation mentioned in sub-paragraph (3)(a) to the chairman of SOCA.

(6) The Secretary of State must consult—

    (a) the chairman of SOCA, and

    (b) the Scottish Ministers.

(7) If the Director General is, under sub-paragraph (1), called upon to retire or resign, he must retire or resign with effect from—

    (a) such date as the Secretary of State may specify, or

    (b) such earlier date as may be agreed between him and the Secretary of State.

(8) If the Secretary of State considers that it is necessary to do so for the maintenance of public confidence in SOCA, he may suspend the Director General from duty.

But before doing so the Secretary of State must have complied with sub-paragraph (6).

(9) Nothing in this paragraph affects any power of the Secretary of State to terminate or suspend the Director General's employment with SOCA in accordance with the terms and conditions of that employment.

Delegation of functions of Director General

11 (1) Anything authorised or required to be done by the Director General may be done by any other member of SOCA's staff who is authorised for the purpose by the Director General (whether generally or specially).

  (2) This paragraph does not apply in any case in relation to which specific provision for the delegation of any function of the Director General is made by this Act or any other enactment.

Remuneration and pensions of staff

12 (1) SOCA shall pay to its employees such remuneration and allowances as it may determine.

  (2) Sub-paragraph (1) does not apply to the Director General (to whom paragraph 9(4) applies instead).

13 (1) SOCA may pay, or make payments in respect of, such pensions, allowances or gratuities to or in respect of its employees or former employees as it may determine.

(2) Employment with SOCA shall be included among the kinds of employment to which a scheme under section 1 of the Superannuation Act 1972 (c. 11) can apply, and accordingly in Schedule 1 to that Act (in which those kinds of employment are listed) insert at the appropriate place—

'Employment by the Serious Organised Crime Agency.'

(3) If any person—

    (a) on ceasing to be employed by SOCA becomes or continues to be one of its members, and

    (b) was, by reference to his employment, a participant in a scheme under section 1 of that Act,

the Minister for the Civil Service may determine that his service as a member of SOCA is to be treated for the purposes of the scheme as if his service as a member were service as an employee of SOCA (whether or not any benefits are payable to or in respect of him by virtue of paragraph 6).

(4) SOCA shall pay to the Minister for the Civil Service, at such times as he may direct, such sums as he may determine in respect of any increase attributable to this paragraph in the sums payable out of money provided by Parliament under that Act.

Insurance

14 The Employers' Liability (Compulsory Insurance) Act 1969 (c. 57) does not require insurance to be effected by SOCA.

PART 3
COMMITTEES, PROCEDURE ETC.

Committees

15 (1) SOCA may establish committees.

    (2) Any committee so established may establish one or more sub-committees.

    (3) Any such committee or sub-committee must be a chaired by a member of SOCA.

    (4) A person who is not a member of SOCA may be appointed to any such committee or sub-committee.

    (5) If a member of any such committee or sub-committee is neither—

        (a) a member of SOCA, nor

        (b) a member of its staff,

    SOCA may pay to him such remuneration and allowances as it may determine.

Delegation to committees and staff

16 (1) SOCA may, to such extent as it may determine, delegate any of its functions to any of its committees or to any members of its staff.

    (2) Any of SOCA's committees may, to such extent as the committee may determine, delegate any function conferred on it to any of its sub-committees or to any member of SOCA's staff.

Proceedings

17 (1) Subject to the following provisions of this paragraph, SOCA may regulate—
  (a) its own proceedings (including quorum), and
  (b) the procedure (including quorum) of its committees and sub-committees.
  (2) Any determination as to the quorum for meetings of SOCA or any of its committees or sub-committees must be made at a meeting of SOCA that is attended by both the chairman and the Director General.
  (3) The quorum for meetings of SOCA shall in the first instance be determined by a meeting of SOCA that is attended by at least five of its members.
18 (1) The validity of any proceedings of SOCA, or any of its committees or sub-committees, shall not be affected by—
  (a) any vacancy among the members of SOCA or the committee or sub-committee;
  (b) any defect in the appointment of any of those members or of the chairman or Director General; or
  (c) any vacancy in the office of the chairman or the Director General.
  (2) The proceedings to which this paragraph apply include those within sub-paragraph (2) (but not (3)) of paragraph 17.

Evidence

19 Any document purporting to be signed on behalf of SOCA shall be received in evidence and, unless the contrary is proved, be taken to be so signed.

PART 4
GENERAL

Status

20 SOCA is not to be regarded—
  (a) as the servant or agent of the Crown, or
  (b) as enjoying any status, immunity or privilege of the Crown;
and SOCA's property is not to be regarded as property of, or property held on behalf of, the Crown.

Incidental powers

21 (1) In connection with exercising its functions SOCA may (subject to the provisions of this Act)—
  (a) enter into contracts and other agreements (whether legally binding or not);
  (b) acquire and dispose of property (including land);
  (c) borrow money; and
  (d) do such other things as SOCA thinks necessary or expedient.
  (2) The power conferred by sub-paragraph (1)(b) includes accepting—
  (a) gifts of money, and
  (b) gifts or loans of other property,
on such terms as SOCA considers appropriate (which may include terms providing for the commercial sponsorship of any of SOCA's activities).

    (3) But SOCA may exercise the power conferred by sub-paragraph (1)(b) or (c) only with the consent of the Secretary of State.

    (4) Such consent may be given—

        (a) with respect to a particular case or with respect to a class of cases;

        (b) subject to such conditions as the Secretary of State considers appropriate.

Section 55   SCHEDULE 2

FUNCTIONS OF INDEPENDENT POLICE COMPLAINTS COMMISSION IN RELATION TO SOCA

1   The Police Reform Act 2002 (c. 30) has effect subject to the following amendments.

2   In section 9(3) (persons ineligible for appointment as members of the Independent Police Complaints Commission)—

        (a) after paragraph (d) insert—

            '(da) he is or has been the chairman or a member of, or a member of the staff of, the Serious Organised Crime Agency;'; and

        (b) in paragraph (e), omit 'is or'.

3   (1) Section 10 (general functions of the Commission) is amended as follows.

    (2) In subsection (1)—

        (a) at the end of paragraph (e) omit 'and';

        (b) in paragraph (f) omit 'the National Criminal Intelligence Service, the National Crime Squad and'; and

        (c) at the end of that paragraph insert '; and

            (g) to carry out functions in relation to the Serious Organised Crime Agency which correspond to those conferred on the Commission in relation to police forces by paragraph (e) of this subsection.'

    (3) In subsection (3)—

        (a) omit paragraph (a);

        (b) after paragraph (b) insert—

            '(ba) any agreement under section 26A of this Act (Serious Organised Crime Agency);'; and

        (c) in paragraph (d) omit 'the National Criminal Intelligence Service, the National Crime Squad or'.

    (4) In subsection (7), omit 'or' at the end of paragraph (a) and at the end of paragraph (b) insert' or

        (c) its function under subsection (1)(g),'.

4   (1) Section 11 (reports) is amended as follows.

    (2) In subsection (6), for paragraphs (b) and (c) substitute—

        '(b) to the Serious Organised Crime Agency; and'.

    (3) For subsection (8) substitute—

        '(8) Where a report under subsection (3) relates to the Serious Organised Crime Agency, the Commission shall send a copy of that report to the Agency.'

    (4) In subsection (10), for paragraphs (d) and (e) substitute—

        '(d) the Serious Organised Crime Agency;'.

5 (1) Section 15 (general duties of police authorities etc.) is amended as follows.

(2) After subsection (1) insert—

'(1A) It shall be the duty of the Serious Organised Crime Agency to ensure that it is kept informed, in relation to the Agency, about all matters falling within subsection (2).'

(3) In subsection (3)—

(a) for paragraph (c) substitute—

'(c) a police authority or chief officer requires the Director General of the Serious Organised Crime Agency to provide a member of the staff of that Agency for appointment under any of those paragraphs,'; and

(b) for 'or Director General to whom the requirement is addressed' substitute 'to whom the requirement is addressed or of the Director General'.

(4) In subsection (4), at the end of paragraph (b) insert 'and' and for paragraphs (c) and (d) substitute—

'(c) the Serious Organised Crime Agency,'.

(5) In subsection (5), at the end of paragraph (b) insert 'and' and for paragraphs (c) and (d) substitute—

'(c) the Serious Organised Crime Agency,'.

(6) In subsection (6)—

(a) for 'the Directors General of the National Criminal Intelligence Service and of the National Crime Squad' substitute 'the Serious Organised Crime Agency';

(b) in paragraph (a), for 'of that Service or Squad' substitute 'a member of the staff of the Agency'; and

(c) omit the words from 'or, as the case may be' to the end of the subsection.

(7) In subsection (7), for the words from 'and in this subsection' onwards substitute 'and where the person whose conduct is under investigation was a member of the staff of the Serious Organised Crime Agency at the time of the conduct, "third force" means any police force other than the force to which the person carrying out the investigation belongs.'

(8) After subsection (7) insert—

'(8) Where the person who requires assistance and cooperation under subsection (5) is a member of the staff of the Serious Organised Crime Agency, a chief officer of a third force may be required to give that assistance and cooperation only with the approval of the Director General of the Agency.

In this subsection, "third force", in relation to an investigation, means any police force other than the force to which the person whose conduct is under investigation belonged at the time of the conduct.

(9) Where—

(a) the person carrying out an investigation is not a member of the staff of the Serious Organised Crime Agency; and

(b) the person whose conduct is under investigation was not a member of the staff of the Agency at the time of the conduct,

the Director General of the Agency may be required to give assistance and cooperation under subsection (5) only with the approval of the chief officer of the force to which the person requiring it belongs.'

6   In section 16 (payment for assistance with investigations), for subsections (5) and (6) substitute—

'(5) In this section (subject to subsection (6))—
    (a) references to a police force and to a police authority maintaining a police force include references to the Serious Organised Crime Agency; and
    (b) in relation to that Agency, references to the chief officer are references to the Director General.
(6) This section shall have effect in relation to cases in which assistance is required to be provided by the Serious Organised Crime Agency as if—
    (a) the reference in subsection (3)(b) to police authorities generally included a reference to the Agency; and
    (b) the reference in subsection (4)(b) to police authorities generally were a reference to the Agency.'

7   Omit section 25 (NCIS and NCS).
8   After section 26 insert—

'26A Serious Organised Crime Agency

(1) The Commission and the Serious Organised Crime Agency must enter into an agreement for the establishment and maintenance in relation to members of the Agency's staff of procedures corresponding or similar to those provided for by or under this Part.
(2) An agreement under this section—
    (a) must not be made or varied except with the approval of the Secretary of State; and
    (b) must not be terminated unless—
        (i) it is replaced by another such agreement, and
        (ii) the Secretary of State approves.
(3) An agreement under this section may contain provision for enabling the Commission to bring and conduct, or otherwise participate or intervene in, any proceedings which are identified by the agreement as disciplinary proceedings in relation to members of the Agency's staff.
(4) An agreement under this section must not confer any function on the Commission in relation to so much of any complaint or conduct matter as relates to the direction and control of the Agency by the Director General or other members of the Agency.
(5) Procedures established in accordance with an agreement under this section shall have no effect in relation to anything done outside England and Wales by any member of the staff of the Agency.'

9   In section 29(3) (interpretation)—
    (a) for paragraph (b) substitute—

      '(b) a member of the staff of the Serious Organised Crime Agency;'; and

    (b) in paragraph (d), for '(temporary service otherwise than with NCIS or NCS)' substitute '(temporary service of various kinds)'.
10   In section 108(7) (extent etc.), omit paragraph (e).
11   (1) Schedule 3 (handling of complaints and conduct matters) is amended as follows.
    (2) In paragraph 16(3), for paragraph (b) substitute—

      '(b) a member of the staff of the Serious Organised Crime Agency,'.

    (3) In paragraph 17(2), for paragraph (b) substitute—

      '(b) a member of the staff of the Serious Organised Crime Agency,'.

Section 58   SCHEDULE 3

                              TRANSFERS TO SOCA

                                  Interpretation

1   In this Schedule—
      'the 1967 Act' means the Police (Scotland) Act 1967 (c. 77);
      'the 1996 Act' means the Police Act 1996 (c. 16);
      'the 1998 Act' means the Police (Northern Ireland) Act 1998 (c. 32);
      'the Commissioners' means the Commissioners for Her Majesty's Revenue and
          Customs;
      'immigration officer' means a person who is an immigration officer within the
          meaning of the Immigration Act 1971 (c. 77);
      'NCIS' means the National Criminal Intelligence Service;
      'NCS' means the National Crime Squad;
      'relevant appointment' means an appointment under section 6, 9, 13, 14, 52, 55,
          58 or 59 of, or Schedule 1 to, the Police Act 1997 (c. 50);
      'transfer scheme' means a scheme made by the Secretary of State under this
          Schedule.

                                     Staff

2   (1) A transfer scheme may provide for a person who—
         (a) holds a relevant appointment,
         (b) is an officer of Revenue and Customs, or
         (c) is an immigration officer,
         to become an employee of SOCA.
    (2) If the person had a contract of employment before becoming an employee of
         SOCA, the scheme may provide for that contract to have effect (subject to any
         necessary modifications) as if originally made between him and SOCA.
    (3) If the person did not have a contract of employment, the scheme may provide for
         the terms and conditions of his relevant appointment or service as an officer of
         Revenue and Customs or an immigration officer to have effect (subject to any
         necessary modifications) as the terms and conditions of his contract of employ-
         ment with SOCA.
    (4) In this paragraph 'relevant appointment' does not include an appointment held
         by a person engaged on relevant service within the meaning of—
         (a) section 38A of the 1967 Act,
         (b) section 97 of the 1996 Act, or
         (c) section 27 of the 1998 Act.
3   A transfer scheme may provide—
         (a) for relevant service within section 38A(1)(ba) of the 1967 Act to have effect
              from a time specified in the scheme as relevant service within section
              38A(1)(bc) of that Act,
         (b) for relevant service within section 97(1)(ca) or (cb) of the 1996 Act to have
              effect from a time specified in the scheme as relevant service within section
              97(1)(cf) of that Act,

(c) for relevant service within section 27(1)(b) of the 1998 Act to have effect from a time specified in the scheme as relevant service within section 27(1) (cb) of that Act.

4 (1) A transfer scheme may provide—

    (a) for the secondment by virtue of which a person holds a relevant appointment to have effect as a secondment to SOCA, and

    (b) for him to serve as a member of the staff of SOCA.

  (2) The scheme may make provision as to the terms and conditions which are to have effect as the terms and conditions of his secondment to SOCA.

5 (1) A transfer scheme may provide—

    (a) for the transfer to SOCA of the rights, powers, duties and liabilities of the employer under or in connection with the contract of employment of a person who becomes a member of the staff of SOCA by virtue of the scheme,

    (b) for anything done before that transfer by or in relation to the employer in respect of such a contract or the employee to be treated as having been done by or in relation to SOCA.

  (2) Sub-paragraph (1) applies with the necessary modifications in relation to a person who before becoming a member of the staff of SOCA—

    (a) did not have a contract of employment, or

    (b) held a relevant appointment by virtue of a secondment.

  (3) A transfer scheme may make provision for periods before a person became an employee of SOCA to count as periods of employment with SOCA (and for the operation of the scheme not to be treated as having interrupted the continuity of that employment).

6 (1) A transfer scheme may provide for a person who—

    (a) holds a relevant appointment or is an officer of Revenue and Customs or an immigration officer, and

    (b) would otherwise become a member of the staff of SOCA by the operation of the scheme,

not to become a member of the staff of SOCA if he gives notice objecting to the operation of the scheme in relation to him.

  (2) A transfer scheme may provide for any person who would be treated (whether by an enactment or otherwise) as being dismissed by the operation of the scheme not to be so treated.

7 (1) A transfer scheme may provide for the termination of a relevant appointment.

  (2) The Secretary of State may make a payment of such amount (if any) as he may determine to the person who held the appointment.

Property, rights and liabilities etc.

8 (1) A transfer scheme may provide for the transfer to SOCA of property, rights and liabilities of any of the following—

    (a) NCIS, its Service Authority and Director General,

    (b) NCS, its Service Authority and Director General,

    (c) the Commissioners, and

    (d) the Secretary of State.

  (2) The scheme may—

(a) create rights, or impose liabilities, in relation to property, rights and liabilities transferred by virtue of the scheme, and

(b) apportion property, rights and liabilities between the Commissioners, or the Secretary of State, and SOCA.

(3) The scheme may provide for things done by or in relation to persons to whom sub-paragraph (4) applies to be—

(a) treated as done by or in relation to SOCA or members of the staff of SOCA,

(b) continued by or in relation to SOCA or members of the staff of SOCA.

(4) This sub-paragraph applies to—

(a) NCIS, its members and Service Authority,

(b) NCS, its members and Service Authority,

(c) the Commissioners and officers of Revenue and Customs, and

(d) the Secretary of State and immigration officers.

(5) The scheme may in particular make provision about the continuation of legal proceedings.

9   A transfer scheme may provide for SOCA to make any payment which—

(a) before a day specified in the scheme could have been made out of the NCIS service fund or the NCS service fund, but

(b) is not a liability which can be transferred by virtue of paragraph 8.

Supplementary

10 (1) A transfer scheme may contain—

(a) further provision in connection with any of the matters to which paragraphs 2 to 9 relate,

(b) the provision mentioned in sub-paragraph (3).

(2) The provision which may be made under sub-paragraph (1)(a) includes provision as to the consequences of the termination of a person's appointment or employment by or by virtue of the scheme.

(3) The provision mentioned in this sub-paragraph is provision—

(a) for the Secretary of State, or any other person nominated by or in accordance with the scheme, to determine any matter requiring determination under or in consequence of the scheme, and

(b) as to the payment of fees charged, or expenses incurred, by any person nominated to determine any matter by virtue of paragraph (a).

11 (1) Before making a transfer scheme which contains any provision relating to persons who fall within paragraph (a), (b) or (c) of paragraph 2(1), the Secretary of State must consult such bodies appearing to represent the interests of those persons as he considers appropriate.

(2) Before making a transfer scheme which contains any provision relating to—

(a) officers of Revenue and Customs, or

(b) property, rights or liabilities of the Commissioners,

the Secretary of State must consult the Commissioners.

Power to make regulations

12   The Secretary of State may by regulations make—

(a) provision as to the consequences of the termination of a person's employment by a transfer scheme (including provision removing any entitlement to compensation which might otherwise arise in such circumstances);

(b) transitory, transitional or saving provision in connection with any provision which is (or in the future may be) included in a transfer scheme by virtue of paragraph 3.

Section 59

SCHEDULE 4

MINOR AND CONSEQUENTIAL AMENDMENTS RELATING TO SOCA

Explosives Act 1875 (c. 17)

1 (1) Section 75 of the Explosives Act 1875 is amended as follows.

(2) In subsection (1)—

(a) after 'chief officer of police,' insert 'the Director General of the Serious Organised Crime Agency,', and

(b) after 'any officer of police,' insert 'designated person,'.

(3) For subsection (2) substitute—

'(2) In subsection (1) "designated person" means a member of the staff of the Serious Organised Crime Agency who is for the time being designated under section 43 of the Serious Organised Crime and Police Act 2005 as a person having the powers of a constable (but this is subject to any limitation specified in such a person's designation under that section).'

Police (Property) Act 1897 (c. 30)

2 (1) Section 2A of the Police (Property) Act 1897 (application to NCS) is amended as follows.

(2) For 'National Crime Squad' (in each place) substitute 'Serious Organised Crime Agency'.

(3) In subsection (2)—

(a) in paragraph (a) for 'member of that Squad' substitute 'member of the staff of that Agency', and

(b) in paragraph (b) for 'Squad' substitute 'Agency'.

(4) In subsection (3)—

(a) in paragraph (a) for 'the Service Authority for that Squad' substitute 'that Agency', and

(b) in paragraph (b) for 'Squad' substitute 'Agency'.

(5) In the heading, for 'NCS' substitute 'SOCA'.

Army Act 1955 (3 & 4 Eliz. 2 c. 18)

3 In section 83BC(2) of the Army Act 1955 (police forces which may be advised by prosecuting authority) omit paragraph (k).

Air Force Act 1955 (3 & 4 Eliz. 2 c. 19)

4 In section 83BC(2) of the Air Force Act 1955 (police forces which may be advised by prosecuting authority) omit paragraph (k).

Naval Discipline Act 1957 (c. 53)

5   In section 52IJ(2) of the Naval Discipline Act 1957 (police forces which may be advised by prosecuting authority) omit paragraph (k).

Public Records Act 1958 (c. 51)

6   In Schedule 1 to the Public Records Act 1958 (definition of public records) in Part 2 of the Table at the end of paragraph 3—
    (a) at the appropriate place insert—
    'Serious Organised Crime Agency.'; and
    (b) omit the entries relating to the Service Authorities for the National Crime Squad and the National Criminal Intelligence Service.

Trustee Investments Act 1961 (c. 62)

7   The Trustee Investments Act 1961 has effect subject to the following amendments.
8   In section 11(4) (local authority investment schemes)—
    (a) in paragraph (a) omit ', the Service Authority for the National Crime Squad', and
    (b) omit paragraph (e).
9   In Part 2 of Schedule 1 (narrower-range investments requiring advice) omit paragraph 9(da).

Offices, Shops and Railway Premises Act 1963 (c. 41)

10 In section 90(4) of the Offices, Shops and Railway Premises Act 1963 (persons taken to be employed for the purposes of the Act)—
    (a) at the end of paragraph (c) insert 'or'; and
    (b) for paragraph (d) substitute—
    '(d) a member of a police force seconded to the Serious Organised Crime Agency to serve as a member of its staff.'

Parliamentary Commissioner Act 1967 (c. 13)

11 In Schedule 2 to the Parliamentary Commissioner Act 1967 (departments etc. subject to investigation) omit the entries relating to the Service Authorities for the National Crime Squad and the National Criminal Intelligence Service.

Police (Scotland) Act 1967 (c. 77)

12 The Police (Scotland) Act 1967 has effect subject to the following amendments.
13 In section 33 (inspectors of constabulary), in subsections (3) and (4), omit 'and the National Criminal Intelligence Service'.
14 (1) Section 38A (constables engaged on service outside their force) is amended as follows.
    (2) In subsection (1)—
        (a) omit paragraph (ba), and
        (b) after paragraph (bb) insert—

'(bc) relevant service as a member of the staff of the Serious Organised Crime Agency on which a person is engaged with the consent of the appropriate authority,'.

(3) In subsection (6)(a) for '(ba) or (bb), (e) or (f)' substitute '(bb), (bc), (e) or (f)'.

15 In section 39(4) (liability for wrongful acts of constables) for 'section 23 of the Police Act 1997' substitute 'section 23 or 25 of the Serious Organised Crime and Police Act 2005'.

16 In section 41(4)(a) (assaults on constables) omit 'or by a member of the National Criminal Intelligence Service or of the National Crime Squad'.

Leasehold Reform Act 1967 (c. 88)

17 In section 28(5) of the Leasehold Reform Act 1967 (bodies retaining or resuming land required for public services) omit paragraph (bc).

Firearms Act 1968 (c. 27)

18 In section 54(3)(c) of the Firearms Act 1968 (application of Parts 1 and 2 to crown servants) for 'National Criminal Intelligence Service or the National Crime Squad' substitute 'staff of the Serious Organised Crime Agency'.

Employment Agencies Act 1973 (c. 35)

19 In section 13(7) of the Employment Agencies Act 1973 (interpretation), in paragraph (f), omit ', the Service Authority for the National Criminal Intelligence Service, the Service Authority for the National Crime Squad'.

Health and Safety at Work etc. Act 1974 (c. 37)

20 In section 51A(2) of the Health and Safety at Work etc. Act 1974 (application of Part 1 of the Act to the police) for paragraph (b) substitute—

'(b) in relation to a member of a police force seconded to the Serious Organised Crime Agency to serve as a member of its staff, means that Agency, and'.

District Courts (Scotland) Act 1975 (c. 20)

21 In section 12(1) of the District Courts (Scotland) Act 1975 (restriction of functions of justices who are councillors etc.) after 'authority' insert 'or a member of staff of the Serious Organised Crime Agency'.

House of Commons Disqualification Act 1975 (c. 24)

22 The House of Commons Disqualification Act 1975 has effect subject to the following amendments.

23 In section 1(1) (disqualification for membership of House of Commons) omit paragraph (da).

24 (1) Schedule 1 (disqualifying offices) is amended as follows.
   (2) In Part 2—
      (a) at the appropriate place insert—
      'The Serious Organised Crime Agency.'; and

    (b) omit the entries relating to the Service Authorities for the National Crime Squad and the National Criminal Intelligence Service.

(3) In Part 3, at the appropriate place insert—

    'Member of the staff of the Serious Organised Crime Agency.'

Northern Ireland Assembly Disqualification Act 1975 (c. 25)

25 The Northern Ireland Assembly Disqualification Act 1975 has effect subject to the following amendments.

26 In section 1(1) (disqualification for membership of Assembly) omit paragraph (da).

27 (1) Schedule 1 (disqualifying offices) is amended as follows.

    (2) In Part 2—

        (a) at the appropriate place insert—

        'The Serious Organised Crime Agency.'; and

        (b) omit the entries relating to the Service Authorities for the National Crime Squad and the National Criminal Intelligence Service.

    (3) In Part 3, at the appropriate place insert—

        'Member of the staff of the Serious Organised Crime Agency.'

Sex Discrimination Act 1975 (c. 65)

28 In section 17 of the Sex Discrimination Act 1975 (police), in subsection (7)—

    (a) in the definition of 'chief officer of police', omit paragraph (aa);

    (b) in the definition of 'police authority', omit paragraph (aa); and

    (c) in the definition of 'police fund', omit the words from', in relation to' (in the second place where they occur) to 'the Police Act 1997'.

Police Pensions Act 1976 (c. 35)

29 The Police Pensions Act 1976 has effect subject to the following amendments.

30 In section 7(2) (payment of pensions and contributions), at the beginning of each of paragraphs (ca) to (cd), insert 'an employee of SOCA and who immediately before he became an employee of SOCA was serving as'.

31 (1) Section 11 (interpretation) is amended as follows.

    (2) In subsection (1), at the beginning of each of paragraphs (ba), (bb), (bc) and (bd), after 'service' insert 'as an employee of SOCA by a person who immediately before he became an employee of SOCA was serving'.

    (3) In subsection (2) for paragraphs (c) and (d) substitute—

        '(c) in relation to any such service as is mentioned in paragraph (ba), (bb), (bc) or (bd) of subsection (1) or any service of the kind described in section 97(1)(cf) of the Police Act 1997 or section 38A (1)(bc) of the Police (Scotland) Act 1967, it means SOCA;'.

    (4) In subsection (5), in the definition of 'central service'—

        (a) in paragraph (a) omit '(ca), (cb),' and after '(cc)' insert ', (cf)', and

        (b) in paragraph (b) for '(ba) or (bb)' substitute '(bb) or (bc)'

    (5) After the definition of 'pension rights' in that subsection add—

        ' "SOCA" means the Serious Organised Crime Agency.'

32 Paragraphs 30 and 31 (and the corresponding entry in Schedule 17) do not affect the operation of the Police Pensions Act 1976 in relation to any person's service of any of the following kinds—

    (a) service as the Director General of the National Criminal Intelligence Service;

    (b) service as the Director General of the National Crime Squad;

    (c) service as a police member of the National Criminal Intelligence Service appointed under subsection (1)(b) of section 9 of the Police Act 1997 (c. 50) by virtue of subsection (2)(a) of that section;

    (d) service as a police member of the National Crime Squad appointed under subsection (1)(b) of section 55 of the Police Act 1997 by virtue of subsection (2)(a) of that section;

    (e) relevant service within paragraph (ca) or (cb) of section 97(1) of the Police Act 1996 (c. 16);

    (f) relevant service within section 38A(1)(ba) of the Police (Scotland) Act 1967 (c. 77).

Race Relations Act 1976 (c. 74)

33 The Race Relations Act 1976 has effect subject to the following amendments.

34 (1) Section 76B (other police bodies) is amended as follows.

    (2) Omit subsection (1).

    (3) In subsection (2) omit the word 'also'.

    (4) After subsection (2) insert—

       '(2A) Constables serving with the Serious Organised Crime Agency do not constitute a body of constables for the purposes of subsection (2).'

35 In Schedule 1A (bodies and other persons subject to general statutory duty)—

    (a) in Part 1 omit paragraphs 59 and 60,

    (b) in Part 2 at the appropriate place under the heading 'Other Bodies, Etc' insert—

       'The Serious Organised Crime Agency.'; and

    (c) in Part 3 omit the entry relating to the Director General of the National Crime Squad.

Sex Discrimination (Northern Ireland) Order 1976 (S.I. 1976/1042) (N.I. 15))

36 The Sex Discrimination (Northern Ireland) Order 1976 has effect subject to the following amendments.

37 In Article 84(8) (police officers) for 'section 23 of the Police Act 1997' substitute 'section 23 or 24 of the Serious Organised Crime and Police Act 2005'.

38 In Article 85 (other police bodies), for paragraph (6) substitute—

    '(6) In this Article in relation to any body of constables—

       (a) "chief officer of police" means the person who has the direction and control of the body;

       (b) "police authority" means the authority by which the members of the body are paid; and

       (c) "police fund" means money provided by that authority.'

Health and Safety at Work (Northern Ireland) Order 1978 (S.I. 1978/1039 (N.I. 9))

39 In Article 47A(2) of the Health and Safety at Work (Northern Ireland) Order 1978 (application of Part II of the Order to the police) omit sub-paragrah (b).

Law Reform (Miscellaneous Provisions) (Scotland) Act 1980 (c. 55)

40 In Part 1 of Schedule 1 to the Law Reform (Miscellaneous Provisions) (Scotland) Act 1980 (persons ineligible for jury service) in Group B, after paragraph (nb) insert—

'(nc) members of staff of the Serious Organised Crime Agency;'.

Stock Transfer Act 1982 (c. 41)

41 In Schedule 1 to the Stock Transfer Act 1982 (securities specified for the purposes of the Act) in paragraph 7(1)—

(a) at the end of paragraph (b) insert 'or'; and

(b) omit paragraph (bb) and the word 'or' before it.

Road Traffic Regulation Act 1984 (c. 27)

42 (1) Section 87 of the Road Traffic Regulation Act 1984 (exemption of fire, ambulance and police vehicles from speed limits) is amended as follows.

(2) The existing text of that section is to be subsection (1).

(3) After that subsection add—

'(2) Subsection (1) above applies in relation to a vehicle being used—

(a) for Serious Organised Crime Agency purposes, or

(b) for training persons to drive vehicles for use for Serious Organised Crime Agency purposes,

as it applies in relation to a vehicle being used for police purposes.

(3) But (except where it is being used for training the person by whom it is being driven) subsection (1) above does not apply in relation to a vehicle by virtue of subsection (2) above unless it is being driven by a person who has been trained in driving vehicles at high speeds.'

Police and Criminal Evidence Act 1984 (c. 60)

43 The Police and Criminal Evidence Act 1984 has effect subject to the following amendments.

44 In section 5 (reports of recorded searches and road checks) omit subsection (1A).

45 In section 55 (intimate searches) omit subsection (14A).

46 In section 63A(1A) (supplementary provision about fingerprints and samples) for paragraphs (b) and (c) substitute—

'(b) the Serious Organised Crime Agency;'.

Prosecution of Offences Act 1985 (c. 23)

47 In section 3(3) of the Prosecution of Offences Act 1985 (functions of Director of Public Prosecutions), in the definition of 'police force', omit ', the National Crime Squad'.

Ministry of Defence Police Act 1987 (c. 4)

48 The Ministry of Defence Police Act 1987 has effect subject to the following amendments.

49 In section 2B(3) (constables serving with other forces), in the definitions of 'chief officer' and 'relevant force', omit paragraphs (c) and (d).

50 After section 2B insert—

'2C Constables serving with Serious Organised Crime Agency

(1) A member of the Ministry of Defence Police serving with the Serious Organised Crime Agency under arrangements to which subsection (2) applies shall—
   (a) be under the direction and control of the Serious Organised Crime Agency, and
   (b) continue to be a constable.

(2) This subsection applies to arrangements made between—
   (a) the Serious Organised Crime Agency, and
   (b) the chief constable of the Ministry of Defence Police.'

Dartford-Thurrock Crossing Act 1988 (c. 20)

51 In section 19(a) of the Dartford-Thurrock Crossing Act 1988 (exemption from tolls) for sub-paragraph (ia) substitute—

'(ia) the Serious Organised Crime Agency;'.

Road Traffic Act 1988 (c. 52)

52 The Road Traffic Act 1988 shall have effect subject to the following amendments.

53 (1) In section 124 (exemption from requirements regarding paid driving instruction) after subsection (1) insert—

'(1A) Section 123(1) and (2) also does not apply to the giving of instruction by a SOCA instructor in pursuance of arrangements made by the Director General of the Serious Organised Crime Agency.

In this subsection "SOCA instructor" means a member of the staff of the Serious Organised Crime Agency whose duties consist of or include the giving instruction in the driving of motor cars to other members of the Agency's staff.'

(2) In subsection (2) of that section, omit the definitions of 'chief officer of police', 'police authority' and 'police force'.

54 In section 144(2) (exemption from requirement of third-party insurance or security) omit paragraph (ba).

Security Service Act 1989 (c. 5)

55 The Security Service Act 1989 has effect subject to the following amendments.

56 In section 1(4) (functions of the Security Service) for',the National Criminal Intelligence Service, the National Crime Squad' substitute', the Serious Organised Crime Agency'.

57 In section 2(2)(c) (duties of the Director General)—
   (a) for 'the Director General of the National Criminal Intelligence Service' substitute 'the Director General of the Serious Organised Crime Agency', and
   (b) for ', the National Criminal Intelligence Service, the National Crime Squad' substitute ', the Serious Organised Crime Agency'.

Official Secrets Act 1989 (c. 6)

58 In section 12(1)(e) of the Official Secrets Act 1989 (meaning of 'Crown servant' in that Act) for 'or of the National Criminal Intelligence Service or the National Crime Squad' substitute 'or of the Serious Organised Crime Agency'.

Aviation and Maritime Security Act 1990 (c. 31)

59 In section 22(4)(b) of the Aviation and Maritime Security Act 1990 (searches in harbour areas) omit sub-paragraph (iii) and the word 'or' before it.

Tribunals and Inquiries Act 1992 (c. 53)

60 The Tribunals and Inquiries Act 1992 has effect subject to the following amendments.
61 In section 7(2) (removal of members of certain tribunals) after '36A' omit '(a) or (b)'.
62 In Schedule 1 (tribunals under supervision of Council on Tribunals) in paragraph 36A omit '(a)' and sub-paragraph (b).

Criminal Appeal Act 1995 (c. 35)

63 (1) Section 22 of the Criminal Appeal Act 1995 (meaning of 'public body' etc.) has effect subject to the following amendments.
   (2) In subsection (2)—
       (a) in paragraph (a) omit', the National Crime Squad',
       (b) in paragraph (b)—
           (i)   at the end of sub-paragraph (i) insert 'and',
           (ii) omit sub-paragraph (ii), and
           (iii) at the end of sub-paragraph (iii) insert 'and',
       (c) in paragraph (c) for ', the City of London police force or the National Crime Squad' substitute 'or the City of London police force', and
       (d) omit paragraphs (d) and (e).
   (3) In subsection (4) for paragraph (aa) substitute—

       '(aa) in relation to the Serious Organised Crime Agency, the Director General of that Agency,'.

Disability Discrimination Act 1995 (c. 50)

64 The Disability Discrimination Act 1995 has effect subject to the following amendments.
65 (1) The section 64A (police) inserted by the Disability Discrimination Act 1995 (Amendment) Regulations 2003 (S.I. 2003/1673) is amended as follows.
   (2) In subsection (7)—
       (a) in the definition of 'chief officer of police', omit paragraph (b),
       (b) in the definition of 'police authority', omit paragraph (b), and
       (c) in the definition of 'police fund', omit paragraph (b).
66 In the section 64A (police) inserted by the Disability Discrimination Act 1995 (Amendment) Regulations (Northern Ireland) 2004 (S.R. 2004/55), in subsection (6)(a), for 'section 23 of the Police Act 1997' substitute 'section 23 or 24 of the Serious Organised Crime and Police Act 2005'.

67 (1) The section 64B (other police bodies) inserted by the Disability Discrimination Act 1995 (Amendment) Regulations (Northern Ireland) 2004 is amended as follows.

(2) For subsection (6) substitute—

'(6) Subject to subsection (8), in this section in relation to any body of constables—

(a) "chief officer of police" means the person who has the direction and control of the body;

(b) "police authority" means the authority by which the members of the body are paid; and

(c) "police fund" means money provided by that authority.'

Police Act 1996 (c. 16)

68 The Police Act 1996 has effect subject to the following amendments.

69 Omit section 23(8) (collaboration agreements).

70 Omit section 24(5) (mutual aid).

71 (1) Section 54 (appointment and functions of inspectors of constabulary) is amended as follows.

(2) In subsection (2) omit 'the National Criminal Intelligence Service and the National Crime Squad'.

(3) For subsection (2B) substitute—

'(2B) The Secretary of State may at any time require the inspectors of constabulary to carry out an inspection under this section of a police force maintained for any police area; and a requirement under this subsection may include a requirement for the inspection to be confined to a particular part of the force in question, to particular matters or to particular activities of that force.'

72 In section 55 (publication of reports) omit subsection (7).

73 (1) Section 57 (common services) is amended as follows.

(2) In subsection (3A)—

(a) for 'National Crime Squad' substitute 'Serious Organised Crime Agency', and

(b) for 'Squad for the Squad' substitute 'Agency for the Agency'.

(3) For subsection (4)(c) substitute—

'(c) if the regulations relate to the Serious Organised Crime Agency, that Agency.'

74 Omit section 59(8) (police federations).

75 Omit section 60(2A) (regulations for police federations).

76 In section 61(1) (police negotiating board) omit paragraphs (aa) and (ba).

77 (1) Section 62 (functions of negotiating board with respect to regulations) is amended as follows.

(2) In subsection (1) omit paragraphs (aa) and (ab).

(3) Omit the subsection (1A) inserted by paragraph 82(2) of Schedule 9 to the Police Act 1997 (c. 50).

(4) Omit subsections (1B) and (1C).

(5) In subsection (2) for 'subsection (1), (1A) or (1B)' substitute 'subsection (1) or (1A)'.

78 (1) Section 63 (police advisory boards) is amended as follows.

(2) Omit subsections (1A) and (1B).

(3) For subsection (3) substitute—

'(3) Before making—
  (a) regulations under section 50 or 52, other than regulations with respect to any of the matters mentioned in section 61(1), or
  (b) regulations under Part 2 of the Police Reform Act 2002,
  the Secretary of State shall supply the Police Advisory Board for England and Wales with a draft of the regulations, and take into consideration any representations made by that Board.'

79 In section 64 (membership of trade unions) omit subsections (4A) and (4B).

80 (1) Section 88 (liability for wrongful acts of constables) is amended as follows.

  (2) In subsection (5)(b) omit 'or section 23 of the Police Act 1997'.

  (3) After subsection (5) insert—

    '(5A) This section shall have effect where, by virtue of section 23 or 24 of the Serious Organised Crime and Police Act 2005, a member of the staff of the Serious Organised Crime Agency who is neither a constable nor an employee of the police authority is provided to a police force as if—
      (a) any unlawful conduct of his in the performance or purported performance of his functions were unlawful conduct of a constable under the direction and control of the chief officer of police of that force; and
      (b) subsection (4) applied to him in the case of the police authority maintaining that force.'

81 In section 89(4)(a) (assaults on constables) omit 'or by a member of the National Criminal Intelligence Service or of the National Crime Squad'.

82 (1) Section 97 (police officers engaged on service outside their force) is amended as follows.

  (2) In subsection (1)—
    (a) omit paragraphs (ca) and (cb),
    (b) the paragraph (cd) inserted by paragraph 30(2) of Schedule 11 to the Proceeds of Crime Act 2002 (c. 29) is to be paragraph (ce), and
    (c) after that paragraph insert—
      '(cf) temporary service as a member of the staff of the Serious Organised Crime Agency on which a person is engaged with the consent of the appropriate authority;'.

  (3) In subsection (6)(a) for the words from 'paragraph' to 'subsection (1)' substitute 'paragraph (a), (aa), (b), (c), (cc), (cd), (ce), (cf), (d), (g) or (h) of subsection (1)'.

  (4) In subsection (8) for the words from 'paragraph' to 'subsection (1)' substitute 'paragraph (aa), (b), (c), (cc), (cd), (ce), (cf) or (d) of subsection (1)'.

83 (1) Section 98 (cross-border aid) is amended as follows.

  (2) In subsections (2) and (3)—
    (a) omit 'or the Director General of the National Crime Squad', and
    (b) omit 'or the National Crime Squad'.

  (3) Omit subsection (3A).

  (4) In subsection (4)—
    (a) omit 'or the National Crime Squad',
    (b) for '(2), (3) or (3A)' substitute '(2) or (3)', and
    (c) omit 'or the Director General of the National Crime Squad'.

  (5) In subsection (5)—
    (a) omit 'or the National Crime Squad' (in both places), and
    (b) omit 'or the Director General of the National Crime Squad'.

  (6) Omit subsection (6A).

Employment Rights Act 1996 (c. 18)

84 The Employment Rights Act 1996 has effect subject to the following amendments.
85 In section 43KA(2) (application of Part 4A of that Act to the police) for paragraphs (b) and (c) substitute—

> '(b) in relation to a member of a police force seconded to the Serious Organised Crime Agency to serve as a member of its staff, that Agency; and'.

86 In section 50(2) (right to time off for public duties) omit paragraph (ca).
87 In section 134A (application of section 100 of that Act to the police) after subsection (2) add—

> '(3) Subsection (1) does not apply to the holding of the office of constable by a member of a police force on secondment to the Serious Organised Crime Agency.'

Juries (Northern Ireland) Order 1996 (S.I. 1996/1141 (N.I. 6))

88 In Schedule 2 to the Juries (Northern Ireland) Order 1996 omit the entry relating to members of the National Criminal Intelligence Service, members of the Service Authority for the National Criminal Intelligence Service and persons employed by the Authority.

Employment Rights (Northern Ireland) Order 1996 (S.I. 1996/1919 (N.I. 16))

89 The Employment Rights (Northern Ireland) Order 1996 has effect subject to the following amendments.
90 In Article 67KA(3) (application of Part VA of that Order to the police) omit sub-paragraph (b).
91 In Article 72A(2) (application of Article 68 of that Order to the police) omit sub-paragraph (b).
92 In Article 169A(2) (application of Article 132 of that Order to the police) omit sub-paragraph (b).

Police (Health and Safety) Act 1997 (c. 42)

93 In section 5(3) of the Police (Health and Safety) Act 1997—
    (a) in the definition of 'relevant authority' omit paragraphs (c) and (d),
    (b) in the definition of 'relevant fund' omit paragraphs (b) and (c), and
    (c) in the definition of 'responsible officer' omit paragraph (b).

Police Act 1997 (c. 50)

94 The Police Act 1997 has effect subject to the following amendments.
95 Omit sections 1 to 87 (provision about NCIS and NCS and their Service Authorities).
96 Omit sections 89 and 90 (general provision about NCS).
97 (1) Section 93 (authorisations to interfere with property) is amended as follows.
    (2) In subsection (1B) after 'officer is a' insert 'member of the staff of the Serious Organised Crime Agency,'.
    (3) In subsection (3) for paragraphs (b) and (c) substitute—

> '(b) if the authorising officer is within subsection (5)(f), by a member of the staff of the Serious Organised Crime Agency,'.

(4) In subsection (5) for paragraphs (f) and (g) substitute—

'(f) the Director General of the Serious Organised Crime Agency, or any member of the staff of that Agency who is designated for the purposes of this paragraph by that Director General;'.

(5) In subsection (6) omit paragraphs (d) and (e).

98 (1) Section 94 (authorisations in absence of authorising officer) is amended as follows.

(2) In subsection (1)—

(a) in paragraph (a) for 'or (e)' substitute', (e) or (f)',

(b) at the end of paragraph (a) insert 'or',

(c) in paragraph (b) for', (d) or (f)' substitute 'or (d)', and

(d) omit paragraph (c) and the word 'or' before it.

(3) In subsection (2) for paragraphs (e) and (ea) substitute—

'(e) where the authorising officer is within paragraph (f) of that subsection, by a person designated for the purposes of this section by the Director General of the Serious Organised Crime Agency;'.

(4) Omit subsections (3) and (4)(c).

99 (1) Section 95 (form and duration of authorisations) is amended as follows.

(2) In subsection (6) for 'or (g)' substitute 'or (f)'.

(3) In subsection (7) for', (d), (f) or (g)' substitute 'or (d)'.

100 (1) Section 97 (authorisations requiring approval) is amended as follows.

(2) In subsection (6A)—

(a) for ', (e) or (g)' substitute 'or (e)', and

(b) for ', Chief Constable or, as the case may be, Director General' substitute 'or, as the case may be, Chief Constable'.

(3) After subsection (6A) insert—

'(6B) The reference in subsection (6) to the authorising officer who gave the authorisation or in whose absence it was given shall be construed—

(a) in the case of an authorisation given by a person within paragraph (f) of section 93(5), as a reference to that person, and

(b) in the case of an authorisation given in the absence of such a person, as a reference to a member of the staff of the Serious Organised Crime Agency who is designated for the purposes of this section by the Director General of that Agency.'

101 In section 105(3) (supplementary provision about appeals) for', (d), (f) or (g)' substitute 'or (d)'.

102 In section 107(4)(b) (exclusions from Chief Commissioner's report) for 'Service Authority for the National Criminal Intelligence Service or the Service Authority for the National Crime Squad' substitute 'Serious Organised Crime Agency'.

103 (1) Section 109 (Police Information Technology Organisation) is amended as follows.

(2) In subsection (3) after 'police forces,' insert—

'(aa) the Serious Organised Crime Agency,'.

(3) In subsection (4) for '(a) or (b)' substitute '(a), (aa) or (b)'.

104 (1) Section 111 (interpretation of Part 5) is amended as follows.

(2) In subsection (1)—

    (a) at the end of paragraph (a) insert 'and', and

    (b) omit paragraphs (c) and (d).

  (3) In subsection (2)—

    (a) at the end of paragraph (b) insert 'and', and

    (b) omit paragraphs (d) and (e).

  (4) In subsection (3)—

    (a) at the end of paragraph (a) insert 'and', and

    (b) omit paragraphs (c) and (d).

105 In section 137(2) (extent) omit paragraphs (b) and (c).

106 Omit Schedules 1 to 2A (Service Authorities for NCIS and NCS).

Race Relations (Northern Ireland) Order 1997 (S.I. 1997/869 (N.I. 6))

107 The Race Relations (Northern Ireland) Order 1997 has effect subject to the following amendments.

108 In Article 72A(8) (police officers) for 'section 23 of the Police Act 1997' substitute 'section 23 or 24 of the Serious Organised Crime and Police Act 2005'.

109 In Article 72B (other police bodies), for paragraph (6) substitute—

    '(6) In this Article, in relation to any body of constables—

      (a) "chief officer of police" means the person who has the direction and control of the body;

      (b) "police authority" means the authority by which the members of the body are paid; and

      (c) "police fund" means money provided by that authority.'

Police (Health and Safety) (Northern Ireland) Order 1997 (S.I. 1997/1774 (N.I. 16))

110 In Article 7(3) of the Police (Health and Safety) (Northern Ireland) Order 1997—

    (a) in the definition of 'the relevant authority', omit sub-paragraph (b),

    (b) in the definition of 'the relevant fund', omit sub-paragraph (a), and

    (c) in the definition of 'the responsible officer', omit sub-paragraph (b).

Audit Commission Act 1998 (c. 18)

111 In section 32(1) of the Audit Commission Act 1998 (documents to be sent by the Audit Commission to the Secretary of State), for the words from 'relates to—' onwards substitute 'relates to a police authority established under section 3 of the Police Act 1996.'

Data Protection Act 1998 (c. 29)

112 In section 56(6) of the Data Protection Act 1998 (prohibition of requirement to produce certain records), in the first entry in the first column of the Table, for paragraphs (d) and (e) substitute—

    '(d) the Director General of the Serious Organised Crime Agency.'

Police (Northern Ireland) Act 1998 (c. 32)

113 The Police (Northern Ireland) Act 1998 has effect subject to the following amendments.

114 (1) Section 27 (members of Police Service of Northern Ireland engaged on other police service) is amended as follows.

(2) In subsection (1)—

(a) omit paragraph (b), and

(b) after paragraph (ca) insert—

'(cb) seconded service as a member of the staff of the Serious Organised Crime Agency on which a member of the Police Service of Northern Ireland is engaged with the consent of the Chief Constable;'.

(3) In subsection (5)(b) for the words from 'subsection (1)(aa)' to 'or (j)' substitute 'subsection (1)(aa), (c), (ca), (cb), (d), (e), (f), (h) or (j)'.

(4) In subsection (7) for '(1)(b), (c) or (ca)' substitute '(1)(c), (ca) or (cb)'.

115 In section 29(5) (liability for wrongful acts of constables) for 'section 23 of the Police Act 1997' substitute 'section 23 or 24 of the Serious Organised Crime and Police Act 2005'.

116 In section 41 (inspectors of constabulary) for subsections (3) and (3A) substitute—

'(3A) The Secretary of State may at any time require the inspectors to carry out an inspection under this section of the Police Service of Northern Ireland; and a requirement under this subsection may include a requirement for the inspection to be confined to a particular part of the Service, to particular matters or to particular activities of the Service.'

117 (1) Section 42 (publication of reports of inspectors of constabulary) is amended as follows.

(2) In subsection (1) omit ', (3)'.

(3) Omit subsection (7).

Crime and Disorder Act 1998 (c. 37)

118 Omit section 113 of the Crime and Disorder Act 1998 (deputy authorising officer under Part 3 of Police Act 1997).

Fair Employment and Treatment (Northern Ireland) Order 1998
(S.I. 1998/3162 (N.I. 21))

119 The Fair Employment and Treatment (Northern Ireland) Order 1998 has effect subject to the following amendments.

120 In Article 94(6) (police officers) for 'section 23 of the Police Act 1997' substitute 'section 23 or 24 of the Serious Organised Crime and Police Act 2005'.

121 In Article 94A (other police bodies), for paragraph (6) substitute—

'(6) In this Article, in relation to any body of constables—

(a) "chief officer of police" means the person who has the direction and control of the body;

(b) "police authority" means the authority by which the members of the body are paid; and

(c) "police fund" means money provided by that authority.'

Immigration and Asylum Act 1999 (c. 33)

122 The Immigration and Asylum Act 1999 has effect subject to the following amendments.

123 In section 20(1) (supply of information to Secretary of State) for paragraphs (b) and (c) substitute—

'(b) the Serious Organised Crime Agency;'.

124 (1) Section 21 (supply of information by Secretary of State) is amended as follows.

(2) In subsection (1) for paragraphs (b) and (c) substitute—

'(b) the Serious Organised Crime Agency, for use for SOCA purposes;'.

(3) For subsections (4) and (5) substitute—

'(4) "SOCA purposes" means any of the functions of the Serious Organised Crime Agency mentioned in section 2, 3 or 5 of the Serious Organised Crime and Police Act 2005.'

Terrorism Act 2000 (c. 11)

125 The Terrorism Act 2000 has effect subject to the following amendments.

126 In section 19(7B) (duty to disclose information)—

(a) for 'person' substitute 'member of the staff of the Serious Organised Crime Agency', and

(b) for 'the National Criminal Intelligence Service' substitute 'that Agency'.

127 In section 20(5) (permission to disclose information)—

(a) for 'person' substitute 'member of the staff of the Serious Organised Crime Agency', and

(b) for 'the National Criminal Intelligence Service' substitute 'that Agency'.

128 In section 21A(14) (failure to disclose: regulated sector)—

(a) for 'person' substitute 'member of the staff of the Serious Organised Crime Agency', and

(b) for 'the National Criminal Intelligence Service' substitute 'that Agency'.

129 In section 21B(7) (protected disclosures)—

(a) for 'person' substitute 'member of the staff of the Serious Organised Crime Agency', and

(b) for 'the National Criminal Intelligence Service' substitute 'that Agency'.

130 In Schedule 14 (exercise of officers' powers), in paragraph 4(1), for paragraph (d) substitute—

'(d) to the Serious Organised Crime Agency;'.

Regulation of Investigatory Powers Act 2000 (c. 23)

131 The Regulation of Investigatory Powers Act 2000 has effect subject to the following amendments.

132 (1) Section 6 (application for issue of an interception warrant) is amended as follows.

(2) In subsection (2)(d) for 'National Criminal Intelligence Service' substitute 'Serious Organised Crime Agency'.

(3) In subsection (3) after 'specified in' insert 'paragraph (a), (b), (c), (e), (f), (g), (h), (i) or (j)'.

133 (1) In section 17(3) (exclusion of matters from legal proceedings) for paragraphs (c) and (d) substitute—

'(c) any member of the staff of the Serious Organised Crime Agency;'.

(2) Sub-paragraph (1) does not affect the operation of section 17 in relation to conduct by any member of the National Criminal Intelligence Service or the National Crime Squad which took place before the commencement of this paragraph.

134 (1) In section 19(2) (unauthorised disclosures) for paragraphs (c) and (d) substitute—

'(c) every member of the staff of the Serious Organised Crime Agency;'.

(2) Sub-paragraph (1) does not affect the operation of section 19 in relation to any person's service as a member of the National Criminal Intelligence Service or the National Crime Squad before the commencement of this paragraph.

135 (1) Section 25 (interpretation) is amended as follows.

(2) In subsection (1), in the definition of 'relevant public authority', for paragraphs (b) and (c) substitute—

'(b) the Serious Organised Crime Agency;'.

(3) After subsection (3) insert—

'(3A) References in this Chapter to an individual holding an office or position with the Serious Organised Crime Agency include references to any member of the staff of that Agency.'

(4) For subsections (4) and (5) substitute—

'(4) The Secretary of State may by order—
    (a) remove any person from the list of persons who are for the time being relevant public authorities for the purposes of this Chapter; and
    (b) make such consequential amendments, repeals or revocations in this or any other enactment as appear to him to be necessary or expedient.

(5) The Secretary of State shall not make an order under this section—
    (a) that adds any person to the list of persons who are for the time being relevant public authorities for the purposes of this Chapter, or
    (b) that by virtue of subsection (4)(b) amends or repeals any provision of an Act, unless a draft of the order has been laid before Parliament and approved by a resolution of each House.'

136 In section 32(6) (authorisation of intrusive surveillance) for paragraphs (k) and (1) substitute—

'(k) the Director General of the Serious Organised Crime Agency and any member of the staff of that Agency who is designated for the purposes of this paragraph by that Director General;'.

137 (1) Section 33 (rules for grant of authorisation) is amended as follows.

(2) In subsection (1)—
    (a) omit', the National Criminal Intelligence Service or the National Crime Squad', and
    (b) omit ', Service or Squad'.

(3) After subsection (1) insert—

'(1A) A person who is a designated person for the purposes of section 28 or 29 by reference to his office or position with the Serious Organised Crime Agency shall not grant an authorisation under that section except on an application made by a member of the staff of the Agency.'

(4) In subsection (3)—

(a) omit', the National Criminal Intelligence Service or the National Crime Squad', and

(b) omit (in both places)', Service or Squad'.

(5) After subsection (3) insert—

'(3A) The Director General of the Serious Organised Crime Agency or a person designated for the purposes of section 32(6)(k) by that Director General shall not grant an authorisation for the carrying out of intrusive surveillance except on an application made by a member of the staff of the Agency.'

(6) In subsection (5)(a) for 'the National Criminal Intelligence Service or the National Crime Squad,' substitute 'a member of the staff of the Serious Organised Crime Agency,'.

(7) In subsection (6)—

(a) in paragraph (e) omit 'and also of the National Criminal Intelligence Service', and

(b) omit paragraph (f).

138 (1) Section 34 (grant of authorisations in absence of senior officer) is amended as follows.

(2) In subsection (1)(a) for 'of the National Criminal Intelligence Service or of the National Crime Squad' substitute 'a member of the staff of the Serious Organised Crime Agency'.

(3) In subsection (2)(a) for ', Service or Squad' substitute 'or Agency'.

(4) In subsection (4) for paragraphs (j) and (k) substitute—

'(j) a person is entitled to act for the Director General of the Serious Organised Crime Agency if he is a person designated for the purposes of this paragraph by that Director General as a person entitled so to act in an urgent case;'.

(5) Omit subsection (5).

(6) Omit subsection (6)(c).

139 (1) Section 35 (notification of certain authorisations) is amended as follows.

(2) In subsection (1) for 'police, customs' substitute 'police, SOCA, customs'.

(3) In subsection (10)—

(a) for 'police, customs' substitute 'police, SOCA, customs', and

(b) in paragraph (a) for ', the National Criminal Intelligence Service or the National Crime Squad' substitute 'or the Serious Organised Crime Agency'.

140 (1) Section 36 (approval required for authorisations to take effect) is amended as follows.

(2) In subsection (1) for paragraphs (b) and (c) substitute—

'(b) a member of the staff of the Serious Organised Crime Agency;'.

(3) In subsection (6)—

(a) in paragraph (b) for 'National Criminal Intelligence Service or the Director General of the National Crime Squad,' substitute 'Serious Organised Crime Agency,', and

(b) for paragraphs (d) and (e) substitute—

'(d) where the authorisation was granted by a person designated for the purposes of section 32(6)(k), or by a person entitled to act for the Director General of the Serious Organised Crime Agency by virtue of section 34(4)(j), that Director General;'.

141 In section 37(1) (quashing of police and customs authorisations) for paragraphs (b) and (c) substitute—

'(b) a member of the staff of the Serious Organised Crime Agency;'.

142 In section 40 (duty to provide information to Surveillance Commissioners) for paragraphs (b) and (c) substitute—

'(b) every member of the staff of the Serious Organised Crime Agency,'.

143 In section 45(6) (cancellation of authorisations)—
(a) at the end of paragraph (b) insert 'and', and
(b) omit paragraphs (d) and (e).

144 In section 46(3) (restriction on authorisations extending to Scotland) after paragraph (da) insert—

'(db) the Serious Organised Crime Agency;'.

145 In section 49(1)(e) (notices requiring disclosure) after 'the police' (in both places) insert ', SOCA'.

146 (1) Section 51 (cases in which key required) is amended as follows.
(2) In subsection (2)—
(a) for 'the police, the customs' substitute 'the police, SOCA, the customs', and
(b) after paragraph (a) insert—

'(aa) in the case of a direction by SOCA, except by or with the permission of the Director General of the Serious Organised Crime Agency;'.

(3) In subsection (3) after 'of police,' insert 'the Director General of the Serious Organised Crime Agency,'.
(4) In subsection (6) after 'of police,' insert 'by the Director General of the Serious Organised Crime Agency,'.

147 In section 54(3) (tipping-off) after 'police' (in both places) insert 'SOCA,'.

148 (1) Section 55 (duties of specified authorities) is amended as follows.
(2) In subsection (1) after paragraph (b) insert—

'(ba) the Director General of the Serious Organised Crime Agency;'.

(3) After subsection (3) insert—

'(3A) Paragraph 11 of Schedule 1 to the Serious Organised Crime and Police Act 2005 does not apply in relation to the duties of the Director General of the Serious Organised Crime Agency under this section.'

149 In section 56(1) (interpretation)—
(a) in the definition of 'chief officer of police' omit paragraphs (j) and (k),
(b) in paragraph (a) of the definition of 'the police' after 'constable' insert '(except a constable who is a member of the staff of the Serious Organised Crime Agency)', and
(c) after the definition of 'section 49 notice' insert—

' "SOCA" means the Serious Organised Crime Agency or any member of the staff of the Serious Organised Crime Agency;'.

150 In section 58(1) (cooperation with Commissioner) for paragraphs (b) and (c) substitute—

'(b) every member of the staff of the Serious Organised Crime Agency,'.

151 In section 65(6) (the Tribunal) for paragraphs (d) and (e) substitute—

'(d) the Serious Organised Crime Agency; or'.

152 In section 68(7) (disclosure to Tribunal) for paragraphs (b) and (c) substitute—

'(b) every member of the staff of the Serious Organised Crime Agency;'.

153 In section 75(6) (authorisations under Part 3 of Police Act 1997) omit paragraph (b).
154 (1) Section 76A (foreign surveillance operations) is amended as follows.
    (2) In subsection (6)(a) for 'National Criminal Intelligence Service' substitute 'Serious Organised Crime Agency'.
    (3) In subsection (11), in the definition of 'United Kingdom officer'—
        (a) in paragraph (b) for 'National Criminal Intelligence Service' substitute 'staff of the Serious Organised Crime Agency', and
        (b) in paragraph (c) omit 'the National Crime Squad or'.
155 (1) In Schedule 1 (relevant authorities) for paragraphs 2 and 3 substitute—

'2 The Serious Organised Crime Agency.'

156 (1) Schedule 2 (persons having appropriate permission) is amended as follows.
    (2) In paragraph 2—
        (a) in sub-paragraph (3) after 'the police' insert ', SOCA', and
        (b) in sub-paragraph (5) after 'Only the police' insert ', SOCA'.
    (3) In paragraph 4(2) after 'the police,' (in each place) insert 'SOCA,'.
    (4) In paragraph 5(3)(b) after 'police' insert ', SOCA'.
    (5) In paragraph 6—
        (a) after sub-paragraph (3) insert—

        '(3A) A member of the staff of the Serious Organised Crime Agency does not by virtue of paragraph 1, 4 or 5 have the appropriate permission in relation to any protected information unless permission to give a section 49 notice in relation to that information has been granted—
            (a) by the Director General; or
            (b) by a member of the staff of the Agency of or above such level as the Director General may designate for the purposes of this sub-paragraph.'; and

        (b) after sub-paragraph (5) add—

        '(6) In sub-paragraph (2) "constable" does not include a constable who is a member of the staff of the Serious Organised Crime Agency.'

Football (Disorder) Act 2000 (c. 25)

157 Omit section 2 of the Football (Disorder) Act 2000 (disclosure of information by NCIS).

Freedom of Information Act 2000 (c. 36)

158 The Freedom of Information Act 2000 has effect subject to the following amendments.
159 In section 23(3) (bodies supplying information which is exempt) omit 'and' at the end of paragraph (k) and after paragraph (l) add—

'(m) the Serious Organised Crime Agency.'

160 In Schedule 1 (list of public authorities), in Part 6, omit the entries relating to the National Crime Squad and the Service Authority for the National Crime Squad.

Criminal Justice and Court Services Act 2000 (c. 43)

161 In section 71(1) and (2)(a) of the Criminal Justice and Court Services Act 2000 (access to driver licensing records) after 'constables' insert 'and members of the staff of the Serious Organised Crime Agency'.

Criminal Justice and Police Act 2001 (c. 16)

162 The Criminal Justice and Police Act 2001 has effect subject to the following amendments.

163 In section 88(8) (functions of Central Police Training and Development Authority) for paragraphs (a) and (b) substitute—

'(a) the Serious Organised Crime Agency;'.

164 (1) Section 104 (vice-chairmen) is amended as follows.
(2) Omit subsection (3).
(3) In subsection (4)—
(a) at the end of paragraph (a) insert 'and', and
(b) omit paragraph (c) and the word 'and' before it.
(4) Omit subsection (8).

165 (1) Section 107 (payment of allowances to authority members) is amended as follows.
(2) Omit subsection (1)(c).
(3) Omit subsection (4).

166 Omit sections 108 to 121 (provision about NCIS and NCS and their Service Authorities).

167 Omit section 138(6)(d) (extent).

Proceeds of Crime Act 2002 (c. 29)

168 The Proceeds of Crime Act 2002 has effect subject to the following amendments.

169 In section 313(1) (restriction on performance by police of functions of the Director of the Assets Recovery Agency) omit paragraphs (c) and (d).

170 In section 330(5)(a) (required disclosure of information regarding money laundering) for 'the Director General of the National Criminal Intelligence Service' substitute 'the Director General of the Serious Organised Crime Agency'.

171 In section 331(5)(a) (required disclosure of information regarding money laundering) for 'the Director General of the National Criminal Intelligence Service' substitute 'the Director General of the Serious Organised Crime Agency'.

172 In section 332(5)(a) (required disclosure of information regarding money laundering) for 'the Director General of the National Criminal Intelligence Service' substitute 'the Director General of the Serious Organised Crime Agency'.

173 In section 336 (giving of consent by a nominated officer) in subsections (2)(a), (3) (a) and (4)(a), for 'the Director General of the National Criminal Intelligence Service' substitute 'the Director General of the Serious Organised Crime Agency'.

174 In section 340(13) (interpretation of references to constable) for 'the Director General of the National Criminal Intelligence Service' substitute 'the Director General of the Serious Organised Crime Agency'.

175 In section 378(5) (interpretation of references to officers) for 'the Director General of the National Criminal Intelligence Service' substitute 'the Director General of the Serious Organised Crime Agency'.

176 In section 436(5) (persons permitted to disclose information to the Director of the Assets Recovery Agency) for paragraphs (b) and (c) substitute—

'(b) the Director General of the Serious Organised Crime Agency;'

177 In section 439(5) (persons permitted to disclose information to the Lord Advocate and Scottish Ministers) for paragraphs (b) and (c) substitute—

'(b) the Director General of the Serious Organised Crime Agency;'.

178 In section 445(2)(b) (external investigations) for 'the Director General of the National Criminal Intelligence Service' substitute 'the Director General of the Serious Organised Crime Agency'.

Police Reform Act 2002 (c. 30)

179 The Police Reform Act 2002 has effect subject to the following amendments.

180 Omit section 8 (powers of Secretary of State in relation to NCIS and NCS).

181 (1) Section 38 (exercise of police powers by civilian employees) is amended as follows.
(2) Omit subsection (3).
(3) In subsection (4) omit 'or a Director General'.
(4) In subsection (7) omit 'or of a Service Authority'.

182 In section 42 (supplementary provisions relating to exercise of police powers) omit subsections (4) and (8).

183 (1) Section 45 (code of practice relating to exercise of police powers) is amended as follows.
(2) In subsection (1) omit 'and by Directors General'.
(3) In subsection (3) omit paragraphs (a), (b), (d) and (e).
(4) In subsection (5) omit 'or a Director General'.

184 In section 47(1) (interpretation) omit the definitions of 'Director General' and 'Service Authority'.

185 (1) Section 82 (police nationality requirements) is amended as follows.
(2) In subsection (1) omit paragraph (c).
(3) In subsection (2)—
(a) at the end of paragraph (a) insert 'or', and
(b) omit paragraph (c) and the word 'or' before it.
(4) In subsection (3)—
(a) at the end of paragraph (c) insert 'and', and
(b) omit paragraph (d).
(5) In subsection (4) for ', Service or Squad' substitute 'or Service'.

186 Omit sections 85 to 91 (NCIS and NCS: general provisions).

187 Omit section 93 (quorum for NCIS and NCS service authorities).

188 (1) Section 102 (liability for wrongful acts of constables) is amended as follows.
(2) In subsection (2) omit paragraphs (c) and (d).
(3) In subsection (5) omit paragraphs (b) and (c).

189 (1) Section 103 (liability in respect of members of teams) is amended as follows.
(2) Omit subsections (2) and (3).

(3) In subsection (6) omit ', the NCIS service fund or the NCS service fund,'.
190 In Schedule 4 (powers exercisable by police civilians), in paragraph 36(1), omit paragraph (b) and the word 'and' before it.

Crime (International Cooperation) Act 2003 (c. 32)

191 Omit section 85 (liability of NCIS in respect of foreign officers) of the Crime (International Cooperation) Act 2003.

Courts Act 2003 (c. 39)

192 In section 41(6)(c) of the Courts Act 2003 (disqualification of lay justices who are members of local authorities) for ', the Service Authority for the National Criminal Intelligence Service or the Service Authority for the National Crime Squad' substitute 'or the Serious Organised Crime Agency'.

Sexual Offences Act 2003 (c. 42)

193 The Sexual Offences Act 2003 has effect subject to the following amendments.
194 In section 94(3) (supply of information for verification) for paragraphs (c) and (d) substitute—

'(c) the Serious Organised Crime Agency.'

195 In section 95(2) (supply of information by Secretary of State) for paragraphs (b) and (c) substitute—

'(b) the Serious Organised Crime Agency.'

Criminal Justice Act 2003 (c. 44)

196 In section 29(5) of the Criminal Justice Act 2003 (persons who may institute criminal proceedings by written charge) after paragraph (ca) insert—

'(cb) the Director General of the Serious Organised Crime Agency or a person authorised by him to institute criminal proceedings;'.

Energy Act 2004 (c. 20)

197 The Energy Act 2004 has effect subject to the following amendments.
198 In section 59(3) (members of civil nuclear constabulary serving with other forces)—
    (a) in the definition of 'chief officer' omit paragraphs (c) and (d), and
    (b) in the definition of 'relevant force' omit paragraphs (c) and (d).
199 After section 59 insert—

'59A Constables serving with Serious Organised Crime Agency

(1) A member of the Constabulary serving with the Serious Organised Crime Agency under arrangements to which subsection (2) applies shall—
    (a) be under the direction and control of the Serious Organised Crime Agency, and
    (b) continue to be a constable.
(2) This subsection applies to arrangements made between the Serious Organised Crime Agency and the chief constable.'

Domestic Violence, Crime and Victims Act 2004 (c. 28)

200 In Schedule 9 to the Domestic Violence, Crime and Victims Act 2004 (authorities within remit of Commissioner for Victims and Witnesses) for paragraphs 13 and 14 substitute—

'13 The Serious Organised Crime Agency.'

Section 82   SCHEDULE 5

PERSONS SPECIFIED FOR THE PURPOSES OF SECTION 82

1   A person who is or might be, or who has been, a witness in legal proceedings (whether or not in the United Kingdom).
2   A person who has complied with a disclosure notice given to him by virtue of section 62(1).
3   (1) A person who has been given an immunity notice under section 71(1) if the notice continues to have effect in relation to him.
    (2) A person who has been given a restricted use undertaking under section 72(1) if the undertaking continues to have effect in relation to him.
4   A person who is or has been a member of a jury.
5   A person who holds or has held judicial office (whether or not in the United Kingdom).
6   A person who is or has been a justice of the peace or who holds or has held a position comparable to that of a justice of the peace in a place outside the United Kingdom.
7   A person who is or has been a member of an international tribunal which has jurisdiction in criminal matters.
8   A person who conducts or has conducted criminal prosecutions (whether or not in the United Kingdom).
9   (1) A person who is or has been the Director of Public Prosecutions for England and Wales.
    (2) A person who is or has been a member of staff of the Crown Prosecution Service for England and Wales.
10 (1) A person who is or has been the Director or deputy Director of Public Prosecutions for Northern Ireland.
    (2) A person who is or has been a person appointed under Article 4(3) of the Prosecution of Offences (Northern Ireland) Order 1972 (S.I. 1972/538 (N.I. 1)) to assist the Director of Public Prosecutions for Northern Ireland.
11 A person who is or has been under the direction and control of the Lord Advocate in the Lord Advocate's capacity as head of the systems of criminal prosecution and investigation of deaths in Scotland.
12 (1) A person who is or has been the Director of Revenue and Customs Prosecutions.
    (2) A person who is or has been a member of staff of the Revenue and Customs Prosecutions Office.
13 A person who is or has been a constable.
14 A person who is or has been designated under—
        (a) section 38(1) of the Police Reform Act 2002 (c. 30) (police powers for police authority employees);

    (b) section 30(1) of the Police (Northern Ireland) Act 2003 (c. 6) (police powers for designated police support staff).

15 A person who is a police custody and security officer (within the meaning of section 9(1A) of the Police (Scotland) Act 1967 (c. 77)) of a police authority in Scotland.

16 A person who—

    (a) is or has been an officer of Revenue and Customs;

    (b) is or has been a member of staff of Her Majesty's Customs and Excise.

17 A person who is or has been a person appointed as an immigration officer under paragraph 1 of Schedule 2 to the Immigration Act 1971 (c. 77).

18 A person who is or has been a member of staff of SOCA.

19 (1) A person who is or has been the Director General of the National Criminal Intelligence Service or the Director General of the National Crime Squad.

    (2) A person who is or has been under the direction and control of the Director General of the National Criminal Intelligence Service or the Director General of the National Crime Squad.

20 (1) A person who is or has been the Director of the Scottish Drug Enforcement Agency.

    (2) A person who is or has been under the direction and control of the Director of the Scottish Drug Enforcement Agency.

21 (1) A person who is or has been the Director of the Assets Recovery Agency.

    (2) A person who is or has been a member of staff of the Assets Recovery Agency or a person with whom the Director of that Agency has made arrangements for the provision of services under section 1(4) of the Proceeds of Crime Act 2002 (c. 29).

22 (1) A person who is or has been the head of the Civil Recovery Unit, that is to say of the organisation known by that name which acts on behalf of the Scottish Ministers in proceedings under Part 5 of the Proceeds of Crime Act 2002 (civil recovery of the proceeds etc. of unlawful conduct).

    (2) A person who is or has been a member of staff of the Civil Recovery Unit.

23 (1) A person who is or has been a person appointed by virtue of section 246(1) of the Proceeds of Crime Act 2002 (c. 29) as an interim receiver.

    (2) A person who assists or has assisted an interim receiver so appointed in the exercise of such functions as are mentioned in section 247 of that Act.

24 (1) A person who is or has been a person appointed by virtue of section 256(1) of the Proceeds of Crime Act 2002 as an interim administrator.

    (2) A person who assists or has assisted an interim administrator so appointed in the exercise of such functions as are mentioned in section 257 of that Act.

25 (1) A person who is or has been the head of the Financial Crime Unit, that is to say of the organisation known by that name which, among other activities, acts on behalf of the Lord Advocate in proceedings under Part 3 of the Proceeds of Crime Act 2002 (confiscation: Scotland).

    (2) A person who is or has been a member of staff of the Financial Crime Unit.

26 A person who is or has been a prison officer.

27 A person who is or has been a covert human intelligence source (within the meaning of section 26(8) of the Regulation of Investigatory Powers Act 2000 (c. 23) or of section 1(7) of the Regulation of Investigatory Powers (Scotland) Act 2000 (asp 11)).

28 A person—

(a) who is a member of the family of a person specified in any of the preceding paragraphs;

(b) who lives or has lived in the same household as a person so specified;

(c) who has or has had a close personal relationship with a person so specified.

Section 109   SCHEDULE 6

MINOR AND CONSEQUENTIAL AMENDMENTS RELATING
TO CHAPTER 6 OF PART 2

Prescription and Limitation (Scotland) Act 1973 (c. 52)

1   In section 19B(3) of the Prescription and Limitation (Scotland) Act 1973 (actions for recovery of property obtained through unlawful conduct etc.)—
    (a) after paragraph (a) insert—

    '(aa) an application is made for a prohibitory property order, or', and

    (b) for 'earlier' substitute 'earliest'.

Limitation Act 1980 (c. 58)

2   In section 27A(3) of the Limitation Act 1980 (time limits for bringing proceedings for recovery order: when proceedings are brought)—
    (a) after paragraph (a) insert—

    '(aa) an application is made for a property freezing order, or', and

    (b) for 'earlier' substitute 'earliest'.

Limitation (Northern Ireland) Order 1989 (S.I. 1989/1339 (N.I. 11))

3   In Article 72A(3) of the Limitation (Northern Ireland) Order 1989 (time limits for bringing proceedings for recovery order: when proceedings are brought)—
    (a) after paragraph (a) insert—

    '(aa) an application is made for a property freezing order, or', and

    (b) for 'earlier' substitute 'earliest'.

Proceeds of Crime Act 2002 (c. 29)

4   The Proceeds of Crime Act 2002 (c. 29) is amended as follows.
5   In section 82(f) (confiscation: England and Wales: property is free property if order under section 246 etc. applies to it)—
    (a) after 'section' insert '245A,' and
    (b) after '246,' insert '255A, 256,'.
6   In section 148(f) (confiscation: Scotland: property is free property if order under section 246 etc. applies to it)—
    (a) after 'section' insert '245A,' and
    (b) after '246,' insert '255A, 256,'.
7   In section 230(f) (confiscation: Northern Ireland: property is free property if order under section 246 etc. applies to it)—

   (a) after 'section' insert '245A,' and

   (b) after '246,' insert '255A, 256,'.

8 In section 241(2)(a) (conduct occurring outside the United Kingdom that is unlawful conduct for the purposes of Part 5)—

   (a) after 'in a country' insert 'or territory', and

   (b) for 'of that country' substitute 'applying in that country or territory'.

9 In section 243 (proceedings for recovery orders in England and Wales or Northern Ireland), after subsection (4) insert—

> '(5) Nothing in sections 245A to 255 limits any power of the court apart from those sections to grant interim relief in connection with proceedings (including prospective proceedings) under this Chapter.'

10 Before section 248 (and its heading) insert the following heading—

'Property freezing orders and interim receiving orders: registration'

11 (1) Section 248 (registration: England and Wales) is amended as follows.

   (2) In subsection (1)(a), for 'interim receiving orders' substitute 'property freezing orders, and in relation to interim receiving orders,'.

   (3) In subsection (1)(b), for 'interim receiving orders' substitute 'property freezing orders, and in relation to applications for interim receiving orders,'.

   (4) In subsection (3), before 'an interim receiving order' insert 'a property freezing order or'.

12 (1) Section 249 (registration: Northern Ireland) is amended as follows.

   (2) In subsection (1), after 'applying for' insert 'a property freezing order or'.

   (3) In subsection (1)(b), for 'an interim receiving order' substitute 'a property freezing order, or an interim receiving order,'.

   (4) After subsection (1) insert—

> '(1A) Upon being served with a copy of a property freezing order, the Registrar must, in respect of any registered land to which a property freezing order or an application for a property freezing order relates, make an entry inhibiting any dealing with the land without the consent of the High Court.'

   (5) In subsection (3), after 'entry made under subsection' insert '(1A) or'.

   (6) In subsection (4)—

     (a) after 'Where' insert 'a property freezing order or', and

     (b) after 'setting aside the' insert 'property freezing order or'.

13 Before section 250 (and its heading) insert the following heading—

'Interim receiving orders: further provisions'

14 (1) Section 252 (interim receiving orders: prohibition on dealings) is amended as follows.

   (2) For subsection (4) (restriction on exclusions for legal expenses) substitute—

> '(4) Where the court exercises the power to make an exclusion for the purpose of enabling a person to meet legal expenses that he has incurred, or may incur, in respect of proceedings under this Part, it must ensure that the exclusion—
>
>   (a) is limited to reasonable legal expenses that the person has reasonably incurred or that he reasonably incurs,
>
>   (b) specifies the total amount that may be released for legal expenses in pursuance of the exclusion, and

(c) is made subject to the required conditions (see section 286A) in addition to any conditions imposed under subsection (3).

(4A) The court, in deciding whether to make an exclusion for the purpose of enabling a person to meet legal expenses of his in respect of proceedings under this Part—

(a) must have regard (in particular) to the desirability of the person being represented in any proceedings under this Part in which he is a participant, and

(b) must, where the person is the respondent, disregard the possibility that legal representation of the person in any such proceedings might, were an exclusion not made, be funded by the Legal Services Commission or the Northern Ireland Legal Services Commission.'

(3) In subsection (6) (power to make exclusions not to be exercised so as to prejudice enforcement authority's rights to recover property), after 'must' insert ', subject to subsection (4A),'.

15 In section 266 (recovery orders), after subsection (8) insert—

'(8A) A recovery order made by a court in England and Wales or Northern Ireland may provide for payment under section 280 of reasonable legal expenses that a person has reasonably incurred, or may reasonably incur, in respect of—

(a) the proceedings under this Part in which the order is made, or

(b) any related proceedings under this Part.

(8B) If regulations under section 286B apply to an item of expenditure, a sum in respect of the item is not payable under section 280 in pursuance of provision under subsection (8A) unless—

(a) the enforcement authority agrees to its payment, or

(b) the court has assessed the amount allowed by the regulations in respect of the item and the sum is paid in respect of the assessed amount.'

16 In section 271(4) (certain payments to trustee for civil recovery to be reduced to take account of loss caused by interim receiving order etc.)—

(a) in paragraph (a), for 'an interim receiving order or' substitute 'a property freezing order, an interim receiving order, a prohibitory property order or an', and

(b) in paragraph (b), for 'interim receiving order or interim administration order' substitute 'order mentioned in paragraph (a)'.

17 In section 272(5) (provision in recovery orders for compensation for loss caused by interim receiving order etc.)—

(a) in paragraph (a), for 'an interim receiving order or' substitute 'a property freezing order, an interim receiving order, a prohibitory property order or an', and

(b) in paragraph (b), for 'interim receiving order or interim administration order' substitute 'order mentioned in paragraph (a)'.

18 In section 280(2) (application of realised proceeds of recovery order)—

(a) after paragraph (a) insert—

'(aa) next, any payment of legal expenses which, after giving effect to section 266(8B), are payable under this subsection in pursuance of provision under section 266(8A) contained in the recovery order,' and

(b) in paragraph (b), for 'second' substitute 'then'.

19 In section 283 (compensation where interim receiving order etc. has applied)—

(a) in subsection (1), for 'an interim receiving order or' substitute 'a property freezing order, an interim receiving order, a prohibitory property order or an', and

    (b) in subsection (5), for 'interim receiving order or interim administration order' substitute 'order mentioned in subsection (1)'.

20 After section 286 insert—

'286A Legal expenses excluded from freezing: required conditions

(1) The Lord Chancellor may by regulations specify the required conditions for the purposes of section 245C(5) or 252(4).

(2) A required condition may (in particular)—

    (a) restrict who may receive sums released in pursuance of the exclusion (by, for example, requiring released sums to be paid to professional legal advisers), or

    (b) be made for the purpose of controlling the amount of any sum released in pursuance of the exclusion in respect of an item of expenditure.

(3) A required condition made for the purpose mentioned in subsection (2)(b) may (for example)—

    (a) provide for sums to be released only with the agreement of the enforcement authority;

    (b) provide for a sum to be released in respect of an item of expenditure only if the court has assessed the amount allowed by regulations under section 286B in respect of that item and the sum is released for payment of the assessed amount;

    (c) provide for a sum to be released in respect of an item of expenditure only if—

        (i) the enforcement authority agrees to its release, or

        (ii) the court has assessed the amount allowed by regulations under section 286B in respect of that item and the sum is released for payment of the assessed amount.

(4) Before making regulations under this section, the Lord Chancellor must consult such persons as he considers appropriate.

286B Legal expenses: regulations for purposes of section 266(8B) or 286A (3)

(1) The Lord Chancellor may by regulations—

    (a) make provision for the purposes of section 266(8B);

    (b) make provision for the purposes of required conditions that make provision of the kind mentioned in section 286A(3)(b) or (c).

(2) Regulations under this section may (in particular)—

    (a) limit the amount of remuneration allowable to representatives for a unit of time worked;

    (b) limit the total amount of remuneration allowable to representatives for work done in connection with proceedings or a step in proceedings;

    (c) limit the amount allowable in respect of an item of expense incurred by a representative or incurred, otherwise than in respect of the remuneration of a representative, by a party to proceedings.

(3) Before making regulations under this section, the Lord Chancellor must consult such persons as he considers appropriate.'

21 In section 287 (financial threshold for starting proceedings), in subsections (3) and (4) (threshold applies to applications made before proceedings started but does not apply after proceedings started or application made), for 'an interim receiving order or' substitute 'a property freezing order, an interim receiving order, a prohibitory property order or an'.

22 (1) Section 316(1) (interpretation of Part 5) is amended as follows.

    (2) After the definition of 'premises' insert—

' "prohibitory property order" has the meaning given by section 255A (2);
"property freezing order" has the meaning given by section 245A (2);'.

(3) In paragraph (b) of the definition of 'respondent', for 'an interim receiving order or' substitute 'a property freezing order, an interim receiving order, a prohibitory property order or an'.

23 In section 432 (insolvency practitioners), in subsections (1)(b), (8)(a) and (9)(a), for 'an interim receiving order made under section 246' substitute 'a property freezing order made under section 245A, an interim receiving order made under section 246, a prohibitory property order made under section 255A'.

Section 111   SCHEDULE 7

POWERS OF ARREST: SUPPLEMENTARY

PART 1
SPECIFIC REPEALS

Unlawful Drilling Act 1819 (60 Geo. 3 & 1 Geo. 4 c. 1)

1   In section 2 of the Unlawful Drilling Act 1819 (power to disperse unlawful meeting), omit ', or for any other person acting in their aid or assistance,'.

Vagrancy Act 1824 (c. 83)

2   Section 6 of the Vagrancy Act 1824 (power to apprehend) shall cease to have effect.

Railway Regulation Act 1842 (c. 55)

3   Section 17 of the Railway Regulation Act 1842 (punishment of persons guilty of misconduct) shall cease to have effect.

Companies Clauses Consolidation Act 1845 (c. 16)

4   In section 156 of the Companies Clauses Consolidation Act 1845 (transient offenders), omit ', and all persons called by him to his assistance,'.

Railways Clauses Consolidation Act 1845 (c. 20)

5   (1) The Railways Clauses Consolidation Act 1845 is amended as follows.
    (2) Section 104 (detention of offenders) shall cease to have effect.
    (3) Section 154 (transient offenders) shall cease to have effect.

Licensing Act 1872 (c. 94)

6   In section 12 of the Licensing Act 1872 (penalty on persons found drunk), omit 'may be apprehended, and'.

Public Stores Act 1875 (c. 25)

7   In section 12 of the Public Stores Act 1875 (powers of arrest and search), omit subsection (1).

London County Council (General Powers) Act 1894 (c. ccxii)

8   In section 7 of the London County Council (General Powers) Act 1894 (arrest for breach of byelaws), omit 'and any person called to the assistance of such constable or person authorised'.

London County Council (General Powers) Act 1900 (c. cclxviii)

9   In section 27 of the London County Council (General Powers) Act 1900 (arrest for breach of byelaws), omit 'and any person called to the assistance of such constable or officer'.

Licensing Act 1902 (c. 28)

10 (1) The Licensing Act 1902 is amended as follows.
    (2) In section 1 (apprehension of persons found drunk), omit 'apprehended and'.
    (3) In section 2 (being drunk in charge of a child), in subsection (1), omit 'may be apprehended, and'.

Protection of Animals Act 1911 (c. 27)

11 In section 12 of the Protection of Animals Act 1911 (powers of constables), omit subsection (1).

Official Secrets Act 1911 (c. 28)

12 Section 6 of the Official Secrets Act 1911 (power of arrest) shall cease to have effect.

Public Order Act 1936 (1 Edw. 8 & 1 Geo. 6 c. 6)

13 In section 7 of the Public Order Act 1936 (enforcement), omit subsection (3),

Street Offences Act 1959 (c. 57)

14 In section 1 of the Street Offences Act 1959 (loitering or soliciting for purposes of prostitution), omit subsection (3).

Criminal Justice Act 1967 (c. 80)

15 In section 91 of the Criminal Justice Act 1967 (drunkenness in a public place), in subsection (1), omit 'may be arrested without warrant by any person and'.

Ministry of Housing and Local Government Provisional Order Confirmation (Greater London Parks and Open Spaces) Act 1967 (c. xxix)

16 In Article 19 (power of detention) of the Order set out in the Schedule to the Ministry of Housing and Local Government Provisional Order Confirmation (Greater London Parks and Open Spaces) Act 1967, omit 'and any person called to the assistance of such constable or officer'.

Theft Act 1968 (c. 60)

17 In section 25 of the Theft Act 1968 (going equipped for stealing etc.), omit subsection (4).

Port of London Act 1968 (c. xxxii)

18 Section 170 of the Port of London Act 1968 (power of arrest) shall cease to have effect.

Criminal Law Act 1977 (c. 45)

19 (1) The Criminal Law Act 1977 is amended as follows.
   (2) In section 6 (violence for securing entry), omit subsection (6).
   (3) In section 7 (adverse occupation of residential premises), omit subsection (6).
   (4) In section 8 (trespassing with a weapon of offence), omit subsection (4).
   (5) In section 9 (trespassing on premises of foreign missions, etc.), omit subsection (7).
   (6) In section 10 (obstruction of certain officers executing process), in subsection (5), omit 'A constable in uniform,'.

Theft Act 1978 (c. 31)

20 In section 3 of the Theft Act 1978 (making off without payment), omit subsection (4).

Animal Health Act 1981 (c. 22)

21 (1) The Animal Health Act 1981 is amended as follows.
   (2) In section 61 (powers of arrest as to rabies), omit subsection (1).
   (3) In section 62 (entry and search under section 61), omit subsection (1).

Local Government (Miscellaneous Provisions) Act 1982 (c. 30)

22 In Schedule 3 to the Local Government (Miscellaneous Provisions) Act 1982 (control of sex establishments), omit paragraph 24.

Aviation Security Act 1982 (c. 36)

23 In section 28 of the Aviation Security Act 1982 (byelaws for designated airports), omit subsection (3).

Police and Criminal Evidence Act 1984 (c. 60)

24 (1) The Police and Criminal Evidence Act 1984 is amended as follows.

(2) In section 118 (general interpretation), in subsection (1), omit the definition of 'arrestable offence'.

(3) Schedule 1A (specific offences which are arrestable offences) shall cease to have effect.

(4) In Schedule 2 (preserved powers of arrest), the following are omitted—

the entry relating to the Military Lands Act 1892 (c. 43),

the entry relating to the Protection of Animals Act 1911 (c. 27),

the entry relating to the Public Order Act 1936 (1 Edw. 8 & 1 Geo. 6 c. 6),

the entry relating to the Street Offences Act 1959 (c. 57),

the entry relating to the Criminal Law Act 1977 (c. 45),

the entry relating to the Animal Health Act 1981 (c. 22).

Sporting Events (Control of Alcohol etc.) Act 1985 (c. 57)

25 In section 7 of the Sporting Events (Control of Alcohol etc.) Act 1985 (powers of enforcement), in subsection (2), omit', and may arrest such a person'.

Public Order Act 1986 (c. 64)

26 (1) The Public Order Act 1986 is amended as follows.

(2) In section 3 (affray), omit subsection (6).

(3) In section 4 (fear or provocation of violence), omit subsection (3).

(4) In section 4A (intentional harassment, alarm or distress), omit subsection (4).

(5) In section 5 (harassment, alarm or distress), omit subsections (4) and (5).

(6) In section 12 (imposing conditions on public processions), omit subsection (7).

(7) In section 13 (prohibiting public processions), omit subsection (10).

(8) In section 14 (imposing conditions on public assemblies), omit subsection (7).

(9) In section 14B (offences in connection with trespassory assemblies), omit subsection (4).

(10) In section 14C (stopping persons from proceeding to trespassory assemblies), omit subsection (4).

(11) In section 18 (use of words or behaviour or display of written material), omit subsection (3).

Road Traffic Act 1988 (c. 52)

27 (1) The Road Traffic Act 1988 is amended as follows.

(2) In section 4 (driving etc. under influence of drink or drugs), omit subsections (6) to (8).

(3) In section 163 of the Road Traffic Act 1988 (power of police to stop vehicles), omit subsection (4).

(4) The repeal of section 4(8) extends also to Scotland.

Football Spectators Act 1989 (c. 37)

28 In section 2 of the Football Spectators Act 1989 (offences relating to unauthorised attendance at designated football matches), omit subsection (4).

Transport and Works Act 1992 (c. 42)

29 In section 30 of the Transport and Works Act 1992 (powers of arrest and entry), omit subsections (1) and (3).

Trade Union and Labour Relations (Consolidation) Act 1992 (c. 52)

30 In section 241 of the Trade Union and Labour Relations (Consolidation) Act 1992 (intimidation or annoyance), omit subsection (3).

Criminal Justice and Public Order Act 1994 (c. 33)

31 (1) The Criminal Justice and Public Order Act 1994 is amended as follows.
    (2) In section 61 (power to remove trespassers on land), omit subsection (5).
    (3) In section 62B (failure to comply with direction under section 62A), omit subsection (4).
    (4) In section 63 (powers to remove persons attending or preparing for a rave), omit subsection (8).
    (5) In section 65 (raves: powers to stop persons from proceeding), omit subsection (5).
    (6) In section 68 (offence of aggravated trespass), omit subsection (4).
    (7) In section 69 (powers to remove persons committing or participating in aggravated trespass), omit subsection (5).
    (8) In section 76 (interim possession orders: trespassing during currency of order), omit subsection (7).

Reserve Forces Act 1996 (c. 14)

32 In Schedule 2 to the Reserve Forces Act 1996 (deserters and absentees without leave), omit paragraph 2(1).

Confiscation of Alcohol (Young Persons) Act 1997 (c. 33)

33 In section 1 of the Confiscation of Alcohol (Young Persons) Act 1997 (confiscation of alcohol), omit subsection (5).

Crime and Disorder Act 1998 (c. 37)

34 In section 31 of the Crime and Disorder Act 1998 (racially or religiously aggravated public order offences), omit subsections (2) and (3).

Criminal Justice and Police Act 2001 (c. 16)

35 In the Criminal Justice and Police Act 2001—
   (a) in section 42 (police directions stopping harassment etc. of a person in his home), omit subsection (8),
   (b) in section 47 (application of offences relating to prostitution advertising to public structures), omit subsection (3).

Anti-social Behaviour Act 2003 (c. 38)

36 In the Anti-social Behaviour Act 2003—
   (a) in section 4 (closure of premises: offences), omit subsection (5),
   (b) in section 32 (supplementary provisions about powers relating to dispersal of groups and removal of persons under 16 to their homes), omit subsection (3).

Hunting Act 2004 (c. 37)

37 Section 7 of the Hunting Act 2004 (arrest) shall cease to have effect.

PART 3
AMENDMENTS RELATING TO REFERENCES TO ARRESTABLE OFFENCES AND SERIOUS ARRESTABLE OFFENCES

Criminal Law Act 1826 (c. 64)

39 In section 28 of the Criminal Law Act 1826 (which confers power to order the payment of compensation to those who have helped apprehend an offender), for 'an arrestable offence' substitute 'an indictable offence'.

Criminal Law Act 1967 (c. 58)

40 (1) The Criminal Law Act 1967 is amended as follows.
   (2) In section 4 (penalties for assisting offenders)—
      (a) in subsection (1)—
         (i) for 'an arrestable offence' substitute 'a relevant offence',
         (ii) for 'other arrestable offence' substitute 'other relevant offence',
      (b) for subsection (1A) substitute—
         '(1A) In this section and section 5 below, "relevant offence" means—
            (a) an offence for which the sentence is fixed by law,
            (b) an offence for which a person of 18 years or over (not previously convicted) may be sentenced to imprisonment for a term of five years (or might be so sentenced but for the restrictions imposed by section 33 of the Magistrates' Courts Act 1980).',
      (c) in subsection (2), for 'an arrestable offence' substitute 'a relevant offence'.
   (3) In section 5 (penalties for concealing offences or giving false information), in subsection (1)—
      (a) for 'an arrestable offence' substitute 'a relevant offence',
      (b) for 'other arrestable offence' substitute 'other relevant offence'.

Port of London Act 1968 (c. xxxii)

41 (1) The Port of London Act 1968 is amended as follows.

(2) In section 2 (interpretation), omit the definition of 'arrestable offence'.

(3) In section 156 (powers of constables), in subsection (2), for 'arrestable', in each place where it occurs, substitute 'indictable'.

Solicitors Act 1974 (c. 47)

42 (1) The Solicitors Act 1974 is amended as follows.

(2) In section 13A (imposition of conditions while practising certificates are in force), in subsection (2)(d), for sub-paragraph (ii) substitute—

'(ii) an indictable offence.'

(3) In section 13B (suspension of practising certificates where solicitors convicted of fraud or serious crime), in subsection (1)(a), for sub-paragraph (ii) substitute—

'(ii) an indictable offence; and'.

Police and Criminal Evidence Act 1984 (c. 60)

43 (1) The Police and Criminal Evidence Act 1984 is amended as follows.

(2) In section 4 (road checks)—

(a) for 'a serious arrestable offence', in each place where it occurs, substitute 'an indictable offence',

(b) in subsection (14), for 'serious arrestable offence' substitute 'indictable offence'.

(3) In section 8 (powers to authorise entry and search), for 'a serious arrestable offence', in both places, substitute 'an indictable offence'.

(4) In section 17 (entry for purpose of arrest etc.), in subsection (1)(b), for 'arrestable' substitute 'indictable'.

(5) In section 18 (entry and search after arrest), in subsection (1), for 'arrestable', in both places, substitute 'indictable'.

(6) In section 32 (search upon arrest), in subsection (2), for paragraph (b) substitute—

'(b) if the offence for which he has been arrested is an indictable offence, to enter and search any premises in which he was when arrested or immediately before he was arrested for evidence relating to the offence.'

(7) In section 42 (authorisation of continued detention), in subsection (1)(b), for 'arrestable' substitute 'indictable'.

(8) In section 43 (warrants of further detention), in subsection (4)(b), for 'a serious arrestable offence' substitute 'an indictable offence'.

(9) In section 56 (right to have someone informed when arrested)—

(a) in each of subsections (2)(a) and (5)(a), for 'a serious arrestable offence' substitute 'an indictable offence',

(b) in subsection (5A)(a), for 'the serious arrestable offence' substitute 'the indictable offence'.

(10) In section 58 (access to legal advice)—

(a) in each of subsections (6)(a) and (8)(a), for 'a serious arrestable offence' substitute 'an indictable offence',

(b) in subsection (8A)(a), for 'the serious arrestable offence' substitute 'the indictable offence'.

(11) In section 114A (power to apply Act to officers of Secretary of State), in subsection (2)(c), for 'a serious arrestable offence', in both places, substitute 'an indictable offence'.

(12) Section 116 (meaning of 'serious arrestable offence') shall cease to have effect.

(13) In Schedule 1 (special procedure material), in paragraph 2(a)(i), for 'a serious arrestable offence' substitute 'an indictable offence'.

(14) Schedule 5 (serious arrestable offences) shall cease to have effect.

Administration of Justice Act 1985 (c. 61)

44 In section 16 of the Administration of Justice Act 1985 (conditional licences for licensed conveyancers), in subsection (1)(ia), for 'a serious arrestable offence (as defined by section 116 of the Police and Criminal Evidence Act 1984)' substitute 'an indictable offence'.

Housing Act 1985 (c. 68)

45 In Part 1 of Schedule 2 to the Housing Act 1985 (which sets out grounds upon which a court may, if it considers it reasonable, order possession of dwelling-houses let under secure tenancies), in Ground 2, in paragraph (b)(ii), for 'arrestable' substitute 'indictable'.

Housing Act 1988 (c. 50)

46 In Part 2 of Schedule 2 to the Housing Act 1988 (which sets out grounds on which a court may order possession of dwelling-houses let on assured tenancies), in Ground 14, in paragraph (b)(ii), for 'arrestable' substitute 'indictable'.

Criminal Justice and Public Order Act 1994 (c. 33)

47 (1) The Criminal Justice and Public Order Act 1994 is amended as follows.

(2) In section 137 (cross-border powers of arrest etc.)—

(a) in subsection (1), for 'conditions applicable to this subsection are' substitute 'condition applicable to this subsection is',

(b) for subsection (4) substitute—

'(4) The condition applicable to subsection (1) above is that it appears to the constable that it would have been lawful for him to have exercised the powers had the suspected person been in England and Wales.',

(c) in subsection (9), for the definition of ' "arrestable offence" and "designated police station" ' substitute—

' "arrestable offence" has the same meaning as in the Police and Criminal Evidence (Northern Ireland) Order 1989 ("the 1989 Order");
"designated police station" has the same meaning as in the Police and Criminal Evidence Act 1984 or, in relation to Northern Ireland, as in the 1989 Order; and'.

(3) In section 138 (provisions supplementing section 137), in subsection (3), for 'subsections (4)(b) and (6)(b)' substitute 'subsection (6)(b)'.

(4) In section 140 (reciprocal powers of arrest), in subsection (1), for 'section 24(6) or (7) or 25' substitute 'section 24'.

(5) This paragraph extends to the whole of the United Kingdom.

Terrorism Act 2000 (c. 11)

48 (1) In Schedule 8 to the Terrorism Act 2000 (detention), in paragraph 8 (which relates to the rights of a person detained under Schedule 7 to or section 41 of that Act)—

(a) in sub-paragraph (4), for 'serious arrestable offence', in each place where it occurs, substitute 'serious offence',

(b) in sub-paragraph (9), for the words before paragraph (a) substitute 'In this paragraph, references to a "serious offence" are (in relation to England and Wales) to an indictable offence, and (in relation to Northern Ireland) to a serious arrestable offence within the meaning of Article 87 of the Police and Criminal Evidence (Northern Ireland) Order 1989; but also include—'.

(2) This paragraph extends to the whole of the United Kingdom.

International Criminal Court Act 2001 (c. 17)

49 (1) The International Criminal Court Act 2001 is amended as follows.

(2) In section 33 (entry, search and seizure), in subsection (2), for 'a serious arrestable offence' substitute '(in the case of Part 2 of the 1984 Act) to an indictable offence or (in the case of Part III of the 1989 Order) to a serious arrestable offence'.

(3) In section 55 (meaning of 'ancillary offence' under the law of England and Wales), in subsection (5), in each of paragraphs (a) and (b), for 'an arrestable offence' substitute 'a relevant offence'.

(4) This paragraph extends to England and Wales and to Northern Ireland (but not to Scotland).

Armed Forces Act 2001 (c. 19)

50 In section 5 of the Armed Forces Act 2001 (power of judicial officer to authorise entry and search of certain premises), in subsection (2)(a), for 'a serious arrestable offence for the purposes of the 1984 Act' substitute 'an indictable offence'.

This paragraph has the same extent as the Armed Forces Act 2001.

Crime (International Cooperation) Act 2003 (c. 32)

51 (1) The Crime (International Cooperation) Act 2003 is amended as follows.

(2) In section 16 (extension of statutory search powers in England and Wales and Northern Ireland), in subsection (1)—

(a) for 'serious arrestable offences' substitute 'indictable offences',

(b) in paragraph (b), for 'a serious arrestable offence' substitute 'an indictable offence'.

(3) In section 17 (warrants in England and Wales or Northern Ireland), in subsection (3)—

    (a) for paragraph (b) substitute—

        '(b) the conduct constituting the offence which is the subject of the proceedings or investigation would (if it occurred in England and Wales) constitute an indictable offence, or (if it occurred in Northern Ireland) constitute an arrestable offence, and',

    (b) in the definition of 'arrestable offence', omit the words 'the Police and Criminal Evidence Act 1984 (c. 60) or (as the case may be)'.

(4) This paragraph extends to the whole of the United Kingdom.

PART 4
OTHER AMENDMENTS

Game Laws (Amendment) Act 1960 (c. 36)

52 (1) The Game Laws (Amendment) Act 1960 is amended as follows.

    (2) In section 2 (power of police to enter on land), in subsection (1)(b), for 'section 25' substitute 'section 24'.

    (3) In section 4 (further provisions as to seizure and forfeiture), in subsection (1), for 'section 25' substitute 'section 24'.

Immigration Act 1971 (c. 77)

53 In section 28A of the Immigration Act 1971 (arrest without warrant), in each of subsections (1) and (9A), for 'A constable or' substitute 'An'.

Customs and Excise Management Act 1979 (c. 2)

54 In section 138 of the Customs and Excise Management Act 1979 (provisions about arrest), in subsection (4)(b), after 'section 24' insert 'or 24A'.

This paragraph has the same extent as that Act.

Animal Health Act 1981 (c. 22)

55 (1) The Animal Health Act 1981 is amended as follows.

    (2) In section 61 (powers of arrest as to rabies)—

    (a) in subsection (2), after 'applies' insert 'for the purposes of section 17(1)(caa) of the Police and Criminal Evidence Act 1984',

    (b) for the heading substitute 'Powers of entry and search in relation to rabies offences'.

    (3) For the heading to section 62 (entry and search under section 61) substitute 'Entry and search in exercise of powers to seize animals'.

Wildlife and Countryside Act 1981 (c. 69)

56 In section 19 of the Wildlife and Countryside Act 1981 (enforcement), in subsection (2), for 'section 25' substitute 'section 24'.

This paragraph extends also to Scotland.

Aviation Security Act 1982 (c. 36)

57 In section 13 of the Aviation Security Act 1982 (power to require aerodrome managers to promote searches at airports), in subsection (5)(a), for '25' substitute '24A'. This paragraph has the same extent as that Act.

Police and Criminal Evidence Act 1984 (c. 60)

58 In section 17 of the Police and Criminal Evidence Act 1984 (entry for purpose of arrest etc.), in subsection (1)—

(a) for paragraph (c)(iiia) substitute—

'(iiia) section 4 (driving etc. when under influence of drink or drugs) or 163 (failure to stop when required to do so by constable in uniform) of the Road Traffic Act 1988;

(iiib) section 27 of the Transport and Works Act 1992 (which relates to offences involving drink or drugs);',

(b) after paragraph (ca) insert—

'(caa) of arresting a person for an offence to which section 61 of the Animal Health Act 1981 applies;'.

Road Traffic Act 1988 (c. 52)

59 In section 184 of the Road Traffic Act 1988 (application of sections 5 to 10 of that Act to persons subject to service discipline), for subsection (2) substitute—

'(2) A member of the provost staff may arrest a person for the time being subject to service discipline without warrant if he has reasonable cause to suspect that that person is or has been committing an offence under section 4.

(2A) The power conferred by subsection (2) is exercisable outside as well as within Great Britain.'

This paragraph has the same extent as section 184 of that Act.

Aviation and Maritime Security Act 1990 (c. 31)

60 In section 22 of the Aviation and Maritime Security Act 1990 (power to require harbour authorities to promote searches in harbour areas), in subsection (10)(a), for '25' substitute '24A'.

This paragraph has the same extent as that Act.

Deer Act 1991 (c. 54)

61 In section 12 of the Deer Act 1991 (powers of search, arrest and seizure), in subsection (2) (b), for 'section 25' substitute 'section 24'.

Gangmasters (Licensing) Act 2004 (c. 11)

63 The Gangmasters (Licensing) Act 2004 is amended as follows—

(a) in section 14 (offences: supplementary), in subsection (1), for 'section 24(4) and (5)' substitute 'section 24A',

(b) in Schedule 2 (application of Act to Northern Ireland), in paragraph 14, for 'section 24(4) and (5)' substitute 'section 24A'.

This paragraph has the same extent as that Act.

Asylum and Immigration (Treatment of Claimants, etc.) Act 2004 (c. 19)

62 The Asylum and Immigration (Treatment of Claimants, etc.) Act 2004 is amended as follows—

(a) in section 2 (entering U.K. without passport, etc.), in subsection (10), for 'a constable or' substitute 'an',

(b) in section 35 (deportation or removal: cooperation), in subsection (5), for 'a constable or' substitute 'an'.

Section 122   SCHEDULE 8

POWERS OF DESIGNATED AND ACCREDITED PERSONS

PART 1
DESIGNATED PERSONS

1 Schedule 4 to the Police Reform Act 2002 (c. 30) (powers exercisable by police civilians) is amended as follows.

Community support officers

2 After paragraph 1 insert—

'Power to require name and address

1A (1) This paragraph applies if a designation applies it to any person.

(2) Such a designation may specify that, in relation to that person, the application of sub-paragraph (3) is confined to one or more only (and not to all) relevant offences or relevant licensing offences, being in each case specified in the designation.

(3) Subject to sub-paragraph (4), where that person has reason to believe that another person has committed a relevant offence in the relevant police area, or a relevant licensing offence (whether or not in the relevant police area), he may require that other person to give him his name and address.

(4) The power to impose a requirement under sub-paragraph (3) in relation to an offence under a relevant byelaw is exercisable only in a place to which the byelaw relates.

(5) A person who fails to comply with a requirement under sub-paragraph (3) is guilty of an offence and shall be liable, on summary conviction, to a fine not exceeding level 3 on the standard scale.

(6) In its application to an offence which is an offence by reference to which a notice may be given to a person in exercise of the power mentioned in paragraph 1(2)(aa), sub-paragraph (3) of this paragraph shall have effect as if for the words "has committed a relevant offence in the relevant police area" there were substituted "in the relevant police area has committed a relevant offence".

(7) In this paragraph, "relevant offence", "relevant licensing offence" and "relevant byelaw" have the meaning given in paragraph 2 (reading accordingly the references to "this paragraph" in paragraph 2(6)).'

3   (1) Paragraph 2 (power to detain etc.) is amended as follows.

(2) For sub-paragraph (2) substitute—

'(2) A designation may not apply this paragraph to any person unless a designation also applies paragraph 1A to him.'

(3) In sub-paragraph (3)—

(a) for 'sub-paragraph (2)' substitute 'paragraph 1A(3)',

(b) at the end add the following new sentence—

'This sub-paragraph does not apply if the requirement was imposed in connection with a relevant licensing offence mentioned in paragraph (a), (c) or (f) of sub-paragraph (6A) believed to have been committed on licensed premises (within the meaning of the Licensing Act 2003).'

(4) After sub-paragraph (3) insert—

'(3A) Where—

(a) a designation applies this paragraph to any person ("the CSO"); and

(b) by virtue of a designation under paragraph 1A the CSO has the power to impose a requirement under sub-paragraph (3) of that paragraph in relation to an offence under a relevant byelaw,

the CSO shall also have any power a constable has under the relevant byelaw to remove a person from a place.

(3B) Where a person to whom this paragraph applies ("the CSO") has reason to believe that another person is committing an offence under section 3 or 4 of the Vagrancy Act 1824, and requires him to stop doing whatever gives rise to that belief, the CSO may, if the other person fails to stop as required, require him to wait with the CSO, for a period not exceeding thirty minutes, for the arrival of a constable.'

(5) In sub-paragraph (4), after '(3)' insert 'or (3B)'.

(6) In sub-paragraph (5)—

(a) omit paragraph (a),

(b) in paragraph (b), after '(3)' insert 'or (3B)'.

(7) In sub-paragraph (6), after the paragraph (ab) inserted by paragraph 13(2) of Schedule 13 to this Act, insert—

'(ac) an offence under section 3 or 4 of the Vagrancy Act 1824; or (ad) an offence under a relevant byelaw; or'.

(8) After sub-paragraph (6) insert—

'(6A) In this paragraph "relevant licensing offence" means an offence under any of the following provisions of the Licensing Act 2003—

(a) section 141 (otherwise than by virtue of subsection (2)(c) or (3) of that section);

(b) section 142;

(c) section 146(1);

(d) section 149(1)(a), (3)(a) or (4)(a);

(e) section 150(1);

(f) section 150(2) (otherwise than by virtue of subsection (3)(b) of that section);

(g) section 152(1) (excluding paragraph (b)).

(6B) In this paragraph "relevant byelaw" means a byelaw included in a list of byelaws which—

(a) have been made by a relevant body with authority to make byelaws for any place within the relevant police area; and

(b) the chief officer of the police force for the relevant police area and the relevant body have agreed to include in the list.

(6C) The list must be published by the chief officer in such a way as to bring it to the attention of members of the public in localities where the byelaws in the list apply.

(6D) A list of byelaws mentioned in sub-paragraph (6B) may be amended from time to time by agreement between the chief officer and the relevant body in question, by adding byelaws to it or removing byelaws from it, and the amended list shall also be published by the chief officer as mentioned in sub-paragraph (6C).

(6E) A relevant body for the purposes of sub-paragraph (6B) is—

    (a) in England, a county council, a district council, a London borough council or a parish council; or in Wales, a county council, a county borough council or a community council;

    (b) the Greater London Authority;

    (c) Transport for London;

    (d) a metropolitan country passenger transport authority established under section 28 of the Local Government Act 1985;

    (e) any body specified in an order made by the Secretary of State.

(6F) An order under sub-paragraph (6E)(e) may provide, in relation to any body specified in the order, that the agreement mentioned in sub-paragraph (6B)(b) and (6D) is to be made between the chief officer and the Secretary of State (rather than between the chief officer and the relevant body).'

(9) Omit sub-paragraph (7).

(10) At the end add—

'(8) The application of any provision of this paragraph by paragraph 3(2), 3A(2) or 7A(8) has no effect unless a designation under this paragraph has applied this paragraph to the CSO in question.'

4   After paragraph 2 insert—

'Powers to search individuals and to seize and retain items

2A Where a designation applies this paragraph to any person, that person shall (subject to sub-paragraph (3)) have the powers mentioned in sub-paragraph (2) in relation to a person upon whom he has imposed a requirement to wait under paragraph 2(3) or (3B) (whether or not that person makes an election under paragraph 2(4)).

(2) Those powers are the same powers as a constable has under section 32 of the 1984 Act in relation to a person arrested at a place other than a police station—

    (a) to search the arrested person if the constable has reasonable grounds for believing that the arrested person may present a danger to himself or others; and to seize and retain anything he finds on exercising that power, if the constable has reasonable grounds for believing that the person being searched might use it to cause physical injury to himself or to any other person;

    (b) to search the arrested person for anything which he might use to assist him to escape from lawful custody; and to seize and retain anything he finds on exercising that power (other than an item subject to legal privilege) if the constable has reasonable grounds for believing that the person being searched might use it to assist him to escape from lawful custody.

(3) If in exercise of the power conferred by sub-paragraph (1) the person to whom this paragraph applies seizes and retains anything by virtue of subparagraph (2), he must—

    (a) tell the person from whom it was seized where inquiries about its recovery may be made; and

    (b) comply with a constable's instructions about what to do with it.'

5 In paragraph 3 (power to require name and address of person acting in anti-social manner), in sub-paragraph (2), for 'sub-paragraph (2) of that paragraph' substitute 'paragraph 1A(3)'.

6 After paragraph 3 insert—

'Power to require name and address: road traffic offences

   3A (1) Where a designation applies this paragraph to any person, that person shall, in the relevant police area, have the powers of a constable—

     (a) under subsection (1) of section 165 of the Road Traffic Act 1988 to require a person mentioned in paragraph (c) of that subsection who he has reasonable cause to believe has committed, in the relevant police area, an offence under subsection (1) or (2) of section 35 of that Act (including that section as extended by paragraphs 11B(4) and 12(2) of this Schedule) to give his name and address; and

     (b) under section 169 of that Act to require a person committing an offence under section 37 of that Act (including that section as extended by paragraphs 11B(4) and 12(2) of this Schedule) to give his name and address.

    (2) Sub-paragraphs (3) to (5) of paragraph 2 apply in the case of a requirement imposed by virtue of sub-paragraph (1) as they apply in the case of a requirement under paragraph 1A(3).

    (3) The reference in section 169 of the Road Traffic Act 1988 to section 37 of that Act is to be taken to include a reference to that section as extended by paragraphs 11B(4) and 12(2) of this Schedule.'

7 In paragraph 4 (power to use reasonable force to detain person)—

     (a) in sub-paragraph (2)(b), after 'paragraph' insert '1A or',

     (b) in sub-paragraph (3), for 'paragraph 2(2)' substitute 'paragraph 1A(3)'.

8 After paragraph 7 insert—

'Search and seizure powers: alcohol and tobacco

   7A (1) Where a designation applies this paragraph to any person ("the CSO"), the CSO shall have the powers set out below.

    (2) Where—

     (a) in exercise of the powers referred to in paragraph 5 or 6 the CSO has imposed, under section 12(2) of the Criminal Justice and Police Act 2001 or under section 1 of the Confiscation of Alcohol (Young Persons) Act 1997, a requirement on a person to surrender alcohol or a container for alcohol;

     (b) that person fails to comply with that requirement; and

     (c) the CSO reasonably believes that the person has alcohol or a container for alcohol in his possession,

    the CSO may search him for it.

    (3) Where—

     (a) in exercise of the powers referred to in paragraph 7 the CSO has sought to seize something which by virtue of that paragraph he has a power to seize;

     (b) the person from whom he sought to seize it fails to surrender it; and

     (c) the CSO reasonably believes that the person has it in his possession,

    the CSO may search him for it.

    (4) The power to search conferred by sub-paragraph (2) or (3)—

     (a) is to do so only to the extent that is reasonably required for the purpose of discovering whatever the CSO is searching for; and

     (b) does not authorise the CSO to require a person to remove any of his clothing in public other than an outer coat, jacket or gloves.

(5) A person who without reasonable excuse fails to consent to being searched is guilty of an offence and shall be liable, on summary conviction, to a fine not exceeding level 3 on the standard scale.

(6) A CSO who proposes to exercise the power to search a person under sub-paragraph (2) or (3) must inform him that failing without reasonable excuse to consent to being searched is an offence.

(7) If the person in question fails to consent to being searched, the CSO may require him to give the CSO his name and address.

(8) Sub-paragraph (3) of paragraph 2 applies in the case of a requirement imposed by virtue of sub-paragraph (7) as it applies in the case of a requirement under paragraph 1A(3); and sub-paragraphs (4) to (5) of paragraph 2 also apply accordingly.

(9) If on searching the person the CSO discovers what he is searching for, he may seize it and dispose of it.

Powers to seize and detain: controlled drugs

7B (1) Where a designation applies this paragraph to any person ("the CSO"), the CSO shall, within the relevant police area, have the powers set out in sub-paragraphs (2) and (3).

(2) If the CSO—

    (a) finds a controlled drug in a person's possession (whether or not he finds it in the course of searching the person by virtue of a designation under any paragraph of this Schedule); and

    (b) reasonably believes that it is unlawful for the person to be in possession of it,

the CSO may seize it and retain it.

(3) If the CSO—

    (a) finds a controlled drug in a person's possession (as mentioned in sub-paragraph (2)); or

    (b) reasonably believes that a person is in possession of a controlled drug,

and reasonably believes that it is unlawful for the person to be in possession of it, the CSO may require him to give the CSO his name and address.

(4) If in exercise of the power conferred by sub-paragraph (2) the CSO seizes and retains a controlled drug, he must—

    (a) if the person from whom it was seized maintains that he was lawfully in possession of it, tell the person where inquiries about its recovery may be made; and

    (b) comply with a constable's instructions about what to do with it.

(5) A person who fails to comply with a requirement under sub-paragraph (3) is guilty of an offence and shall be liable, on summary conviction, to a fine not exceeding level 3 on the standard scale.

(6) In this paragraph, "controlled drug" has the same meaning as in the Misuse of Drugs Act 1971.

7C (1) Sub-paragraph (2) applies where a designation applies this paragraph to any person ("the CSO").

(2) If the CSO imposes a requirement on a person under paragraph 7B (3)—

    (a) sub-paragraph (3) of paragraph 2 applies in the case of such a requirement as it applies in the case of a requirement under paragraph 1A(3); and

    (b) sub-paragraphs (4) to (5) of paragraph 2 also apply accordingly.'

9 After paragraph 8 insert—

'Entry to investigate licensing offences

8A (1) Where a designation applies this paragraph to any person, that person shall have the powers of a constable under section 180 of the Licensing Act 2003 to enter and search premises other than clubs in the relevant police area, but only in respect of a relevant licensing offence (as defined for the purposes of paragraph 2).

(2) Except as mentioned in sub-paragraph (3), a person to whom this paragraph applies shall not, in exercise of the power conferred by sub-paragraph (1), enter any premises except in the company, and under the supervision, of a constable.

(3) The prohibition in sub-paragraph (2) does not apply in relation to premises in respect of which the person to whom this paragraph applies reasonably believes that a premises licence under Part 3 of the Licensing Act 2003 authorises the sale of alcohol for consumption off the premises.'

10 After paragraph 11A insert—

'Power to control traffic for purposes other than escorting a load of exceptional dimensions

11B (1) Where a designation applies this paragraph to any person, that person shall have, in the relevant police area—

(a) the power of a constable engaged in the regulation of traffic in a road to direct a person driving or propelling a vehicle to stop the vehicle or to make it proceed in, or keep to, a particular line of traffic;

(b) the power of a constable in uniform engaged in the regulation of vehicular traffic in a road to direct a person on foot to stop proceeding along or across the carriageway.

(2) The purposes for which those powers may be exercised do not include the purpose mentioned in paragraph 12(1).

(3) Where a designation applies this paragraph to any person, that person shall also have, in the relevant police area, the power of a constable, for the purposes of a traffic survey, to direct a person driving or propelling a vehicle to stop the vehicle, to make it proceed in, or keep to, a particular line of traffic, or to proceed to a particular point on or near the road.

(4) Sections 35 and 37 of the Road Traffic Act 1988 (offences of failing to comply with directions of constable engaged in regulation of traffic in a road) shall have effect in relation to the exercise of the powers mentioned in sub-paragraphs (1) and (3), for the purposes for which they may be exercised and by a person whose designation applies this paragraph to him, as if the references to a constable were references to him.

(5) A designation may not apply this paragraph to any person unless a designation also applies paragraph 3A to him.'

11 After paragraph 13 insert—

'Power to place traffic signs

13A (1) Where a designation applies this paragraph to any person, that person shall have, in the relevant police area, the powers of a constable under section 67 of the Road Traffic Regulation Act 1984 to place and maintain traffic signs.

(2) Section 36 of the Road Traffic Act 1988 (drivers to comply with traffic directions) shall apply to signs placed in the exercise of the powers conferred by virtue of sub-paragraph (1).'

12 After paragraph 15 insert—

'Photographing of persons arrested, detained or given fixed penalty notices

15ZA Where a designation applies this paragraph to any person, that person shall, within the relevant police area, have the power of a constable under section 64A(1A) of the 1984 Act (photographing of suspects etc.) to take a photograph of a person elsewhere than at a police station.'

Investigating officers

13 In paragraph 16 (search warrants)—
   (a) in paragraph (a), for 'in the relevant police area' substitute 'whether in the relevant police area or not',
   (b) in paragraph (e), for 'in respect of premises in the relevant police area' substitute', but in respect of premises in the relevant police area only,'.

14 After paragraph 16 insert—

   '16A Where a designation applies this paragraph to any person—
      (a) the persons to whom a warrant may be addressed under section 26 of the Theft Act 1968 (search for stolen goods) shall, in relation to persons or premises in the relevant police area, include that person; and
      (b) in relation to such a warrant addressed to him, that person shall have the powers under subsection (3) of that section.
   16B Where a designation applies this paragraph to any person, subsection (3), and (to the extent that it applies subsection (3)) subsection (3A), of section 23 of the Misuse of Drugs Act 1971 (powers to search and obtain evidence) shall have effect as if, in relation to premises in the relevant police area, the reference to a constable included a reference to that person.'

15 In paragraph 17 (access to excluded and special procedure material)—
   (a) in paragraph (b)(ii), at the end add '(in the case of a specific premises warrant) or any premises, whether in the relevant police area or not (in the case of an all premises warrant);',
   (b) in paragraph (bc), for 'in respect of premises in the relevant police area' substitute', but in respect of premises in the relevant police area only,'.

Detention officers

16 After paragraph 33 insert—

   'Taking of impressions of footwear

   33A Where a designation applies this paragraph to any person—
      (a) he shall, at any police station in the relevant police area, have the powers of a constable under section 61A of the 1984 Act (impressions of footwear) to take impressions of a person's footwear without the appropriate consent; and
      (b) the requirement by virtue of section 61A(5)(a) of the 1984 Act that a person must be informed by an officer that an impression of his footwear may be the subject of a speculative search shall be capable of being discharged, in the case of a person at such a station, by his being so informed by the person to whom this paragraph applies.'

PART 2
ACCREDITED PERSONS

17 Schedule 5 to the Police Reform Act 2002 (c. 30) (powers exercisable by accredited persons) is amended as follows.

18 In paragraph 2 (power to require giving of name and address), in sub-paragraph (3), after paragraph (a) insert—

   '(aa) an offence under section 3 or 4 of the Vagrancy Act 1824; or'.

19 After paragraph 3 insert—

'Power to require name and address: road traffic offences

3A (1) An accredited person whose accreditation specifies that this paragraph applies to him shall, in the relevant police area, have the powers of a constable—

(a) under subsection (1) of section 165 of the Road Traffic Act 1988 to require a person mentioned in paragraph (c) of that subsection who he has reasonable cause to believe has committed, in the relevant police area, an offence under subsection (1) or (2) of section 35 of that Act (including that section as extended by paragraphs 8B(4) and 9(2) of this Schedule) to give his name and address; and

(b) under section 169 of that Act to require a person committing an offence under section 37 of that Act (including that section as extended by paragraphs 8B(4) and 9(2) of this Schedule) to give his name and address.

(2) The reference in section 169 of the Road Traffic Act 1988 to section 37 of that Act is to be taken to include a reference to that section as extended by paragraphs 8B(4) and 9(2) of this Schedule.'

20 After paragraph 8A insert—

'Power to control traffic for purposes other than escorting a load of exceptional dimensions

8B (1) A person whose accreditation specifies that this paragraph applies to him shall have, in the relevant police area—

(a) the power of a constable engaged in the regulation of traffic in a road to direct a person driving or propelling a vehicle to stop the vehicle or to make it proceed in, or keep to, a particular line of traffic;

(b) the power of a constable in uniform engaged in the regulation of vehicular traffic in a road to direct a person on foot to stop proceeding along or across the carriageway.

(2) The purposes for which those powers may be exercised do not include the purpose mentioned in paragraph 9(1).

(3) A person whose accreditation specifies that this paragraph applies to him shall also have, in the relevant police area, the power of a constable, for the purposes of a traffic survey, to direct a person driving or propelling a vehicle to stop the vehicle, to make it proceed in, or keep to, a particular line of traffic, or to proceed to a particular point on or near the road.

(4) Sections 35 and 37 of the Road Traffic Act 1988 (offences of failing to comply with directions of constable engaged in regulation of traffic in a road) shall have effect in relation to the exercise of the powers mentioned in sub-paragraphs (1) and (3), for the purposes for which they may be exercised and by a person whose accreditation specifies that this paragraph applies to him, as if the references to a constable were references to him.

(5) A person's accreditation may not specify that this paragraph applies to him unless it also specifies that paragraph 3A applies to him.'

21 After paragraph 9 insert—

'Photographing of persons given fixed penalty notices

9ZA An accredited person whose accreditation specifies that this paragraph applies to him shall, within the relevant police area, have the power of a constable under section 64A(1A) of the 1984 Act (photographing of suspects etc.) to take a photograph, elsewhere than at a police station, of a person to whom the accredited person has given a penalty notice (or as the case may be a fixed penalty notice) in exercise of any power mentioned in paragraph 1(2).'

Section 122   SCHEDULE 9

ADDITIONAL POWERS AND DUTIES OF DESIGNATED PERSONS

1   Schedule 4 to the Police Reform Act 2002 (c. 30) (powers exercisable by police civilians) is amended as follows.

Community Support Officers

2   In paragraph 2 (power to detain etc.), after sub-paragraph (4) insert—

'(4A) If a person has imposed a requirement under sub-paragraph (3) or (3B) on another person ('P'), and P does not make an election under sub-paragraph (4), the person imposing the requirement shall, if a constable arrives within the thirty-minute period, be under a duty to remain with the constable and P until he has transferred control of P to the constable.

(4B) If, following an election under sub-paragraph (4), the person imposing the requirement under sub-paragraph (3) or (3B) ('the CSO') takes the person upon whom it is imposed ('P') to a police station, the CSO—

(a) shall be under a duty to remain at the police station until he has transferred control of P to the custody officer there;

(b) until he has so transferred control of P, shall be treated for all purposes as having P in his lawful custody; and

(c) for so long as he is at the police station, or in its immediate vicinity, in compliance with, or having complied with, his duty under paragraph (a), shall be under a duty to prevent P's escape and to assist in keeping P under control.'

3   In paragraph 4 (power to use reasonable force to detain person)—

(a) in sub-paragraph (2)(b), after 'relevant offences' insert 'or relevant licensing offences',

(b) in sub-paragraph (3), after 'making off' insert 'and to keep him under control.'

4   After paragraph 4 insert—

'4ZA Where a designation applies this paragraph to any person, that person may, if he has imposed a requirement on any person to wait with him under paragraph 2(3B) or by virtue of paragraph 7A(8) or 7C(2)(a), use reasonable force to prevent that other person from making off and to keep him under control while he is either—

(a) subject to that requirement; or

(b) accompanying the designated person to a police station in accordance with an election made under paragraph 2(4).

4ZB Where a designation applies this paragraph to any person, that person, if he is complying with any duty under sub-paragraph (4A) or (4B) of paragraph 2, may use reasonable force to prevent P (as identified in those sub-paragraphs) from making off (or escaping) and to keep him under control.'

Investigating officers

5   In paragraph 22 (power to transfer persons into custody of investigating officers), in sub-paragraph (2)—

(a) in paragraph (b), after 'duty' insert 'to keep that person under control and',

(b) in paragraph (c), at the end add 'and under his control'.

6   After paragraph 22 insert—

'Powers in respect of detained persons

22A Where a designation applies this paragraph to any person, he shall be under a duty, when in the course of his employment he is present at a police station—

(a) to assist any officer or other designated person to keep any person detained at the police station under control; and

(b) to prevent the escape of any such person,

and for those purposes shall be entitled to use reasonable force.'

Detention officers

7   After paragraph 33A (inserted by paragraph 16 of Schedule 8 to this Act) insert—

'Powers in respect of detained persons

3B Where a designation applies this paragraph to any person, he shall be under a duty, when in the course of his employment he is present at a police station—

(a) to keep under control any person detained at the police station and for whom he is for the time being responsible;

(b) to assist any officer or other designated person to keep any other person detained at the police station under control; and

(c) to prevent the escape of any such person as is mentioned in paragraph (a) or (b), and for those purposes shall be entitled to use reasonable force.

3C Where a designation applies this paragraph to any person, he shall be entitled to use reasonable force when—

(a) securing, or assisting an officer or another designated person to secure, the detention of a person detained at a police station in the relevant police area, or

(b) escorting within a police station in the relevant police area, or assisting an officer or another designated person to escort within such a police station, a person detained there.'

Escort officers

8   (1) Paragraph 34 (power to take an arrested person to a police station) is amended as follows.

(2) In sub-paragraph (1)(c)—

(a) in paragraph (ii), after 'duty' insert 'to keep the person under control and',

(b) in paragraph (iii), at the end add 'and under his control'.

(3) After sub-paragraph (1)(c) add—

'(d) a person who has taken another person to a police station in exercise of the power conferred by virtue of paragraph (a)—

(i) shall be under a duty to remain at the police station until he has transferred control of the other person to the custody officer at the police station;

(ii) until he has so transferred control of the other person, shall be treated for all purposes as having that person in his lawful custody;

(iii) for so long as he is at the police station or in its immediate vicinity in compliance with, or having complied with, his duty under sub-paragraph (i), shall be under a duty to prevent the escape of the other person and to assist in keeping him under control; and

    (iv) shall be entitled to use reasonable force for the purpose of complying with his duty under sub-paragraph (iii).'

9 (1) Paragraph 35 (escort of persons in police detention) is amended as follows.

  (2) In sub-paragraph (3)—

    (a) in paragraph (b), after 'duty' insert 'to keep the person under control and',

    (b) in paragraph (c), at the end add 'and under his control'.

  (3) After sub-paragraph (3) insert—

   '(3A) A person who has escorted another person to a police station or other place in accordance with an authorisation under sub-paragraph (1) or (2)—

    (a) shall be under a duty to remain at the police station or other place until he has transferred control of the other person to a custody officer or other responsible person there;

    (b) until he has so transferred control of the other person, shall be treated for all purposes as having that person in his lawful custody;

    (c) for so long as he is at the police station or other place, or in its immediate vicinity, in compliance with, or having complied with, his duty under paragraph (a), shall be under a duty to prevent the escape of the other person and to assist in keeping him under control; and

    (d) shall be entitled to use reasonable force for the purpose of complying with his duty under paragraph (c).'

Staff custody officers

10 After paragraph 35A (inserted by section 120(5) of this Act) insert—

'Powers in respect of detained persons

35B Where a designation applies this paragraph to any person, he shall be under a duty, when in the course of his employment he is present at a police station—

    (a) to keep under control any person detained at the police station and for whom he is for the time being responsible;

    (b) to assist any officer or other designated person to keep any other person detained at the police station under control; and

    (c) to prevent the escape of any such person as in mentioned in paragraph (a) or (b),

  and for those purposes shall be entitled to use reasonable force.'

Section 144   SCHEDULE 10

PARENTAL COMPENSATION ORDERS

PART 1
ENGLAND AND WALES

1 The Crime and Disorder Act 1998 (c. 37) is amended as provided in paragraph 2 to 5.

2 After section 13 insert—

'13A Parental compensation orders

  (1) A magistrates' court may make an order under this section (a "parental compensation order") if on the application of a local authority it is satisfied, on the civil standard of proof—

    (a) that the condition mentioned in subsection (2) below is fulfilled with respect to a child under the age of 10; and

    (b) that it would be desirable to make the order in the interests of preventing a repetition of the behaviour in question.

(2) The condition is that the child has taken, or caused loss of or damage to, property in the course of—

    (a) committing an act which, if he had been aged 10 or over, would have constituted an offence; or

    (b) acting in a manner that caused or was likely to cause harassment, alarm or distress to one or more persons not of the same household as himself.

(3) A parental compensation order is an order which requires any person specified in the order who is a parent or guardian of the child (other than a local authority) to pay compensation of an amount specified in the order to any person or persons specified in the order who is, or are, affected by the taking of the property or its loss or damage.

(4) The amount of compensation specified may not exceed £5,000 in all.

(5) The Secretary of State may by order amend subsection (4) above so as to substitute a different amount.

(6) For the purposes of collection and enforcement, a parental compensation order is to be treated as if it were a sum adjudged to be paid on the conviction by the magistrates' court which made the order of the person or persons specified in the order as liable to pay the compensation.

(7) In this section and sections 13B and 13C below, 'local authority' has the same meaning as in the 1989 Act.

13B Parental compensation orders: the compensation

(1) When specifying the amount of compensation for the purposes of section 13A(3) above, the magistrates' court shall take into account—

    (a) the value of the property taken or damaged, or whose loss was caused, by the child;

    (b) any further loss which flowed from the taking of or damage to the property, or from its loss;

    (c) whether the child, or any parent or guardian of his, has already paid any compensation for the property (and if so, how much);

    (d) whether the child, or any parent or guardian of his, has already made any reparation (and if so, what it consisted of);

    (e) the means of those to be specified in the order as liable to pay the compensation, so far as the court can ascertain them;

    (f) whether there was any lack of care on the part of the person affected by the taking of the property or its loss or damage which made it easier for the child to take or damage the property or to cause its loss.

(2) If property taken is recovered before compensation is ordered to be paid in respect of it—

    (a) the court shall not order any such compensation to be payable in respect of it if it is not damaged;

    (b) if it is damaged, the damage shall be treated for the purposes of making a parental compensation order as having been caused by the child, regardless of how it was caused and who caused it.

(3) The court shall specify in the order how and by when the compensation is to be paid (for example, it may specify that the compensation is to be paid by instalments, and specify the date by which each instalment must be paid).

(4) For the purpose of ascertaining the means of the parent or guardian, the court may, before specifying the amount of compensation, order him to provide the court, within such period as it may specify in the order, such a statement of his financial circumstances as the court may require.

(5) A person who without reasonable excuse fails to comply with an order under subsection (4) above is guilty of an offence and is liable on summary conviction to a fine not exceeding level 3 on the standard scale.

(6) If, in providing a statement of his financial circumstances pursuant to an order under subsection (4) above, a person—

    (a) makes a statement which he knows to be false in a material particular;

    (b) recklessly provides a statement which is false in a material particular; or

    (c) knowingly fails to disclose any material fact,

he is liable on summary conviction to a fine not exceeding level 4 on the standard scale.

(7) Proceedings in respect of an offence under subsection (6) above may, despite anything in section 127(1) of the 1980 Act (limitation of time), be commenced at any time within two years from the date of the commission of the offence or within six months of its first discovery by the local authority, whichever period expires earlier.

13C Parental compensation orders: supplemental

(1) Before deciding whether or not to make a parental compensation order in favour of any person, the magistrates' court shall take into account the views of that person about whether a parental compensation order should be made in his favour.

(2) Before making a parental compensation order, the magistrates' court shall obtain and consider information about the child's family circumstances and the likely effect of the order on those circumstances.

(3) Before making a parental compensation order, a magistrates' court shall explain to the parent or guardian of the child in ordinary language—

    (a) the effect of the order and of the requirements proposed to be included in it;

    (b) the consequences which may follow (under subsection (4)(b) below) as a result of failure to comply with any of those requirements;

    (c) that the court has power (under subsection (4)(a) below) to review the order on the application either of the parent or guardian or of the local authority.

(4) A magistrates' court which has made a parental compensation order may make an order under subsection (5) below if while the order is in force—

    (a) it appears to the court, on the application of the local authority, or the parent or guardian subject to the order, that it is appropriate to make an order under subsection (5); or

    (b) it is proved to the satisfaction of the court, on the application of the local authority, that the parent or guardian subject to it has failed to comply with any requirement included in the order.

(5) An order under this subsection is an order discharging the parental compensation order or varying it—

    (a) by cancelling any provision included in it; or

    (b) by inserting in it (either in addition to or in substitution for any of its provisions) any provision that could have been included in the order if the court had then had power to make it and were exercising the power.

(6) Where an application under subsection (4) above for the discharge of a parental compensation order is dismissed, no further application for its discharge shall be made under that subsection by any person except with the consent of the court which made the order.

(7) References in this section to the magistrates' court which made a parental compensation order include any magistrates' court acting in the same local justice area as that court.

13D Parental compensation orders: appeal

(1) If a magistrates' court makes a parental compensation order, the parent or guardian may appeal against the making of the order, or against the amount of compensation specified in the order.

(2) The appeal lies to the Crown Court.

(3) On the appeal the Crown Court—

   (a) may make such orders as may be necessary to give effect to its determination of the appeal;

   (b) may also make such incidental or consequential orders as appear to it to be just.

(4) Any order of the Crown Court made on an appeal under this section (other than one directing that an application be re-heard by a magistrates' court) shall, for the purposes of section 13C above, be treated as if it were an order of the magistrates' court from which the appeal was brought and not an order of the Crown Court.

(5) A person in whose favour a parental compensation order is made shall not be entitled to receive any compensation under it until (disregarding any power of a court to grant leave to appeal out of time) there is no further possibility of an appeal on which the order could be varied or set aside.

13E Effect of parental compensation order on subsequent award of damages in civil proceedings

(1) This section has effect where—

   (a) a parental compensation order has been made in favour of any person in respect of any taking or loss of property or damage to it; and

   (b) a claim by him in civil proceedings for damages in respect of the taking, loss or damage is then to be determined.

(2) The damages in the civil proceedings shall be assessed without regard to the parental compensation order, but the claimant may recover only an amount equal to the aggregate of the following—

   (a) any amount by which they exceed the compensation; and

   (b) a sum equal to any portion of the compensation which he fails to recover.

(3) The claimant may not enforce the judgment, so far as it relates to such a sum as is mentioned in subsection (2)(b) above, without the permission of the court.'

3 (1) Section 8 (parenting orders) is amended as follows.

 (2) In subsection (1), after paragraph (a) insert—

'(aa) a parental compensation order is made in relation to a child's behaviour;'.

 (3) In subsection (6)(a)—

   (a) after 'paragraph (a)' insert', (aa)',

   (b) after 'child safety order,' insert 'parental compensation order,'.

4 In section 18 (interpretation of Chapter 1), in subsection (1), after the definition of 'local child curfew scheme' insert—

' "parental compensation order" has the meaning given by section 13A(1) above;'.

5 In section 114 (orders and regulations), in subsection (3), after 'section' insert '13A(5),'.

6 The amendments made by paragraph 2 of this Schedule do not apply in relation to any conduct which occurred before the coming into force of that paragraph.

PART 2
NORTHERN IRELAND

7 The Criminal Justice (Children) (Northern Ireland) Order 1998 (S.I. 1998/1504 (N.I. 9)) is amended as provided in paragraphs 8 and 9.

8 After Article 36 insert—

'**36ZA Parental compensation orders**

(1) A magistrates' court may make an order under this Article (a "parental compensation order") if on the application of a person of a description specified for the purpose in an order made by the Secretary of State (referred to in this Article and in Articles 36ZB and 36ZC as the "applicant") the court is satisfied, on the civil standard of proof—

(a) that the condition mentioned in paragraph (2) is fulfilled with respect to a child under the age of 10; and

(b) that it would be desirable to make the order in the interests of preventing a repetition of the behaviour in question.

(2) The condition is that the child has taken, or caused loss of or damage to, property in the course of—

(a) committing an act which, if he had been aged 10 or over, would have constituted an offence; or

(b) acting in a manner that caused or was likely to cause harassment, alarm or distress to one or more persons not of the same household as himself.

(3) A parental compensation order is an order which requires any person specified in the order who is a parent or guardian of the child to pay compensation of an amount specified in the order to any person or persons specified in the order who is, or are, affected by the taking of the property or its loss or damage.

(4) The amount of compensation specified may not exceed £5,000 in all.

(5) The Secretary of State may by order amend paragraph (4) so as to substitute a different amount.

(6) For the purposes of collection and enforcement, a parental compensation order is to be treated as if it were a sum adjudged to be paid on the conviction by the magistrates' court which made the order of the person or persons specified in the order as liable to pay the compensation.

(7) An order under paragraph (1) or (5) is subject to annulment in pursuance of a resolution of either House of Parliament in the same manner as a statutory instrument; and, accordingly, section 5 of the Statutory Instruments Act 1946 (c. 36) applies to such an order.

36ZB Parental compensation orders: the compensation

(1) When specifying the amount of compensation for the purposes of Article 36ZA(3), the magistrates' court shall take into account—

(a) the value of the property taken or damaged, or whose loss was caused, by the child;

(b) any further loss which flowed from the taking of or damage to the property, or from its loss;

(c) whether the child, or any parent or guardian of his, has already paid any compensation for the property (and if so, how much);

(d) whether the child, or any parent or guardian of his, has already made any reparation (and if so, what it consisted of);

(e) the means of those to be specified in the order as liable to pay the compensation, so far as the court can ascertain them;

(f) whether there was any lack of care on the part of the person affected by the taking of the property or its loss or damage which made it easier for the child to take or damage the property or to cause its loss.

(2) If property taken is recovered before compensation is ordered to be paid in respect of it—

(a) the court shall not order any such compensation to be payable in respect of it if it is not damaged;

(b) if it is damaged, the damage shall be treated for the purposes of making a parental compensation order as having been caused by the child, regardless of how it was caused and who caused it.

315

(3) The court shall specify in the order how and by when the compensation is to be paid (for example, it may specify that the compensation is to be paid by instalments, and specify the date by which each instalment must be paid).

(4) For the purpose of ascertaining the means of the parent or guardian, the court may, before specifying the amount of compensation, order him to provide the court, within such period as it may specify in the order, such a statement of his financial circumstances as the court may require.

(5) A person who without reasonable excuse fails to comply with an order under paragraph (4) is guilty of an offence and is liable on summary conviction to a fine not exceeding level 3 on the standard scale.

(6) If, in providing a statement of his financial circumstances pursuant to an order under paragraph (4), a person—
   (a) makes a statement which he knows to be false in a material particular;
   (b) recklessly provides a statement which is false in a material particular; or
   (c) knowingly fails to disclose any material fact,
   he is liable on summary conviction to a fine not exceeding level 4 on the standard scale.

(7) Proceedings in respect of an offence under paragraph (6) may, despite anything in Article 19 of the Magistrates' Courts (Northern Ireland) Order 1981 (limitation of time), be commenced at any time within two years from the date of the commission of the offence or within six months of its first discovery by the applicant, whichever period expires earlier.

(8) Paragraphs (1)(e) and (4) to (7) do not apply in the case of an order specifying an authority as liable to pay the compensation.

36ZC Parental compensation orders: supplmental

(1) Before deciding whether or not to make a parental compensation order in favour of any person, the magistrates' court shall take into account the views of that person about whether a parental compensation order should be made in his favour.

(2) Before making a parental compensation order, the magistrates' court shall obtain and consider information about the child's family circumstances and the likely effect of the order on those circumstances.

(3) Before making a parental compensation order, a magistrates' court shall explain to the parent or guardian of the child in ordinary language—
   (a) the effect of the order and of the requirements proposed to be included in it;
   (b) the consequences which may follow (under paragraph (4)(b)) as a result of failure to comply with any of those requirements;
   (c) that the court has power (under paragraph (4)(a)) to review the order on the applica-tion either of the parent or guardian or of the applicant.

(4) A magistrates' court which has made a parental compensation order may make an order under paragraph (5) if while the order is in force—
   (a) it appears to the court, on the application of the applicant, or the parent or guardian subject to the order, that it is appropriate to make an order under paragraph (5); or
   (b) it is proved to the satisfaction of the court, on the application of the applicant, that the parent or guardian subject to it has failed to comply with any requirement included in the order.

(5) An order under this paragraph is an order discharging the parental compensation order or varying it—
   (a) by cancelling any provision included in it; or
   (b) by inserting in it (either in addition to or in substitution for any of its provisions) any provision that could have been included in the order if the court had then had power to make it and were exercising the power.

(6) Where an application under paragraph (4) for the discharge of a parental compensation order is dismissed, no further application for its discharge shall be made under that paragraph by any person except with the consent of the court which made the order.

(7) References in this Article to the magistrates' court which made a parental compensation order include any magistrates' court acting for the same county court division as that court.

36ZD Parental compensation orders: appeal

(1) If a magistrates' court makes a parental compensation order, the parent or guardian may appeal against the making of the order, or against the amount of compensation specified in the order.

(2) The appeal lies to the county court.

(3) On the appeal the county court—

  (a) may make such orders as may be necessary to give effect to its determination of the appeal;

  (b) may also make such incidental or consequential orders as appear to it to be just.

(4) Any order of the county court made on an appeal under this Article (other than one directing that an application be re-heard by a magistrates' court) shall, for the purposes of Article 36ZC, be treated as if it were an order of the magistrates' court from which the appeal was brought and not an order of the county court.

(5) A person in whose favour a parental compensation order is made shall not be entitled to receive any compensation under it until (disregarding any power of a court to grant leave to appeal out of time) there is no further possibility of an appeal on which the order could be varied or set aside.

36ZE Effect of parental compensation order on subsequent award of damages in civil proceedings

(1) This Article has effect where—

  (a) a parental compensation order has been made in favour of any person in respect of any taking or loss of property or damage to it; and

  (b) a claim by him in civil proceedings for damages in respect of the taking, loss or damage is then to be determined.

(2) The damages in the civil proceedings shall be assessed without regard to the parental compensation order, but the claimant may recover only an amount equal to the aggregate of the following—

  (a) any amount by which they exceed the compensation; and

  (b) a sum equal to any portion of the compensation which he fails to recover.

(3) The claimant may not enforce the judgment, so far as it relates to such a sum as is mentioned in paragraph (2)(b), without the leave of the court.'

9 In Article 2 (interpretation), in paragraph (2), in the appropriate place insert—

' "parental compensation order" has the meaning given by Article 36ZA(1);'.

10 The amendments made by paragraph 8 of this Schedule do not apply in relation to any conduct which occurred before the coming into force of that paragraph.

Section 159   SCHEDULE 11

INVESTIGATIONS INTO CONDUCT OF POLICE OFFICERS: ACCELERATED PROCEDURE IN SPECIAL CASES

1 Schedule 3 to the Police Reform Act 2002 (c. 30) is amended as follows.

2 In paragraph 20(1)—

   (a) for 'until' substitute' until—

      (a) the appropriate authority has certified the case as a special case under paragraph 20B(3) or 20E(3), or'; and

   (b) the words from 'a report' to the end become paragraph (b).

3 After paragraph 20 insert—

'Accelerated procedure in special cases

20A(1) If, at any time before the completion of his investigation, a person appointed or designated to investigate a complaint or recordable conduct matter believes that the appropriate authority would, on consideration of the matter, be likely to consider that the special conditions are satisfied, he shall proceed in accordance with the following provisions of this paragraph.

   (2) If the person was appointed under paragraph 16, he shall submit to the appropriate authority—

      (a) a statement of his belief and the grounds for it; and

      (b) a written report on his investigation to that point;

and if he was appointed following a determination made by the Commission under paragraph 15 he shall send a copy of the statement and the report to the Commission.

   (3) If the person was appointed under paragraph 17 or 18 or designated under paragraph 19, he shall submit to the appropriate authority—

      (a) a statement of his belief and the grounds for it; and

      (b) a written report on his investigation to that point;

and shall send a copy of the statement and the report to the Commission.

   (4) A person submitting a report under this paragraph shall not be prevented by any obligation of secrecy imposed by any rule of law or otherwise from including all such matters in his report as he thinks fit.

   (5) A statement and report may be submitted under this paragraph whether or not a previous statement and report have been submitted; but a second or subsequent statement and report may be submitted only if the person submitting them has grounds to believe that the appropriate authority will reach a different determination under paragraph 20B(2) or 20E(2).

   (6) After submitting a report under this paragraph, the person appointed or designated to investigate the complaint or recordable conduct matter shall continue his investigation to such extent as he considers appropriate.

   (7) The special conditions are that—

      (a) the person whose conduct is the subject matter of the investigation may have committed an imprisonable offence and that person's conduct is of a serious nature;

      (b) there is sufficient evidence, in the form of written statements or other documents, to establish on the balance of probabilities that conduct justifying dismissal took place; and

      (c) it is in the public interest for the person whose conduct is the subject matter of the investigation to cease to be a member of a police force, or to be a special constable, without delay.

   (8) In sub-paragraph (7)—

      (a) in paragraph (a), "imprisonable offence" means an offence which is punishable with imprisonment in the case of a person aged 21 or over; and

      (b) in paragraph (b), "conduct justifying dismissal" means conduct which is so serious that disciplinary proceedings brought in respect of it would be likely to result in a dismissal.

(9) In paragraphs 20B to 20H "special report" means a report submitted under this paragraph.

Investigations managed or carried out by Commission: action by appropriate authority

20B (1) This paragraph applies where—
    (a) a statement and special report on an investigation carried out under the management of the Commission, or
    (b) a statement and special report on an investigation carried out by a person designated by the Commission,
    are submitted to the appropriate authority under paragraph 20A(3).

(2) The appropriate authority shall determine whether the special conditions are satisfied.

(3) If the appropriate authority determines that the special conditions are satisfied then, unless it considers that the circumstances are such as to make it inappropriate to do so, it shall—
    (a) certify the case as a special case for the purposes of Regulation 11 of the Police (Conduct) Regulations 2004 (S.I. 2004/645); and
    (b) subject to any request made under paragraph 20G(1), take such steps as are required by that Regulation in relation to a case so certified.

(4) The reference in sub-paragraph (3) to Regulation 11 includes a reference to any corresponding provision replacing that Regulation.

(5) If the appropriate authority determines that the special conditions are satisfied then it shall notify the Director of Public Prosecutions of its determination and send him a copy of the special report.

(6) The appropriate authority shall notify the Commission of a certification under sub-paragraph (3).

(7) If the appropriate authority determines—
    (a) that the special conditions are not satisfied, or
    (b) that, although those conditions are satisfied, the circumstances are such as to make it inappropriate at present to bring disciplinary proceedings,
    it shall submit to the Commission a memorandum under this sub-paragraph.

(8) The memorandum required to be submitted under sub-paragraph (7) is one which—
    (a) notifies the Commission of its determination that those conditions are not satisfied or (as the case may be) that they are so satisfied but the circumstances are such as to make it inappropriate at present to bring disciplinary proceedings; and
    (b) (in either case) sets out its reasons for so determining.

(9) In this paragraph "special conditions" has the meaning given by paragraph 20A(7).

Investigations managed or carried out by Commission: action by Commission

20C (1) On receipt of a notification under paragraph 20B(6), the Commission shall give a notification—
    (a) in the case of a complaint, to the complainant and to every person entitled to be kept properly informed in relation to the complaint under section 21; and
    (b) in the case of a recordable conduct matter, to every person entitled to be kept properly informed in relation to that matter under that section.

(2) The notification required by sub-paragraph (1) is one setting out—
    (a) the findings of the special report;
    (b) the appropriate authority's determination under paragraph 20B (2); and
    (c) the action that the appropriate authority is required to take as a consequence of that determination.

(3) Subsections (5) to (7) of section 20 shall have effect in relation to the duties imposed on the Commission by sub-paragraph (1) as they have effect in relation to the duties imposed on the Commission by that section.

(4) Except so far as may be otherwise provided by regulations made by virtue of sub-paragraph (3), the Commission shall be entitled (notwithstanding any obligation of secrecy imposed by any rule of law or otherwise) to discharge the duty to give a person mentioned in sub-paragraph (1) notification of the findings of the special report by sending that person a copy of that report.

20D(1) On receipt of a memorandum under paragraph 20B(7), the Commission shall—

    (a) consider the memorandum;

    (b) determine, in the light of that consideration, whether or not to make a recommendation under paragraph 20H; and

    (c) if it thinks fit to do so, make a recommendation under that paragraph.

(2) If the Commission determines not to make a recommendation under paragraph 20H, it shall notify the appropriate authority and the person appointed under paragraph 18 or designated under paragraph 19 of its determination.

Other investigations: action by appropriate authority

20E (1) This paragraph applies where—

    (a) a statement and a special report on an investigation carried out by an appropriate authority on its own behalf, or

    (b) a statement and a special report on an investigation carried out under the supervision of the Commission,

are submitted to the appropriate authority under paragraph 20A(2) or (3).

(2) The appropriate authority shall determine whether the special conditions are satisfied.

(3) If the appropriate authority determines that the special conditions are satisfied then, unless it considers that the circumstances are such as to make it inappropriate to do so, it shall—

    (a) certify the case as a special case for the purposes of Regulation 11 of the Police (Conduct) Regulations 2004 (S.I. 2004/645); and

    (b) subject to any request made under paragraph 20G(1), take such steps as are required by that Regulation in relation to a case so certified.

(4) The reference in sub-paragraph (3) to Regulation 11 includes a reference to any corresponding provision replacing that Regulation.

(5) If the appropriate authority determines that the special conditions are satisfied then it shall notify the Director of Public Prosecutions of its determination and send him a copy of the special report.

(6) Where the statement and report were required under paragraph 20A (2) to be copied to the Commission, the appropriate authority shall notify the Commission of a certification under sub-paragraph (3).

(7) If the appropriate authority determines—

    (a) that the special conditions are not satisfied, or

    (b) that, although those conditions are satisfied, the circumstances are such as to make it inappropriate at present to bring disciplinary proceedings,

it shall notify the person appointed under paragraph 16 or 17 of its determination.

(8) In this paragraph "special conditions" has the meaning given by paragraph 20A(7).

20F (1) If the appropriate authority certifies a case under paragraph 20E(3), it shall give a notification—

    (a) in the case of a complaint, to the complainant and to every person entitled to be kept properly informed in relation to the complaint under section 21; and

(b) in the case of a recordable conduct matter, to every person entitled to be kept properly informed in relation to that matter under that section.

(2) The notification required by sub-paragraph (1) is one setting out—
   (a) the findings of the report;
   (b) the authority's determination under paragraph 20E(2); and
   (c) the action that the authority is required to take in consequence of that determination.

(3) Subsections (5) to (7) of section 20 shall have effect in relation to the duties imposed on the appropriate authority by sub-paragraph (1) as they have effect in relation to the duties imposed on the appropriate authority by that section.

(4) Except so far as may be otherwise provided by regulations made by virtue of sub-paragraph (3), the appropriate authority shall be entitled (notwithstanding any obligation of secrecy imposed by any rule of law or otherwise) to discharge the duty to give a person mentioned in sub-paragraph (1) notification of the findings of the special report by sending that person a copy of that report.

Special cases: Director of Public Prosecutions

20G(1) On receiving a copy of a special report under paragraph 20B(5) or 20E (5), the Director of Public Prosecutions may request the appropriate authority not to bring disciplinary proceedings without his prior agreement, if the Director considers that bringing such proceedings might prejudice any future criminal proceedings.

(2) The Director of Public Prosecutions—
   (a) shall notify the appropriate authority of any decision of his to take, or not to take, action in respect of the matters dealt with in a special report copied to him under paragraph 20B(5) or 20E(5); and
   (b) where the special report was copied to him under paragraph 20B (5), shall send a copy of that notification to the Commission.

(3) It shall be the duty of the Commission to notify the persons mentioned in sub-paragraph (5) if criminal proceedings are brought against any person by the Director of Public Prosecutions in respect of any matters dealt with in a special report copied to him under paragraph 20B(5).

(4) It shall be the duty of the appropriate authority to notify the persons mentioned in sub-paragraph (5) if criminal proceedings are brought against any person by the Director of Public Prosecutions in respect of any matters dealt with in a special report copied to him under paragraph 20E(5).

(5) Those persons are—
   (a) in the case of a complaint, the complainant and every person entitled to be kept properly informed in relation to the complaint under section 21; and
   (b) in the case of a recordable conduct matter, every person entitled to be kept properly informed in relation to that matter under that section.

Special cases: recommendation or direction of Commission

20H(1) Where the appropriate authority has submitted, or is required to submit, a memorandum to the Commission under paragraph 20B(7), the Commission may make a recommendation to the appropriate authority that it should certify the case under paragraph 20B(3).

(2) If the Commission determines to make a recommendation under this paragraph, it shall give a notification—
   (a) in the case of a complaint, to the complainant and to every person entitled to be kept properly informed in relation to the complaint under section 21; and

    (b) in the case of a recordable conduct matter, to every person entitled to be kept properly informed in relation to that matter under that section.

(3) The notification required by sub-paragraph (2) is one setting out—

    (a) the findings of the special report; and

    (b) the Commission's recommendation under this paragraph.

(4) Subsections (5) to (7) of section 20 shall have effect in relation to the duties imposed on the Commission by sub-paragraph (2) as they have effect in relation to the duties imposed on the Commission by that section.

(5) Except so far as may be otherwise provided by regulations made by virtue of sub-paragraph (4), the Commission shall be entitled (notwithstanding any obligation of secrecy imposed by any rule of law or otherwise) to discharge the duty to give a person mentioned in sub-paragraph (2) notification of the findings of the special report by sending that person a copy of the report.

(6) It shall be the duty of the appropriate authority to notify the Commission whether it accepts the recommendation and (if it does) to certify the case and proceed accordingly.

(7) If, after the Commission has made a recommendation under this paragraph, the appropriate authority does not certify the case under paragraph 20B(3)—

    (a) the Commission may direct the appropriate authority so to certify it; and

    (b) it shall be the duty of the appropriate authority to comply with the direction and proceed accordingly.

(8) Where the Commission gives the appropriate authority a direction under this paragraph, it shall supply the appropriate authority with a statement of its reasons for doing so.

(9) The Commission may at any time withdraw a direction given under this paragraph.

(10) The appropriate authority shall keep the Commission informed of whatever action it takes in response to a recommendation or direction.

20I (1) Where—

    (a) the Commission makes a recommendation under paragraph 20H in the case of an investigation of a complaint, and

    (b) the appropriate authority notifies the Commission that the recommendation has been accepted,

the Commission shall notify the complainant and every person entitled to be kept properly informed in relation to the complaint under section 21 of that fact and of the steps that have been, or are to be, taken by the appropriate authority to give effect to it.

(2) Where in the case of an investigation of a complaint the appropriate authority—

    (a) notifies the Commission that it does not accept the recommendation made by the Commission under paragraph 20H, or

    (b) fails to certify the case under paragraph 20B(3) and to proceed accordingly,

it shall be the duty of the Commission to determine what (if any) further steps to take under paragraph 20H.

(3) It shall be the duty of the Commission to notify the complainant and every person entitled to be kept properly informed in relation to the complaint under section 21—

    (a) of any determination under sub-paragraph (2) not to take further steps under paragraph 20H; and

    (b) where it determines under that sub-paragraph to take further steps under that paragraph, of the outcome of the taking of those steps.'

4   In paragraph 25, after sub-paragraph (2) insert—

   '(2A) In sub-paragraph (2)—

    (a) references to the findings of an investigation do not include a reference to findings on a report submitted under paragraph 20A; and

(b) references to the report of an investigation do not include a reference to a report submitted under that paragraph.'

Section 160   SCHEDULE 12

INVESTIGATIONS OF DEATHS AND SERIOUS INJURIES
DURING OR AFTER CONTACT WITH THE POLICE

1   The Police Reform Act 2002 (c. 30) has effect subject to the following amendments.
2   (1) Section 10(2) (general functions of the Commission) is amended as follows.
    (2) After paragraph (b) insert—

    '(ba) the recording of matters from which it appears that a person has died or suffered serious injury during, or following, contact with a person serving with the police;'.

    (3) In paragraph (c), after 'paragraph (b)' insert 'or (ba)'.
3   In section 12 (matters to which Part 2 applies), after subsection (2) insert—

    '(2A) In this Part "death or serious injury matter" (or "DSI matter" for short) means any circumstances (other than those which are or have been the subject of a complaint or which amount to a conduct matter)—
      (a) in or in consequence of which a person has died or has sustained serious injury; and
      (b) in relation to which the requirements of either subsection (2B) or subsection (2C) are satisfied.
    (2B) The requirements of this subsection are that at the time of the death or serious injury the person—
      (a) had been arrested by a person serving with the police and had not been released from that arrest; or
      (b) was otherwise detained in the custody of a person serving with the police.
    (2C) The requirements of this subsection are that—
      (a) at or before the time of the death or serious injury the person had contact (of whatever kind, and whether direct or indirect) with a person serving with the police who was acting in the execution of his duties; and
      (b) there is an indication that the contact may have caused (whether directly or indirectly) or contributed to the death or serious injury.
    (2D) In subsection (2A) the reference to a person includes a person serving with the police, but in relation to such a person 'contact' in subsection (2C) does not include contact that he has whilst acting in the execution of his duties.'

4   In the following provisions, for 'and conduct matters' substitute', conduct matters and DSI matters'—
    (a) the cross-heading preceding section 13;
    (b) the heading for section 13 (handling of complaints and conduct matters); and
    (c) that section itself.
5   (1) Section 16(2) (assistance for which payment is required) is amended as follows.
    (2) In paragraph (a), for the words from 'an investigation relating to' to the end substitute—

    '(i) an investigation relating to the conduct of a person who, at the time of the conduct, was a member of the other force, or
    (ii) an investigation of a DSI matter in relation to which the relevant officer was, at the time of the death or serious injury, a member of the other force; and'.

(3) In paragraph (b), for the words from 'an investigation' to the end substitute—

'(i) an investigation relating to the conduct of a person who, at the time of the conduct, was not a member of that force, or

(ii) an investigation of a DSI matter in relation to which the relevant officer was, at the time of the death or serious injury, not a member of that force.'

6 In section 18 (inspection of police premises on behalf of the Commission), in subsection (2)(a), after 'conduct matters' insert 'or DSI matters'.

7 (1) Section 21 (duty to provide information) is amended as follows.

(2) In subsection (1), for 'or recordable conduct matter' substitute', recordable conduct matter or DSI matter'.

(3) In subsection (1)(a), after 'subsection (2)' insert 'or (2A)'.

(4) In subsection (2), after 'if' insert '(in the case of a complaint or recordable conduct matter)'.

(5) After subsection (2) insert—

'(2A) A person falls within this subsection if (in the case of a DSI matter)—

(a) he is a relative of the person who has died;

(b) he is a relative of the person who has suffered serious injury and that person is incapable of making a complaint;

(c) he himself is the person who has suffered serious injury.'

(6) In subsection (3)—

(a) after 'subsection (2)' insert 'or (2A)'; and

(b) for 'or recordable conduct matter' (in both places) substitute ', recordable conduct matter or DSI matter'.

(7) In subsection (5), for 'or conduct matter' substitute ', conduct matter or DSI matter'.

(8) In subsections (6) and (7), for 'or recordable conduct matter' substitute ', recordable conduct matter or DSI matter'.

(9) After subsection (9)(b) insert—

'(ba) whether the Commission or the appropriate authority has made a determination under paragraph 21A of Schedule 3;'.

(10) In subsection (9)(c), after 'paragraph 22' insert 'or 24A'.

(11) In subsection (10), for 'or recordable conduct matter' substitute ', recordable conduct matter or DSI matter'.

8 (1) Section 22 (power of Commission to issue guidance) is amended as follows.

(2) In subsection (2)(b)(ii), after 'recordable conduct matters' insert 'or DSI matters'.

(3) In subsection (5)—

(a) in paragraph (a), after 'recordable conduct matters' insert 'or DSI matters';

(b) in paragraphs (b) and (d)(ii), after 'recordable conduct matter' insert 'or DSI matter'; and

(c) in paragraph (e)(i), for 'or conduct matter' substitute ', conduct matter or DSI matter'.

9 (1) Section 23(2) (regulations) is amended as follows.

(2) In paragraph (b), after 'recordable conduct matters' insert 'and DSI matters'.

(3) For paragraph (h) substitute—

'(h) for combining into a single investigation the investigation of any complaint, conduct matter or DSI matter with the investigation or investigations of any one or more, or any combination, of the following—
   (i) complaints (whether or not relating to the same conduct),
   (ii) conduct matters, or
   (iii) DSI matters,
and for splitting a single investigation into two or more separate investigations;'.

(4) In paragraph (j), for 'or conduct matter' substitute ', conduct matter or DSI matter'.

(5) In paragraph (n)(ii), after 'recordable conduct matters' insert 'or DSI matters'.

10 (1) Section 29 (interpretation) is amended as follows.

  (2) In subsection (1)—

    (a) for the definition of 'the appropriate authority' substitute—

     ' "the appropriate authority"—
       (a) in relation to a person serving with the police or in relation to any complaint, conduct matter or investigation relating to the conduct of such a person, means—
         (i) if that person is a senior officer, the police authority for the area of the police force of which he is a member; and
         (ii) if he is not a senior officer, the chief officer under whose direction and control he is;'; and
       (b) in relation to a death or serious injury matter, means—
         (i) if the relevant officer is a senior officer, the police authority for the area of the police force of which he is a member; and
         (ii) if he is not a senior officer, the chief officer under whose direction and control he is;'; and

    (b) after the definition of 'conduct matter' insert—

     ' "death or serious injury matter" and "DSI matter" have the meaning given by section 12;'.

  (3) After subsection (1) insert—

    '(1A) In this Part "the relevant officer", in relation to a DSI matter, means the person serving with the police (within the meaning of section 12 (7))—
      (a) who arrested the person who has died or suffered serious injury,
      (b) in whose custody that person was at the time of the death or serious injury, or
      (c) with whom that person had the contact in question;
     and where there is more than one such person it means, subject to subsection (1B), the one who so dealt with him last before the death or serious injury occurred.
    (1B) Where it cannot be determined which of two or more persons serving with the police dealt with a person last before a death or serious injury occurred, the relevant officer is the most senior of them.'

11 Schedule 3 (handling of complaints and conduct matters) is amended as set out in the following paragraphs.

12 After paragraph 14 insert—

'PART 2A
HANDLING OF DEATH AND SERIOUS INJURY (DSI) MATTERS

Duty to record DSI matters

14A(1) Where a DSI matter comes to the attention of the police authority or chief officer who is the appropriate authority in relation to that matter, it shall be the duty of the appropriate authority to record that matter.

(2) If it appears to the Commission—

    (a) that any matter that has come to its attention is a DSI matter, but

    (b) that that matter has not been recorded by the appropriate authority,

the Commission may direct the appropriate authority to record that matter; and it shall be the duty of that authority to comply with the direction.

Duty to preserve evidence relating to DSI matters

14B (1) Where—

    (a) a DSI matter comes to the attention of a police authority, and

    (b) the relevant officer in relation to that matter is the chief officer of the force maintained by that authority,

it shall be the duty of that authority to secure that all such steps as are appropriate for the purposes of Part 2 of this Act are taken, both initially and from time to time after that, for obtaining and preserving evidence relating to that matter.

(2) Where—

    (a) a chief officer becomes aware of a DSI matter, and

    (b) the relevant officer in relation to that matter is a person under his direction and control,

it shall be his duty to take all such steps as appear to him to be appropriate for the purposes of Part 2 of this Act for obtaining and preserving evidence relating to that matter.

(3) The chief officer's duty under sub-paragraph (2) must be performed as soon as practicable after he becomes aware of the matter in question.

(4) After that, he shall be under a duty, until he is satisfied that it is no longer necessary to do so, to continue to take the steps from time to time appearing to him to be appropriate for the purposes of Part 2 of this Act for obtaining and preserving evidence relating to the matter.

(5) It shall be the duty of a police authority to comply with all such directions as may be given to it by the Commission in relation to the performance of any duty imposed on it by virtue of sub-paragraph (1).

(6) It shall be the duty of the chief officer to take all such specific steps for obtaining or preserving evidence relating to any DSI matter as he may be directed to take for the purposes of this paragraph by the police authority maintaining his force or by the Commission.

Reference of DSI matters to the Commission

14C (1) It shall be the duty of the appropriate authority to refer a DSI matter to the Commission.

(2) The appropriate authority must do so within such period as may be provided for by regulations made by the Secretary of State.

(3) A matter that has already been referred to the Commission under this paragraph on a previous occasion shall not be required to be referred again under this paragraph unless the Commission so directs.

Duties of Commission on references under paragraph 14C

14D (1) It shall be the duty of the Commission, in the case of every DSI matter referred to it by a police authority or a chief officer, to determine whether or not it is necessary for the matter to be investigated.

(2) Where the Commission determines under this paragraph that it is not necessary for a DSI matter to be investigated, it may if it thinks fit refer the matter back to the appropriate authority to be dealt with by that authority in such manner (if any) as that authority may determine.'

13 In paragraph 15(1)(a) and (8) (power of the Commission to determine the form of an investigation), for 'or recordable conduct matter' substitute ', recordable conduct matter or DSI matter'.

14 (1) Paragraph 16 (investigations by the appropriate authority on its own behalf) is amended as follows.

(2) In sub-paragraph (1), for 'or recordable conduct matter ' substitute ', recordable conduct matter or DSI matter'.

(3) In sub-paragraph (2)(a), after 'recordable conduct matter' insert 'or under paragraph 14D(2) in relation to any DSI matter'.

(4) In sub-paragraph (3), after '(4)' insert 'or (5)'.

(5) In sub-paragraph (4), for 'matter' substitute 'conduct matter'.

(6) After sub-paragraph (4) add—

'(5) The person appointed under this paragraph to investigate any DSI matter—
(a) in relation to which the relevant officer is a chief officer, must not be a person under that chief officer's direction and control;
(b) in relation to which the relevant officer is the Commissioner of Police of the Metropolis or the Deputy Commissioner of Police of the Metropolis, must be the person nominated by the Secretary of State for appointment under this paragraph.'

15 (1) Paragraph 17 (investigations supervised by the Commission) is amended as follows.

(2) In sub-paragraph (1), for 'or recordable conduct matter' substitute', recordable conduct matter or DSI matter'.

(3) In sub-paragraph (6), for 'matter' substitute 'conduct matter'.

(4) After sub-paragraph (6) insert—

'(6A) The person appointed under this paragraph to investigate any DSI matter—
(a) in relation to which the relevant officer is a chief officer, must not be a person under that chief officer's direction and control;
(b) in relation to which the relevant officer is the Commissioner of Police of the Metropolis or the Deputy Commissioner of Police of the Metropolis, must be the person nominated by the Secretary of State for appointment under this paragraph.'

16 (1) Paragraph 18 (investigations managed by the Commission) is amended as follows.

(2) In sub-paragraph (1), for 'or recordable conduct matter' substitute ', recordable conduct matter or DSI matter'.

(3) In sub-paragraph (2), for '(6)' substitute '(6A)'.

17 (1) Paragraph 19 (investigations by the Commission itself) is amended as follows.

(2) In sub-paragraph (1), for 'or recordable conduct matter' substitute ', recordable conduct matter or DSI matter'.

(3) After sub-paragraph (3) insert—

'(3A) The person designated under sub-paragraph (2) to be the person to take charge of an investigation of a DSI matter in relation to which the relevant officer is the Commissioner of Police of the Metropolis or the Deputy Commissioner of Police of the Metropolis must be the person nominated by the Secretary of State to be so designated under that subparagraph.'

18 In paragraph 20(1) (restrictions on proceedings pending the conclusion of an investigation), after '22' insert 'or 24A'.

19 In paragraph 21(4) (power of the Commission to discontinue an investigation), for 'or recordable conduct matter ' substitute', recordable conduct matter or DSI matter'.

20 After paragraph 21 insert—

'Procedure where conduct matter is revealed during investigation of DSI matter

21A (1) If during the course of an investigation of a DSI matter it appears to a person appointed under paragraph 18 or designated under paragraph 19 that there is an indication that a person serving with the police ("the person whose conduct is in question") may have—
   (a) committed a criminal offence, or
   (b) behaved in a manner which would justify the bringing of disciplinary proceedings,
   he shall make a submission to that effect to the Commission.

(2) If, after considering a submission under sub-paragraph (1), the Commission determines that there is such an indication, it shall—
   (a) notify the appropriate authority in relation to the DSI matter and (if different) the appropriate authority in relation to the person whose conduct is in question of its determination; and
   (b) send to it (or each of them) a copy of the submission under sub-paragraph (1).

(3) If during the course of an investigation of a DSI matter it appears to a person appointed under paragraph 16 or 17 that there is an indication that a person serving with the police ("the person whose conduct is in question") may have—
   (a) committed a criminal offence, or
   (b) behaved in a manner which would justify the bringing of disciplinary proceedings,
   he shall make a submission to that effect to the appropriate authority in relation to the DSI matter.

(4) If, after considering a submission under sub-paragraph (3), the appropriate authority determines that there is such an indication, it shall—
   (a) if it is not the appropriate authority in relation to the person whose conduct is in question, notify that other authority of its determination and send to that authority a copy of the submission under sub-paragraph (3); and
   (b) notify the Commission of its determination and send to it a copy of the submission under sub-paragraph (3).

(5) Where the appropriate authority in relation to the person whose conduct is in question—
   (a) is notified of a determination by the Commission under sub-paragraph (2),
   (b) (in a case where it is also the appropriate authority in relation to the DSI matter) makes a determination under sub-paragraph (4), or
   (c) (in a case where it is not the appropriate authority in relation to the DSI matter) is notified by that other authority of a determination by it under sub-paragraph (4),
   it shall record the matter under paragraph 11 as a conduct matter (and the other provisions of this Schedule shall apply in relation to that matter accordingly).'

21 For paragraph 22 (final reports on investigations) substitute—

'Final reports on investigations: complaints, conduct matters and certain DSI matters

22 (1) This paragraph applies on the completion of an investigation of—
   (a) a complaint,
   (b) a conduct matter, or

      (c) a DSI matter in respect of which the Commission or the appropriate authority has made a determination under paragraph 21A (2) or (4).

(2) A person appointed under paragraph 16 shall submit a report on his investigation to the appropriate authority.

(3) A person appointed under paragraph 17 or 18 shall—

      (a) submit a report on his investigation to the Commission; and

      (b) send a copy of that report to the appropriate authority.

(4) In relation to a DSI matter in respect of which a determination has been made under paragraph 21A(2) or (4), the references in sub-paragraphs (2) and (3) of this paragraph to the appropriate authority are references to—

      (a) the appropriate authority in relation to the DSI matter; and

      (b) (where different) the appropriate authority in relation to the person whose conduct is in question.

(5) A person designated under paragraph 19 as the person in charge of an investigation by the Commission itself shall submit a report on it to the Commission.

(6) A person submitting a report under this paragraph shall not be prevented by any obligation of secrecy imposed by any rule of law or otherwise from including all such matters in his report as he thinks fit.'

22 (1) In the heading preceding paragraph 23, after 'investigation report' insert 'under paragraph 22'.

    (2) In paragraph 23(1)—

      (a) in paragraph (a), for '(2)' substitute '(3)'; and

      (b) in paragraph (b), for '(3)' substitute '(5)'.

    (3) After paragraph 23(12) insert—

      '(13) In relation to a DSI matter in respect of which a determination has been made under paragraph 21A(2) or (4), the references in this paragraph to the appropriate authority are references to the appropriate authority in relation to the person whose conduct is in question.'

23 (1) In the heading preceding paragraph 24, after 'investigation report' insert 'under paragraph 22'.

    (2) In paragraph 24(1)—

      (a) in paragraph (a), for '22(1)' substitute '22(2)'; and

      (b) in paragraph (b), for '22(2)' substitute '22(3)'.

    (3) After paragraph 24(10) insert—

      '(11) In relation to a DSI matter in respect of which a determination has been made under paragraph 21A(2) or (4), the references in this paragraph to the appropriate authority are references to the appropriate authority in relation to the person whose conduct is in question.'

24 After paragraph 24 insert—

'Final reports on investigations: other DSI matters

  24A (1) This paragraph applies on the completion of an investigation of a DSI matter in respect of which neither the Commission nor the appropriate authority has made a determination under paragraph 21A(2) or (4).

      (2) A person appointed under paragraph 16, 17 or 18 or designated under paragraph 19 shall—

         (a) submit a report on the investigation to the Commission; and

         (b) send a copy of that report to the appropriate authority.

      (3) A person submitting a report under this paragraph shall not be prevented by any

obligation of secrecy imposed by any rule of law or otherwise from including all such matters in his report as he thinks fit.

(4) On receipt of the report, the Commission shall determine whether the report indicates that a person serving with the police may have—

    (a) committed a criminal offence, or

    (b) behaved in a manner which would justify the bringing of disciplinary proceedings.

Action by the Commission in response to an investigation report under paragraph 24A

24B (1) If the Commission determines under paragraph 24A(4) that the report indicates that a person serving with the police may have—

    (a) committed a criminal offence, or

    (b) behaved in a manner which would justify the bringing of disciplinary proceedings,

it shall notify the appropriate authority in relation to the person whose conduct is in question of its determination and, if it appears that that authority has not already been sent a copy of the report, send a copy of the report to that authority.

(2) Where the appropriate authority in relation to the person whose conduct is in question is notified of a determination by the Commission under sub-paragraph (1), it shall record the matter under paragraph 11 as a conduct matter (and the other provisions of this Schedule shall apply in relation to that matter accordingly).

24C (1) If the Commission determines under paragraph 24A(4) that there is no indication in the report that a person serving with the police may have—

    (a) committed a criminal offence, or

    (b) behaved in a manner which would justify the bringing of disciplinary proceedings,

it shall make such recommendations or give such advice under section 10 (1)(e) (if any) as it considers necessary or desirable.

(2) Sub-paragraph (1) does not affect any power of the Commission to make recommendations or give advice under section 10(1)(e) in other cases (whether arising under this Schedule or otherwise).'

Section 161   SCHEDULE 13

ABOLITION OF ROYAL PARKS CONSTABULARY: SUPPLEMENTARY

PART 1
TRANSFERS TO METROPOLITAN POLICE AUTHORITY

Interpretation

1   In this Part of this Schedule—

'the Authority' means the Metropolitan Police Authority, and
'transfer scheme' means a scheme made by the Secretary of State under this Schedule.

Establishment of eligibility for transfer

2   The Secretary of State may by regulations impose requirements in relation to persons serving as park constables with the Royal Parks Constabulary for the purpose of establishing whether they are eligible—

      (a) to be employed by the Authority, or

      (b) to serve as a members of the police force for the metropolitan police district.

3 (1) The Secretary of State may terminate the Crown employment of any person who fails to comply with or satisfy any requirement imposed in relation to him by regulations made under paragraph 2.

    (2) A person whose Crown employment is terminated under sub-paragraph (1) is not to be treated (whether for the purposes of any enactment or otherwise) as being dismissed by virtue of that termination.

Relevant persons

4 (1) A transfer scheme may provide for any relevant person to become an employee of the Authority on the appointed day.

    (2) The scheme may make provision—

      (a) for the termination of the relevant person's Crown employment on the appointed day,

      (b) as to the terms and conditions which are to have effect as the terms and conditions of the relevant person's contract of employment with the Authority,

      (c) transferring to the Authority the rights, powers, duties and liabilities of the employer under or in connection with the relevant person's Crown employment,

      (d) for things done before the appointed day by or in relation to the employer in respect of the relevant person or his Crown employment to be treated from that day as having been done by or in relation to the Authority,

      (e) for the period during which the relevant person has been in Crown employment to count as a period of employment with the Authority (and for the operation of the transfer scheme not to be treated as having interrupted the continuity of that employment), and

      (f) for the termination of the Crown employment of a relevant person who would otherwise be transferred by the scheme but who has informed the Secretary of State that he does not wish to be so transferred.

    (3) The scheme may provide for a person who would be treated (whether by an enactment or otherwise) as being dismissed by the operation of the scheme not to be so treated.

5 (1) A transfer scheme may provide for the appointment as a member of the police force for the metropolitan police district of any relevant person who becomes an employee of the Authority by virtue of the scheme.

    (2) The appointment does not take effect until the person has been attested as a constable for the metropolitan police district in accordance with section 29 of the Police Act 1996 (c. 16).

    (3) On being so attested his contract of employment with the Authority is terminated by virtue of this sub-paragraph.

    (4) He is not to be treated (whether for the purposes of any enactment or otherwise) as being dismissed by virtue of the operation of sub-paragraph (3).

Property, rights and liabilities, etc.

6 (1) The transfer scheme may provide for the transfer of property, rights and liabilities of the Secretary of State to the Authority on the appointed day.

  (2) The scheme may include provision for anything (including any legal proceedings) which relates to anything transferred by virtue of sub-paragraph (1) to be continued from the appointed day by or in relation to the Authority.

Consultation

7 Before making a transfer scheme which contains any provision relating to persons serving as park constables with the Royal Parks Constabulary the Secretary of State must consult such bodies appearing to represent the interests of those persons as he considers appropriate.

Termination of employment

8 The Secretary of State may by regulations make provision as to the consequences of the termination of a person's Crown employment under paragraph 3(1) or by a transfer scheme (including provision removing any entitlement to compensation which might otherwise arise in such circumstances).

PART 2
AMENDMENTS

Royal Parks (Trading) Act 2000 (c. 13)

9 In section 4 of the Royal Parks (Trading) Act 2000 (seizure of property) after subsection (3) add—

  '(4) In the application of this section to a specified park—
    (a) the reference in subsection (1) to a park constable has effect as a reference to a constable, and
    (b) subsections (2) and (3) do not apply.
  (5) In subsection (4) "specified park" has the same meaning as in section 162 of the Serious Organised Crime and Police Act 2005.'

Regulation of Investigatory Powers Act 2000 (c. 23)

10 In Schedule 1 to the Regulation of Investigatory Powers Act 2000 (relevant authorities) omit paragraph 27D and the cross-heading before it.

Police Reform Act 2002 (c. 30)

11 The Police Reform Act 2002 has effect subject to the following amendments.

12 (1) Section 82 (police nationality requirements) is amended as follows.
  (2) In subsection (1)—
    (a) at the end of paragraph (e) insert 'or', and
    (b) omit paragraph (f).

(3) In subsection (3)(e) for 'the Civil Nuclear Constabulary or the Royal Parks Constabulary' substitute 'or the Civil Nuclear Constabulary'.

(4) Omit subsection (5).

13 (1) Schedule 4 (powers exercisable by police civilians) is amended as follows.

(2) In paragraph 2(6) after paragraph (aa) insert—

'(ab) an offence committed in a specified park which by virtue of section 2 of the Parks Regulation (Amendment) Act 1926 is an offence against the Parks Regulation Act 1872; or'.

(3) After paragraph 7C insert—

'Park Trading offences

7D (1) This paragraph applies if—

(a) a designation applies it to any person ("the CSO"), and

(b) the CSO has under paragraph 2(3) required another person ("P") to wait with him for the arrival of a constable.

(2) If the CSO reasonably suspects that P has committed a park trading offence, the CSO may take possession of anything of a non-perishable nature which—

(a) P has in his possession or under his control, and

(b) the CSO reasonably believes to have been used in the commission of the offence.

(3) The CSO may retain possession of the thing in question for a period not exceeding 30 minutes unless P makes an election under paragraph 2(4), in which case the CSO may retain possession of the thing in question until he is able to transfer control of it to a constable.

(4) In this paragraph "park trading offence" means an offence committed in a specified park which is a park trading offence for the purposes of the Royal Parks (Trading) Act 2000.'

(4) In paragraph 36 after sub-paragraph (3) insert—

'(3A) In this Schedule "specified park" has the same meaning as in section 162 of the Serious Organised Crime and Police Act 2005.'

Section 163   SCHEDULE 14

AMENDMENTS OF PART 5 OF POLICE ACT 1997

1 Part 5 of the Police Act 1997 (c. 50) (certificates of criminal records etc.) is amended as follows.

2 In section 114(3) for 'Section 113(3) to (5)' substitute 'Sections 113A(3) to (6) and 113C to 113F'.

3 In section 116—

(a) in the application to Scotland of subsection (2)(b) for 'to which subsection (3) or (4) of section 115 applies' substitute 'of such description as may be prescribed';

(b) in subsection (3) for 'Section 115(6) to (10)33 substitute 'Sections 113B (3) to (11) and 113C to 113F'.

4 In section 119—

(a) in subsection (1A) for 'section 113(3A) or (3C) or (3EA) or (3EC)' substitute 'section 113C(3) or 113D(3)';

(b) in subsection (2) for '115' substitute '113B'.

5   In section 119A(2) for the words from 'under' to 'adults' substitute 'in a list mentioned in section 113C(3) or 113D(3)';

6   In section 120—

    (a) in subsection (3)(b) for '113 or 115' substitute '113A or 113B';

    (b) in subsection (5)(b) for '113 or 115' substitute '113A or 113B';

    (c) in subsection (7) or '113' substitute '113A'.

7   In section 120ZA(4)(b) for '113 or 115' substitute '113A or 113B'.

8   In section 120A (as inserted by section 134(1) of the Criminal Justice and Police Act 2001 (c. 16))—

    (a) in subsection (3)(b) for 'section 113(3A) or (3C) or (3EA) or (3EC)' substitute 'section 113C(3) or 113D(3)';

    (b) in subsection (5) for '113' substitute '113A'.

9   In section 120A (as inserted by section 70 of the Criminal Justice (Scotland) Act 2003 (asp 7))—

    (a) in subsection (3)(a) for '113' substitute '113A';

    (b) in subsection (3)(b) for '113(3C)' substitute '113C(3) or 113D(3)';

    (c) after subsection (6) (as inserted by section 165(2) of this Act) insert—

      '(7) In the case of such a body the reference in subsection (5) to a police authority must be construed as a reference to such body as is prescribed.'

10 In section 121 for 'under section 114(2), 115(4) or (10), 116(2), 122(1) or (2) or 125' substitute 'in relation to the making of regulations or orders'.

11 In section 122(3) and (4)(b) for '113 or 115' substitute '113A or 113B'.

12 In section 124—

    (a) in subsections (1), (2), (3), (4) and (6) for '113 or 115' substitute '113A or 113B';

    (b) in subsection (5) for '115(8)' substitute '113B(5)';

    (c) in subsection (6)(e) for '113' substitute '113A'.

13 In section 124B—

    (a) in subsection (1) for '113' substitute '113A';

    (b) in subsection (3) for '113(5)' substitute '113A(6)'.

14 In section 125, at the end add—

    '(6) If the power mentioned in subsection (1) is exercised by the Scottish Ministers, the reference in subsection (3) to each House of Parliament must be construed as a reference to the Scottish Parliament.'

Section 171   SCHEDULE 15

PRIVATE SECURITY INDUSTRY ACT 2001: SCOTTISH EXTENT

1   The Private Security Industry Act 2001 (c. 12) is amended as follows.

2   In section 2 (directions etc. by the Secretary of State)—

    (a) in subsection (2), the existing words 'shall consult the Authority' become paragraph (a) and after that paragraph add ' and

      (b) where any of those directions relates wholly or mainly to the exercise of the Authority's activities in or as regards Scotland, shall obtain the consent of the Scottish Ministers.'; and

(b) in subsection (3), the existing words 'the Secretary of State with such information about its activities as he may request' become paragraph (a) and after that paragraph add ' and

(b) the Scottish Ministers with such information about its activities in or as regards Scotland as they may request.'

3 After section 2 insert—

'2A Authority to be treated as cross-border public authority etc. for certain purposes

For the purposes of—

(a) section 5(5B) of the Parliamentary Commissioner Act 1967 (restriction on investigatory powers of Parliamentary Commissioner for Administration);

(b) section 23(2)(b) of the Scotland Act 1998 (power of Scottish Parliament to require persons outside Scotland to give evidence or produce documents);

(c) section 70(6) of that Act of 1998 (accounts prepared by cross-border authorities);

(d) section 91(3)(d) of that Act of 1998 (provision for investigation of certain complaints); and

(e) section 7(5) of the Scottish Public Services Ombudsman Act 2002 (restriction on investigatory powers of ombudsman),

the Authority is to be treated as a cross-border public authority within the meaning of that Act of 1998.'

4 In section 3 (conduct prohibited without a licence), after subsection (3) insert—

'(3A) In the application of this Act to Scotland—

(a) the reference in subsection (3) to the Secretary of State must be construed as a reference to the Scottish Ministers; but

(b) before making any order under subsection (3) the Scottish Ministers are to consult the Secretary of State.'

5 In section 7 (licensing criteria), after subsection (5) insert—

'(5A) Before giving approval under subsection (5), the Secretary of State shall consult the Scottish Ministers.'

6 In section 11 (appeals in licensing matters)—

(a) in subsection (1), after 'court' insert '(in Scotland, to the sheriff)';

(b) in subsection (4), the existing words from 'a magistrates' ' to 'Crown Court' become paragraph (a) and after that paragraph insert ' or

(b) the sheriff makes a decision on an appeal under that subsection, an appeal to the Sheriff Principal,'; and

(c) in subsection (6)(d), the existing words from 'the appropriate' to the end become sub-paragraph (i) and after that sub-paragraph add ' or

(ii) the sheriff or the Sheriff Principal may direct pending an appeal from a determination made on an appeal to the sheriff.'

7 In section 13 (licensing at local authority level), at the end add—

'(8) This section does not apply to Scotland.'

8 In section 15(1) (duty to secure arrangements are in force for granting certain approvals), at the end of paragraph (a) add 'or in Scotland'.

9 In section 18 (appeals relating to approvals)—

(a) in subsection (1), after 'court' insert '(in Scotland, to the sheriff)';

(b) in subsection (4), the existing words from 'a magistrates' to 'Crown Court' become paragraph (a) and after that paragraph insert ' or

    (b) the sheriff makes a decision on an appeal under that subsection, an appeal to the Sheriff Principal,'; and

(c) in subsection (5)(d), the existing words from 'the appropriate' to the end become sub-paragraph (i) and after that sub-paragraph add ' or

    (ii) the sheriff or the Sheriff Principal may direct pending an appeal from a determination made on an appeal to the sheriff.'

10 In section 23 (criminal liability of directors etc.), the existing words become subsection (1) and after that subsection add—

    '(2) Where an offence under any provision of this Act is committed by a Scottish partnership and is proved to have been committed with the consent or connivance of, or to be attributable to any neglect on the part of—

    (a) a partner; or

    (b) any person who was purporting to be a partner;

    he (as well as the partnership) shall be guilty of that offence and liable to be proceeded against and punished accordingly.'

11 In section 24 (consultation with Security Industry Authority before making orders or regulations etc.)—

(a) after subsection (1) insert—

    '(1A) But in Scotland "prescribed" in paragraph 8(3)(d) of Schedule 2 to this Act includes prescribed by regulations made by the Scottish Ministers';

(b) in subsection (2), after 'Secretary of State' insert 'or the Scottish Ministers';

(c) in subsection (3), after paragraph (b) insert 'or

    (c) an order or regulations made by the Scottish Ministers,';

(d) after subsection (3) insert—

    '(3A) A statutory instrument containing an order or regulations made by the Scottish Ministers, other than an order under section 26(2), shall be subject to annulment in pursuance of a resolution of the Scottish Parliament.';

(e) in subsection (4), after 'consult' insert 'the Scottish Ministers (except where the order is made by virtue of section 3(2)(j)) and'; and

(f) in subsection (5)(b), at the end add '(or where the order is, or regulations are, made by the Scottish Ministers, as the Scottish Ministers think fit)'.

12 In section 26 (short title, commencement and extent)—

(a) after subsection (2) insert—

    '(2A) In the application of this Act to Scotland—

    (a) the reference in subsection (2) to the Secretary of State must be construed as a reference to the Scottish Ministers; but

    (b) before making any order under subsection (2) the Scottish Ministers are to consult the Secretary of State.'; and

(b) in subsection (4), after 'Wales' insert 'and to Scotland'.

13 In Schedule 1 (the Security Industry Authority)—

(a) in paragraph 1 (membership and chairman), at the end add—

    '(4) Before appointing the chairman, the Secretary of State shall consult the Scottish Ministers.';

(b) in paragraph 3 (removal from office), the existing words become sub-paragraph (1) and after that sub-paragraph insert—

'(2) Before removing a person from office as chairman of the Authority, the Secretary of State shall consult the Scottish Ministers.';

(c) in paragraph 6 (staff etc.), after sub-paragraph (2), insert—

'(2A) Before giving consent under sub-paragraph (2), the Secretary of State shall consult the Scottish Minister.';

(d) in paragraph 14 (money), after sub-paragraph (1) insert—

'(1A) The Scottish Ministers may make payments to the Authority out of the Scottish Consolidated Fund in relation to the exercise by the Authority of its functions in or as regards Scotland.';

(e) in paragraph 16 (accounts)—
   (i) in sub-paragraph (3), after second 'State' insert ', to the Scottish Minister'; and
   (ii) after sub-paragraph (3) insert—

'(3A) The Scottish Ministers shall present documents received by them under sub-paragraph (3) to the Scottish Parliament.'; and

(f) in paragraph 17 (annual report)—
   (i) in sub-paragraph (1), after 'State' insert 'and to the Scottish Ministers'; and
   (ii) at the end add—

'(3) The Scottish Ministers shall lay a copy of each such report before the Scottish Parliament.'

14 In Schedule 2 (activities liable to control under the Private Security Industry Act 2001 (c. 12))—

(a) in paragraph 3 (immobilisation of vehicles), at the end add—

'(4) This paragraph does not apply to any activities carried out in Scotland.';

(b) in paragraph 4 (private investigations), after sub-paragraph (4) insert—

'(4A) This paragraph does not apply to any activities of a person who is an advocate or solicitor in Scotland in the provision of legal services—
   (a) by him;
   (b) by any firm of which he is a partner or by which he is employed;
   (c) by any body corporate of which he is a director or member or by which he is employed.';

(c) after paragraph 4 insert—

'Taking precognitions

4A (1) This paragraph applies (subject to sub-paragraph (2)) to the taking, other than on behalf of the Crown, of a precognition for the purposes of, or in anticipation of—
   (a) criminal or civil proceedings in Scotland; or
   (b) proceedings on an application under section 65(7) or (9) of the Children (Scotland) Act 1995.
(2) This paragraph does not apply to any activities of a person who is an advocate or solicitor in Scotland.';

(d) in paragraph 8(2) (door supervisors etc. for public houses, clubs and comparable venues) after paragraph (e) add—

'(f) any premises specified in a public house licence (within the meaning of the Licensing (Scotland) Act 1976) which is for the time being in force;
(g) any premises specified in an hotel licence (within the meaning of that Act) which is for the time being in force;

(h) any premises specified in an entertainment licence (within the meaning of that Act) which is for the time being in force if they comprise a dance hall;

(i) any premises comprised in a place to which an occasional licence granted under section 33(1) of that Act (occasional licence for premises other than licensed premises or clubs) to the holder of a public house licence or hotel licence extends;

(j) any premises comprised in a place to which an occasional permission granted under section 34(1) of that Act (occasional permission for sale of alcohol in the course of catering for events arising from or related to the activities of a voluntary organisation) extends;

(k) any premises comprised in a place or class of place for the time being specified by resolution under section 9(5)(b) of the Civic Government (Scotland) Act 1982 (resolution specifying place or class of place falling to be licensed if to be used as place of public entertainment);

(l) any premises comprised in a place where an activity for the time being designated under section 44(1) of that Act (additional activities for which a licence is required) is carried on provided that, in the case of an activity designated under paragraph (a) of that section, the requisite resolution under section 9 of that Act has been obtained;'; and

(e) after paragraph 9 add—

'Taking precognitions

10 This paragraph applies to any activities which are activities of a security operative by virtue of paragraph 4A of this Schedule.'

Section 174 | **SCHEDULE 16**

REMAINING MINOR AND CONSEQUENTIAL AMENDMENTS (SEARCH WARRANTS)

Incitement to Disaffection Act 1934 (c. 56)

1 In section 2 of the Incitement to Disaffection Act 1934 (which makes provision about search warrants), in subsection (2), for 'one month' substitute 'three months'.

Public Order Act 1936 (1 Edw. 8 & 1 Geo. 6 c. 6)

2 In section 2 of the Public Order Act 1936 (prohibition of quasi-military organisations), in subsection (5), for 'one month' substitute 'three months'.

Wireless Telegraphy Act 1949 (c. 54)

3 In section 15 of the Wireless Telegraphy Act 1949 (entry and search of premises), in subsection (1), for 'one month' substitute 'three months'.

Licensing Act 1964 (c. 26)

4 Until their repeal by the Licensing Act 2003 (c. 17), the following provisions of the Licensing Act 1964 have effect as if for 'one month' there were substituted 'three months'—

section 54 (search warrants relating to clubs),
section 85(1) (search warrants relating to parties organised for gain),
section 187(1) (search warrants relating to sale of alcohol).

Biological Weapons Act 1974 (c. 6)

5   In section 4 of the Biological Weapons Act 1974 (powers to search etc.), in subsection (1)(a), for 'one month' substitute 'three months'.

Copyright, Designs and Patents Act 1988 (c. 48)

6   (1) The Copyright, Designs and Patents Act 1988 is amended as follows.
     (2) In section 109 (search warrants), in subsection (3)(b), for '28 days' substitute 'three months'.
     (3) In section 200 (search warrants), in subsection (3)(b), for '28 days' substitute 'three months'.
     (4) In section 297B (search warrants), in subsection (3)(b), for '28 days' substitute 'three months'.

Computer Misuse Act 1990 (c. 18)

7   In section 14 of the Computer Misuse Act 1990 (search warrants), in subsection (3)(b), for 'twenty-eight days' substitute 'three months'.

Trade Marks Act 1994 (c. 26)

8   In section 92A of the Trade Marks Act 1994 (search warrants), in subsection (3) (b), for '28 days' substitute 'three months'.

Section 174   SCHEDULE 17

REPEALS AND REVOCATIONS

PART 1
REPEALS COMING INTO FORCE ON ROYAL ASSENT

Short title and chapter	*Extent of repeal*
Police Reform Act 2002 (c. 30)	Section 95. In Schedule 8, the reference to section 5 of the Police (Health and Safety) Act 1997 (c. 42).

PART 2
OTHER REPEALS AND REVOCATIONS

Short title and chapter or title and number	Extent of repeal or revocation
Unlawful Drilling Act 1819 (60 Geo. 3 & 1 Geo. 4 c. 1)	In section 2, the words ', or for any other person acting in their aid or assistance,'.
Vagrancy Act 1824 (c. 83)	Section 6.
Railway Regulation Act 1842 (c. 55)	Section 17.
Companies Clauses Consolidation Act 1845 (c. 16)	In section 156, the words ', and all persons called by him to his assistance,'.
Railways Clauses Consolidation Act 1845 (c. 20)	Sections 104 and 154.
Licensing Act 1872 (c. 94)	In section 12, the words 'may be apprehended, and'.
Public Stores Act 1875 (c. 25)	Section 12(1).
London County Council (General Powers) Act 1894 (c. ccxii)	In section 7, the words 'and any person called to the assistance of such constable or person authorised'.
London County Council (General Powers) Act 1900 (c. cclxviii)	In section 27, the words 'and any person called to the assistance of such constable or officer'.
Licensing Act 1902 (c. 28)	In section 1, the words 'apprehended and'. In section 2(1), the words 'may be apprehended, and'.
Protection of Animals Act 1911 (c. 27)	Section 12(1).
Official Secrets Act 1911 (c. 28)	Section 6.
Public Order Act 1936 (1 Edw. 8 & 1 Geo. 6 c. 6)	Section 7(3).
Army Act 1955 (3 & 4 Eliz. 2 c. 18)	Section 83BC(2)(k).
Air Force Act 1955 (3 & 4 Eliz. 2 c. 19)	Section 83BC(2)(k).
Naval Discipline Act 1957 (c. 53)	Section 52IJ(2)(k).
Public Records Act 1958 (c. 51)	In Schedule 1, in Part 2 of the Table at the end of paragraph 3, the entries relating to the Service Authorities for the National Crime Squad and the National Criminal Intelligence Service.
Street Offences Act 1959 (c. 57)	Section 1(3).
Trustee Investments Act 1961 (c. 62)	In section 11(4), in paragraph (a), the words ', the Service Authority for the National Crime Squad', and paragraph (e). In Part 2 of Schedule 1, paragraph 9(da).
Parliamentary Commissioner Act 1967 (c. 13)	In Schedule 2, the entries relating to the Service Authorities for the National Crime Squad and the National Criminal Intelligence Service.
Police (Scotland) Act 1967 (c. 77)	In section 33, in subsections (3) and (4), the words 'and the National Criminal Intelligence Service'. Section 38A(1)(ba). In section 41(4)(a), the words 'or by a member of the National Criminal Intelligence Service or of the National Crime Squad'.

Short title and chapter or title and number	Extent of repeal or revocation
Criminal Justice Act 1967 (c. 80)	In section 91(1), the words 'may be arrested without warrant by any person and'.
Leasehold Reform Act 1967 (c. 88)	Section 28(5)(bc).
Ministry of Housing and Local Government Provisional Order Confirmation (Greater London Parks and Open Spaces) Act 1967 (c. xxix)	In Article 19 of the Order set out in the Schedule, the words 'and any person called to the assistance of such constable or officer'.
Theft Act 1968 (c. 60)	Section 25(4).
Port of London Act 1968 (c. xxxii)	In section 2, the definition of 'arrestable offence'.
	Section 170.
Employment Agencies Act 1973 (c. 35)	In section 13(7)(f), the words ', the Service Authority for the National Criminal Intelligence Service, the Service Authority for the National Crime Squad'.
House of Commons Disqualification Act 1975 (c. 24)	Section 1(1)(da).
	In Schedule 1, in Part 2, the entries relating to the Service Authorities for the National Crime Squad and the National Criminal Intelligence Service.
Northern Ireland Assembly Disqualification Act 1975 (c. 25)	Section 1(1)(da).
	In Schedule 1, in Part 2, the entries relating to the Service Authorities for the National Crime Squad and the National Criminal Intelligence Service.
Sex Discrimination Act 1975 (c. 65)	In section 17(7), in the definition of 'chief officer of police', paragraph (aa), in the definition of 'police authority', paragraph (aa) and, in the definition of 'police fund' the words from ', in relation to' (in the second place where they occur) to 'the Police Act 1997'.
Police Pensions Act 1976 (c. 35)	In section 11(5), in paragraph (a) of the definition of 'central service', '(ca), (cb),'.
Race Relations Act 1976 (c. 74)	In section 76B, subsection (1) and, in subsection (2), the word 'also'.
	In Schedule 1A, in Part 1, paragraphs 59 and 60 and, in Part 3, the entry relating to the Director General of the National Crime Squad.
Criminal Law Act 1977 (c. 45)	Section 6(6).
	Section 7(6).
	Section 8(4).
	Section 9(7).
	In section 10(5), the words 'A constable in uniform,'.
Theft Act 1978 (c. 31)	Section 3(4).
Health and Safety at Work (Northern Ireland) Order 1978 (S.I. 1978/1039 (N.I. 9))	In Article 47A(2), sub-paragraph (b).
Animal Health Act 1981 (c. 22)	Section 61(1).
	Section 62(1).
Local Government (Miscellaneous Provisions) Act 1982 (c. 30)	In Schedule 3, paragraph 24.
Aviation Security Act 1982 (c. 36)	Section 28(3).

Short title and chapter or title and number	*Extent of repeal or revocation*
Stock Transfer Act 1982 (c. 41)	In Schedule 1, in paragraph 7(1), paragraph (bb) and the word 'or' before it.
Police and Criminal Evidence Act 1984 (c. 60)	Section 5(1A).
	In section 15(2)(a)(i), the word 'and' at the end.
	Section 25.
	Section 55(14A).
	In section 66(1)(a)(i), the word 'or' at the end.
	Section 116.
	In section 118(1), the definition of 'arrestable offence'.
	In Schedule 1, in paragraph 14(a), the words 'to which the application relates'.
	Schedule 1A.
	In Schedule 2, the entries relating to the Military Lands Act 1892 (c. 43), the Protection of Animals Act 1911 (c. 27), the Public Order Act 1936 (1 Edw. 8 & 1 Geo. 6 c. 6), the Street Offences Act 1959 (c. 57), the Criminal Law Act 1977 (c. 45) and the Animal Health Act 1981 (c. 22).
	Schedule 5.
	In Schedule 6, paragraph 17.
Prosecution of Offences Act 1985 (c. 23)	In section 3(3), in the definition of 'police force', the words', the National Crime Squad'.
Sporting Events (Control of Alcohol etc.) Act 1985 (c. 57)	In section 7(2), the words ', and may arrest such a person'.
Public Order Act 1986 (c. 64)	Section 3(6).
	Section 4(3).
	Section 4A(4).
	Section 5(4) and (5).
	Section 12(7).
	Section 13(10).
	Section 14(7).
	Section 14B(4).
	Section 14C(4).
	Section 18(3).
Ministry of Defence Police Act 1987 (c. 4)	In section 2B(3), in the definitions of 'chief officer' and 'relevant force', paragraphs (c) and (d).
Criminal Justice Act 1988 (c. 33)	Section 140(1)(a) and (b).
	In Schedule 15, paragraphs 98 and 102.
Road Traffic Act 1988 (c. 52)	Section 4(6) to (8).
	In section 124(2), the definitions of 'chief officer of police', 'police authority' and 'police force'.
	Section 144(2)(ba).
	Section 163(4).
Road Traffic (Consequential Provisions) Act 1988 (c. 54)	In Schedule 3, paragraph 27(5).
Football Spectators Act 1989 (c. 37)	Section 2(4).
Aviation and Maritime Security Act 1990 (c. 31)	In section 22(4)(b), sub-paragraph (iii) and the word 'or' before it.
	In Schedule 3, paragraph 8.

Short title and chapter or title and number	*Extent of repeal or revocation*
Football (Offences) Act 1991 (c. 19)	Section 5(1).
Road Traffic Act 1991 (c. 40)	In Schedule 4, paragraph 39.
Local Government Finance Act 1992 (c. 14)	In section 43(7)(b), ',(5A)'.
Transport and Works Act 1992 (c. 42)	Section 30(1) and (3).
	Section 40.
Trade Union and Labour Relations (Consolidation) Act 1992 (c. 52)	Section 241(3).
Tribunals and Inquiries Act 1992 (c. 53)	In section 7(2), after '36A', '(a) or (b)'.
	In Schedule 1, in paragraph 36A, '(a)' and sub-paragraph (b).
Criminal Justice and Public Order Act 1994 (c. 33)	Section 61(5).
	Section 62B(4).
	Section 63(8).
	Section 65(5).
	Section 68(4).
	Section 69(5).
	Section 76(7).
	Section 85(1), (2) and (3).
	Section 155.
	Section 166(4).
	Section 167(7).
	In Schedule 10, paragraph 59.
Drug Trafficking Act 1994 (c. 37)	In Schedule 1, paragraph 9 and, in paragraph 25, the words 'section 9(6) of' and the words after '1990'.
Criminal Appeal Act 1995 (c. 35)	In section 22(2), in paragraph (a), the words ', the National Crime Squad', paragraph (b)(ii) and paragraphs (d) and (e).
Criminal Procedure (Consequential Provisions) (Scotland) Act 1995 (c. 40)	In Schedule 4, paragraph 76(2).
Disability Discrimination Act 1995 (c. 50)	In the section 64A inserted by the Disability Discrimination Act 1995 (Amendment) Regulations 2003 (S.I. 2003/1673), in subsection (7), in the definitions of 'chief officer of police', 'police authority' and 'police fund', paragraph (b).
Reserve Forces Act 1996 (c. 14)	In Schedule 2, paragraph 2(1).
Police Act 1996 (c. 16)	Section 23(8).
	Section 24(5).
	In section 54(2), the words 'the National Criminal Intelligence Service and the National Crime Squad'.
	Section 55(7).
	Section 59(8).
	Section 60(2A).
	Section 61(1)(aa) and (ba).
	In section 62, subsection (1)(aa) and (ab), the subsection (1A) inserted by paragraph 82(2) of Schedule 9 to the Police Act 1997, and subsections (1B) and (1C).

Short title and chapter or title and number	*Extent of repeal or revocation*
Police Act 1996 (c. 16)—*continued*	In section 63, subsections (1A) and (1B).
	In section 64, subsections (4A) and (4B).
	In section 88(5)(b), the words 'or section 23 of the Police Act 1997'.
	In section 89(4)(a), the words 'or by a member of the National Crimina Intelligence Service or of the National Crime Squad'.
	Section 97(1)(ca) and (cb).
	In section 98, in subsections (2) and (3), the words 'or the Director General of the National Crime Squad' and 'or the National Crime Squad', subsection (3A), in subsection (4) the words 'or the National Crime Squad' and 'or the Director General of the National Crime Squad', in subsection (5) the words 'or the National Crime Squad' (in both places) and 'or the Director General of the National Crime Squad' and subsection (6A).
Employment Rights Act 1996 (c. 18)	Section 50(2)(ca).
Offensive Weapons Act 1996 (c. 26)	Section 1(1).
Public Order (Amendment) Act 1996 (c. 59)	The whole Act.
Juries (Northern Ireland) Order 1996 (S.I. 1996/1141 (N.I. 6))	In Schedule 2, the entry relating to members of the National Criminal Intelligence Service, members of the Service Authority for the National Criminal Intelligence Service and persons employed by the Authority.
Employment Rights (Northern Ireland) Order 1996 (S.I. 1996/1919 (N.I. 16))	Article 67KA(3)(b).
	Article 72A(2)(b).
	Article 169A(2)(b).
Confiscation of Alcohol (Young Persons) Act 1997 (c. 33)	Section 1(5).
Police (Health and Safety) Act 1997 (c. 42)	In section 5(3), in the definition of 'relevant authority' paragraphs (c) and (d), in the definition of 'relevant fund' paragraphs (b) and (c) and, in the definition of 'responsible officer', paragraph (b).
Police Act 1997 (c. 50)	Sections 1 to 87.
	Sections 89 and 90.
	In section 93(6), paragraphs (d) and (e).
	In section 94, in subsection (1) paragraph (c) and the word 'or' before it and subsections (3) and (4)(c).
	In section 111, in subsection (1), paragraphs (c) and (d), in subsection (2), paragraphs (d) and (e) and, in subsection (3), paragraphs (c) and (d).
	Section 113.
	Section 115.
	In section 125 as it applies to Scotland, subsection (3) and, in subsection (4), the words 'to which subsection (3) does not apply'.
	In section 137(2), paragraphs (b) and (c).
	Schedules 1 to 2A.

Short title and chapter or title and number	Extent of repeal or revocation
Police Act 1997 (c. 50)—*continued*	In Schedule 9, paragraphs 1, 4 to 6, 11, 14(b), 15, 16, 20, 26, 29(2), 30(2), 31, 44, 46 to 48, 54, 58 to 62, 69, 70, 71 (2)(a), (c), (d) and (3), 73, 74, 76, 77, 79 to 84, 86(3) and (4), 87, 88 and 92.
Police (Health and Safety) (Northern Ireland) Order 1997 (S.I. 1997/1774 (N.I. 6))	In Article 7(3), in the definition of 'the relevant authority', sub-paragraph (b), in the definition of 'the relevant fund', sub-paragraph (a) and, in the definition of 'the responsible officer', sub-paragraph (b).
Police (Northern Ireland) Act 1998 (c. 32)	Section 27(1)(b). In section 42, in subsection (1)', (3)', and subsection (7). In Schedule 4, paragraph 22.
Crime and Disorder Act 1998 (c. 37)	In section 1C, subsections (6) to (8). Section 27(1). Section 31(2) and (3). Section 113.
Protection of Children Act 1999 (c. 14)	Section 8.
Terrorism Act 2000 (c. 11)	In Schedule 15, paragraph 5(11).
Care Standards Act 2000 (c. 14)	Section 90. Section 102. Section 104. In Schedule 4, paragraph 25.
Regulation of Investigatory Powers Act 2000 (c. 23)	In section 33, in subsection (1) the words ', the National Criminal Intelligence Service or the National Crime Squad' and ', Service or Squad', in subsection (3) the words ', the National Criminal Intelligence Service or the National Crime Squad' and (in both places) ', Service or Squad' and, in subsection (6), in paragraph (e) the words 'and also of the National Criminal Intelligence Service' and paragraph (f). In section 34, subsections (5) and (6)(c). In section 45(6), paragraphs (d) and (e). In section 56(1), in the definition of 'chief officer of police', paragraphs (j) and (k) Section 75(6)(b). In section 76A(11)(c) the words 'the National Crime Squad or'. In Schedule 1, paragraph 27D and the cross-heading before it. In Schedule 4, paragraph 8(4)(c) and (5).
Football (Disorder) Act 2000 (c. 25)	Section 2. In Schedule 2, paragraph 2.
Police (Northern Ireland) Act 2000 (c. 32)	In Schedule 6, in paragraph 20, sub-paragraphs (4) to (7).
Freedom of Information Act 2000 (c. 36)	In section 23(3), the word 'and' at the end of paragraph (k). In Schedule 1, in Part 6, the entries relating to the National Crime Squad and the Service Authority for the National Crime Squad.

Short title and chapter or title and number	Extent of repeal or revocation
Criminal Justice and Court Services Act 2000 (c. 43)	In Schedule 7, paragraph 77.
Health and Social Care Act 2001 (c. 15)	Section 19.
Criminal Justice and Police Act 2001 (c. 16)	Section 42(8). Section 47(3). In section 104, subsection (3), in subsection (4) paragraph (c) and the word 'and' before it, and subsection (8). In section 107, subsections (1)(c) and (4). Sections 108 to 121. Section 138(6)(d). In Schedule 4, paragraph 7(3)(b). Schedule 5. In Schedule 6, paragraphs 1 to 21, 55, 56, 60, 61 and 77.
Anti-terrorism, Crime and Security Act 2001 (c. 24)	Section 39(8).
Regulation of Care (Scotland) Act 2001 (asp 8)	In Schedule 3, paragraph 21.
International Development Act 2002 (c. 1)	In Schedule 3, paragraphs 3(3), 11(3) and 12(3).
National Health Service Reform and Health Care Professions Act 2002 (c. 17)	In Schedule 2, paragraph 64.
Proceeds of Crime Act 2002 (c. 29)	In section 313(1), paragraphs (c) and (d). In section 330, subsection (5)(b), and, in subsection (9) (b), the words after 'employment'. Section 331(5)(b). In section 332(1) and (3), '337 or'. Section 332(5)(b). In section 337(5)(b), the words after 'employment'. In section 338, subsection (1)(b) (except the word 'and' at the end) and, in subsection (5)(b), the words after 'employment'. Section 339(5) and (6). In section 447(3)(a), the word 'or' at the end. In Schedule 11, paragraphs 3(3), 14(4), 30(3) and (4) and 34(3) and (4).
Police Reform Act 2002 (c. 30)	Section 8. In section 9(3)(e) the words 'is or'. In section 10, in subsection (1), at the end of paragraph (e) the word 'and', in paragraph (f) the words 'the National Criminal Intelligence Service, the National Crime Squad and', in subsection (3), paragraph (a) and, in paragraph (d), the words 'the National Criminal Intelligence Service, the National Crime Squad or' and, in subsection (7), the word 'or' at the end of paragraph (a). In section 15(6), the words from 'or, as the case may be' to the end of the subsection. Section 25.

Short title and chapter or title and number	Extent of repeal or revocation
Police Reform Act 2002 (c. 30)—*continued*	In section 38, subsection (3), in subsection (4) the words 'or a Director General' and, in subsection (7), the words 'or of a Service Authority'.
	Section 42(4) and (8).
	In section 45, in subsection (1) the words 'and by Directors General', in subsection (3) paragraphs (a), (b), (d) and (e) and, in subsection (5), the words 'or a Director General'.
	In section 47(1), the definitions of 'Director General' and 'Service Authority'.
	Section 48.
	Section 49(1).
	In section 82, subsection (1)(c) and (f), in subsection (2), paragraph (c) and the word 'or' before it, subsection (3) (d) and subsection (5).
	Sections 85 to 91.
	Section 93.
	In section 102, in subsection (2), paragraphs (c) and (d) and, in subsection (5), paragraphs (b) and (c).
	In section 103, subsections (2) and (3) and, in subsection (6), the words ', the NCIS service fund or the NCS service fund,'.
	Section 108(7)(e).
	Schedule 1.
	In Schedule 4, paragraph 2(5)(a) and (7), and in paragraph 36(1), paragraph (b) and the word 'and' before it.
	In Schedule 5, in paragraph 1(2)(aa), the words 'except in respect of an offence under section 12 of the Licensing Act 1872 or section 91 of the Criminal Justice Act 1967'.
	Schedule 6.
	In Schedule 7, paragraphs 16, 17, 19(2) and (3), 21 and 22(2).
Education Act 2002 (c. 32)	Part 2 of Schedule 12.
	In Schedule 13, paragraphs 7 and 8.
	In Schedule 21, paragraphs 72 and 73.
Adoption and Children Act 2002 (c. 38)	Section 135.
	In Schedule 3, paragraph 93.
Licensing Act 2003 (c. 17)	In Schedule 6, paragraphs 93 and 116.
Aviation (Offences) Act 2003 (c. 19)	Section 1(1).
Communications Act 2003 (c. 21)	Section 181(1).
Crime (International Cooperation) Act 2003 (c. 32)	In section 17(3), the words 'the Police and Criminal Evidence Act 1984 (c. 60) or (as the case may be)'.
	Section 85.
Anti-social Behaviour Act 2003 (c. 38)	Section 4(5).
	Section 23(5).
	Section 32(3).
	Section 37(3).
Courts Act 2003 (c. 39)	In Schedule 8, paragraphs 12 and 281(2).

Short title and chapter or title and number	*Extent of repeal or revocation*
Sexual Offences Act 2003 (c. 42)	In Schedule 6, paragraph 28(3) and (4).
Criminal Justice Act 2003 (c. 44)	Section 3.
	In Schedule 35, paragraphs 3 and 4.
Protection of Children (Scotland) Act 2003 (asp 5)	Section 12.
Criminal Justice (Scotland) Act 2003 (asp 7)	Section 70(3).
Protection of Children and Vulnerable Adults (Northern Ireland) Order 2003 (S.I. 2003/417 (N.I. 4))	Article 17(4) to (6).
	Article 47(3) to (5).
Energy Act 2004 (c. 20)	In section 59(3), in the definition of 'chief officer', paragraphs (c) and (d) and, in the definition of 'relevant force', paragraphs (c) and (d).
	In Schedule 14, paragraph 11(b).
Domestic Violence, Crime and Victims Act 2004 (c. 28)	Section 10(1).
	In Schedule 10, paragraph 24.
Hunting Act 2004 (c. 37)	Section 7.
Prevention of Terrorism Act 2005 (c. 2)	Section 9(9).
Serious Organised Crime and Police Act 2005 (c. 15)	Section 112(6) and (7).
	Section 126(2) and (3).
	Section 130(1).
	Section 136(5).

Index

accomplice evidence 4.03 *see also* **offenders assisting investigations and prosecutions**
all premises warrant 6.32
animal rights protestors 7.02
  interference with business contracts which damage animal research organisations 1.03, 8.02–8.04, 8.07
  intimidation of persons connected with animal research organisations 8.05
  protection of animal rights organisations 8.02–8.09
anti-social behaviour orders (ASBOs)
  adjournment of proceedings 7.32
  application 7.31
  breach 7.31
  contracting out 7.36
  discharge 7.33
  generally 1.09, 7.31–7.33
  human rights 7.35
  interim orders 7.32
  introduction 7.31
  parental compensation orders 7.38–7.40
  proof of order 7.32
  reporting restrictions 7.34, 7.35
  variation 7.33
  witness protection 7.37
arrest, powers of
  expansion 1.09
  without warrant
    constables 6.04–6.21
    other persons 6.04, 6.22–6.27
ASBOS *see* **anti-social behaviour orders (ASBOs)**
assembly, freedom of 7.03–7.05
assisting investigations *see* **offenders assisting investigations and prosecutions**
attempts
  investigation powers 3.10
Australia 3.68, 3.69–3.75

banking confidentiality 3.35, 3.36
begging 6.56

Canada 3.68
cartel offences 4.08
cash, appeal in proceedings for forfeiture of 5.42–5.45

code of practice
  Serious Organised Crime Agency (SOCA) 2.10
community support officers
  powers 1.03, 6.56
confidentiality undertaking
  disclosure notices 3.67
conspiracy
  investigation powers 3.10
Criminal Records Bureau (CRB)
  amendments to provisions 8.42
  children, suitability to work with 8.43
  criminal records certificates 8.43
  Department of Work and Pension's database, access to 8.44
  Driver and Vehicle Licensing Agency, access to information held by 8.44
  enhanced criminal record certificates 8.43
  establishment 8.41
  fees 8.45
  Passport Agency, access to information held by 8.44
  police authority, definition of 8.45
  purpose 8.41
  urgent cases 8.43
  vulnerable adults, suitability to work with 8.43

defence
  tactics 1.10
demonstrations
  Parliament, in vicinity of 1.09, 7.02, 7.25–7.30
designated sites, trespass on 7.02, 7.18–7.24
Director of Public Prosecutions
  compulsory powers granted to 3.04, 3.05
  investigation powers 3.04, 3.05
disciplinary proceedings
  police 8.35, 8.36
disclosure notices
  see also **investigation powers**
  authorisation 3.14
  banking confidentiality 3.35, 3.36
  conditions 3.12
  confidentiality undertaking 3.67
  contents 3.15, 3.17
  demonstrations in vicinity of Parliament 1.09, 7.02, 7.25–7.30
  documents, requests for 3.16

disclosure notices—*contd*
  drafting 3.17
  excluded material 3.34
  human rights 3.19
  knowingly or recklessly making false or
    misleading statement 3.63
  legal professional privilege 3.04, 3.24–3.33
  nature of inquiry being conducted 3.18
  non-compliance 3.17, 3.59–3.65
  non-suspects 3.13
  offences 3.59–3.65
  Parliament, demonstration in vicinity of
    1.09, 7.02, 7.25–7.30
  person under investigation 3.18
  power to issue 3.04, 3.12
  production of documents 3.21, 3.22
  purpose 3.12
  requirements 3.15
  retention of documents 3.04
  self-incrimination, protection against
    3.37–3.42
    derivative use of statements 3.51–3.54
    limits on 3.43–3.50
  service 3.66
  use of 3.20
drink-driving offences 8.22–8.27
drivers
  drink-driving offences 8.22–8.27
  uninsured 8.17–8.21
  unlicensed 8.17–8.21

enforcement powers 3.04
  enter and seize documents, power to
    3.55–3.58
enter and seize documents, power to 3.55–3.58
excluded material
  disclosure notices 3.34
  search warrants 6.33
exclusion zones 6.28–6.30
expression, freedom of 7.03–7.05

fair trial, right to a 3.37
'faith hate' provisions 1.01
false or misleading information
  disclosure notices 3.63
  financial reporting order (FRO) 5.02, 5.15
financial reporting order (FRO)
  ancillary nature 5.03
  availability 5.01
  commencement 5.09
  contents 5.13
  duration 5.01, 5.12
  effect 5.02, 5.11–5.14
  extent of disclosure 5.04
  false or misleading information 5.02, 5.15
  human rights 5.04
  introduction 5.01
  making 5.05–5.10

  non-compliance 5.02, 5.15
  Northern Ireland 5.10
  offences 5.02
  penalties 5.02, 5.15
  revocation 5.21, 5.22
  Scotland 5.10
  variation 5.21, 5.22
  verifying information 5.16–5.20
  White Paper 5.03
fingerprints 6.44–6.47
fireworks
  stop and search for prohibited fireworks
    6.36
footwear impressions 6.48, 6.49
forfeiture orders, overseas
  enforcement 5.23–5.27
fraud
  Serious Organised Crime Agency (SOCA)
    2.06, 2.07
freezing orders
  international obligations 5.28–5.35
  proceeds of crime 5.39–5.41
FRO *see* **financial reporting order (FRO)**

Greenaway report 8.17

harassment
  extension of law 1.03
  home, harassment of a person at 7.12–7.17
  Protection from Harassment Act 1997,
    amendment to 7.07–7.11
  purpose of amendments to law 7.02,
    7.06
health and safety
  police 8.33, 8.34
Her Majesty's Customs and Excise 1.02, 1.05,
  2.01
human rights
  anti-social behaviour orders (ASBOs)
    7.35
  fair trial, right to a 3.37
  financial reporting order (FRO) 5.04
  freedom of assembly 7.03–7.05
  freedom of expression 7.03–7.05
  photographing suspects 6.41
  public order and conduct in public places
    7.02
  search warrants 6.35
  Serious Organised Crime Agency (SOCA)
    2.26–2.29
  uninsured drivers, seizure of cars of 8.21

immunity from prosecution
  offenders assisting investigations and
    prosecutions 4.04–4.08
**interference with business contracts which
    damage animal research organisations**
    1.03, 8.02–8.04, 8.07

international obligations
mutual assistance in freezing property or evidence 5.28–5.35
overseas forfeiture orders, enforcement of 5.23–5.27
intimate samples 6.50, 6.51
investigation powers
see also **disclosure notices**
amount of potential loss 3.09
appeal, no 3.06
attempts 3.10
bodies exercising 3.05, 3.06
compulsory powers 1.06, 3.01
conspiracy 3.10
criticism of powers 3.11
delegation 3.05
Director of Public Prosecutions 3.05
Director of Revenue and Customs Prosecutions 3.05
excluded material 3.34
failure to comply with 3.01
judicial review 3.06
justification 1.06
legal professional privilege 3.04, 3.24–3.33
lifestyle offences 3.08
Lord Advocate 3.05
minor offences 3.11
offences to which new powers apply 3.04, 3.07–3.11
overview 3.04
privilege 3.24–3.33
rationale 1.06, 3.02
safeguards, no 3.06
self-incrimination, protection against 3.37–3.42
derivative use 3.51–3.54
limits on 3.43–3.50
terrorist offences 3.07
use of material obtained 3.04
VAT, fraudulent evasion of 3.09

judicial review
investigation powers 3.06

legal professional privilege
investigation powers 3.04, 3.24–3.33
licensing offences 6.56
lifestyle offences
investigation powers 3.08
local policing information, publication of 8.29–8.31
Lord Advocate
investigation powers 3.05

money laundering
disclosures to identify persons and property 5.51–5.65
failure-to-report provisions 5.51–5.65

form of disclosures 5.66
manner of disclosures 5.66
offences 1.03
overseas conduct legal under local law, defence where 5.46
threshold amounts 5.49, 5.50
Motor Insurers' Information Centre 8.17
moving images 6.39, 6.43

National Crime Squad 1.02, 1.05, 2.01
National Criminal Intelligence Service 1.02, 1.05, 2.01
New Zealand 3.68
Northern Ireland 4.03
financial reporting order (FRO) 5.10
Norway 3.68

offenders assisting investigations and prosecutions
advance indication of sentence 4.12
generally 1.07, 1.08
guidelines 4.03
immunity from prosecution 4.04–4.08
immunity notice 4.06
Northern Ireland experience 4.03
Queen's evidence 4.01, 4.03
reduction in sentence 4.11–4.15
restricted use undertaking 4.09, 4.10
review of sentence 4.16–4.19
Salmon undertaking 4.09
sentencing
advance indication of sentence 4.12
exclusion of public from proceedings 4.20
reduction 4.11–4.15
review of sentence 4.16–4.19
specified prosecutor 4.05
supergrasses 4.03
undertakings as to use of evidence 4.09, 4.10
use of power to grant immunity 4.07
White Paper 4.01
organised crime
meaning 1.02
overseas forfeiture orders, enforcement of 5.23–5.27

parental compensation orders 7.38–7.40
Parliament, demonstrations in vicinity of 1.09, 7.02, 7.25–7.30
photographing of suspects 6.37–6.43
plea bargaining 4.12
police
accelerated procedure into investigation of 8.35, 8.36
death or serious injury after contact with 8.37
disciplinary proceedings 8.35, 8.36
exclusion zones 6.28–6.30
fingerprints 6.44–6.47

police—*contd*
footwear impressions 6.48, 6.49
health and safety 8.33, 8.34
intimate samples 6.50, 6.51
local policing information, publication of
8.29–8.31
photographing of suspects 6.37–6.43
powers
accredited persons 6.56
arrest *see* **arrest, powers of**
designated persons 6.56
exclusion zones 6.28–6.30
fingerprints 6.44–6.47
footwear impressions 6.48, 6.49
intimate samples 6.50, 6.51
moving images 6.39, 6.43
overview of Part 3 SOCPA 6.01–6.03
photographing of suspects 6.37–6.43
search warrant 6.31–6.35
staff custody officers 6.52–6.55
stop and search for prohibited fireworks
6.36
search warrant 6.31–6.35
Serious Organised Crime Agency (SOCA),
cooperation with 1.05
staff custody officers 6.52–6.55
stop and search for prohibited fireworks
6.36
police authorities
Secretary of State, payments by 8.28
**Police Information Technology Organisation
(PITO)** 8.17
proceeds of crime
cash, appeal in proceedings for forfeiture of
5.42–5.45
civil recovery 5.39–5.41
confiscation orders in magistrates' courts
5.37, 5.38
freezing orders 5.39–5.41
generally 5.36
money laundering
disclosures to identify persons and
property 5.51–5.65
failure-to-report provisions 5.51–5.65
form of disclosures 5.66
manner of disclosures 5.66
overseas conduct legal under local law,
defence where 5.46
threshold amounts 5.49, 5.50
protection arrangements *see under* **witnesses**
public order and conduct in public places
anti-social behaviour *see* **anti-social
behaviour orders (ASBOs)**
freedom of assembly 7.03–7.05
freedom of expression 7.03–7.05
harassment *see* **harassment**
human rights 7.02
meaning 7.01

purpose of provisions 7.01
rationale for introduction of measures
7.02
trespass on designated sites 7.02, 7.18–7.24
publication of local policing information
8.29–8.31

Queen's evidence 4.01, 4.03

reporting restrictions
anti-social behaviour orders (ASBOs) 7.34,
7.35
restricted use undertaking 4.09, 4.10
road traffic accidents 6.56
Royal Parks Constabulary (RPC)
abolition 8.38–8.40

Salmon undertaking 4.09
samples
intimate 6.50, 6.51
Scotland
financial reporting order (FRO) 5.10
private security industry 8.51
search warrants 3.04
all premises warrant 6.32
application 6.32
enter and seize documents, power to
3.55–3.58
excluded material 6.33
human rights 6.35
non-compliance 3.55–3.58
offences 3.59–3.65
police powers 6.31–6.35
special procedure material 6.33
specific premises warrant 6.32
super warrant 6.31
wilful obstruction 3.64
self-incrimination, protection against 3.37–3.42
derivative use 3.51–3.54
limits on 3.43–3.50
sentencing
offenders assisting investigations and
prosecutions
advance indication of sentence 4.12
exclusion of public from proceedings 4.20
reduction 4.11–4.15
review of sentence 4.16–4.19
reduction 4.11–4.15
review 4.16–4.19
Serious Organised Crime Agency (SOCA)
annual plan 2.10
'British FBI' 2.03
code of practice 2.10
cooperation of police with 1.05
designated offences 2.35
directed arrangements 2.32
disclosure of information 2.09, 2.20–2.22
establishment 1.02, 2.01, 2.02

experts 1.05
fraud 2.06, 2.07
functions
  general considerations 2.10
  generally 1.02
  information relating to crime 2.08, 2.09
  serious organised crime 2.05–2.07
headline measure 1.05
human rights compatibility 2.26–2.29
information
  disclosure by SOCA 2.20–2.22
  generally 2.19
  human rights compatibility 2.26–2.29
investigation powers *see* **investigation powers**
non-designated offences 2.35
performance targets 2.10
police, relationship with 2.30–2.33
powers 2.11, 2.12
powers of staff 2.14–2.16
prosecutions arising out of investigations
  2.34–2.37
rationale 2.02
remit 1.02, 2.01, 2.05–2.10
responsibilities 2.01
staff 1.05, 2.01
  powers 2.14–2.16
strategic priorities 2.10
structure 2.13
supervision of 2.17, 2.18
voluntary arrangements 2.32
Serious Organised Crime and Police Act 2005
see also Appendix for full text
background 1.01–1.05
errors in numbering 1.04
minor offences and 1.02
overview 1.01–1.05
Parliamentary passage 1.01
purpose 1.02
SOCA *see* **Serious Organised Crime Agency
(SOCA)**
Soham murders inquiry 8.44
special procedure material 3.36, 6.33
specific premises warrant 6.32
specified prosecutor 4.05
staff custody officers 6.52–6.55
stop and search for prohibited fireworks 6.36

terrorist offences
  investigation powers 3.07

trespass on designated sites 7.02, 7.18–7.24

uninsured driving 8.17–8.21
United States 3.68, 3.76–3.80

vehicle registration 8.11–8.16

warrants
  enter and seize documents, power to
    3.55–3.58
  non-compliance 3.55–3.58
  offences 3.55–3.58
White Paper *One Step Ahead: A 21st Century
  Strategy to Defeat Organised Crime*
  1.02, 1.08, 1.10, 1.11, 3.02, 4.01, 4.21,
  5.03
wilful obstruction
  search warrants 3.64
witnesses
  attendance in court, securing 8.47–8.50
  cooperation from 1.07, 1.08
  definition 4.39
  protection 4.01, 4.21–4.39
    anti-social behaviour orders (ASBOs)
     7.37
    associated persons 4.39
    cancellation of arrangement 4.25
    defences 4.31
    disclosing information relating to
     arrangement and new identities
     4.29–4.33
    duty to assist protection providers
     4.28
    duty to provide information 4.38, 4.39
    establishing arrangements 4.25
    existing powers, use of 4.23
    joint protection arrangements 4.26
    liability, protection from 4.34
    offences 4.29–4.33
    protected persons 4.39
    protection arrangements 4.23–4.27
    protection provider 4.23
    strategy 4.22
    transfer of protection arrangements 4.27
    transitional provisions 4.35–4.37
    variation of arrangement 4.25
    White Paper 4.21
  summonses 8.47–8.50
  witness orders 8.47